Sociolinguistic Research

Sociolinguistic Research: Application and Impact provides a unique overview of international research projects, showcasing their positive outcomes and offering critical insights and constructive critiques into the meaning of 'impact' in contemporary research. The book includes:

- original findings from cutting-edge research from scholars such as Mary Bucholtz, Walt Wolfram, and Peter Patrick;
- coverage of organisational contexts including education, government, justice, heritage, and the workplace;
- activities including after-school programmes, workplace training courses, social media campaigns, and video productions;
- application of research to professional practice including teaching (primary school to university), adjudication, police interviewing, and governmental policymaking;
- contributors' personal reflections on the research process and its outcomes, including constructive critiques of institutional definitions of impact.

With chapters spanning research across five continents, *Sociolinguistic Research: Application and Impact* is essential reading for sociolinguistic researchers, students embarking on sociolinguistic research, and anyone interested in the practical application of research on language and society.

Robert Lawson is Senior Lecturer in the School of English at Birmingham City University, UK.

Dave Sayers is Senior Lecturer in the Department of Humanities at Sheffield Hallam University, UK, an Honorary Research Fellow in the School of Social Sciences at Cardiff University, UK, and a registered Expert Advisor to the Welsh Government.

Sociolinguistic Research

Application and impact

Edited by Robert Lawson
and Dave Sayers

LONDON AND NEW YORK

First published 2016
by Routledge
2 Park Square, Milton Park, Abingdon, Oxon OX14 4RN

and by Routledge
711 Third Avenue, New York, NY 10017

Routledge is an imprint of the Taylor & Francis Group, an informa business

British Library Cataloguing in Publication Data
A catalogue record for this book is available from the British Library

Library of Congress Cataloging-in-Publication Data
Sociolinguistic research : application and impact / edited by
   Robert Lawson and Dave Sayers.
      pages cm
   Includes bibliographical references and index.
   1. Sociolinguistics—Research.   I. Lawson, Robert, 1982–
editor.   II. Sayers, Dave, editor.
   P40.3.S63 2016
   306.44072—dc23
   2015035998

ISBN: 978-0-415-74850-6 (hbk)
ISBN: 978-0-415-74852-0 (pbk)
ISBN: 978-1-315-67176-5 (ebk)

Typeset in Goudy
by Apex CoVantage, LLC

For Rebecca and Kerry, our endlessly patient better halves. Quite apart from being a constant source of support to us, as non-academic practitioners they have achieved impact in a different league to ours.

Contents

Figures

Tables

Foreword

For assembling this excellent edited collection, we are indebted to Robert Lawson and Dave Sayers. But when they issued their original Call for Papers in the *Variationist List [Var-L]* on January 18, 2012, noting that "very few people outside academia have ever heard of sociolinguistics – let alone its influence beyond the groves of academe," not everyone agreed. Rudy Troike (University of Arizona, Tucson), for instance, pointed to early work in the USA by William Labov, Roger Shuy, Roseann Gonzalez, and others that helped to dispel myths about African American English, and to improve testing, teaching, and interpreting in classrooms, the armed services, and courts. Celeste Rodriguez Louro (University of Western Australia, Crawley) noted counter-examples from Australia too, citing work by Diana Eades and her colleagues on Australian Aboriginal communication style in court cases, and on problems with the process of assessing the nationality of people seeking refugee status in Australia.

Responding on *Var-L* for both editors, Robert Lawson acknowledged the existence of sociolinguistic activism in the UK as well, for instance, in work by Peter Trudgill, Ron Macaulay, Sue Fox, and others on English in education and resources for teachers. But he argued that the goal of the volume was to *highlight* this kind of activism by bringing it together in one coherent volume, and to focus more explicitly on engagement, a relatively new phrasing and focus of applied work. The editors have fulfilled this goal admirably. But before developing this point, I'd like to comment on the relative significance of applied research in sociolinguistics and/or language variation and change more generally.

Some of the earliest community studies by US sociolinguists – e.g. Shuy et al. (1967), Labov et al. (1968), Wolfram (1969) – were funded by the US Department of Education and/or the Center for Applied Linguistics as a means of better understanding and redressing educational inequities linked to vernacular dialects. Despite this, applied issues have usually taken a back seat to analytical and theoretical issues in sociolinguistics, although several leading figures managed to combine all three. The diminution of application relative to theory is especially prevalent in the so-called First World, e.g. N. America, W. Europe, Japan, Australia, and New Zealand. (In Third World countries, e.g. in the Caribbean and West Africa, linguists, as part of a relatively small intelligentsia, and with students, contacts, and interests in education or government, are much more fre-quently drawn into educational, nation-development, and other applied issues.)

For instance, although Labov's applied work from the first twenty years of his linguistics career (e.g. Labov 1969, 1982) is almost as well known as his earliest descriptive or theoretical work (e.g. Labov 1963, 1980), this is not true of his work over the last twenty years. His three-volume *Principles of Linguistic Change* (Labov 1994, 2001a, 2010b) is deservedly famous, but his invaluable work on improv-ing reading for AAVE speakers (e.g. Labov 1995, 2001b; Labov and Baker 2010) is much less so. Moreover, outside of his current/recent colleagues and students, few linguists know of the vibrant Penn Reading Initiative he spearheaded at the University of Pennsylvania, or its associated *Reading Road* instructional program (http://www.ling.upenn.edu/pri/). And fewer still know of the *Portals Real World Reading Bounce A* stories he crafted to help elementary students master "silent e" (*hat* vs. *hate*) and other challenges of the English orthography (Labov 2008, 2010a), although these books are very widely used in schools in California and Texas.

Speaking more broadly, there is only one book (Trudgill 1984) carrying the title *Applied Sociolinguistics*, which pursued "the application of linguistic research to the solution of practical, education and social problems of all types" (p. 1). And most introductory sociolinguistics texts include at most a chapter or two at the end about applications to societal problems. One can see this, to varying extents, in the three most recent Handbooks. Chambers and Schilling's (2013) *Handbook of Language Variation and Change* (which most readers will recognize as a moniker for quantitative sociolinguistics) includes a final chapter by Wolfram on "Community Commitment and Responsibility." Wolfram's chapter is the only one in the book's final section, "Sociolinguists and Their Communities," and as the only chapter dealing with applied sociolinguists, it represents 3.8% (1/26) of the book's contents – an improvement on the 2002 first edition, which had no such chapter. Bayley et al.'s (2013) *Oxford Handbook of Sociolinguistics* is better in this regard, with the fifteen chapters in the book's final two sections ("Language Policy, Language Ideology, and Language Attitudes" and "Sociolinguistics, The Professions and Public Interest") representing 37.5% (15/40) of the book's con-tents. Wodak et al.'s (2011) *SAGE Handbook of Sociolinguistics* is somewhere in between. It has a five-chapter final section on "Applications," as well as various policy and practice-relevant chapters in other sections, for an overall percentage of about 28%.

One reason for the under-representation of "applied issues" in sociolinguistics (apart from individual scholars' interests and inclinations) is the relative status of theory and application in linguistics departments and in academia more gener-ally. In many research universities, not least in North America, theory is highly valued, and applied issues at best ignored. Within linguistics, the situation was exacerbated for many years by the centrality of "theoretical linguistics" (core syn-tax, phonology, semantics and pragmatics) and the marginality of "hyphenated linguistics." Over the past two decades, this linguistics-specific distinction has weakened considerably, for various reasons (more "theory" by sociolinguists and psycholinguists, more interest in corpora/usage data by "theoretical linguists," more collaboration between them), but the primacy of "theory" in research universities remains.

Another possible reason for the under-representation of applied issues in sociolinguistics texts is the existence of "applied linguistics" as a separate subfield, with its own conferences and including, for instance, applied linguistics Handbooks from publishers including Blackwell (Davies and Elder 2004), Oxford (Kaplan 2010) and Routledge (Simpson 2001). Routledge has a whole series of specialized applied Handbooks, dealing separately with interpreting, multilingualism, language testing, Hispanic applied linguistics, and so on. It would take us too far afield to discuss the relations between applied linguistics and sociolinguistics in detail, but a few quick observations are in order.

The first is that while this varies by continent and individual, many sociolinguists don't consider themselves applied linguists, or attend applied linguistics conferences. The reverse is also true. Shuy (2015: 434) notes, for instance, that he was "often pigeonholed as a sociolinguist and not thought of as an applied linguist," partly because of the traditional focus of applied linguistics on [second] "language learning, teaching and testing." Shuy's paper is rich in suggestions for broadening the vision and reach of applied linguistics, and for increasing its relation to theoretical linguistics and enhancing its prestige, and this is indeed the focus of the entire special issue of *Applied Linguistics* in which it appears. (See, for instance, Hellerman's 2015 introduction and other papers in the issue.) This expanded tent is one in which many sociolinguists with an applied bent could comfortably find themselves, and indeed, applied sociolinguists could benefit from a similar soul-searching and reconceptualization, as this volume itself demonstrates.

Whatever the reasons for the traditional under-representation of applied sociolinguistics, we are at a historical point where the academic rewards for applied work (in terms of promotion, research grants, funding for individuals and departments) are gradually increasing. And sociolinguists, who typically gather data in speech communities and communities of practice in the "real world," are very well positioned to pursue and demonstrate "impact." The rise of "impact" as a key element in the five-year research evaluation by which universities in the UK are assessed is documented in revealing detail by Lawson and Sayers (this volume). From their account, 2014 was a pivotal year, not only because of the name change from Research Assessment Exercise to Research Excellence Framework, but also because "esteem" was replaced then as a criterion by "impact." As they note, "impact" includes not only a 2010 definition as "effect on, change or benefit to the economy, society, culture, public policy or services, health, the environment or quality of life, beyond academia," but an additional 2012 criterion that "public debate has been stimulated or informed by research."

Universities in the USA are not required to demonstrate "impact" in their assessment exercises in quite the same way as our UK counterparts are, but the National Science Foundation, especially since 2013, assesses grant proposals both in terms of "Intellectual Merit" and "Broader Impacts," the latter defined as "the potential to benefit society and contribute to the achievement of specific, desired societal outcomes" (http://www.nsf.gov/bfa/dias/policy/merit_review/overview.pdf and http://www.nsf.gov/od/oia/publications/Broader_Impacts.pdf). So we are increasingly subject to the same pressures or incentives.

Of course, for many, perhaps all of us, interest in sociolinguistic application or impact does not derive solely from recent carrots or sticks, but from longer standing stirrings to "do justice" and "love mercy" (Micah 6:8), especially since the people "whose data fuel our theories and descriptions" (Rickford 1997: 186) are often poor, and oppressed or disadvantaged in schools, housing, courtrooms, interactions with the police, and opportunities to offer significant improvements to their children. These stirrings are reflected in Labov's (1982: 172) *principle of debt incurred* ("An investigator who has obtained linguistic data from members of a speech community has an obligation to use the knowledge based on that data for the benefit of the community, when it has need of it") and Wolfram's (1993: 227) *principle of linguistic gratuity* ("Investigators who have obtained linguistic data from members of a speech community should actively pursue positive ways in which they can return linguistic favors to the community").

The chapters in this volume richly exemplify the spirit of the older principles and the intent of the newer impact criteria. Given the editors' detailed summaries in their joint essay, and my own wish to avoid specific comparisons, it is unnecessary for me to discuss the contents of this book chapter by chapter. I would say, however, that I am impressed, as a group, by the range of their research foci and/or goals (reduced discrimination, improved teaching and learning, fairer courtroom verdicts and refugee decisions, more language-enriched public exhibits, better language policy) and by the variety of their institutional settings (schools, museums, workplaces, social media, entire countries). The geographical settings constitute a relatively broad range too, from Canada and the USA, to the UK, other parts of Europe, Australia, and New Zealand. Gabon, Pakistan, and Indonesia get some coverage too, although it would be terrific to see more so-called Second and Third World countries included in future editions.

What is really new and exciting about this volume is the explicit and extended discussion in each chapter of the five Ws and H of "impact" (Who, What, When, Where, Why, and How), explored in insightful and stimulating ways. I have already started to tell my students and colleagues about the terrific chapters in this book, and we are all avidly awaiting its publication. The editors tell me they plan to follow this book with the creation of an open access journal provisionally named *Applied Sociolinguistics*. If that comes to fruition, it could productively extend this book's focus on how we conceptualize and carry out "applied" work in sociolinguistics, and on the proportion and standing of application relative to analysis and theory.

Professor John R. Rickford, Stanford University

References

Bayley, Robert, Richard Cameron, and Ceil Lucas (eds.). 2013. *The Oxford Handbook of Sociolinguistics*. Oxford: Oxford University Press.

Chambers, J. K., and Natalie Schilling (eds.). 2013. *The Handbook of Language Variation and Change*, 2nd ed. Oxford: Blackwell.

Davies, Alan, and Catherine Elder (eds.). 2004. *The Handbook of Applied Linguistics*. Oxford: Blackwell.

Hellerman, John. 2015. "Three contexts for my work as co-editor: Introduction to the special issue." *Applied Linguistics* 36 (4): 419–424.

Kaplan, Robert B. (ed.). 2010. *The Oxford Handbook of Applied Linguistics*, 2nd ed. Oxford: Oxford University Press.

Labov, William. 1963. "The social motivation of language change." *Word* 18: 1–42.

Labov, William. 1969. "The logic of non-standard English." *Georgetown Monograph on Languages and Linguistics* 22: 1–44. Reprinted in *Language and Social Context*, 1972, ed. by Pier Paolo Giglioli, 179–215. Harmondsworth: Penguin.

Labov, William. 1980. "The social origins of sound change." In *Locating Language in Time and Space*, ed. by William Labov, 251–265. New York: Academic Press.

Labov, William. 1982. "Objectivity and commitment in linguistic science: The case of the Black English trial in Ann Arbor." *Language in Society* 11 (2): 165–202.

Labov, William. 1994. *Principles of Linguistic Change Vol. 1: Internal Factors*. Oxford: Blackwell.

Labov, William. 1995. "Can reading failure be reversed? A linguistic approach to the question." In *Literacy among African American Youth*, ed. by Vivian L. Gadsden and Daniel A. Wagner, 39–68. Cresskill, NJ: Hampton.

Labov, William. 2001a. *Principles of Linguistic Change Vol. 2: Social Factors*. Oxford: Blackwell.

Labov, William. 2001b. "Applying our knowledge of African American English to the problem of raising reading levels in inner city schools." In *Sociocultural and Historical Contexts of African American English*, ed. by Sonja L. Lanehart, 299–317. Philadelphia: John Benjamins.

Labov, William. 2008. *Portals Real World Reading Bounce A*. Boston: Houghton Mifflin Harcourt.

Labov, William. 2010a. *Portals Real World Reading Bounce B*. Boston: Houghton Mifflin Harcourt.

Labov, William. 2010b. *Principles of Linguistic Change Vol. 3: Cognitive and Cultural Factors*. Oxford: Blackwell.

Labov, William, and Bettina Baker. 2010. "What is a reading error?" *Applied Psycholinguistics* 31 (4): 735–757.

Labov, William, Paul Cohen, Clarence Robins, and John Lewis. 1968. *A Study of the Non-standard English of Negro and Puerto Rican Speakers in New York City: Cooperative Research Report 3288*. Vols I and II. Philadelphia: U.S. Regional Survey (Linguistics Laboratory, University of Pennsylvania).

Rickford, John R. 1997. "Unequal partnership: Sociolinguistics and the African American speech community." *Language in Society* 26 (2): 161–197.Shuy, Roger W. 2015. "Applied linguistics past and future." *Applied Linguistics* 36 (4): 434–443.

Shuy, Roger W., Walt Wolfram, and William K. Riley. 1967. "Linguistic correlates of social stratification in Detroit speech." USOE Final Report No. 6–1347.

Simpson, James (ed.). 2001. *The Routledge Handbook of Applied Linguistics*. Oxon: Routledge.

Trudgill, Peter (ed.). 1984. *Applied Sociolinguistics*. London: Academic Press.

Wodak, Ruth, Barbara Johnstone, and Paul Kerswill (eds.). 2011. *The SAGE Handbook of Sociolinguistics*. London: Sage.

Wolfram, Walt. 1969. *A Sociolinguistic Description of Detroit Negro Speech*. Washington, DC: Center for Applied Linguistics.

Wolfram, Walt. 1993. "Ethical considerations in Language Awareness Programs." *Issues in Applied Linguistics* 4 (2): 225–255.

Acknowledgements

After four years, thousands of emails, dozens of Skype calls, and several visits to the pub, we're proud to have eventually completed this project. It has been a significant undertaking, and so our first big 'thank you' is to each other. If you are planning to edit a book, we would highly recommend recruiting a co-editor.

Beyond mutual back-patting, our sincere thanks go to Routledge for seeing potential in a slightly unusual book proposal. At Routledge our main contacts were Nadia Seemungal, Rachel Daw, and Helen Tredget; all were extremely helpful and encouraging during the various stages of writing and editing. We would also like to thank Nicola Lennon for her work in collating the index, and Autumn Spalding for her excellent work with seeing the book through production.

In order to field-test the theme of the book, and the way we were framing the chapters, we gave presentations on the subject of impact in sociolinguistics to the British Association of Applied Linguistics (University of Warwick), i-Mean (University of Warwick), the Linguistics Association of Great Britain (Queen's College, Oxford), and the Sociolinguistic Symposium (University of Jyväskylä). We thank all the organisers for inviting us along and our audiences for their extremely valuable feedback and insights.

Our contributors have all been remarkably patient with our nagging over progress and incessant requests for changes. Most importantly they all delivered on time, which for an academic volume is practically a miracle. They deserve great praise for their work.

Every chapter had at least two anonymous peer reviewers. You know who you are, and thanks to all of you. Thanks also to Joan Beal, who very kindly offered to look over the entire completed manuscript to check its consistency and structure. Her minimal comments were a testament to the high quality of the contributions. Any remaining housekeeping errors are ours.

– Robert Lawson and Dave Sayers, 2016

Contributors

Mary Bucholtz is Professor of Linguistics in the Department of Linguistics at the University of California, Santa Barbara. She has written extensively on language and gender, language and race, language and identity, and youth language. She is the author of *White Kids: Language, Race, and Styles of Youth Identity* (CUP, 2011) and the editor of *Language and Woman's Place: Text and Commentaries* (OUP, 2004), among other volumes. She also sits on the editorial board of a number of international journals of sociocultural linguistics.

Dolores Inés Casillas is Associate Professor in the Department of Chicana and Chicano Studies at the University of California, Santa Barbara. Her book *Sounds of Belonging: U.S. Spanish-language Radio and Public Advocacy* (NYU Press, 2014) examines how immigration politics throughout the twentieth century have shaped and transformed the character and growth of US Spanish-language radio. She has published essays on radio humor, 'accent' use within popular culture, immigration-based broadcasts, and the politics of language.

Hywel Coleman is Honorary Senior Research Fellow in the School of Education at the University of Leeds. His work focuses on the intersection of language and education, particularly language-in-education policy in the developing world. Recent experience has been in Indonesia (where he is based), Pakistan, Morocco, Gabon, Senegal, and Côte d'Ivoire. He has published monographs and edited volumes exploring these issues, including *Society and the Language Classroom* (CUP, 1996), *Change and Language* (with Lynne Cameron, Multilingual Matters, 1996), *Dreams and Realities: Developing Countries and the English Language* (British Council, 2011), and *The English Language in Francophone West Africa* (British Council, 2013). He is a Trustee of the Language and Development Conferences and was awarded an OBE in 2000 for services to education in Indonesia.

Jules Dickinson is a practitioner-researcher. Her PhD thesis, awarded by Heriot-Watt University, was on the impact of sign language interpreters in workplace settings. She currently works as a Senior Interpreter at

Nottinghamshire Deaf Society, and is an Honorary Research Fellow of Heriot-Watt University.

Fiona Douglas lectures in English language at the University of Leeds. Her research interests straddle sociolinguistics, digital humanities, and corpus linguistics, and she is primarily interested in regional non-standard and dialect varieties. She has published on Scots and Scottish English varieties, newspaper language, and corpus-building methodologies.

Kate Haworth is Lecturer in Applied Linguistics at the Centre for Forensic Linguistics, Aston University, Birmingham. She is also a non-practising barrister. Her research interests include all aspects of language and communication in legal contexts, especially spoken interaction and the use of language data as evidence. Her research to date has focused on police interviews with suspects, a topic on which she has published and presented widely.

Bronwen Innes lectures in Linguistics at the University of Auckland, New Zealand. Her work falls within the field of language and law, with particular foci on forensic linguistics and language use in the courtroom. She was awarded a New Zealand Law Foundation research grant in 2007 to examine language use among judges, specifically the construction and content of trial summaries for juries.

Robert Lawson is Senior Lecturer in Sociolinguistics at Birmingham City University and former Fulbright Scottish Studies Scholar. He has publications in a number of major journals, including the *Journal of Sociolinguistics*, *Gender and Language*, and *English World-Wide* and is editor of *Sociolinguistics in Scotland* (Palgrave, 2014).

Jin Sook Lee is Professor of Education at the University of California, Santa Barbara. Her research focuses on the cultural, sociopolitical, and sociopsychological factors that shape the language learning experiences of immigrant children. She is co-editor of *The Education of Language Minority Immigrants in the US* (Multilingual Matters, 2009) and serves on the editorial board of the *International Journal of Multilingual Research*. She is a recent recipient of a Fulbright Senior Scholars Research Award in Applied Linguistics.

Catherine Levasseur is a doctoral student at Université de Montréal, with an M.A. in Anthropology from Laval University. Her research is on bilingual and multilingual children attending minority French schools in British Columbia, Canada. Her preliminary results are being used to influence policy and practice on the ground. She also works as a lecturer on the M.Ed. course at the University of British Columbia.

Nicci MacLeod is a Research Associate in Forensic Linguistics at Aston University, Birmingham. Her research focuses on the way power is manifested through linguistic structure, particularly within legal and investigative contexts. Her work on discourse markers and narrative evaluations in police interviews has been published in the *British Journal of Forensic Practice* and *Critical Approaches to Discourse Analysis across Disciplines*.

Peter Patrick is Professor of Sociolinguistics and Member of the Human Rights Centre at the University of Essex, and affiliated with the Observatoire International des Droits Linguistique/International Observatory on Language Rights. He has worked on language variation and change, pidgin and creole studies, urban dialectology, sociolinguistics methods, and language rights. His recent work focuses on evaluating language testing of asylum seekers. He has deployed sociolinguistic methods in non-academic contexts, through testimony in criminal cases, studies of clinical communication, and interventions in the asylum process. He is one of the founding members of the Language & Asylum Research Group.

Dave Sayers is Senior Lecturer in the Department of Humanities at Sheffield Hallam University. His teaching is in sociolinguistics and his research interests include language policy (especially Welsh and Cornish) and variationist sociolinguistics. From 2009–2015 he was an Honorary Research Fellow at Swansea University. He is currently an Honorary Research Associate at Cardiff University (in association with the Wales Institute for Social & Economic Research, Data & Methods) and has been published in journals including the *Journal of Sociolinguistics* and *Language Problems & Language Planning*. He is also a registered Expert Adviser with the Welsh Government.

Walt Wolfram is the William C. Friday Distinguished Professor of English at North Carolina University, and Director of the North Carolina Language and Life Project. His research focuses on the social and ethnic dialects of the USA, particularly North Carolina. He is also interested in the communication of sociolinguistic information to public audiences. To this end, he has been involved in the production of television documentaries, the construction of museum exhibits, and the development of innovative social studies of dialect awareness curricula – endorsed by the North Carolina Department of Public Instruction. He has also served as President of the Linguistics Society of America, the American Dialect Society, and the Southeastern Conference on Linguistics.

Introduction

Robert Lawson, ORCID NO. 0000–0003–1415–517X
Dave Sayers, ORCID NO. 0000–0003–1124–7132

Preliminaries

The purpose of this book is to show how research across sociolinguistics can achieve something called 'impact,' and to provide a window into the journey that any researcher takes in pursuing this ascendant priority. Before we go on, though, we first want to point out that readers should expect the very broadest definition of 'sociolinguistic research': that is, simply research on the relationship between language and society. For a book like this we saw no reason to sit inside disciplinary silos. The end result, we hope, has turned out to be as deeply insightful as it is broadly pitched. We also feel obliged to forewarn readers that we have urged our contributors to step beyond some customary practices of academic writing: to focus less on methodology and empirical data and more on personal reflections about the research process, and to give explicit guidance for other researchers considering impact as a goal.

If these departures from convention were not risky enough, we have encouraged contributors to employ the active voice as far as possible, even to write in the first person. Moreover, we asked our contributors to reflect on the meaning of 'impact' for them, in comparison (and in contrast) to its meaning for funding organisations, governments, university management, and other institutional overseers. Impact is a term often derided in academia, scoffed at by scratchy scholars annoyed at yet another imposition on their academic freedoms. We are here neither to cheerlead for institutional definitions of impact, nor to rail against this prevalent buzzword entirely. We hope, instead, with these examples of sociolinguistic research that have actually helped real people, to argue how impact might be better articulated. For the most part, in making this argument, we let the chapters do the talking. We have resisted the temptation to pepper the volume with editorial summaries, or introductions and conclusions to each section. Instead, we limit our sermon to the beginning, then leave you alone to take in the chapters and consider their mutual relevance.

The final bit of unorthodoxy is that these preliminary notes, and the next section introducing the contributors' chapters, constitute the entirety of our introduction. But where is the substantive editorial essay exploring the book's disciplinary and political context? That's all in Chapter 1. We made this separation to address a perennial problem with introductions: nobody reads them. Like all editors, we feel our contextual essay is far too important to be merrily leafed past. Steering readers around like this may come across as gamesmanship; but then, since nobody will read this introduction, nobody will notice.

Overview of chapters

In the early stages of planning this book, we knew we were straying into some unusual territory. To our delight we received a wide range of excellent chapter proposals, which gave us the luxury of accepting only those that met very high standards – both in general academic terms and with respect to the theme of impact. Our next job was to decide how to arrange the ones we accepted. They seemed to fall into reasonably clear categories, although as always there was some ambiguity. We arrived at three Parts. The chapters in Part I discuss research that principally concerns education, in traditional teaching contexts and further afield. Chapters 2 and 3 involve work in schools, while Chapters 4 and 5 concern public education projects about language and dialect. Also of note: Chapters 2, 4 and 5 all involve significant roles for university students, bridging the gap between research and teaching. Part II was perhaps the hardest to define. These chapters concern the ways that sociolinguistic research has been used to influence professional practice in organisations and/or wider umbrella professional bodies. Of course, the same could be said about the chapters in Parts I and III. One aspect that distinguishes the chapters in Part II is that they deal with organisations that, historically, have perhaps been less thoroughly engaged with by sociolinguists: Chapter 6 concerns deaf employees and their employers; Chapter 7 jury trials; Chapter 8 police interviews; and Chapter 9 the media (traditional and 'new'). So these are 'institutions' of varying kinds, the uniting thread being engagement with practitioners to influence their practice. Part III returns to an area more traditionally linked with sociolinguistics: governmental language policy. Chapter 10 discusses engagement with language policymakers in Wales; Chapter 11 compares and contrasts efforts to influence language policy in three different developing countries; Chapter 12 looks at the UK Government's policies and practices in relation to asylum seekers whose origins are determined based on evidence of their language and dialect. We discuss each chapter in a little more detail below.

In Chapter 2, Mary Bucholtz, Dolores Inés Casillas, and Jin Sook Lee present a discussion of the *School Kids Investigating Language in Life and Society* (SKILLS) project in Santa Barbara County, California. Drawing on the notion of "accompaniment," the project introduces young people from African American, Asian American, European American, and Native American heritages to sociolinguistic methods and concepts. They then use these concepts to explore everyday language in their immediate social surroundings. In doing so, the project helps participants "develop a deeper understanding of their own and others' linguistic heritage and expertise as language users while strengthening their academic skills and participating in mentoring relationships and friendships with university grad-uate and undergraduate students that often extend well beyond the end of the program each year" (p. 31). Not only is the SKILLS project an excellent example of how sociolinguistics can be integrated within an education programme, but it also demonstrates how young people can leverage sociolinguistic knowledge to challenge social and linguistic inequality.

In Chapter 3, Catherine Levasseur reports on her doctoral research examining tensions and paradoxes in French-medium schooling in British Columbia, Can-ada. She focuses particularly on school children whose parents have 'ayant droit' status (i.e. the right to register their children in a French language school). As she highlights, some of these children have more limited competence in French than their status suggests, and so they are placed on a *francisation* programme. Despite being legally recognised as Francophone, these students are "most often not recognized as native French speakers and thus their right to be enrolled in a [Francophone] school is regularly questioned" (p. 47). Through a series of sen-sitively conducted focus groups with the children themselves, Levasseur shows how these children construct their identities in between, or even outside, Fran-cophone and Anglophone labels. Given that these children are expected to be the next generation of Francophones, the findings raise a number of important questions. Levasseur's impact centres on her engagement with parents and teach-ers, helping them come to a more nuanced understanding of language, identity, and what it means to be Francophone.

In Chapter 4, Fiona Douglas discusses the *Language, History, Place* project, a collaboration between the University of Leeds and three Yorkshire folk museums. The project aims to widen access to a range of dialect material hosted at the uni-versity, and reciprocally collecting visitors' own knowledge, opinions, and voices regarding local dialect use. The project also aims to reconnect these historical dialect materials "with the physical objects from the museums' collections" so that "the past can be brought to life, and valuable new connections and mean-ings made" (p. 71). As noted earlier, Douglas' chapter contributes to the case (reflected in Chapters 2 and 5) for including student work within definitions of impact. She notes the work of her undergraduate students in collecting and col-lating dialect material from visitors, and using this to produce a range of resources including videos for public consumption.

Part I ends with Chapter 5. In relating the groundbreaking and multi-award-winning work of the *North Carolina Language and Life Project* (NCLLP), Walt Wolfram outlines how sociolinguists can utilise diverse multi-media tools to facilitate public engagement with sociolinguistic research. The NCLLP includes a wide range of resources such as video productions, oral history compilations, museum exhibits, and much more. In particular, Wolfram offers a persuasive argu-ment as to how these forms of outreach and engagement can help counter wide-spread prescriptivist prejudices, and replace "misguided notions and erroneous beliefs about language diversity with information about the authentic nature of language variation" (p. 87). Wolfram also highlights how such public education endeavours can be augmented by more formal educational pathways. These include formal curricula on language in schools through to language diversity sessions designed for university staff, students, and faculty.

Taken together, the chapters in Part I concern influences of education, and influences on education. A recurrent theme is also the way impact can be achieved by bridging research and teaching in higher education. These chapters also show how critical such forms of outreach are for widening participation in sociolinguistic research, and, as advanced in Wolfram's chapter, for the very survival of linguistics as an autonomous discipline.

Part II opens with Chapter 6. Jules Dickinson investigates problems faced by deaf employees and their interpreters in the workplace. She focuses on workplace humour, and how the impossibility of translating a wry smile or a cheeky aside into sign language can cumulatively build up to significant exclusion from workplace communication. Humour is a vital part of building a workplace community and promoting group solidarity, so this can have serious implications in terms of deaf employees' wellbeing. As Dickinson points out, "Overall deaf people report negative emotions and feelings such as frustration, dissatisfaction, loneliness, and anger in relation to their workplace experiences. These mainly result from the communication barriers in this setting . . . reflecting deaf people's experiences of interacting with hearing people generally" (p. 127). Following on from detailed conversation analysis, she presents a series of practical steps to address these concerns, including awareness-raising among hearing employees, the integration of her research material into interpreting and sign language courses, and a range of other workshops and training events.

Practitioner training forms the central focus in Chapter 7, where Bronwen Innes discusses a key speech act in law court discourse: the judge's summing-up. The summing-up occurs prior to the jury retiring to reach its verdict. The judge discusses legal precedents relevant to the case, and outlines the main elements of the prosecution and defence. As Innes' research shows, this speech act is characterised by a constellation of knotty linguistic features including complex noun phrases, specialised legal language, and a high rate of lexical density. All this can confuse jurors and blur their understanding of the case, thereby limiting their ability to arrive at an informed decision. By adapting the findings of her work into training for judges, she shows that small changes in linguistic practice can help judges "contribute positively to better outcomes for justice" (p. 144).

Continuing the focus on legal contexts, Nicci MacLeod and Kate Haworth in Chapter 8 present their sociolinguistic research on police interviews, and how, similarly to Innes, they used this to develop training for several police forces across England. By using real-life examples from police interviews, the course trains police interviewers to identify the kinds of interactional strategies interviewers adopt, and to understand the effect these choices have on interviewees, and on interview outcomes. Drawing on commentary and feedback from police officers who attended the training course, MacLeod and Haworth evaluate the current impact of their work and identify potential future applications for the training scheme.

As they summarise at the end of their chapter, there is a "clear requirement both for more sociolinguistic research in the area of police interviewing and for more widespread engagement with police practitioners in general" (pp. 167–168). Their ongoing work is an important step towards addressing this deficit.

Chapter 9 by Robert Lawson moves on to look at the relationship between mass media, social media, and research dissemination in the public domain. Using recent media coverage of the supposed rise of 'vocal fry' among young American women, the chapter shows how sociolinguistic expertise can be side-lined in favour of promoting particular language ideologies, and outlines how social media can be used by sociolinguists to counter these ideologies. Using this context as a starting point, the chapter goes on to argue that dissemination is a key part of the 'impact chain' and discusses advantages and disadvantages of using traditional and social media to disseminate research beyond academic audiences. The chapter also offers some recommendations on using social media, including blogging and altmetrics, and argues that these forms of outreach can help facilitate potential future impact.

The chapters in Part II show how engagement with practitioners can lead to unforeseen impact even within the project, for example the way Dickinson's deaf interviewees found the very process of recounting their communicative difficul-ties to be therapeutic. These chapters also show how the process of engagement can inform changes to the research process, for example the many requests that Innes' judges had for the kinds of training they would find most useful. All this contributes to our understanding of how impact can shape, and be shaped by, professional practice.

Part III presents work related to impact in language policy research. Chapter 10 by Dave Sayers is part research account, part self-help guide for under-employed sociolinguists still aspiring to impact. It argues that even without an academic career, or even much hope of achieving one, it is possible to pursue impact with sociolinguistic research. The chapter begins with an account of research on Welsh language policy, and of showing Welsh language policymakers the slightly discom-forting findings. The chapter broadens out into a discussion of how trained socio-linguists who do not currently have a formal university affiliation, or any research funding, can still effectively engage with policymakers. This guidance covers hon-orary affiliations, contacting key decision-makers, and building academic cred-ibility, among other issues. It is still perfectly possible to pursue impact "given the right attitude to opportunities, some perseverance, and good temper" (p. 195).

Hywel Coleman in Chapter 11 examines the motivations, methods and find-ings of research projects commissioned by the British Council on the role of English in three developing countries: Indonesia, Gabon, and Pakistan. These case studies are presented as having different levels of impact, and lessons are drawn from their successes and shortcomings. The chapter concludes with some observations about the difficulties arising when the researcher's recom-mendations do not align with those of the organisation or government that commissioned the research.

Finally in Chapter 12, Peter Patrick presents a discussion of ongoing work in the field of Language Analysis for Determination of Origin (LADO). The development of sociolinguistically informed analyses of language is an important shift within the immigration system, especially since "the fate of people claiming asylum due to 'fear of persecution' is partly determined by 'language analysis' processes whose scientific basis is questioned by linguists" (p. 236). In the context of the complexities of using a speaker's language competency to scrutinise their claim of origin, Patrick's chapter shows how sociolinguistics is ideally placed to positively contribute to the life opportunities of individuals. He also demonstrates how he and his collaborators have used their work to challenge institutional approaches to LADO, and to encourage systemic change.

The chapters of Part III all discuss research that has gone against prevailing governmental paradigms, and the struggle of presenting such challenging findings to those in power. Another aspect of these chapters is the importance of chance encounters. In all three chapters, certain opportune events or contacts helped on the road to impact. This may seem discouraging to readers if so much hangs on sheer luck, but a lesson from all these encounters is the importance of simply making yourself visible in different ways, and seizing opportunities as they arise.

Chapter 1

Where we're going, we don't need roads

The past, present, and future of impact

Robert Lawson, ORCID no. 0000–0003–1415–517X
Dave Sayers, ORCID no. 0000–0003–1124–7132

Sociolinguistics: The unsung hero of impact

Compared to other subfields of linguistics, sociolinguistics has been relatively outward-facing since its inception. In one sense, this follows naturally when collecting data from people in everyday situations. Yet few can accuse sociolinguistics of being particularly meddlesome in the political process; nor has the discipline as a whole been overwhelmingly preoccupied with improving people's lives. In fact, despite significantly furthering our academic understanding of linguistic variation and change, language policy and planning, language and identity, language and gender, and so on, very few people outside academia have ever heard of sociolinguistics – let alone its influence beyond the groves of academe.

But wait a minute. Isn't there a strong tradition of sociolinguistic work that has aimed, amongst other things, to fight language discrimination, to stand up for downtrodden minorities, and to champion linguistic equality? Doesn't an emancipatory ethos resonate right from the earliest sociolinguistic research? Labov's (1969) *The Logic of Nonstandard English* is not only a staunch defence of a stigmatised linguistic group, but also an attempt to challenge factually inaccurate theories of language use in the inner city. This tradition has been carried on through the work of pioneering figures like Deborah Cameron, Jenny Cheshire, Joshua Fishman, Ben Rampton, Peter Trudgill, Walt Wolfram, and others. Returning to Labov, his (1982) *principle of debt incurred,* as well as Wolfram's (1993) *principle of linguistic gratuity* (see also Wolfram et al. 2008; Wolfram, this volume), have guided community-based language research in giving back to communities, and seeing participants as fundamentally involved stakeholders rather than as simply passive objects of inquiry (see also Cameron et al. 1992: 22; Wolfram et al. 2004). Cameron et al. (1992) have provided a significant advance in using academic research to empower research participants, as well as wider interest groups and local communities. The list goes on, of those sociolinguists who have established a long record in pursuing human wellbeing as a central tenet of their work. Happily this list includes a number of our current contributors.

Yet despite a good deal of work countering nefarious myths about linguistic deficiency, standing up for neglected groups and so on, that tradition has seldom been narrated coherently; it has not been brought together and celebrated for what it is. Nor has this laudable work been particularly clearly articulated in current parlance: 'impact.' As Peter Trudgill put it in a characteristically laconic response to our original call for papers for this volume, sent to an email list: "In those happier days, when we had no idea what 'impact' was, we were nevertheless concerned to make an impact." (Thanks to Peter for consenting to this being reproduced here.) Indeed, his 1984 edited volume *Applied Sociolinguistics*, which showcased a range of sociolinguistic research with applications beyond academia, was a rare specimen. Since then, the collocation of 'applied' and 'sociolinguistics' has not gained the purchase he might have hoped. If anything it has come to mean simply the application of sociolinguistic theory to cases of human interaction, resulting in predominantly academic outputs (e.g. the contributions to Giles et al. 1991). Trudgill's volume has not been identifiably followed up. In that respect, one of our more ostentatiously precocious aims is to step into his shoes.

Only very recently has there been renewed specific attention to the application of sociolinguistic research to non-academic contexts, and often still in somewhat germinal form. Grujicic-Alatriste's 2015 edited volume *Linking Discourse Studies to Professional Practice* begins by offering a framework for how to apply research findings, then each chapter considers how that framework might be used to apply their findings in different contexts. Yet the chapters mostly remain in quite hypothetical territory, planning for future application rather than reporting on application and impact achieved. The volume is still innovative and novel, but with the current book we hope to progress on to examples of research already applied and impact already achieved, while also giving space to plans for future application and impact.

Another recent addition, Corrigan and Mearns' (2016) *Taming Digital Voices and Texts Volume 3: Databases for Public Engagement*, approaches the impactful application of language corpora in different contexts. Their chapters progress into the actual application of research. Discussing the use of corpus resources in education and in professional training contexts, the volume resonates with our own on many levels. It is perhaps the closest complement to our book. Corrigan and Mearns' chapters focus on corpus linguistics, whilst our chapters cover sociolinguistics more broadly, so the two books complement one another nicely.

This general quietude about the history of impact in sociolinguistics is a curious state of affairs, especially given dramatic recent changes to the research funding landscape – tied up with wider political developments around the world (as discussed in the next section). 'Impact' is now a significant funding criterion for all research as funding bodies increasingly turn their attention to its real-world application. The weighting of impact as a percentage of research quality is therefore likely to grow (Kerridge 2013; Witty 2013: 37). How can sociolinguistics adapt to this? How can we build on the tradition of benevolent sociolinguistic intervention and embed this into more of our research?

We put this book together with four main aims. In no particular order, the first is to showcase and celebrate the application and impact of sociolinguistic research in a variety of national and international contexts, to see how this basic imperative to do good with research transcends political boundaries. Second, we very passionately want to emphasise that impact can be achieved across the full range of career stages and with very different levels of resources. Some might assume that impact is impossible without a major funded research project and an army of eager research assistants, but some of our chapters show that demonstrably positive outcomes are possible with a modest budget, or none at all, and by hitherto unknown researchers even without academic employment. This is particularly important given the pressure that most early career researchers feel from the current research assessment regime (Mathieson 2015). Our third aim is to encourage sociolinguists using all manner of methodologies and subdisciplinary foci to consider embedding impact within their research, to imagine how their research might be leveraged (even in a small way) to address issues of human wellbeing. This is not to suggest that every sociolinguistic research project should have impact at its centre. Rather, we hope to show that a number of traditionally academically focused methodologies can – with relatively modest adaptations – be used to achieve positive changes in people's lives. We hope to inspire, not harangue. Last, but by no means least, our fourth aim is to address specific gripes with the contemporary articulation of impact and to offer constructive ideas for how this could be reframed. One of these, high on our list, is the stipulation that impact can only happen outside of the university, and must be informed by research, not teaching – that 'the university' and 'the community' are separate entities. As Crispin Thurlow (2015) put it emphatically in a recent talk on these intersections, "The university is the real world, dammit!" A number of our chapters show how impact can be achieved by postgraduate and undergraduate students, given appropriate guidance, and that this can take place within a wider programme of research and teaching. With ever greater calls for synergy between research and teaching, this is fertile ground for constructive critique of the contemporary impact agenda.

New public management and the history of impact

In this section, we outline the history of impact within the public sector, its roots in an emergent paradigm of state governance 'New Public Management' (NPM), and its eventual integration into academia. Our intention is to show how and why impact has grown to be such a key priority for policymakers, funding agencies, higher education institutions and researchers. Along the way, we discuss certain criticisms directed at the impact agenda, particularly from within the arts and humanities. We focus principally on the UK higher education context, though many of the principles translate further afield – as our chapters from around the world bear out.

The history of research impact can be traced back to the rise of New Public Management, a model of state governance that originated in New Zealand in the

1980s (Schedler and Proeller 2002: 163) and came to influence government poli-cymaking worldwide in the following three decades (see e.g. Cloke et al. 2010: 112). Among the early defining features of NPM was the "best value" regime (Martin 2002), an imperative to seek continuous improvement to public services, regardless of specific deficiencies, and to measure these quantifiably. This signalled "[a] movement away from input controls, rules and procedures towards output measurements and performance targets" (Hope Sr. 2002: 211). Critically, that had the effect of simultaneously de-emphasising anything that could not be mea-sured in this way. As Broadbent and Laughlin (2001: 102) have it: " 'Account-ing logic' . . . produces an aura of factual representation, . . . 'neutral, objective, independent and fair' information. . . . It . . . emphasizes . . . common measurable yardsticks." Such accounting logic is hindered by the "lack of ability to define outputs" (Broadbent and Laughlin 2001: 102); and to this problem "two logical solutions exist" (p. 103):

> One is to admit that the prerequisites for control approaches based on markets or hierarchies are inappropriate . . . . The other, characteristic of . . . NPM, is to systematize the tasks in question and standardize the outputs, i.e. to reinvent the tasks . . . for the application of such logic.

The importance of inspection and demonstrating productivity are crucial here:

> Over the last 30 years in the UK . . . [w]e have moved from large, state-owned bureaucracies . . . to quasi-independent operational units . . . to networks of organizations which can operate with a fair degree of autonomy providing they meet specified performance targets. Persistent failure, however, invites state intervention.
>
> (Dawson and Dargie 2002: 53)

In many ways, NPM emerged as the blending of two paradigms: the Thatcher-Reagan era pursuit of shrinking the state, and a centrist ideology of broadened state intervention. Mixing the two created a government doctrine designed to micro-manage behaviour and change society, but with a managerialist attention to productivity and intense introspection based on measurable performance.

As a policymaking framework, NPM quickly spread not only to the UK, but to Australia, the USA and Scandinavia (Dawson and Dargie 2002), mainland Europe (Schedler and Proeller 2002), and "most Western democracies" (Mar-tin 2002: 129). It subsequently spread to Mexico (Barragan and Roemer 2001), South Africa (Mwaniki 2004), sub-Saharan Africa (Hope Sr. 2002), East Asia (Cheung 2002), and a range of developing countries (McCourt 2002). In sum, it has become "a standard international model for public administration reform" (Schedler and Proeller 2002: 163).

NPM seemed propelled by its own inertia. Meanwhile, heightened scrutiny inside government was increasingly matched from outside, via the media and pressure groups (Dawson and Dargie 2002: 37). All this began to create a climate in which the expenditure of public money must not only demonstrate success in terms of *outputs* but also *outcomes*, tangible changes effected.

The ascendency of 'impact' as a watchword in the contemporary funding environment can be seen as a direct corollary of the emergence of NPM. The popularity of NPM has been attributed to the intuitive attractiveness of ideals like efficiency, accountability, and progress, and the sheer difficulty of arguing against them:

> Academics who traditionally had the public sphere to themselves found it invaded by concepts of management. [T]his . . . posed a crude choice, either critique and reject [NPM] . . . or adopt it as your own. . . . Conceptual discussions of NPM in the late 1990s suggest that many commentators have taken the latter choice, not least, one may surmise, because to appear to stand against ways to improve efficiency and so on would be to assume the role of a Luddite and lose the ear of those whom they may be trying to influence.
>
> (Dawson and Dargie 2002: 41)

All this serves to demonstrate the rise of a qualitatively different sociopolitical context from the time of Trudgill's 1984 *Applied Sociolinguistics* volume mentioned earlier, with concomitant changes to the pressures and incentives faced by researchers.

Currently, approximately every five years all UK universities undergo a major peer-reviewed evaluation of their research, designed to rank universities and departments by their relative research strengths and to allocate "quality-related" (QR) funding from the Higher Education Funding Council for England (HEFCE), the Higher Education Funding Council for Wales (HEFCW), the Scottish Further and Higher Education Funding Council (SHEFC), and the Department for Employment and Learning Northern Ireland (DELNI). (For the most part, HEFCE has assumed the lead role in defining impact, and so we focus on HEFCE below.) The influence of NPM within UK higher education spurred a state of concentrated fervour between 2006 and 2014, with the introduction of what has since come to be known as the "impact agenda" (Martin 2011). Understanding this period involves tracing the history of a wider regime of governmental scrutiny over academic research, with which the impact agenda came to dovetail.

Tracing a series of key reforms in British higher education, Kogan and Hanney (2000) pinpoint 1977 as a precipice in the historically expansive freedoms – academic, organisational, and financial – that universities had enjoyed: "Step by step from the mid-1970s, the universities' almost unique freedom in finance was reduced, and by the end of the 1970s the notion of a sacrosanct unit of resource was coming under criticism" (p. 85). In July 1981, central government began to take direct control of "points such as access and efficiency" in higher education (p. 87). Kogan and Hanney (2000: 89) note the newly fervent austerity of the

Secretary of State for Education, Sir Keith Joseph, "driven . . . by a monetarist ideology," at a time when "questions were being voiced by ministers . . . over whether much of the HE [Higher Education] output was economically valueless . . . and . . . should be both reduced in scale and somehow drastically reformed." Accordingly, the 1981 funding allocations to universities "were significant in that they incorporated differential quality judgements, thus beginning the explicit stratifying of universities and departments which became more open in the 1986 research assessment exercise" (or RAE).

The RAE, initially discussed as a "research selectivity exercise," was a product of its time, of civil service mandarins conjuring policies in evening lamplight, over steak and claret. Its genesis is retold in delicious detail in Kogan and Hanney (2000: 97–98). They quote Christopher Ball, then Warden of Keble College, Oxford (Warden = Master or Principle), recounting his conversations with Peter Swinnerton-Dyer, chairman of the University Grants Committee, and David Phillips, chairman of the Advisory Board for the Research Councils.

> [We] used to have dinner together, and plan our . . . strategy. One evening, Peter said, '. . . I can no longer defend the funding of universities . . . without real accountability to government . . . why does the university system need all these unspecific funds? . . .' . . . So we discussed it and I suppose at that dinner we invented the research selectivity exercise.

The anecdote goes on to note that selectivity was originally only intended for the more expensive science and technology subjects, but the "heads of the disciplinary group in social studies and arts" said they "can't be left out. It would appear to the public that our research is unimportant (ibid.)." And so a sense of challenged legitimacy, concern about losing face, and perhaps some bridled egos, led to what might seem a counter-intuitive acceptance of evaluation metrics by the entire research community.

The first RAE was completed in 1986. It evaluated university departments against three criteria: research outputs (articles, monographs, edited volumes, etc.); research environment (number of PhD students, external funding, etc.); and indicators of esteem (number of Professorial chairs, advisory roles taken up, research awards and fellowships, etc.). Further RAEs were undertaken in 1989, 1992, 1996, 2001, and 2008. As New Public Management took greater hold of government during the 1990s and into the 2000s, especially as the reins of power changed from Conservative to New Labour, the purpose of research assessment changed. In the mid-1980s the context was funding cuts; but by the early 2000s funding for higher education was increasing (Chowdry and Sibieta 2011: 7; Universities UK 2013: 55). Hence a change in the rationale for research assessment: from its origins as a way to fairly distribute reductions in funding, towards a way to fairly allocate increased resources. Recalling the benchmarks of NPM – best value, quantifiable measurement of performance, perpetual review – we can see how this contoured the evolving RAE:

The evolution of the RAE took place during the debate surrounding performance indicators. All institutions were increasingly being asked to justify their performance and account for their use of resources to external funding bodies. The evaluation of research performance in the UK during the 1980s and 1990s should be viewed alongside changes in the structure of university funding, the increasing importance attached to assessing quality and the development of performance indicators to facilitate this.

(Bence and Oppenheim 2005: 141)

The 2014 iteration of this exercise saw a name change to Research Excellence Framework (REF). Like its predecessors, its main aim was to develop a picture of research capability across all academic subjects within UK higher education and "to produce indicators of research excellence for all disciplines which can be used to benchmark quality against international standards" (Eastwood 2007). Compared to previous reviews, however, REF 2014 replaced "esteem" with the new category of "impact." One intention behind this new category was to foreground how research is used by stakeholders beyond an immediate academic context, to ensure that academic research is accountable, transparent and visible (Martin 2011; Watermeyer 2016: 361). In many ways, this was a perfectly natural evolution and extension of a scrutinising ethos that had been growing since the 1970s. A parallel motivation in replacing esteem with impact was to shift the emphasis away from (potentially obsolete) past achievements and towards current application. As Steve Fuller – a sociologist at Warwick University – put it in a blog post in 2009: "No more coasting on reputations made twenty years ago!"

But mostly, at its moment of conception in 2006, impact arose from an intriguing political compromise. As Jump (2013, after Brown and Carasso 2013) relates, the then Chancellor (later Prime Minister) Gordon Brown wanted to reduce the ballooning cost of the RAE by replacing peer review entirely with a more automated process based on "metrics such as citations, research income and postgraduate numbers." The task of mounting a counter-argument fell to Rama Thirunamachandran, HEFCE Director of Research, Innovation and Skills 2002–2008. Thirunamachandran offered to introduce 'impact' as a more nuanced measure of performance, as a way to encourage the Treasury in Whitehall to drop its proposal. As Thirunamachandran recounted, the question of where "£1.6 billion a year in QR [quality-related] funding" was actually going could "only be articulated in terms of impact and, to some extent, it was a sort of unstated compact that if we could demonstrate and assess impact, the sort of mindless cry for metrics would subside from the Whitehall end" (Jump 2013). Again, the hallmarks of NPM hove into view here, requiring performance to be measured against centrally defined benchmarks. (See Olssen and Peters 2005 for extensive further discussion of the political history of NPM, and related ideologies, in higher education.)

Work on the 2008 RAE was well underway by 2006, and so it continued without introducing impact. The idea of impact therefore only rose to wider attention in 2009 during the early planning stages of REF 2014. It was somewhat clumsily publicised at first, and quickly drew the ire of academics and other commentators who imagined a final nail falling into the coffin of academic freedom. Scholars in the arts and humanities, some of whom had embraced research assessment in the 1980s (as outlined earlier), became its sharpest critics, feeling that it would reduce research planning to mundane short-term cost-benefit analyses (Belfiore 2014). Such researchers may not immediately situate their work as having a public impact, at least according to official definitions. Moreover, as Cook (2011: 35) argues, it is incumbent upon academics to critique establishment values, not slavishly adhere to them. What of research that raises important points but does not align with – or even directly threatens – existing policies or commercial interests (Cook 2011: 44)? That may be deemed unimportant, and deprioritised accordingly. In 2009, the issue hit the headlines when the high profile (and relatively highbrow) comedian David Mitchell wrote a newspaper article in response to the REF plans:

> So what sort of pointless study is this new system going to weed out? Why, all the ones that don't have a solid social or economic goal, of course. The government isn't going to pay for clever people just to sit in universities indulging their curiosity. . . . Nothing good ever got invented by accident, apart from some silly fun stuff like the slinky, post-it notes, penicillin, warfarin and X-rays. . . . The trouble is that, for a moment, it sounds perfectly sensible to demand that researchers justify their means in terms of their projected ends, but so, for a moment, does Noddy's idea of building the roof of a house first so that it keeps the rain off while you build the walls.

Steve Fuller, cited earlier (2009), had lauded the spirit of replacing esteem with impact to enable newer academics to build a reputation, but he echoed Mitchell's criticisms of bean-counting myopia. He opined that this would choke off the spirit of independent inquiry which for millennia had spurred serendipitous discoveries – and that, anyway, research in the arts and humanities is valuable in a number of ways beyond finance, economics or policy (cf. Coulombeau 2013; Williams 2014).

The next development was the publication in 2010 of a document by the Economic and Social Research Council about integrating social science research into the evidence base for forming government policy (ESRC 2010). The following year, HEFCE issued guidance with a specific definition for impact: "an effect on, change or benefit to the economy, society, culture, public policy or services, health, the environment or quality of life, beyond academia as the result of excellent research" (HEFCE 2011: 26). Then an interesting and strategically shrewd change took place. Cognizant of the above criticisms and other such views, although HEFCE's subsequent final criteria for assessing impact (HEFCE 2012) principally focused on demonstrable changes to government policy and/or professional practice, they included one criterion that stood out: "Public debate has been stimulated or informed by research" (p. 28). If a researcher could demonstrate this then they could claim impact without changing – without even intending to change – policy or practice. Impact therefore ended up as a broader benchmark, simply measuring changes to behaviour influenced by research. Stirring civic debate, even if that has zero effect on government policy, is still a change in behaviour. Research has reached out and done something, beyond the rarefied world of journals and conferences. The concrete effect of this shift was the requirement in REF 2014 for university departments to include a series of "impact case studies" in their submissions (HEFCE 2013). These would set out the impact that occurred as a result of research, with claims supported by evidence including testimonials by end users, statistical analysis and so forth (see Penfield et al. 2014).

But this is still firmly within the New Public Management framework, prioritising and measuring social outcomes as a direct linear result of fiscal expenditure. Contribution to knowledge on its own – impact on academia, however extensive – remained explicitly excluded from the criteria (HEFCE 2012: 48). With all this in mind, one key remaining criticism of the impact agenda is that it promotes pervasive instrumentalisation, constraining research value to the achievement of measurable social value, utility or end products (Belfiore 2014). For funding bodies, a logical consequence is that such benefits must be foreseeable in advance, in order to be included and assessed in funding bids. Such benefits also need to be demonstrable within the lifetime of the research, or shortly thereafter. It is both impermissible and impossible to speculate about how research might influence society at some future point.

As discussed earlier, deference to "accounting logic" has the effect of de-emphasising anything that cannot be measured in this way (Broadbent and Laughlin 2001: 102). A knock-on effect of this can be seen in the way funding for 'STEM' subjects (science, technology, engineering and maths) was raised as a strategic priority for both central Government and HEFCE (HM Government 2012: 23), while funding for arts and humanities was cut (Morgan 2010; Belfiore 2013: 19).

Meanwhile, as Penfield et al. (2014: 22) outline, higher education institutions warmly embraced impact. For them, it promised a new measure of relative performance among their departments. It would show how their research contributed to local, national, and international communities, thus bolstering their case for continued tax-payer funding – and more widely for the allocation of research money. Finally, explicitly recording how impact was achieved could function as a guide to researchers wishing to pursue this in their own work.

Academic dissent is not immune from pressure, and the common good only motivates so much resistance. In the context of a fiercely competitive academic job market with less room for quarrelsome malcontents, academics in the arts and humanities have increasingly felt compelled to justify their work and to demonstrate its social and economic worth (Belfiore and Upchurch 2013a: 16; Brunning 2013). Indeed, there has been quite a clamour not only to demonstrate impact within individual research projects, but also to dedicate whole projects and programmes to it – for example the *Impact of Social Sciences* project at the London

School of Economics (http://blogs.lse.ac.uk/impactofsocialsciences/). A growing number of institutions are setting up dedicated outreach programmes, entrepreneurial workshops, and engagement courses, all directed towards facilitating impact. Research that achieves impact is increasingly recognised as an exemplar of good practice. For example, in 2014 Swansea University announced a series of annual Impact Awards celebrating examples of impact across various fields, including public policy, commerce, public engagement, and health. In 2013, the Economic and Social Research Council introduced a *Celebrating Impact Prize* and an *Impact Champion of the Year Award*. In 2014, the ESRC announced a series of funding opportunities to "accelerate the impact of research" (ESRC 2014). These are examples of actions guided by broader macro-level incentives, reacting to the way impact is linked to funding and pushing in that direction for understandable reasons of self-preservation. Yet, this has not been matched by funding or awards for critically exploring the influence of impact on research motivated by this new regime.

A further risk is that impact goes from being one factor in research quality to being conflated with it entirely. Cook (2011: 35) contends that "impact is not necessarily a measure of academic worth," but it is recurrently claimed that the more impact, the better the research (cf. Allen 2014). This is a fairly easy and intuitive claim to advance, but change is a matter of perspective and not all change is necessarily good (Cook 2011: 45; Penfield et al. 2014: 22). Nor are the best changes always the quickest; the distant speck of a star could be outshone by the nearby dazzle of a candle. Moreover, research in different fields cannot be measured against the same yardsticks (Penfield et al. 2014: 25–26). Even with HEFCE's inclusion of the one standout criterion on "public debate" as a form of impact (noted earlier), as Belfiore (2013: 38) points out the overarching wider focus palpably remains "impact on either the economy or on policy-making." That can sideline more ineffable and evanescent forms of impact. Taken together, the impact agenda may constitute a form of governmental dictat on the research academics pursue (Cook 2011: 54).

As reviewed so far, there is a lively debate about the position – and imposition – of impact. But there are redeeming factors, at least in the spirit of increasing the attention to how research might be used to effect positive social change:

> In shifting the focus from the intermediate good of published outputs to the final good of scholarly impact . . . there may indeed be important behavioural and cultural changes to our practice as scholars. [T]his opening up of the impact agenda can create greater legitimacy for a portfolio approach to publishing for those scholars deadened by the retreat to defining scholarship just in terms of publication in A-rated scholarly journals.
>
> (Pettigrew 2011: 348)

This reframing of scholarly focus has opened up new avenues for academics to develop research profiles explicitly orientated towards engagement and positive social outcomes. Pettigrew (2011: 351–352) further argues that this particular approach to research goes hand in hand with networking, connecting with disparate stakeholders, and cultivating social and cultural capital for positive ends. As Baron (2010) argues (cf. Rickford, this volume), the traditional division between theoretical knowledge and real-world application has hindered effective public engagement. The impact framework goes some way towards bridging this gap.

Another important detail is that the evidencing of impact has at least satisfied the NPM framework and its insistence on measuring performance, thereby stemming what could otherwise have simply been a much more drastic haemorrhaging of research funding. After all, there are still deep-seated suspicions that academia remains a leisurely pursuit with few serious constraints, even rife with profligacy. Recalling the suspicions about waste and inefficiency identified earlier as arising in the 1980s, this frothing irascibility remains alive and well today – in society at large and in the halls of power – fuelled by the return of fiscal austerity and government-wide funding cuts. On 8 January 2015, a Member of Parliament, Brian Binley, was quoted by a journalist from the *Times Higher Education* calling for improved "productivity" of universities, adding for good measure that academics have had "too many high tables, had it too easy for too long" (https://twitter.com/JMorganTHE/status/553164930292396033). Even after the MPs' expenses scandal of 2009, academics remain the target of this kind of antiquated potshot. Binley faced no reprimand or backlash for this (save for a few barbed retorts from academics on social media), so he was not expressing an extreme view. Like it or not, there is still work to do in deconstructing a popular and persistent stereotype of the aloof ivory tower dweller, the begowned dilettante cosseted from the concerns of the real world (cf. Belfiore 2013: 38). Pursuing impact may help in part to address that myth, and in the process bolster the case for research funding in an increasingly cut-throat fiscal environment. Jump (2013, after Brown and Carasso 2013) relates the view of Rama Thirunamachandran (introduced earlier) that the assessment regime has increased the overall quality of UK research, and that this in turn has "also convinced successive governments to invest vastly more resources in university research."

This, of course, does nothing to counter the impact agenda. The unappealing choice for now is whether to accept one's porridge or starve in protest while others feast. There is no sign of collective revolt. But as we hope this book shows, pursuing impact can be more than slavish adherence to imposed priorities. It can lead to a stronger and more constructive position, enabling us as researchers to critique – from a position of superior insight – what it means to achieve something called impact.

To sum up then, impact has emerged from a complex history: scrutiny over academic activity (variously motivated); wider cost-cutting across government; and the ascendency of New Public Management, a governance framework that requires measurable outcomes for all fiscal expenditure. There is a mixed picture in assessing the rise (and rise) of impact. Some of its underlying motivations are generally laudable; others have drawn more heated reactions. Inherent benefits include the general push to emphasise how research can achieve positive outcomes. Rather more tautological benefits include satiating a system of governance (NPM) that may have oversimplified what matters in society. There are clear risks, like swaying incentives towards easy wins and discouraging research whose benefits may be nebulous at first but potentially significant in the longer term. A final criticism is that impact, according to HEFCE, can only be achieved by the academic researcher, not the participants or anyone else involved. As various chapters in this volume suggest, school children, undergraduates, members of local communities, and other individuals who may not be classed as academic researchers but who are centrally involved in a research project can achieve meaningful impact. This kind of palpable outcome through research remains unacknowledged in the UK definition of impact, even if it would not have come about without the research.

Taking all of the above criticisms together, the impact agenda is often seen as overly simplistic, or as undervaluing research that lacks immediately obvious fireworks at the end. This is a concerning place to be, not least because it risks hollowing out the meaning of academic research and the role of the university in wider civic life. Instrumentalisation has not entirely won the day, but it is still vitally important to seek ways to define and operationalise impact in broader terms (cf. Belfiore and Upchurch 2013b; Penfield et al. 2014).

Wherever you stand, we return to the point that arguing for change will be easier if it is based on worked examples. The rise of impact seems assured: the author of a government-commissioned report in 2013 recommends "a presumption of increase in the weighting for impact evidence to 25% [from 20%] in the next REF, subject to evaluation of the current REF" (Witty 2013: 37; cf. Kerridge 2013). It therefore seems likely that funding agencies will continue to view impact as a strategic priority, particularly in the context of economic austerity where accountability is paramount. Where academics can intervene is in highlighting specific limitations of the impact agenda, and demonstrating more nuanced and inclusive understandings of what could be a progressive and positive measure. It is precisely that task we aim to undertake in this book. Each chapter provides a significant contribution to such a constructive critique, demonstrating palpable positive outcomes through sociolinguistic research, with important contrasts to overarching institutional definitions of impact. By drawing out these kinds of comparisons and contrasts, we hope that sociolinguists generally will be in a stronger position to develop counter-narratives to the impact agenda.

Changing times, changing contexts: Rearticulating impact in sociolinguistics

As we have discussed so far, impact is a high priority in higher education and likely to remain so for the foreseeable future. In some senses, impact has been rather crudely articulated in instrumentalist terms; but it has its redeeming features, and the principle of working to improve human wellbeing is worth salvaging. We believe that the chapters in this book demonstrate how impact can be pursued in a way that is relevant, useful and beneficial to people's lives. In doing so, we hope to move the discussion away from relatively narrow definitions of impact, towards a broader consideration of human wellbeing and social justice.

More strategically, the research presented in this volume also helps further the evidence base for the relevance of sociolinguistics within contemporary society, particularly in the face of changeable funding priorities. As Wolfram (p. 104) points out, language research of all stripes is in danger of being lost to the ether, particularly if it struggles to articulate its importance to universities, employers, the general public, funding bodies, and so on. Public perceptions of sociolinguistics remain relatively constrained. Public educational and outreach programmes can help, but a key challenge remains for sociolinguists to augment such efforts with other forms of dissemination, collaboration, and engagement activities. In particular, sociolinguistics is at its best when working with communities, local organisations, schools, museums, historical societies, employers, third sector groups, policymakers, civil servants, etc., and actively engaging them in the research process. That basic imperative to help people in their lives is a vibrant tradition and a continuing strength for sociolinguistics. We hope to celebrate that strength here, and in the process show how sociolinguistics can move from the periphery to the centre of the debate about what impact is, and could be.

References

Allen, Ansgar. 2014. "Who benefits from the impact agenda?" Accessed 25 February 2015. Available from: http://www.timeshighereducation.co.uk/comment/opinion/who-benefits-from-the-impact-agenda/2016732.article.

Baron, Nancy. 2010. *Escape from the Ivory Tower: A Guide to Making Your Science Matter.* Washington, DC: Island Press.

Barragan, Esteban Moctezuma, and Andres Roemer. 2001. *A New Public Management in Mexico: Towards a Government That Produces Results.* London: Ashgate.

Belfiore, Eleonora. 2013. "The 'rhetoric of gloom' v. the discourse of impact in the humanities: Stuck in a deadlock?" In *Humanities in the Twenty-First Century: Beyond Utility and Markets,* ed. by Eleonora Belfiore and Anna Upchurch, 17–44. Basingstoke: Palgrave Macmillan.

Belfiore, Eleonora. 2014. "'Impact', 'value' and 'bad economics': Making sense of the problem of value in the arts and humanities." *Arts and Humanities in Higher Education* 13 (3).

Belfiore, Eleonora, and Anna Upchurch. 2013a. "The humanities and their impact." In *Humanities in the Twenty-First Century: Beyond Utility and Markets,* ed. by Eleonora Belfiore and Anna Upchurch, 15–16. Basingstoke: Palgrave Macmillan.

Belfiore, Eleonora, and Anna Upchurch (eds.). 2013b. *Humanities in the Twenty-First Century: Beyond Utility and Markets.* Basingstoke: Palgrave Macmillan.

Bence, Valerie, and Charles Oppenheim. 2005. "The evolution of the UK's Research Assessment Exercise: Publications, performance and perceptions." *Journal of Educational Administration and History* 37 (2): 137–155.

Broadbent, Jane, and Richard Laughlin. 2001. "Public service professionals and the New Public Management: Control of the professions in the public services." In *New Public Management: Current Trends and Future Prospects*, ed. by Kathleen McLaughlin, Stephen P. Osborne, and Ewan Ferlie, 95–108. London: Routledge.

Brown, Roger, and Helen Carasso. 2013. *Everything for Sale? The Marketisation of UK Higher Education*. London: Routledge.

Brunning, Luke. 2013. "How can we have an Education Secretary so hostile to those who work in higher education?" Accessed 23 March 2015. Available from: http://www.independent.co.uk/voices/comment/how-can-we-have-an-education-secretary-so-hostile-to-those-who-work-in-higher-education-8548819.html.

Cameron, Deborah, Elizabeth Fraser, Penelope Harvey, M.B.H. Rampton, and Kay Richardson. 1992. *Researching Language: Issues of Power and Method*. London: Routledge.

Cheung, Anthony B. L. 2002. "The politics of New Public Management: Some experience from reforms in East Asia." In *New Public Management: Current Trends and Future Prospects*, ed. by Kathleen McLaughlin, Stephen P. Osborne, and Ewan Ferlie, 243–273. London: Routledge.

Chowdry, Haroon, and Luke Sibieta. 2011. "Trends in education and schools spending." Institute for Fiscal Studies. Accessed 29 June 2015. Available from: http://www.ifs.org.uk/bns/bn121.pdf.

Cloke, Paul, Jon May, and Sarah Johnsen. 2010. *Swept up Lives? Re-envisioning the Homeless City*. Chichester: Wiley-Blackwell.

Cook, Guy. 2011. "British applied linguistics: Impacts of and impacts on." In *The Impact of Applied Linguistics: Proceedings of the 44th Annual Meeting of the British Association for Applied Linguistics*, ed. by Jo Angouri, Michael Daller, and Jeanine Treffers-Daller, 35–58.

Corrigan, Karen P., and Adam Mearns (eds.). In press. *Creating and Digitizing Language Corpora, Volume 3: Corpora for Public Engagement*. Basingstoke: Palgrave-Macmillan.

Coulombeau, Sophie. 2013. "In defence of the humanities: Why this Government is wrong to scorn an arts education." Accessed 23 March 2015. Available from: http://www.independent.co.uk/voices/comment/in-defence-of-the-humanities-why-this-government-is-wrong-to-scorn-an-arts-education-8597863.html.

Dawson, Sandra, and Charlotte Dargie. 2002. "New Public Management: A discussion with special reference to UK health." In *New Public Management: Current Trends and Future Prospects*, ed. by Kathleen McLaughlin, Stephen P. Osborne, and Ewan Ferlie, 34–56. London: Routledge.

Eastwood, David. 2007. "Future framework for research assessment and funding." Accessed 26 February 2015. Available from: https://web.archive.org/web/20120218164052/http://www.hefce.ac.uk/pubs/circlets/2007/cl06_07/.

Economic and Social Research Council (ESRC). 2010. "Getting social science research into the evidence base in Government." Accessed 26 February 2015. Available from: https://www2.warwick.ac.uk/fac/cross_fac/ias/activities/ace/resources/impact_-_miles_2.pdf.

Economic and Social Research Council (ESRC). 2013. "Researchers celebrated for outstanding impact." Accessed 26 February 2015. Available from: http://www.esrc.ac.uk/research/celebrating-impact-prize/.

Economic and Social Research Council (ESRC). 2014. "ESRC impact acceleration accounts." Accessed 23 March 2015. Available from: http://www.esrc.ac.uk/funding/funding-opportunities/impact-acceleration-accounts/.

Fuller, Steve. 2009. "The debate over the desirability of 'pointless' research continues to rage." Accessed 28 April 2015. Available from: https://blogs.warwick.ac.uk/swfuller/entry/the_debate_over/.

Giles, Howard, Justine Coupland, and Nikolas Coupland. 1991. *Contexts of Accommodation: Developments in Applied Sociolinguistics*. Cambridge: Cambridge University Press.

Grujicic-Alatriste, Lubie (ed.). 2015. *Linking Discourse Studies to Professional Practice*. Bristol: Multilingual Matters.

HEFCE (Higher Education Funding Council England). 2011. "Decisions on assessing research impact." Accessed 23 March 2015. Available from: http://www.ref.ac.uk/media/ref/content/pub/assessmentframeworkandguidanceonsubmissions/GOS%20including%20addendum.pdf.

HEFCE (Higher Education Funding Council England). 2012. "Panel criteria and working methods." Accessed 26 February 2015. Available from: http://www.ref.ac.uk/media/ref/content/pub/panelcriteriaandworkingmethods/01_12.pdf.

HEFCE (Higher Education Funding Council England). 2013. "Impact case studies." Accessed 23 March 2015. Available from: http://www.ref.ac.uk/about/guidance/faq/impactcasestudiesref3b.

HM Government. 2012. "Government response to the House of Lords Select Committee on Science and Technology Report." Accessed 23 March 2015. Available from: http://www.parliament.uk/documents/lords-committees/science-technology/STEMsubjects/GovtresponseHEinSTEMreportupdate.pdf.

Hope Sr., Kempe Ronald. 2002. "The New Public Management: A perspective from Africa." *New Public Management: Current Trends and Future Prospects*, ed. by Kathleen McLaughlin, Stephen P. Osborne, and Ewan Ferlie, 210–226. London: Routledge.

Jump, Paul. 2013. "Evolution of the REF." Accessed 30 April 2015. Available from: https://www.timeshighereducation.com/features/evolution-of-the-ref/2008100.article.

Kerridge, Simon. 2013. "To 2020 and beyond." Accessed 2 April 2015. Available from: http://www.researchresearch.com/index.php?option=com_news&template=rr_2col&view=article&articleId=1339882.

Kogan, Maurice, and Stephen Hanney. 2000. *Reforming Higher Education*. London: Jessica Kingsley Publishers.

Labov, William. 1969. "The logic of non-standard English." *Georgetown Monograph on Languages and Linguistics* 22: 1–44. Reprinted in *Language and Social Context*, 1972, ed. by Pier Paolo Giglioli, 179–215. Harmondsworth: Penguin.

Martin, Ben R. 2011. "The Research Excellence Framework and the 'impact agenda': Are we creating a Frankenstein monster?" *Research Evaluation* 20 (3): 247–254.

Martin, Steve. 2002. "Best value: New Public Management or new direction?" In *New Public Management: Current Trends and Future Prospects*, ed. by Kathleen McLaughlin, Stephen P. Osborne, and Ewan Ferlie, 129–140. London: Routledge.

Mathieson, Charlotte. 2015. "A culture of 'publish or perish'? How the REF affects early career researchers." Paper presented at Next Steps for the REF, Royal Society, London, UK.

McCourt, Willy. 2002. "New Public Management in developing countries." In *New Public Management: Current Trends and Future Prospects*, ed. by Kathleen McLaughlin, Stephen P. Osborne, and Ewan Ferlie, 227–242. London: Routledge.

Mitchell, David. 2009. "Pointless studies are the key to evolution." Accessed 29 June 2016. Available from: http://www.theguardian.com/commentisfree/2009/sep/27/david-mitchell-pointless-studies-survey.

Morgan, John. 2010. "Fears made flesh: Only STEM teaching grants spared CSR scythe." Accessed 23 March 2015. Available from: https://www.timeshighereducation.com/news/fears-made-flesh-only-stem-teaching-grants-spared-csr-scythe/413956.article.

Mwaniki, Modest Munene. 2004. *Language Planning in South Africa: Towards a Language Management Approach.* PhD thesis, University of the Free State.

Olssen, Mark, and Michael A. Peters. 2005. "Neoliberalism, higher education and the knowledge economy: From the free market to knowledge capitalism." *Journal of Education Policy* 20 (3): 313–345.

Penfield, Teresa, Matthew J. Baker, Rosa Scoble, and Michael C. Wykes. 2014. "Assessment, evaluations, and definitions of research impact: A review." *Research Evaluations* 23 (1): 21–32.

Pettigrew, Andrew M. 2011. "Scholarship with impact." *British Journal of Management* 22 (3): 347–354.

Saussure, Ferdinand de. 1983. *Course in General Linguistics,* trans. Roy Harris. London: Duckworth.

Schedler, Kuno, and Isabella Proeller. 2002. "The New Public Management: A perspective from mainland Europe." In *New Public Management: Current Trends and Future Prospects,* ed. by Kathleen McLaughlin, Stephen P. Osborne, and Ewan Ferlie, 163–180. London: Routledge.

Swansea University. 2014. "Impact awards 2014." Accessed 26 February 2015. Available from: http://www.swansea.ac.uk/research/impactawards/.

Thurlow, Crispin. 2015. "Where did all the teachers go? Confronting the divisive implications of impact, community engagement, etc." Paper presented at i-Mean 4, University of Warwick, UK.

Trudgill, Peter (ed.). 1984. *Applied Sociolinguistics.* London: Academic Press.

Universities UK. 2013. "The funding environment for universities: An assessment." Accessed 30 March 2015. Available from: http://www.universitiesuk.ac.uk/highereducation/Documents/2013/FundingEnvironmentForUniversities.pdf.

Watermeyer, Richard. 2016. "Impact in the REF: Issues and obstacles." *Studies in Higher Education* 41 (2): 199–214.

Williams, Rowan. 2014. "Rowan Williams: There's no fooling about impact." Accessed 26 February 2015. Available from: http://www.timeshighereducation.co.uk/story.aspx?storyCode=2012699.

Witty, Andrew. 2013. "Final report and recommendations: Encouraging a British invention revolution." Accessed 1 May 2015. Available from: https://www.gov.uk/government/uploads/system/uploads/attachment_data/file/249720/bis-13-1241-encouraging-a-british-invention-revolution-andrew-witty-review-R1.pdf.

Wolfram, Walt. 1993. "Ethical considerations in Language Awareness Programs." *Issues in Applied Linguistics* 4 (2): 225–255.

Wolfram, Walt, Jeffery Reaser, and Charlotte Vaughn. 2008. "Operationalizing linguistic gratuity: From principle to practice." *Language and Linguistic Compass* 2 (6): 1109–1134.

Wolfram, Walt, Ryan Rowe, and Drew Grimes. 2004. "Sociolinguistic involvement in community perspective: Opportunity and obligation." Paper presented at LAVIS III, North Carolina State University.

Part I

Impact in education

Chapter 2

Beyond empowerment

Accompaniment and sociolinguistic justice in a youth research program

Mary Bucholtz, ORCID NUMBER 0000–0001–7343–3374
Dolores Inés Casillas, ORCID NUMBER 0000–0001–9217–462X
Jin Sook Lee, ORCID NUMBER 0000–0001–9812–4922

Introduction

For many scholars hoping to make a real-world impact through sociolinguistic research, the ultimate goal of such work is the empowerment of research participants. Building on the similar concepts of conscientization and critical or liberatory pedagogy (Freire 1970), the rise of the notion of empowerment in scholarship during the 1980s coincided with the emergence of a range of general critical perspectives on race and ethnicity, gender and sexuality, capitalism and social class, (post-)colonialism, and other structures of inequality. Throughout the next decade, empowerment discourse swept across the academy, including not only fields centrally concerned with inequity such as race and ethnic studies, gender studies, education, sociology, and anthropology, as well as the more socially oriented subfields of linguistics, but also such areas as social services, international development, and even corporate management.

Within sociolinguistics, the idea of empowerment has primarily circulated via the work of Deborah Cameron and her colleagues, who propose a three-part taxonomy of relationships between researcher and researched, which they label *ethics*, *advocacy*, and *empowerment* (Cameron et al. 1992, 1993). In their shorthand characterization, traditional social science scholarship, or "research *on*," positions research subjects as no more than research objects and reduces the obligations of researchers to a matter of professional ethics, or the protection of basic rights overseen by institutional review boards, such as confidentiality and informed consent. The second type of relationship, advocacy, adds to and reframes the ethical model by emphasizing "research *for*" participants. In the advocacy framework, linguists seek to use the insights of their scholarship in the public realm to influence opinion and policy, with research participants positioned as beneficiaries and researchers as their spokespersons. Finally, when scholars set aside objectivizing methodologies and restructure the research relationship as a partnership in which participants as well as scholars set the agenda, such work involves not only "research *on* and research *for*" but also "research *with*" – in other words, empowerment. (Cameron and her colleagues explicitly reject "research *by*" participants, which they associate with action research, an approach that they view as too removed from academic dialogues and too uncritical of participants' perspectives to be of significant scholarly value [Cameron et al. 1993].)

The authors' thoughtful discussion and explicit engagement with issues of power in sociolinguistic scholarship opened up a (still) much-needed conversation within the field regarding the purposes and obligations of research. Even as they argue for empowerment as the most desirable form of sociolinguistic research in many contexts, Cameron and her colleagues note the difficulties with this perspective, including such fundamental questions as what counts as power, what counts as research, and what counts as knowledge. Although their argument has been embraced by many researchers, some commentators defend the scholarly status quo, while others, despite sympathizing with the authors' commitment to social change, doubt the possibility of empowering research. Indeed, in a later article Cameron herself raises significant concerns about the idea of empowerment but ultimately affirms its importance as a goal for sociolinguists (Cameron 1998; cf. Siegel 2006).

Beyond sociolinguistics and related fields, however, the idea of empowerment has come in for more extensive critique, primarily among those who, like its proponents, view scholarship as a crucial site for explicit sociopolitical engagement (e.g., Troyna 1994; Cheater 1999; Cruikshank 1999). For such critics, both the macropolitics and the micropolitics of empowerment discourse are deeply problematic. The macropolitical critique stems from the concern that the notion of empowerment often reproduces the hegemony of neoliberalism by focusing on individual actors rather than collective action (Calvès 2009). Consequently, critics argue, such discourse does nothing to dismantle systems of power but merely produces good neoliberal subjects, who are imagined to be self-empowered to pull themselves up by their own bootstraps with minimal governmental intervention. The micropolitical critique focuses instead on language. One strand of such criticism argues that the very term *empowerment,* which often carries self-aggrandizing and patronizing overtones, refers to a transitive act of beneficence from the more powerful to the less powerful that leaves the institutional inequalities of supposedly empowering interactions intact (Gore 1993). A second language-related concern is that the concept of empowerment is frequently elaborated through a variety of speech-centered metaphors, such as "giving voice" to disempowered groups or engaging in "dialogue" with them (Bhavnani 1988; Ellsworth 1989). Critics of these sorts of metaphors note that they erase the diversity of participants' perspectives (Cook-Sather 2007) as well as social actors' decidedly nonmetaphorical and profoundly material experience as producers of discourse in social settings (Weidman 2003). Such metaphors may thus imply that sociopolitically marginalized groups lack the capacity to speak, let alone act, on their own behalf without expert assistance, or that members of these groups speak with a single voice.

Given the significant problems with the concept of empowerment, we find a useful alternative in the idea of accompaniment as advanced by George Lipsitz and his coauthors (Fischlin et al. 2013; Tomlinson and Lipsitz 2013).

These scholars extend the concept from its use in the writings of Salvadoran archbishop Óscar Romero on human rights to offer a broad perspective on all forms of political action and social change:

> In Central American social movements, the word *accompaniment* (connected to the verb *acompañar*) designates an approach to collective mobilization. In contrast to the atomized individualism of liberal capitalism and the elitist vanguardism of Leninist left-wing parties, the idea of accompaniment envisions political action as a journey taken together, an excursion in which people from different backgrounds and experiences can work together respectfully as equals. . . . Like the musical practice whose name it shares, accompaniment in politics enacts the social relations it envisions. It succeeds best when it engages people in unpredictable and ephemeral yet meaningful acts of listening, speaking, and sharing. . . . Through accompaniment, some of our biggest achievements will come through small acts.
>
> (Fischlin et al. 2013: 235)

In this framing, accompaniment, above all, is a joint activity, illustrated through such metaphors as collective travel or musical performance; as Lipsitz and Barbara Tomlinson write in a piece urging scholars to engage in sustained collaborative efforts toward social justice, "Accompaniment recognizes the inescapably and quintessentially *social* nature of scholarship and citizenship" (Tomlinson and Lipsitz 2013: 10; original emphasis). They argue that academic acts of accompaniment necessarily involve collaboration across both scholarly and social boundaries, with researchers engaging substantively with perspectives and practices quite different from their own within as well as beyond the academy: "People from different walks of life have different skills, different speech patterns, and different problem-solving strategies. Working together entails a sometimes painfully slow process of learning from each other, of working hard to forge mutually beneficial relations and relationships" (Tomlinson and Lipsitz 2013: 12). Thus accompaniment is an ongoing, negotiated social process of learning to talk and work together, in which all participants contribute different forms of expertise and understanding and from which they benefit in different ways. Researchers of language, culture, and society are especially well positioned to participate in a relationship of accompaniment, given such scholars' commitment to recognizing and valuing diverse linguistic and interactional practices.

In our own efforts to forge university collaborations with public school students and teachers in Southern California centering on language as a sociocultural phenomenon, we have found the concept of accompaniment much more useful than the notion of empowerment in guiding our work. Whereas empowerment implies an endpoint to politically engaged activities (i.e., when a group has "become empowered"), accompaniment underscores the ongoing, incomplete nature of social justice efforts. Further, accompaniment highlights the mutuality of social relationships across parameters of difference. This perspective leads us to reconceptualize the usual relationship between adults and young people from a one-way transmission of information and knowledge to a multidirectional exchange of ideas and understandings. That is, rather than seeking to "empower" youth, our work has a more modest goal: to acknowledge and engage with the young people we work with as sociopolitical agents who already have rich life experiences and insights that we can learn from and contribute to as we accompany them for a short time along their educational paths. Finally, accompaniment does not conceptualize political engagement as a mere addendum to the more valuable work of research – or vice versa – but positions both activities as equally necessary for scholars who work in the social realm. As researchers of the sociocultural dimensions of language, we have found accompaniment to be a valuable guiding principle for conducting socially transformative scholarship on language without the potential pitfalls of empowerment discourse.

Sociolinguistic justice and educational equity

Our own journey of accompaniment begins with our intellectual collaboration across our home disciplines, as scholars whose professional affiliations range from linguistics to Chicana and Chicano studies to education. What brings us together as researchers is our shared recognition of the close connection between linguistic inequality and social inequality and our commitment to sociolinguistic justice, a concept that developed through our work with local communities. We understand sociolinguistic justice as a fundamentally bottom-up collaborative effort by linguistically subordinated communities and individuals that inevitably involves negotiation and debate; sociolinguistic justice therefore includes accompaniment among members of local communities as well as potentially between such communities and outsiders, including academic researchers.

Elsewhere, members of our research team have discussed five interrelated goals of sociolinguistic justice: (1) the valorization of language variation and diversity; (2) the legitimation of local linguistic varieties in the public sphere; (3) the opportunity to use and learn about one's own linguistic varieties, however these are conceived; (4) access to politically powerful varieties; and (5) recognition of the linguistic expertise of all language users (Bucholtz et al. 2014). Importantly, all of these goals are driven by an underlying fundamental goal: (6) a critical understanding of the social, historical, and political processes that reproduce linguistic inequality, as well as the ways in which such processes are often obscured or distorted through the workings of language ideologies. Although scholarly projects that aim for sociolinguistic justice may focus on only one or two of these goals, the close connection among them means that efforts in one area often further the other goals as well.

With respect to the linguistically marginalized California youth with whom we have worked most extensively, obstacles to sociolinguistic justice are often rooted in the educational system, in which young people's ways of using language are typically devalued, misrecognized, and targeted for eradication (cf. Levasseur, this volume, on the explicit sanctioning of English in French immersion education). This issue is of course familiar to sociolinguists and other researchers concerned with language, and many scholars have advocated pedagogical approaches that can directly or indirectly foster sociolinguistic justice in schools and other learning settings (e.g., Rickford and Rickford 1995; Egan-Robertson and Bloome 1998; Wheeler 1999; Smitherman 2000; Denham and Lobeck 2005, 2010; Siegel 2006; Alim 2007; Reaser and Wolfram 2007; Wolfram et al. 2007; Labov 2010; Charity Hudley and Mallinson 2011, 2014; Watson 2013; Lidz and Kronrod 2014; McCarty and Nicholas 2014). A number of these undertakings valorize young people's own linguistic and cultural knowledge and experiences and take these as a starting point for further learning, an approach that has been theorized as crucial for socially transformative pedagogy (e.g., González et al. 2005; Paris 2012; Paris and Alim 2014).

This student-centered perspective also informs our own pedagogical approach. Most speakers of minoritized linguistic varieties, especially those who are racially and/or economically subordinated, have experienced the deprecation of their linguistic and cultural practices; for youth of color in California, this situation is worsened by a long history of racist and xenophobic laws that have profoundly shaped educational policy and practice (Fillmore 2004). Such young people must overcome considerable structural obstacles to attend college, including economic hardship, lack of mentoring, lack of academic opportunities due to educational segregation or "tracking," and racism (cf. Carter 2014). When they do manage to pursue higher education, these students contribute significantly to the academic community not only through their diverse life experiences but also through their unique and valuable linguistic and cultural expertise. This expertise is of special importance to sociolinguistic knowledge, given the ability of such students to identify, document, and analyze a rich array of under-investigated linguistic phenomena in their local communities (e.g., slang, phonological changes in progress, code-switching practices, language attitudes and ideologies), as well as their firsthand insight into the politics of language and inequality.

Yet the linguistic and cultural expertise of youth is often not simply overlooked but actively marginalized and dismissed within traditional educational settings (Watson 2013). This situation discourages many young people with substantial academic promise from pursuing higher education, a result that does lasting harm not only to the students themselves but also to their families and communities, to the larger society, and to scholarly advancement. In the collaborative program that we have developed, we pursue the six interlocking goals of sociolinguistic justice together with youth and their teachers by recognizing students as linguistic and cultural experts and by working with them both to examine their own and others' substantial knowledge and to challenge the devaluation of that knowledge within existing systems of power.

The SKILLS program

The School Kids Investigating Language in Life and Society (SKILLS) program, established at the University of California, Santa Barbara in 2010, combines research, training, academic preparation, and activism. SKILLS brings teams of graduate student teaching fellows and undergraduate mentors together with young people, teachers, and staff in schools and after-school programs throughout Santa Barbara County. In a recent implementation of the 20-week program (January–June 2014), SKILLS was based in three high schools and two after-school programs in five different municipalities within the county. On average, SKILLS involves around 100 students per year, mostly of high school age. Reflecting the demographics of public schools in the region, SKILLS students are primarily second-generation immigrant Latinas and Latinos from working-class homes who are the first generation of their families to be college-bound. However, the program has served students ranging in age from 6 through 19 and representing varied socioeconomic and ethnoracial backgrounds, including participants of African American, Asian American, European American, and Native American heritages.

Most of the students in the program, as children of Mexican immigrants, regularly experience linguistic subordination firsthand. Not only have they witnessed their parents' economic marginalization in the United States as Spanish-speaking laborers, but the students themselves have often been routed through the California educational system's English Language Development program, which focuses exclusively on standard academic English and dismisses the Mexican Spanish, Chicano Spanish, and Chicano English that youth bring from their peer groups and communities. As a result of this monolingual educational policy, many Latina and Latino students are experiencing or have already undergone rapid language shift from Spanish to English, leading to communication barriers with their grandparents – and in some cases, even with their parents. Those who have managed to retain their communicative ability in Spanish, meanwhile, speak a variety that is not institutionally valued, so that even those who have the opportunity to study Spanish in the school setting are taught that their home variety is incorrect. Moreover, students from other ethnoracial and linguistic backgrounds may speak varieties of English that are stigmatized in the academic context, and nearly all have a family history of linguistic subordination and/or language shift either in their own or in earlier generations, limiting young people's access to and appreciation of their linguistic and cultural heritage (cf. Coleman, this volume, on how educational neglect of minority languages in developing countries leads to language shift).

We have developed the SKILLS program in response to how these inequities affect the lives of youth in our local community, which likely reflect the realities in many other communities as well. The heart of the program is an innovative inquiry-based curriculum collaboratively developed by graduate student team members and annually revised at each site based on instructors' and students' needs and interests, the expertise of each teaching team, and our own continually developing understanding of the most effective topics and pedagogical strategies for engaging students. Throughout the program, SKILLS students explore and extend sociolinguistic concepts by carrying out empirical research and community action projects. At the same time, participants develop a deeper understanding of their own and others' linguistic heritage and expertise as language users while strengthening their academic skills and participating in mentoring relationships and friendships with university graduate and undergraduate students that often extend well beyond the end of the program each year.

Recognizing that young people have linguistic and cultural expertise that should be fostered by both educators and scholars, SKILLS acknowledges youth as intellectual agents, and frames their learning process within the program as research inquiry and knowledge-sharing rather than as schoolwork. The student-researchers must obtain informed consent from their research participants, and they are trained to carry out every step in the research process, from developing research questions, to collecting and analyzing data using technological tools, to sharing the results in a variety of written and oral formats. Throughout this process, they critically examine the relationship of language to both identity and power. The academic bar is set very high – at most sites, students receive college credit for their participation – and the SKILLS students, who have often been classified by their schools as academically "deficient" in some way, regularly meet and exceed these expectations.

SKILLS draws on fundamental tools, concepts, and frameworks of the broad interdisciplinary field of sociocultural linguistics (Bucholtz and Hall 2008) and relates these to students' everyday life experience; it also draws theoretical and political inspiration from socially transformative pedagogy such as the now-banned Mexican American studies curriculum in Arizona and other social justice-oriented programs (e.g., Cammarota and Aguilera 2012; Cabrera et al. 2013). The SKILLS program is loosely structured around four units: language in the peer group; language in the family; language in the community; and language in the world. In each unit, students carry out an original empirical research project or community action project, or a combination of the two. For example, in the first unit students may examine youth slang in their friendship groups or raise public awareness of the systematicity of code-switching among young bilinguals. In the second unit, students may conduct a linguistic oral history of a family elder or develop a plan for how to maintain Spanish in the home. In the third unit, students may critically analyze the presence of Spanish-language and bilingual signage in area organizations and businesses, or they may carry out a collaborative video-based ethnography of language and culture in a local community of practice. In the final unit they may debate bilingual language policy or create a video or a radio public service announcement to combat linguistic racism.

The results of students' work are shared with community members, families, and scholars through presentations at the annual SKILLS Day conference at UCSB. In addition, students' work is made available to a wider audience through inclusion on the SKILLS website, along with lesson plans and other materials related to the program (http://www.skills.ucsb.edu). The public dissemination of students' research and activism further underscores their status as linguistic and cultural experts and agents of social change. Finally, students' work forms the basis of larger research projects involving faculty, graduate students, and undergraduates from the SKILLS team, so that their work goes on to have further impacts on scholarship oriented to social change (e.g., Bucholtz forthcoming).

Despite its academic emphasis, SKILLS is not conceptualized simply as an outreach program but rather as a collaboration with youth and adults in the Santa Barbara community to work against social, linguistic, and educational inequities. Socially, the program aims to unsettle the conventional status of young people in society by positioning students as producers rather than consumers of knowledge and by publicly recognizing their authority as linguistic experts. Linguistically, the program challenges the use of language as a tool for perpetuating inequality by working with youth participants to examine and expose processes of sociolinguistic injustice in their own lives and more broadly. Educationally, the program seeks to remedy systemic inequities in access to higher education by acknowledging and further developing students' academic abilities and working with them to address the structural challenges they face in earning a college degree. In these intertwined efforts to create social change, we strive to act in accompaniment with student-researchers, teachers and administrators, families, and our own graduate and undergraduate students.

SKILLS as accompaniment

To illustrate the idea of accompaniment, we offer instances in which SKILLS instructors and students have negotiated the goals and practices of the program in order to make their joint work toward sociolinguistic justice as beneficial as possible. Each of our examples also involves (at least) one of the six goals of sociolinguistic justice and how the SKILLS program aims to advance that goal.

The first and overarching goal of sociolinguistic justice is the valorization of all linguistic varieties, or broad awareness and appreciation of diverse ways of using language. SKILLS addresses this goal through its sustained focus on the minoritized languages and dialects used by the students in the program, in conjunction with discussion of other marginalized linguistic varieties in California and elsewhere. In our work with the primarily Latina and Latino youth within SKILLS, this goal necessarily centers on the Spanish language. Classroom discussions with students, however, quickly showed us that simply promoting the value of Spanish as a monolithic linguistic system rather than as a diverse set of ways of using language would be not only ineffective but potentially detrimental to students' learning experience. Many students enter the program feeling ashamed of their Spanish knowledge, either because they speak an English-influenced variety that is stigmatized by native Mexican Spanish speakers, or because their knowledge of the language is primarily receptive and hence often goes unrecognized as a form of competency. Valorizing Spanish – as well as other minoritized languages – in the context of SKILLS, then, involves discussing such topics as contact-induced change as a process of linguistic innovation rather than linguistic corruption; the considerable linguistic ability required for receptive bilingualism; and larger sociopolitical structures and processes rather than personal or familial failing as the primary driver of language shift. Such reframing helps students to understand their relationship to Spanish as one of ability rather than inability and their varied experiences as socially shared and power-saturated rather than individualized and nonpolitical. Thus our most basic act of accompaniment is to acknowledge and incorporate students' complex linguistic realities into the program and to avoid taking an oversimplified approach to linguistic valorization that may unintentionally ignore or depreciate young people's ways of using language.

The second goal of sociolinguistic justice is the legitimation of the linguistic varieties of local communities through their authorized use in public, institutional settings such as schools. This goal directly challenges the monolingual regime that has been imposed on California's educational system. By the time they reach high school in California, the majority of bilingual students avoid Spanish even in many private interactions at school; hence, the use of Spanish in a formal educational context is a significant political act. We have worked to legitimate all forms of Spanish in SKILLS classrooms alongside English and other varieties, beginning with some graduate student instructors' own incorporation of Spanish into their academic talk within the program. This act of accompaniment is especially powerful for SKILLS students to experience because they themselves know firsthand the risk involved in the public use of Spanish. Indeed, whether graduate students are native speakers of U.S.-based or other Spanish varieties or second-language learners, they acknowledge their feelings of vulnerability in using the language, either because of their own linguistic insecurity as speakers of non-normative varieties (Zentella 2007) or because of the ideological clash involved in using such a politicized and racialized language in the "white public space" (Hill 1999) represented by the school.

The goal of linguistic legitimation is further promoted in the SKILLS program by encouraging students to use their own linguistic varieties not only as resources for data collection and analysis, but also for publicly sharing the results of their research. In student presentations in the classroom, at Family Night events at local schools, and at the SKILLS Day conference on the university campus, students choose which variety or varieties they want to use to communicate their academic ideas and arguments. Students and instructors also ensure that such public forums are as linguistically inclusive as possible. For example, at one Family Night event, the graduate student instructors serving as MCs addressed parents and other family members in Spanish as well as English, with bilingual volunteers on hand to provide individualized interpretation in each language; meanwhile, the SKILLS students presented their work in various forms of English, Spanish, and Spanglish, the mixed code preferred by many bilingual youth. In the final part of the event, an in-depth audience discussion conducted primarily in

Spanish enabled Spanish-dominant parents to participate more actively and extensively in the academic lives of their children than is possible in most other school-sponsored activities. This unusual opportunity also enabled students to see their parents as skilled language users in an institutional, public setting. Through these and other strategies, the SKILLS program works in accompaniment with students, families, and schools to legitimate local forms of language as valid for academic and public discourse (cf. Douglas, this volume, on including university student work in definitions of impact).

The third goal of sociolinguistic justice, which is closely related to the two foregoing goals, is for all language users to be able both to use and to learn about the language varieties of their background, to whatever extent they wish. However, in dialogue with students we soon recognized the danger of linguistically and ethnoracially essentializing them by emphasizing specific varieties instead of incorporating their full linguistic repertoires. Most obviously, the focus on a few varieties marginalizes students from other backgrounds; but just as importantly, even students who are in the ethnoracial majority within the classroom do not necessarily identify strongly with their linguistic heritage, narrowly construed. For example, some Latina and Latino teenagers in the program have shown less interest in their familial connection to Spanish than in other forms of language that they consider more central to their identities, such as youth slang, a foreign language learned at school, or a variety tied to their youth-cultural interests, such as British English or Japanese. Similarly, at a SKILLS partner site that serves members of a local band of Chumash Indians, some students we worked with were eager to learn the tribal language through after-school classes with community elders, while others felt stereotyped and constrained by discussions of their Native heritage. Rather than imposing essentialized categories on students, then, we encourage them to explore their own linguistic – and nonlinguistic – interests in classroom discussions, activities, and projects, even when these diverge considerably from our own initial expectations and plans. Through these efforts to expand our original vision of what counts as students' language and culture, and hence to accompany students where they want to go rather than where we think they should go, we understand the identities of the young people we work with in a much deeper way, and the youth themselves are able to find greater personal meaning within the program.

The fourth goal of sociolinguistic justice, access to politically powerful ways of speaking, is incorporated into program activities through the development of the student-researchers' spoken and written academic English (and, often, Spanish) abilities via regular academic presentations and written documents in a variety of genres and formats. Moreover, students have helped us to more fully appreciate that the disciplinary jargon of linguistics can be a powerful resource for them, both in legitimating their experiences as valid topics of scholarly interest and in endowing their public discourse about those experiences with academic authority. We avoid burdening students with lists of keywords that they must memorize and define as in a traditional classroom; indeed, the curriculum involves no decontextualized tests or quizzes, only context-rich projects, activities, and discussions. However, we have found that the use of one or two carefully chosen key terms in introducing each topic gives young people a new way of talking and thinking about the linguistic phenomena they experience every day, such as language brokering (Orellana 2009) or family language policy (King et al. 2008). At the same time, we encourage students to share their own metalinguistic terminology, and we recognize such terms as legitimate in the classroom as long as they do not carry offensive connotations. For example, we embrace the term *Spanglish*, which some linguists reject (e.g., Otheguy and Stern 2011), as a socially meaningful, non-derogatory term for the complex linguistic practices of many Latinas and Latinos (cf. Martínez 2013). We use the term as an entry point for investigating with youth the various aspects of this bilingual way of speaking, from the integration of English loanwords into Spanish to systematic code-switching between the two languages. Thus within the SKILLS program, accompanying student-researchers as they explore politically powerful varieties includes ensuring that they have access to the powerful language of linguistics itself.

The fifth goal of sociolinguistic justice involves recognition of the linguistic expertise of all language users, including young people. Most crucially, participants' research projects within SKILLS are acknowledged as original contributions to scholarship, and so instead of using pseudonyms as in traditional forms of research, we give student-researchers full credit for their work on the SKILLS website and in any publications, with their and their parents' permission. This research often yields productive new insights and lines of inquiry: For example, a student project on language brokering revealed the increasingly central role of technology in this practice (Aviles et al. 2014), an important development that is as yet all but unexplored by adult researchers. Such acts of accompaniment reverse the traditional expert–novice classroom relationship by creating opportunities for the adult participants to learn from youth experts.

Finally, all of these goals are driven by a commitment to scrutinizing the processes of power that underlie sociolinguistic injustice. We join our youth partners in difficult discussions of the historical roots and ongoing workings of social inequality in relation to language, race, class, immigration, and other issues, and we accompany them as they share painful experiences from their own lives. In this process, a genuine commitment to accompaniment as human connection across difference is a vital component of our work. Rather than speaking from the safe analytic distance of traditional academic discourse in such conversations, we seek to engage with students first and foremost through their own and our subjective responses to these potent issues and then work together to find tools to expose and challenge inequality. In this way, we are able to connect and collaborate while acknowledging how the privilege of our positions as university faculty and students can sometimes limit or distort our understanding.

Building on our work throughout the program, the final SKILLS Day conference offers a setting in which the student-researchers most profoundly and publicly experience themselves as recognized experts. At this event, youth participants at different partner sites come together to share their research and activism work with university faculty and students as well as family and community members. Taking up the role of expert in this largely adult context is daunting for most students, especially in light of the fact that very few young people have experience with public speaking. Yet the student-researchers regularly report that these presentations serve as an exhilarating capstone to the entire program, as they discover their ability to command the attention and respect of an audience on the basis of their own knowledge and ideas. And because students from multiple sites participate in SKILLS Day, they have the opportunity to enter into sustained scholarly discussions and debates with peers, jointly examining knowledge claims in a way familiar to academics but new to most high school students. This experience thus helps young people to see themselves and be seen by peers as well as by adults as authoritative contributors to knowledge and important agents of social change.

Social change through SKILLS

Although the SKILLS program strives to promote sociolinguistic justice in our local community in a variety of ways, this goal of course can never be fully achieved. We evaluate the effects of our ongoing work through a variety of means, including surveys of students before and after their participation in SKILLS, matched with a comparison group whenever possible; video recordings and analyses of classroom interactions; tracking of students' academic performance both during and after the program; and written and/or oral comments from all program participants, including master teachers and UCSB graduate and undergraduate students as well as SKILLS students. Survey results reveal, for example, that compared to their peers, students in SKILLS report feeling more prepared for college in a range of areas, as well as having a greater knowledge of and appreciation for their own and others' linguistic and cultural backgrounds (Table 2.1).

And although systematic tracking of academic trajectories presents a number of difficulties, the information we have been able to obtain about students' pathways after high school suggests that SKILLS participants enter college at higher rates than their peers. Such measures suggest that the program yields general benefits for participants, and we continue to collect and analyze data that will enable us to evaluate and improve the program in an ongoing way.

However, a focus on generalizations and outcomes underplays the significance of individual students' experiences at specific moments during SKILLS as they participate in the process of accompaniment. The transformative potential of these moments may not be visible in surveys administered immediately after the program's conclusion; indeed, we regularly hear from students and their teachers that SKILLS influenced their lives in unexpected ways even long after their participation had officially ended. We have not yet found a practical way to measure these longer-term effects, but doing so is a high priority for our team.

Table 2.1 Mann-Whitney *U* Test comparing intervention and comparison groups across select outcomes (adapted from Wigginton 2013)

Comparison	p value	z statistic	Mean	
			Intervention	Comparison
In my classes I often learn about the linguistic behavior of different groups.	< 0.001	−5.56	2.16	3.51
My classes overall have improved my understanding of different cultural, racial, and/or ethnic groups.	< 0.001	−3.52	1.97	2.68
My classes overall have improved my understanding of the ways people use language.	< 0.001	−5.63	1.75	2.93
My classes overall have improved my understanding of myself, my experiences, and my history.	< 0.001	−4.73	1.84	2.81
My classes have taught me a lot about my town, city, or community.	< 0.001	−2.97	2.50	3.09
My classes have taught me a lot about my family history.	< 0.003	−4.21	2.69	3.64
I feel comfortable giving oral presentations.	< 0.001	−3.83	1.69	2.59
I feel comfortable collecting and analyzing data.	< 0.001	−3.53	1.50	2.12
I feel comfortable writing academic papers.	< 0.005*	−2.82	1.75	2.27

*Significant differences at $p < .005$

In considering the effects of the program, then, we focus not simply on institutional impact but just as importantly on the incremental work of social transformation at the individual level. With regard to institutional change, although SKILLS is deliberately not designed to affect policy in a top-down fashion, our work with schools helps lay the foundation for systematic educational change as teachers, administrators, and parents see the beneficial effects of youth-centered learning. Moreover, SKILLS has shaped educational practice and policy at participating schools by teaching linguistics content in high school classrooms, something that to our knowledge has never before been implemented in California's public schools. Because the SKILLS program trains teachers in the discipline of linguistics (including providing graduate and professional development coursework for university credit whenever possible), it is able to change teachers' perspectives on language and help them to appreciate their students' linguistic capabilities. Further, the program challenges the longstanding ideology that only students classified by schools as high-achieving are able to perform at the college level. Our primary target population is youth whose abilities have not been recognized through traditional education and we ensure that these students get a jump start on college by earning college credit, just like their more structurally advantaged 'high-achieving' peers. The program also seeks to reach a wider audience by making all its curricular materials and research projects available on the SKILLS website so that they can be used in a variety of ways by other educators, scholars, and students around the world.

With regard to individual change, SKILLS is transformative for the youth who participate in it, both in helping them to recognize their own and others' vast linguistic and cultural knowledge and appreciating its value, and in preparing them to further develop and share their expertise through higher education. Students who do not aspire to a degree or career in linguistics – that is, the vast majority of SKILLS participants – and even those who do not initially aim for college at all benefit from the experience of critically examining language from a youth-centered sociocultural perspective. And students who may have rarely received positive feedback from teachers discover academic abilities of which they were previously unaware and which may draw them toward higher education. In addition to the academic impact of the program, students are often deeply affected at the emotional level by what they learn in SKILLS. Discussions of language shift and loss, linguistic discrimination, and language politics are not simply academic for these young people but part of the landscape of their everyday lives. The chance to evaluate these experiences critically and analytically with linguistic tools enables youth to engage in debates over language in the public sphere in an informed way, while the opportunity to learn more about their own families' and communities' language use is also personally moving for many students and helps strengthen intergenerational bonds.

Finally, and crucially for the accompaniment perspective, SKILLS is both institutionally and individually transformative for the university students and faculty who work together within the program each year. We have witnessed with admiration and awe the dedication, creativity, and wisdom of our graduate and undergraduate team members, who find in the program the kind of personally meaningful learning experience that is unfortunately all too rare in traditional university coursework. Their contributions to SKILLS have greatly strengthened the program, and through their example they have taught us a tremendous amount about how to be innovative and passionate teachers and mentors. Indeed, for us as scholars with a commitment to social change, embracing the idea of accompaniment has profoundly changed our own teaching and research in ways that extend well beyond our work related to the program. At the same time, our experiences have helped us to appreciate the potential for locally based community partnerships such as the SKILLS program to effect real social change.

Conclusion: Fostering accompaniment in sociolinguistic research

The SKILLS program seeks to address a fundamental sociolinguistic injustice of socially and racially stratified multilingual societies: the devaluation of the talents and abilities of youth who speak politically subordinated linguistic varieties. Rather than seeking to "empower" such young people, who are already powerful agents of social change in their own right, we aim to work in accompaniment with them and their teachers, families, and communities in order to achieve the goals of sociolinguistic justice: the valorization and legitimation of all ways of using language, access to both locally meaningful and institutional powerful varieties, the recognition of all language users as linguistic experts, and an understanding of the material and ideological bases of linguistic inequality.

The accompaniment process pervades all aspects of the SKILLS program. At the most fundamental level, accompaniment continually occurs as all participants – regardless of their institutional status as students or instructors – take up roles as experts or novices in particular topics or domains within the program and thereby learn from one another even as they gain additional expertise (Lee and Bucholtz 2015). Accompaniment is also evident in interaction within the classroom, as students collaborate across social boundaries of race and ethnicity, class, gender, sexuality, immigrant generation, and youth-cultural style. And it is central to the work that students do within the program as they enlist peers, parents, and others as research participants in their investigations of the role of language in social life. Above all, accompaniment involves mutual recognition and negotiation. Whereas the goal of empowerment can too often devolve into power relations as usual, as well-intentioned powerful outsiders impose their own political agendas and perspectives on those they hope to empower, accompaniment requires that scholars who aim for social justice set aside their own agendas, give up their certainties, expose their vulnerabilities, and engage in joint activities that lead to shared understanding, collective meaning-making, and social change. Accompaniment is necessarily gradual, and the process is as crucial as the outcome. The real-world impact of such work, admittedly, is often hard to see, and as we have discussed, despite our best efforts it may at times reinforce as much as undermine existing structures of power.

In the foregoing discussion, it would have been tempting for us to succumb to the triumphalist rhetoric that tends to dominate accounts of scholarly efforts to enact social change, or to the equally tempting confessionalist discourse of failure, error, and naïveté by academic do-gooders. But both of these framings place scholars, not communities and their members, at the center of the story. The idea of accompaniment emphasizes that social interaction is a vital component of social action.

Our goal in this chapter has been to describe the workings of a particular community partnership as an illustration of the accompaniment perspective rather than to make broad-based recommendations that can be generalized to other settings. Elsewhere, we offer practical advice for teams of scholars interested in forging partnerships with educators and students (Bucholtz et al. 2015). Here, however, we summarize the lessons we have learned about how to foster a relationship of accompaniment in any educational partnership focused on sociolinguistic justice:

1   Work to valorize partners' and participants' full linguistic repertoires, including those ways of using language that they themselves value highly and those that they and/or the broader society devalue or may not recognize as a form of linguistic expertise. Meanwhile, as students come to see their linguistic practices from new vantage points, it is important for their academic partners to accompany them by rethinking our own received wisdom about language (such as who counts as a fluent speaker, what qualifies as bilingual ability, or how to conceptualize language itself [cf. García and Leiva 2014]).

2   Legitimate the use of students' non-hegemonic linguistic varieties in both formal and informal learning settings for the expression of ideas and knowledge. To the extent that it is acceptable to students, it can be a powerful act of accompaniment for academics to try to use these varieties ourselves, perhaps especially if we are not adept in them, and to explore the difficulties of such efforts with students (cf. Gutiérrez et al. 2011).

3   Don't make assumptions about students' identities or which forms of language are most meaningful to them, especially when these differ from our own expectations and/or areas of expertise. Get to know students as individuals and give them the space to set the terms of what they want to learn based on their own needs and goals.

4   Offer students access to powerful ways of speaking, including specialized academic language, as well as the opportunity to decide for themselves which aspects of these resources are useful for them.

5   Recognize students as linguistic experts, knowledge producers, and agents of change, while embracing the role of learner. Accompany students through the process of intellectual discovery and critical engagement by asking questions, offering suggestions, and then standing back to let them do their work.

6   Make issues of power, inequality, and ideology central to the discussion of language, and accept that this entails difficult and uncomfortable conversations that academics often prefer to avoid. Accompany students in meaningful dialogues in which all participants are recognized as real human beings with emotions and experiences and not mere academic thinking machines.

What we have learned in our work of accompaniment within the SKILLS program can be reduced to a single principle: *Follow, don't lead* – or, in Tomlinson and Lipsitz's words, "sometimes accompaniment means *saying less so that others can be heard*" (2013: 12; original emphasis). When we set aside our own scholarly and political agendas, keep quiet, and let our youth partners teach us what is important to them (and, of course, these priorities are often different for different groups and individual students), we learn from them and discover how they can best learn from us and from one another. As sociolinguists and other scholars continue to engage with communities and polities to effect social change, it is crucial that such work not be reduced either to charitable acts of service or to mere "applications" of scholarship. Rather, acts of accompaniment reside at the very heart of scholarly theory and inquiry, shaping and giving meaning to the knowledge we produce. If scholars and communities are truly to work together toward social, educational, and linguistic justice, a commitment to accompaniment is an important starting point.

Acknowledgements

We are grateful to the many members of the SKILLS team past and present, including the students, teachers, and administrators at our partner sites and our graduate and undergraduate team members. We especially thank the graduate students in our 2013–14 interdisciplinary seminar The Politics of Race and Language in Learning Contexts for their insights. In addition, we gratefully acknowledge the support of UC/ACCORD and the Verizon Foundation, as well as our many UCSB funders: the Academic Senate, the Graduate Division's Crossroads Initiative, the Institute for Social, Behavioral, and Economic Research, the Office of Education Partnerships, and numerous campus offices supporting student-based outreach and research activities. Special thanks to Meghan Corella Morales for impeccable copy-editing and valuable suggestions. Finally, we thank the volume editors and the two anonymous reviewers of this chapter for their extremely helpful comments.

References

Alim, H. Samy. 2007. "Critical Hip-hop language pedagogies: Combat, consciousness, and the cultural politics of communication." *Journal of Language, Identity, and Education* 6 (2): 161–176.

Aviles, Elizabeth, Diana Escobar, Raquel Garcia, and Inés Mendoza. 2014. "Language brokering: Emotions, contributions and technology." Paper presented at the annual SKILLS day conference, University of California, Santa Barbara.

Bhavnani, Kum-Kum. 1988. "Empowerment and social research: Some comments." *Text* 8 (1–2): 41–50.

Bucholtz, Mary. Forthcoming. "On being called out of one's name: Indexical bleaching as a technique of deracialization." In *Racing Language, Languaging Race: Language and Ethnoracial Identities in the 21st Century*, ed. by H. Samy Alim, John R. Rickford, and Arnetha F. Ball. Stanford, CA: Stanford University Press.

Bucholtz, Mary, Dolores Inés Casillas, and Jin Sook Lee. 2015. "Team collaboration and educational partnership in sociocultural linguistics." *American Speech* 90 (2): 230–245.

Bucholtz, Mary, and Kira Hall. 2008. "All of the above: New coalitions in sociocultural linguistics." *Journal of Sociolinguistics* 12 (4): 401–431.

Bucholtz, Mary, Audrey Lopez, Allina Mojarro, Elena Skapoulli, Christopher Vander-Stouwe, and Shawn Warner-Garcia. 2014. "Sociolinguistic justice in the schools: Student researchers as linguistic experts." *Language and Linguistics Compass* 8 (4): 144–157.

Cabrera, Nolan L., Elisa L. Meza, Andrea J. Romero, and Roberto Cintli Rodríguez. 2013. "'If there is no struggle, there is no progress': Transformative youth activism and the School of Ethnic Studies." *Urban Review* 45 (1): 7–22.

Calvès, Anne-Emmanuèle. 2009. "'Empowerment': Généalogie d'un concept clé du discours contemporain sur le développement." *Revue Tiers Monde* 4 (200): 735–749.

Cameron, Deborah. 1998. "Problems of empowerment in linguistic research." *Cahiers de l'ILSL* 10: 23–38.

Cameron, Deborah, Elizabeth Frazer, Penelope Harvey, M.B.H. Rampton, and Kay Richardson. 1992. *Researching Language: Issues of Power and Method.* London: Routledge.

Cameron, Deborah, Elizabeth Frazer, Penelope Harvey, Ben Rampton, and Kay Richardson. 1993. "Ethics, advocacy and empowerment: Issues of method in researching language." *Language and Communication* 13 (2): 81–94.

Cammarota, Julio, and Michelle Aguilera. 2012. "'By the time I get to Arizona': Race, language, and education in America's racist state." *Race, Ethnicity and Education* 15 (4): 485–500.

Carter, Phillip M. 2014. "National narratives, institutional ideologies, and local talk: The discursive production of Spanish in a 'new' US Latino community." *Language in Society* 43 (2): 209–240.

Charity Hudley, Anne H., and Christine Mallinson. 2011. *Understanding English Language Variation in U.S. Schools.* New York: Teachers College Press.

Charity Hudley, Anne H., and Christine Mallinson. 2014. *We Do Language: English Language Variation in the Secondary English Classroom.* New York: Teachers College Press.

Cheater, Angela P. (ed.). 1999. *The Anthropology of Power: Empowerment and Disempowerment in Changing Structures.* Oxon: Routledge.

Cook-Sather, Alison. 2007. "Resisting the impositional potential of student voice work: Lessons for liberatory educational research from poststructuralist feminist critiques of critical pedagogy." *Discourse: Studies in the Cultural Politics of Education* 28 (3): 389–403.

Cruikshank, Barbara. 1999. *The Will to Empower: Democratic Citizens and Other Subjects.* Ithaca, NY: Cornell University Press.

Denham, Kristin, and Anne Lobeck (eds.). 2005. *Language in the Schools: Integrating Linguistic Knowledge into K-12 Teaching.* Mahwah, NJ: Lawrence Erlbaum Associates.

Denham, Kristin, and Anne Lobeck (eds.). 2010. *Linguistics at School: Language Awareness in Primary and Secondary Education.* Cambridge: Cambridge University Press.

Egan-Robertson, Ann, and David Bloome (eds.). 1998. *Students as Researchers of Culture and Language in Their Own Communities.* Cresskill, NJ: Hampton Press.

Ellsworth, Elizabeth. 1989. "Why doesn't this feel empowering? Working through the repressive myths of critical pedagogy." *Harvard Educational Review* 59 (3): 297–324.

Fillmore, Lily Wong. 2004. "Language in education." In *Language in the USA: Themes for the Twenty-First Century*, ed. by Edward Finegan and John R. Rickford, 339–360. Cambridge: Cambridge University Press.

Fischlin, Daniel, Ajay Heble, and George Lipsitz. 2013. *The Fierce Urgency of Now: Improvisation, Rights, and the Ethics of Cocreation.* Durham, NC: Duke University Press.

Freire, Paulo. 1970. *Pedagogy of the Oppressed.* New York: Continuum.

García, Ofelia, and Camila Leiva. 2014. "Theorizing and enacting translanguaging for social justice." In *Heteroglossia as Practice and Pedagogy*, ed. by Adrian Blackledge and Angela Creese, 199–216. Dordrecht: Springer.

González, Norma, Luis Moll, and Cathy Amanti (eds.). 2005. *Funds of Knowledge: Theorizing Practices in Households, Communities, and Classrooms.* Mahwah, NJ: Lawrence Erlbaum Associates.

Gore, Jennifer M. 1993. *The Struggle for Pedagogies: Critical and Feminist Discourses as Regimes of Truth.* Oxon: Routledge.

Gutiérrez, Kris D., Andrea C. Bien, Makenzie K. Selland, and Daisy M. Pierce. 2011. "Polylingual and polycultural learning ecologies: Mediating emergent academic literacies for dual language learners." *Journal of Early Childhood Literacy* 11 (2): 232–261.

Hill, Jane H. 1999. "Language, race, and white public space." *American Anthropologist* 100 (3): 680–689.

King, Kendall A., Lyn Fogle, and Aubrey Logan-Terry. 2008. "Family language policy." *Language and Linguistics Compass* 2 (5): 907–922.

Labov, William. 2010. *PORTALS: An Intervention Program for Grades 4–8.* Boston: Houghton-Mifflin Harcourt.

Lee, Jin Sook, and Mary Bucholtz. 2015. "Language socialization across learning spaces." In *Handbook of Classroom Discourse and Interaction*, ed. by Numa Markee, 319–336. Oxford: Wiley-Blackwell.

Lidz, Jeffrey, and Yakov Kronrod. 2014. "Expanding our reach and theirs: When linguists go to high school." *Language and Linguistics Compass* 8 (10): 449–463.

Martínez, Ramón Antonio. 2013. "Reading the world in *Spanglish*: Hybrid language practices and ideological contestation in a sixth-grade English language arts classroom." *Linguistics and Education* 24 (3): 276–288.

McCarty, Teresa L., and Sheilah E. Nicholas. 2014. "Reclaiming indigenous languages: A reconsideration of the roles and responsibilities of schools." *Review of Research in Education* 38: 106–136.

Orellana, Marjorie Faulstich. 2009. *Translating Childhoods: Immigrant Youth, Language, and Culture.* New Brunswick, NJ: Rutgers University Press.

Otheguy, Ricardo, and Nancy Stern. 2011. "On so-called Spanglish." *International Journal of Bilingualism* 15 (1): 85–100.

Paris, Django. 2012. "Culturally sustaining pedagogy: A needed change in stance, terminology, and practice." *Educational Researcher* 41 (3): 93–97.

Paris, Django, and H. Samy Alim. 2014. "What are we seeking to sustain through culturally sustaining pedagogy? A loving critique forward." *Harvard Educational Review* 84 (1): 85–100.

Reaser, Jeffrey, and Walt Wolfram. 2007. *Voices of North Carolina: Language and Life from the Atlantic to the Appalachians.* Raleigh, NC: North Carolina Language and Life Project.

Rickford, John R., and Angela E. Rickford. 1995. "Dialect readers revisited." *Linguistics and Education* 7 (2): 107–128.

Siegel, Jeff. 2006. "Language ideologies and the education of speakers of marginalized language varieties: Adopting a critical awareness approach." *Linguistics and Education* 17 (2): 157–174.

Smitherman, Geneva. 2000. *Talkin that Talk: Language, Culture and Education in African America.* London: Routledge.

Tomlinson, Barbara, and George Lipsitz. 2013. "American studies as accompaniment." *American Quarterly* 65 (1): 1–30.

Troyna, Barry. 1994. "Blind faith? Empowerment and educational research." *International Studies in Sociology of Education* 4 (1): 3–24.

Watson, Vajra M. 2013. "Censoring freedom: Community-based professional development and the politics of profanity." *Equity and Excellence in Education* 46 (3): 387–410.

Weidman, Amanda. 2003. "Gender and the politics of voice: Colonial modernity and classical music in South India." *Cultural Anthropology* 18 (2): 194–232.

Wheeler, Rebecca S. (ed.). 1999. *Language Alive in the Classroom*. Westport, CT: Praeger.

Wigginton, Raquel. 2013. *School Kids Investigating Language in Life and Society: Pilot Evaluation Report*. MA dissertation, University of California, Santa Barbara.

Wolfram, Walt, Carolyn Temple Adger, and Donna Christian. 2007. *Dialects in Schools and Communities*, 2nd ed. Oxon: Routledge.

Zentella, Ana Celia. 2007. "Dime con quíén hablas y te diré quién eres: Linguistic (in) security and Latino unity." In *The Blackwell Companion to Latino Studies*, ed. by Juan Flores and Renato Rosaldo, 25–39. Oxford: Wiley-Blackwell.

Chapter 3

When children challenge what's 'obvious'

Identities, discourses, and representations from the perspective of schoolchildren in Vancouver, Canada

Catherine Levasseur, ORCID NUMBER 0000–0002–2867–1960

Introduction

The right to schooling is at the center of most legal battles for linguistic minority communities in Canada. Schools are institutions in which schoolchildren are not only learning through the medium of the minority language, but also where members of the linguistic community can meet, network, and share experiences. Schools, as socialization agents, are often considered to be key means to maintain, promote, and assure the future of the linguistic community. In short, it is considered to be the most powerful resistance against linguistic assimilation (Heller 2002; Magnan and Pilote 2007; Landry et al. 2010). In this respect, children enrolled in these schools face expectations, not only regarding their learning, but also their identification. More specifically, it is expected that they will grow up to be proud and active members of the linguistic minority (cf. Bucholtz et al., this volume, and Coleman, this volume, on school students with non-prestigious varieties and languages). In British Columbia (B.C.), a Western Canada province where I conducted my doctoral research, the situation is no different. Schooling and socialization of the new generation of French speakers is an ongoing issue for the local minority language community.

For the above reasons, the adoption of the *Canadian Charter of Rights and Freedom* (hereafter the *Charter*) in 1982 is regarded as a milestone. Sections 16, 20, and 23 of the *Charter* specifically stated equal rights of both English and French in Canada. Moreover, the *Charter* compelled provincial governments to recognize the rights of their official language minority communities and ensure education in their language (Landry et al. 2008). Section 23 also defined the required criteria necessary to have the right to register children in a minority language school. This status is recognized under the term 'ayant droit,' literally meaning 'who has right.'

Before the *Charter*, education in French was already available in B.C., via two different programs: the French Immersion program and the Francophone program (*Programme cadre de français*, PCDF). French immersion schools were (and still are) under the jurisdiction of the provincial public school boards, which are run in English. Immersion schools thus typically welcome schoolchildren from all backgrounds. The PCDF was established in 1979 to provide French education for the Francophone community. However, it was managed by local public school districts (Jacquet 2009: 101; *Conseil scolaire francophone de la Colombie-Britannique* 2014). After many years of claims by parents and educators, the B.C. Francophone school district (*Conseil scolaire francophone*, CSF), was established in 1995. Since then, the CSF has managed all public Francophone schools in the Province and the PCDF is no longer active. The CSF is now fully in charge of primary and secondary education programs, which are recognized by the provincial Ministry of Education.

The 2011 Canadian census shows 70,000 first-language speakers of French in B.C. – approximately 1.6% of the B.C. population. Half of these are located in the Vancouver mainland (*Statistique Canada* 2011). Individuals who declare themselves as French speakers thus have different linguistic and cultural profiles. This is similar to the general population of the main urban centers in Canada, which, like Vancouver, welcome a significant number of migrants (Dagenais 2003; Gerin-Lajoie 2004; Magnan and Pilote 2007; Jacquet 2009). Indeed, a quarter of those who declare themselves as French first-language speakers in B.C. also declare at least one other first language. Landry et al. (2010: 24) estimate that 72% of B.C. French speakers declare speaking English most often at home – significantly more than other provinces such as New Brunswick (11%), Ontario (42%), and Manitoba (56%).

In this context, Francophone schools in B.C. are often the main setting where children speak French and learn about Francophone cultures and traditions. Given the fact that schoolchildren are expected to be the next generation of French speakers, and members of the Francophone community, it is important to understand how they see themselves within this community.

My involvement in the Vancouver Francophone community

The choice of research topic for my doctoral thesis emerged from my experience as a French language instructor. Originally from French-dominant Québec, I relocated to Vancouver, teaching French as an additional language to adults in a 'family francization' program. These classes targeted parents who did not speak French, but had children in a French immersion or Francophone school. I learned that parents felt the need to learn more French not only to communicate with their children and support their schoolwork, but also to help legitimize their children's enrollment at these schools. Speaking French greatly improved their relationships with school teachers and parents, especially in Francophone schools where French is expected to be the only language spoken.

I also learned that many of these parents obtain the 'ayant droit' status and register their children in a CSF school even if they speak little or no French at home. Their children often arrive at kindergarten with limited French. For this reason, the CSF decided to offer a francization program, modeled on ESL equivalents.

The francization programs are different in each province and are still in development in many regions of Canada (Cormier and Lowe 2010). In B.C., the program can differ slightly by school, but is mostly standardized by a Guidebook created in 2006 (*Conseil scolaire francophone de la Colombie-Britannique* 2006). Francization is offered for all children at kindergarten, regardless of their language competence. The CSF 2010 and 2011 annual reports (*Conseil scolaire francophone de la Colombie-Britannique* 2010, 2011) estimate that 31% of children attending a CSF school in 2010–2011 were assigned as in need of linguistic aid (francization). At the end of the school year, schoolchildren take a francization test to determine enrollment on the francization program the following year. Starting with grade one, francization classes are instructed as 'pull-out' classes, occurring about twice a week. Schoolchildren remain in the francization program for up to five years, or until they succeed at the francization test, after which they are ineligible for further linguistic aid.

Importantly, enrolled children are registered in the CSF schools due to their parents' status as 'ayant droits.' In other words, these children are legally recognized as Francophone. Yet, francization students are most often not recognized as native French speakers by educators, parents, and other education stakeholders, and thus their right to enroll in a CSF school is regularly questioned. This throws into question a more crucial factor that goes beyond the 'ayant droit' status. These concerns are directly linked to self-representation and identity: are these schoolchildren 'real Francophones'? Are they legitimate members of the Francophone community?

For this reason, I shifted my focus from parents to schoolchildren on the francization program. I wanted to know what it meant for them to be 'Francophone.' My hope was to produce work that mattered to educators, parents, and the schoolchildren themselves. As the research unfolded, I was increasingly convinced that the data had potential to challenge what was considered 'obvious' in this minority education system: the very definition of being Francophone.

Research project overview

My research is greatly influenced by Heller (2001, 2002, 2007), Dagenais (2003), Gerin-Lajoie (2004), Jacquet et al. (2008), Sabatier (2010), and Arrighi and Boudreau (2013). This body of work questions the place of multilingualism and multiculturalism in a minority context. It also raises pertinent issues around inclusion and exclusion, as well as legitimacy and authenticity at school in the Francophone communities across Canada.

For research purposes, I considered the 'Francophone community' as an imagined community (Dagenais 2003; Pavlenko 2003; Anderson 2006), created, maintained, and challenged through discourses and representations (Barth 1969;

Pilote and Magnan 2012). This imagined community then becomes available to individuals in their identification process (Pavlenko 2003).

Anderson's (2006: 4) concept of imagined communities was initially meant to study nationalism, or "nation-ness": "To understand [nation-ness and national-ism] properly we need to carefully consider how they have come into historical being, in what ways their meanings have changed over time, and why, today, they command such profound emotional legitimacy." Nations bring together members who see themselves as united and similar, even though they do not know each other. Anderson (2006: 6) adds that his concept can also be applied to "all com-munities larger than primordial villages of face-to-face contact (and perhaps even these)."

A community is typically imagined with clear borders (Anderson 2006: 7). I wanted to understand what criteria were employed to determine who could be a legitimate member of the Francophone community. Further, I wanted to find out if the schoolchildren recognized those linguistic communities and their borders, whether they considered themselves as legitimized members, and what they had to say about it.

An ethnographic approach to inquire about linguistic identity

My research was based on eight months of ethnographic fieldwork in 2010–2011, at Beaulieu School (a pseudonym), a primary school in a Vancouver sub-urb. The research was approved by Montreal University's ethical committee. All participants' names below are pseudonyms.

I chose this institution because of its mission as a community school and its long history with French education in the area. It was one of the first to provide the PCDF, well before the creation of the CSF. Today, as the only Francophone school in the area, many schoolchildren commute in from other towns. This illustrates families' preference for this specific school over a local school. The attraction of CSF schools is not unique to Beaulieu. At the time of research, the CSF was the only public school board in B.C. to enjoy growing registrations. Most English-speaking school boards faced declines. The French immersion programs were also attracting an increasing number of students, but the schools in this program represent only 8% of all public schools in B.C., and this marginal number did not influence the general tendency of the registration decline (*Conseil scolaire francophone de la Colombie-Britannique* 2010; B.C. Ministry of Education 2014). Many 'ayant droits' parents prefer to send their children to CSF schools despite their own limited competen-cies in French, for different reasons. Many parents I interviewed considered English-French bilingualism as a Canadian value, or saw French as a family or heritage language. Others were hoping to raise their children's employment or study opportunities. I discuss parents' motivation at greater length elsewhere (Levasseur forthcoming).

Beaulieu School also plays an important role as a community center, where families meet and participate in activities through the medium of French. The cultural and community events are well attended and contribute to a sense of belonging in the Francophone community.

A real-world problem

In the first weeks of my fieldwork, I made my research known amongst the school community. I met principals, teachers, and parents, to inform local stakeholders about my research and to gain their acceptance. This also helped me gauge parents' and teachers' interest in the project.

Happily, both parents and teachers expressed the need for research on the francization program and Francophone identity. These questions were related to forthcoming decisions concerning the future of French Education in B.C. The ultimate goal was to protect and support the Francophone community. Stakeholders thus questioned the selection of families as 'ayant droit' and its impact on the school community profile and experience. Including all 'ayant droit' families, regardless of children's linguistic competence, was perceived as a risk for the overall quality of language education and experience as a Francophone community. If most schoolchildren and parents speak more English than French, would the students adopt French as their main language? Would students adopt a Francophone linguistic identity if they were living their lives in English? Were the CSF schools becoming immersion schools? Such were the questions raised by stakeholders.

These meetings confirmed the relevance and timeliness of my research. I felt that I could tackle a 'real-world problem,' even if I could not answer all the questions above. My aim was to better understand identity representations of children enrolled on the francization program, and their relationship to the French language.

Recruitment and data collection

The recruitment period ran from October 2010 to early February 2011. Invitation letters with enclosed bilingual consent forms were sent to all parents with children on the francization program. From the initial response I recruited six schoolchildren, mostly 1–2 graders (6–8 years old). I began the workshops with them while sending out further invitations, this time targeting 3–6 graders. By the end, I had recruited twelve schoolchildren aged 6–11, eight girls and four boys, representing eleven families. All participants were enrolled on the francization program at Beaulieu, apart from three who had been enrolled but no longer were. All participants declared speaking French and English, and most of them at least one other language. The profile of each participant is shown in Table 3.1. Note that the number of years in francization included the 2010–2011 school year. It does not, however, include years spent in francization in other schools. The order of languages spoken at home does not represent the level of competencies.

Table 3.1 Participants' profiles (children)

Group	Name	Gender	Age	Grade	Years in francization	Languages spoken at home
C	Amy	Girl	6 y. old	1st	2	French; English; Hungarian
C	Laura	Girl	7 y. old	1st	2	French; English
D	Briana	Girl	6 y. old	1st	2	French; English
D	Gabriel	Boy	6 y. old	1st	2	French; English
D	Olivier	Boy	7 y. old	2nd	1	French; English
A	Sandra	Girl	9 y. old	3rd	3	French; English; Hungarian
A	Kevin	Boy	9 y. old	3rd	1	French; English; Polish; Ukrainian
A	Ana	Girl	9 y. old	3rd	3	French; English; Spanish
A	Anaïs	Girl	8 y. old	3rd	2	French; English; Polish
B	Sarah	Girl	9 y. old	4th	2	French; English
B	Eric	Boy	9 y. old	4th	4	French; English; German
B	Valérie	Girl	11 y. old	5th	5	French; English; Japanese

Schoolchildren were at the center of my research interests, but I also investigated the school community, the francization program, and the profiles of the families. I wanted to create a wider backdrop reflecting language and identity ideologies, representations and discourses, and then compare these with the children's responses. I thus recruited approximately twenty-five adults for interviews including: teachers; school staff; representatives of the Beaulieu Parents' Association; CSF representatives; and leaders of the B.C Francophone Parents Federation (FPFCB). I also made contact with nine parents of children participating in my research, representing seven of the eleven families.

The first part of the data collection was based on observations at the school. I took field notes during regular classes, francization classes, lunchtime, recess, special events, and other activities. These allowed me to grasp the language dynamics between teachers, parents, and schoolchildren, and understand the school language policies and identity discourses.

The second part was inspired by the work of Pilote (2004), Moore (2006), and Perregaux (2009), all of whom used drawings to facilitate children's expression of discourses and representations. I divided participants into four age groups. Each met monthly for a lunchtime workshop, of which there were seven in all. Participants discussed language uses, identity representations, experiences at school and within the francization program, etc. Activities like drawing, role-play, and craft-making guided the discussions.

The success of these workshops was down to the trust built with the participants, despite my authoritative position as an adult. They all called me 'Madame Catherine,' as they addressed their teachers. As a consequence, during the first few workshops they made an effort to give me the 'right answers,' what they thought was expected from them, especially about the languages they used at school and home. They did not initially feel comfortable telling me they used languages in ways they were not supposed to. Extract 1 with Amy and Laura, two first graders, illustrates how the participants avoid providing answers that could 'put them in trouble.' All quotes have been translated into English. English words used in the original are italicized (only occurring in extracts 4–6). 'CL' stands for 'Catherine Levasseur.' The transcription conventions used in the excerpts are available at the end of the chapter.

Extract 1 — Amy and Laura discussing languages used at school

1	CL:	French! At school, perfect/ Are there any other languages/ at school/ that you speak sometimes?
	Amy:	Hum/ English _a little_
	CL:	_A little_
5	Amy:	But, I don't want to write [it]
	CL:	Ok it's all right/ why don't you want to write it?
	Amy:	Because/ it's like NEVER I speak English at school
	CL:	Ok All right/ and
	Laura:	And the same for me
10	CL:	It's the same for you Laura?
	Laura:	Yes

Over time, they realized they could speak more freely with me, even switching between French and English. They started sharing insightful opinions and experiences. This gradual change was a testimony of their understanding of rules, policies, expectations, and norms regarding language which they faced at school. The following extract is with Amy and Laura, in the sixth workshop (i.e. after six months of building trust with the pupils). When asked what languages teachers spoke in class, they finally told me teachers *should not be using English,* instead of just giving me the 'right answer' that teachers *only speak French* at school.

Extract 2 — Amy and Laura discussing languages spoken by teachers

1	CL:	And teachers here in the school/ which languages do they speak?/ Do you know?
	Amy:	Only in _French_
	Laura:	_French_ and sometimes English
5	Amy:	Yes!
		[. . .]
	Laura:	Sometimes/ hum/ other languages/ because hum/ sometimes there is people who do not understand this word that she/ what he says/ he says/ what?/ And after he needs to say again
10		and after he says/ what?/an after / he says in English and he says/ Oooohhh! THAT!

	CL:	Ok/ It helps them understand?
	Laura:	Yes
		[. . .]
15	CL:	Yes?/ You find this strange Amy? Why?
	Amy:	Because/ when it's in a school/ in French/ it's strange/ because/ hum// he has to speak English but/ he has to/ in French/ well he speaks English/ and/ he has to/ make us learn in French and it's a school in Fren/ in French _so we are not
20		allowed/ of hum/ and _
	Laura:	_and he said in English!// class_
	Amy:	And also/ He is not allowed to speak English

These changes unravelling during the fieldwork show the relevance and validity of the data collected with schoolchildren. They were able to express themselves and discuss difficult topics such as identity and language representations, languages practices and norms, etc. Even at this early stage of schooling, they understood many of the issues discussed by adults. In addition, their own positions were quite different from what was expected from them, as I discuss later.

The imagined linguistic communities as viewed by schoolchildren

Through all the interviews and workshops, adults and schoolchildren were invited to share their views on what it means to be Francophone. After analyzing the transcripts using both content and discourse analysis (Fairclough 1993; Boutet and Maingueneau 2005; Keller 2007), it became clear that four categories were used to determine the boundaries between the three main imagined linguistic communities at school, i.e. 'Francophone,' the 'Francophile,' and the 'Anglophone.' The four categories are: 1) national origin; 2) first language or mother tongue; 3) language competence in French; and 4) language practices. For the purpose of this chapter, I only present the categories used to define the Francophone imagined linguistic community from the perspective of the schoolchildren. Other categories are discussed in Levasseur (forthcoming).

The first way schoolchildren described Francophone identity was by national origin, stating clearly that a 'real francophone' is someone living or born either in Québec or France. In extract 3, Sarah and Eric name class friends they consider Francophone because of their national identity:

Extract 3 — Valérie, Sarah and Eric talking about 'who is Francophone?'

1	CL:	Who is Francophone here in school?
	Valérie:	_Everyone_
	Eric:	_Salam!_
	Sarah:	_Théo!_

5	Valérie:	_Everyone who speaks_
	Sarah:	_Thibaud and Théo_
	Eric:	Salam
	Valérie:	Everyone who speaks French
	CL:	And why are you thinking of Thibaud first?
10	Sarah:	Because he/ he
	Eric:	He was born in France
	Sarah:	Hum/ borne in France/ and he doesn't speak English
	CL:	OK
	Sarah:	And Théo/ he's in my class and he doesn't speak English

Another notable assertion in this extract is that Francophones speak French, not English. In the following extract, they are even more specific: French has to be the first language, or at least learned during early childhood.

Extract 4 — Sarah talking about French as first language

1	CL:	So how would you describe yourself?
	Sarah:	Hum/ not Francophone
	CL:	Is there a word to say hum/ what you are?
	Sarah:	Hum/
5	Eric:	Anglophone
	Sarah:	A person who speaks French
	Valérie:	Ok *bye*
	CL:	So a person who speaks French
	Sarah:	Yes! But I'm not Francophone
10	CL:	And what would be needed?/ What is needed to be Francophone in that case?
	Sarah:	Like your first language or like your second that you have learned like/ you have like/ three years old// This is/ Francophone

As Anaïs and Sandra elaborate in the following extract, a Francophone must not only just speak French, but do so well enough to communicate 'with everyone,' intimating native fluency.

Extract 5 — Anaïs and Sandra talking about speaking French as a native speaker

1	CL:	So/ [. . .] from your point of view/ what does it mean to be Francophone?
	Anaïs:	Mhhh/ _speaking/ speaking in French_
	Sandra:	_Speaking in French_// and have an/ and have a
5		background/
	CL:	Have a background like what?

	Sandra:	An origin like knowing French and speak it with other people
	Anaïs:	And you can speak it with like
10	San:	And you can speak it with everyone
	Anaïs:	And you can have two languages
	CL:	Yes?
	Sandra:	Yeah
	Anaïs:	And you can go to France and you can just speak with
15		everyone
	Sandra:	Yeah like not like OH! I don't know/ French/ can you speak in English and she will be like hum haaan/ *What?*

Sandra and Anaïs also consider that parents could help them feel more Francophone by speaking more French every day at home. In the last extract below, Sandra mocks her mother who reproached her *in English* for not using French often enough:

Extract 6 — Anaïs and Sandra, on the need to speak more French at home

1	CL:	And what can your parents do to make you feel more Francophone?
	Sandra:	Speaking in French
	Anaïs:	Me too
5	Sandra:	And SPEAK more in French starting now/ because my mom is like *you're failing school you've got / you've got to talk more French*/ Oh my God/ I speak in English!/ Oh my God I speak in *anglaishh*

By describing what it is to be Francophone in those terms, schoolchildren use exactly the same criteria as the adults in their interviews (see Levasseur forthcoming). Through its practices, discourses, and representations, the school system and its actors – especially parents and educators – teach children how they should act, speak, and be part of the Francophone community. They should be Québecers or French, have French as their first language, master it as native speakers and use it at all time. My observations led me to understand that this representation of an imagined community is shared and passed on by the school in various ways.

The strict policy of using French in school can be found in the Student Planner given to all students at the beginning of the academic year. There is also a sign at the main entrance saying "Here we speak French", which reinforces the boundary between the 'French inside world' and the 'English outside world.' Moreover, this language policy discourages languages other than French, reinforcing a belief that a Francophone must be monolingual. Cultural events such as the winter musical show, the 'maple syrup dinner' *(cabane à sucre)*, and the spring carnival are other ways of teaching children what being Francophone means. These events contribute to showcasing Québec and French cultures as the main Francophone models to emulate. These are just a few examples demonstrating the role the school plays in socializing future members of the Francophone community. Schoolchildren are thus 'doing their homework.' They recognize the borders that determine who's in and who's out and they position themselves accordingly.

So, on which sides of the border do the francization schoolchildren stand? As Sarah expressed in Extract 4, all participants except Valérie described themselves as non-Francophone. This is not really surprising if we consider their profiles and linguistic repertoires. None of my participants were born in Québec or France. They had all grown up in B.C. and lived in the Vancouver mainland, where they use English daily and are exposed to many more languages. Vancouver is also where an important part of their social life takes place. They all express, in different ways, a sense of belonging to the city, especially through its sports teams. Most participants spoke little or no French on entering school at five years old. Indeed, at least six of them have French as their third language. They are definitely not monolinguals and are often considered deficient French speakers in oral expression and writing competency. These findings illustrate how discourses and representations shared at school about the definition of 'being Francophone' largely reflect stereotypes, not the cultural diversity of the families whose children attend the CSF schools.

It is to be expected that schoolchildren schooled in a CSF school and socialized as future members of the Francophone community either *adopt* or *reject* the identity models available to them. However, in this case, they are not really *rejecting* the label 'Francophone.' Rather, as they told me, they simply *could not be* Francophone. The Francophone community exists, they recognize its shape and characteristics, but they do not feel they belong in it. In other words, they do not feel legitimized members of this linguistic community. But, as illustrated in extract 4, they do not necessarily adopt the 'Anglophone' category either. Sarah is not comfortable in either linguistic identity. She prefers "a person who speaks French." This shows the inadequacy of the traditional dichotomy between English and French speakers in understanding the identification process of these young speakers.

I realized that this was where my research could contribute towards changing ideologies, practices, and policies – in short, to have an impact. If the school community desires schoolchildren to become full, active, proud members of the Francophone community and to support the school mission, something had to change. Models had to change. Discourses had to change. Practices had to change. A place was needed to make room for other ways of being Francophone.

Aiming at achieving impact

'Achieving impact' in research is often understood in a 'cost-benefit' perspective. This vision of impact is often adopted by funding agencies and governments wishing to measure the value of research (Lynch-Cerullo and Cooney 2011; Morgan 2014). Agencies try to measure research benefits in terms of national economy, public health, or the other 'greater needs' of a nation. In social sciences, impact is also measured in terms of effectiveness or performance (Lynch-Cerullo and Cooney 2011). Not all conceptualizations of research impact are limited to a pure economic framework (Morgan 2014). However, agencies and governments are still mostly trying to evaluate the extent to which funding (sociolinguistic) research can benefit society in general and the extent to which the research process is effective in achieving social change. According to this view, 'impact' is long-term change observed at the end of a three-step process: 1) the research process; 2) outputs (products of the research); and 3) outcomes (changes observed as a result of the research).

My understanding of social change has been greatly influenced by participatory approaches, where a common principle is that researchers work closely with the community. This means working in a more horizontal structure where stakeholders have some control of the research and its outcomes (Funk et al. 2012; Fontan et al. 2013). They should be the beneficiaries of social change. Participatory approaches are, of course, not miraculous. They cannot be applied to all cases and scenarios. They have their challenges and their flaws, and the results are not always as what one hopes for (Waller and Bitou 2011; Funk et al. 2012; Fontan et al. 2013).

In this respect, avoiding top-down authoritative solutions is an important principle that guides the participatory researcher's practice. However, the desire for impact, outcomes, and social change implies making a judgment in an authoritative voice. We consider that something *has to change* and, more often than not, we have an idea about *what* that change should be. Even if we facilitate the local stakeholders to find solutions through our research findings and interpretations, then we are already leading the way. This is why, as I discuss in the following sections, it is important to take a reflexive standpoint in any research project that aims at social change.

Aiming at changes: From results to outputs

My research enabled me to frequently share my academic outputs, mostly presentations in local, national, and international conferences. I also gave lectures on undergraduate and graduate courses in fields including education and social work. These helped me pursue outcomes and impact. I took part in national and international debates on minority languages and identity in the framework of multilingual discourses (Moore 2006; Billiez 2007; Magnan and Pilote 2007; Block 2008; Sabatier 2010) and nationalist discourses (Heller 2002, 2007; Anderson 2006). As I discuss in the following section, my contribution to the scientific circles has been valuable in two different ways: 1) it has brought fresh perspectives to academic debates, since academic discourses on minorities are often used as political tools by stakeholders; and 2) it can help future professionals in education to question their own representations and discourses, which will consequently influence their practices.

I wondered then how my research could initiate changes and have outcomes at Beaulieu, at the CSF, and more broadly in the Francophone community of Vancouver. I wanted to reach out to stakeholders involved in this debate, who were concerned about the role and future of the French language in B.C. The next section details the initiatives undertaken in this respect.

Impact and outcomes: Why and towards what?

The idea of producing research outcomes that mattered to the local community grew alongside the research process. At first, I was simply hoping to shed light on an issue not well studied in the field, i.e. the identity representations of school-children in the B.C. francization program. Then, I believed the results needed to be shared with the local stakeholders such as the people actually living, working, teaching, and growing up in Francophone Vancouver. These were the ones who could best use the results. From this, they could reflect on their situation and consider how they might want to change (or not).

As the fieldwork progressed, I also felt more pressure to be 'useful' and to produce results that could be applied in the school or the community. Parents, teachers, principals, and other staff asked me about the research and the early findings. Many expressed hope that I could provide them with solutions and recommendations about what they saw as problems in school. Some hoped I could find ways to improve the francization program. Others thought I could help make the schoolchildren speak more French at school and be more involved in cultural activities. I felt quite helpless facing these demands. I was not working in a pure education or didactic framework. My goal was not to produce a program, a guidebook, or class activities. I was more interested in social dynamics, ideologies, discourses, and their impact on social relationships at school. I was interested in issues like inclusion and exclusion, language representations, identities, borders, and mostly about interests and conflicts. As Heller (2002) would describe it – who's in and who's out? And who benefits or loses? These questions were not leading me towards recommendations readily applicable in classes, as teachers and parents would have liked. Nevertheless, I still believed I could contribute in my own ways to the issues raised.

I realized that if the school wanted the schoolchildren to speak more French, and more importantly to feel they were fully included in the local Francophone community, some things *had to change*. All my data pointed to one conclusion: schoolchildren did not feel included in the traditional definition of 'Franco-phone.' Even considering identification as a dynamic, complex, non-linear, and life-long process (Hengst 1997; Brubaker and Junqua 2001), I felt that the school was missing its target. Even at elementary school, children did not feel included. The fact that they clearly understood the model, passed on to them as the 'perfect Francophone,' and yet distanced themselves from it, showed me that the school mission was off to a bad start.

Based on my data, I felt that *adult* discourses and representations should change. What seemed obvious to them about what it meant to be Francophone was questioned by the next generation of French speakers. Schoolchildren's experiences of being Francophone were different from their parents' or teachers'. Therefore, my position was that adults needed to be more inclusive towards the children's diversity and let go of that 'perfect, real, legitimate, and authentic' Francophone model that no longer fits. I was, and still am, dreaming about multicultural and multilingual Canadian *Francophonies*.

Facilitating changes: How?

With all that in mind, the next question was: how could I facilitate change in representations and discourses that could eventually lead to changes of practices and policies? And how could I ensure that my data (and the participants) led the way, and not my own wishes? The task at hand was not easy so I put in place four different strategies, discussed below.

Dissemination of early findings and group discussion

The first strategy was a presentation of the early findings at the school, before leaving the field. A meeting was organized for all school staff interested in the research. The meeting had different purposes. First was to respond to the school's request to hear about the research results. Second was to leave the school community with a better understanding of what I had been working on, and the issues investigated. The third purpose was to receive first-hand feedback on what I had learned. Last but not least was to encourage debate between school staff – with different interests and positions – about the issues raised in the research.

After a presentation of the main results, participants questioned some of my interpretations and lines of analysis. For example, I considered some language practices as resistance to the rules, such as saying "*je suis fini*" [I'm done/dead/over] instead of "*j'ai fini*" [I'm done/I have finished]. Teachers interpreted these practices as a lack of effort or knowledge on the part of the students. Then, the discussion turned to a debate concerning 'what to do next.' This part of the discussion was particularly interesting. They were touched by two topics in particular: the need to make the school more welcoming to English-speaking parents; and the need to be more understanding and inclusive about the English spoken at school by the schoolchildren. They tried to find strategies that could help students feel included even if they spoke English within the limitations of the school mission and policies. One solution explored was the possibility of teaching a third language, to disrupt the tense duality between English and French.

I was glad that the presentation had sparked debate and a solution-seeking process from teachers and staff. They took control, and moved away from my results to their own reality and experiences, taking on the parts that were more relevant to them.

Using media as a means of outreach to the local community

The second strategy was to get media coverage for my research, in order to feed into wider civic debate in B.C. and elsewhere. Easier said than done, especially for a postgraduate student. This is when luck and strategy combined paid off.

In June 2013, I presented at a national Human Sciences conference in Victoria, B.C. What I had not anticipated was the conference communication team sending my abstract to local and regional media as a possible topic of interest. And this is how I got calls for interviews from *Radio-Canada* Vancouver (radio and television). *Radio-Canada* is a national public broadcaster and the Vancouver regional antenna is one of the very few (if not only) broadcasters operating in French. It is considered the main source of information for the Francophone community. This was a major opportunity to share my research results with a wide audience.

The timing could not have been better: in June 2013, a debate was going on in the CSF about the criteria used to define families as 'ayant droit.' The CSF was favorable towards relaxing the criteria in order to include more families. They faced opposition from many stakeholders who favored a stricter application of the criteria. By taking part in media interviews, I could contribute to the debate in presenting my own analysis about the question of inclusion and exclusion at the CSF.

This media coverage enabled me to meet a number of people, such as university professors, teachers, and parents, who told me they had heard the interviews. Interestingly, it was largely a result of participating in an academic conference which gave me the opportunity to talk to the media. I now believe that participating in academic activities should not be underestimated as it can greatly help to obtain outcomes.

Results dissemination workshops: Giving back to the participants

The third strategy was the one I considered most important. It consisted of organizing workshops at Beaulieu with all stakeholders involved in the research, as well as others who were interested. I invited all participants (parents, teachers, and schoolchildren), Beaulieu staff, CSF and FPFCB representatives, and researchers from the main universities of Vancouver.

I planned three identical workshops, all run in the school library: two in French and one in English. I wanted to make sure English speakers could fully participate without feeling excluded or judged by the French speakers. Invitation letters (in both French and English) were sent to stakeholders. An invitation was also published in the school newsletter.

In total, fifteen participants attended the workshops. In the end, the English-medium workshop was run in French as the participants were more comfortable in French. Despite the relatively low number of participants, I was pleased about the diversity of stakeholder representation. Individuals representing all groups of the research participants and institutions were present, except the schoolchildren (discussed later). In addition, members of the CSF Teachers Union were present. This diversity of profiles and groups of interests was key to the success of the workshops. Attendees could compare and contrast their views on the issues raised by my findings. They could later share their thoughts with colleagues, friends, and family.

I called these 'workshops' because I wanted them to be interactive. I was aiming at facilitating debates, exchanges, and discussions. I wanted the participants to experience my research methodology and, in doing so, have a better understanding of my work with the schoolchildren. As I was dealing with discourses and representations, I thought it would contribute to making my work more understandable and accessible. Moreover, this interactive format would help the participants feel connected to the findings, recognizing their own ways of addressing the questions of languages and identity. Consequently, they would see how the research results could bring fresh ideas to the issues they cared about.

The workshops were divided into three sections: introduction, activities, and case studies. At the beginning, I did a short presentation on the research design and my main lines of analysis but without talking about the results. It was important not to present my interpretations early on in the meeting in order to let the attendees express themselves more freely during the activities.

The second section involved inviting attendees to participate in activities similar to the ones I did with the schoolchildren. The activities aimed at exploring different aspects of the attendees' language representations, followed by an activity exploring more directly the Francophone identity representation. All activities were discussed in small groups, and then linked to my findings, to see their own representations in relation to those analyzed in the study.

The last section of the workshop consisted of presenting case studies from the schoolchildren. This aimed to show the attendees the wide variety of schoolchildren's profiles when it comes to languages and identities. Attendees had previously discussed the criteria used to describe the Francophone linguistic identity. Now they were able to see the distance between the idea of Francophone identity as imagined and propagated by a large number of stakeholders, and the idea held by the schoolchildren themselves. In this way I encouraged participants to question their own understanding of what it meant to be Francophone and its effect on the identification process of schoolchildren in the francization program.

Before leaving, attendees were invited to fill out an evaluation form. This helped me evaluate the research itself as well as the relevance of the workshop activities and their format. Finally, I used the evaluation form to ask the attendees what they would take away with them from the session and what should or could be learned from it. I was pleased to see that most wrote a comment regarding the need to be open-minded about the definition of Francophone and to be more aware of the model presented to the schoolchildren.

In order to further gauge the impact of the workshops, I plan to do a follow-up with these participants in the near future. But, for the time being, the evaluation forms showed me that many stakeholders left the meetings already shaken in their beliefs about linguistic identities and about their way of understanding and promoting Francophone identity at school. In my understanding of outcomes and impact, this is the first step towards long-term changes and it shows the potential of this kind of dissemination workshop as a tool to promote social change.

Professional publications as a means of outreach to educators

The last strategy I put in place to reach out beyond academic circles and the school community was to publish a paper in a professional education journal (Levasseur 2012). The paper mostly focuses on school monolingual policies and their effects on schoolchildren's language use at school. The journal is mostly read by teachers in the province of Québec, but is also distributed and read across Canada. Publishing this paper will hopefully give food for thought to current and future French teachers. These are the ones who work with schoolchildren for whom French is a second or third language but who are expected to use it as the only means of communication. This publication was a way of contributing to the ongoing debates in Francophone schools across the country about the role of French as the sole language of communication.

Conclusion

My experience in this research led me to consider and plan for the future, as change occurs slowly and impact is only visible in the long-term. If I consider my work, as a doctoral researcher, like planting the seed of change, what can be done next to help it flourish?

During the years that followed my fieldwork, the feedback I received from stakeholders in the Vancouver Francophone community showed that my results echoed what they had experienced in their school and in their home. The next step would be a postdoctoral project to enrich the data collection and analysis. Collecting data in another setting, with another group of students, school, city, and province – perhaps working with other researchers on the same topic – would then make it possible to compare and contrast sets of data. It would greatly improve the scope of the results and help to develop a more comprehensive interpretation of young French Canadians' identity representations and discourses.

Another option would be to run a second round of fieldwork at Beaulieu. A follow-up with all participants through meetings, workshops, or interviews could help keep the discussion going. It could allow involvement of stakeholders not previously involved in the research process. Furthermore, a long-term follow-up could help bolster the use of a participatory approach.

A follow-up with schoolchildren would indeed greatly enrich the data collection and it would be possible to observe changes in representations and discourses through time. During the dissemination workshops of 2013, I wished children could have taken an active part. They were by then two years older, so it would have been interesting to hear them react to what they had said during the fieldwork, to see if they might explain it differently, and if they might change their statements. It would have been a rich experience to have them heard directly by their parents, their teachers, their educators, and so on. The context did not permit that, mostly due to confidentiality. Going back to the field would allow me to organize such an event and have all the authorizations needed.

Another way to contribute to long-term change and to keep the discussion going would be to go back to Vancouver and engage with the community. This could happen by various means. I could continue to participate in conferences and give talks in local academic settings or with stakeholders in French education. Being involved in the continuing education program for teachers, counselors, and principals, etc., would provide opportunities to facilitate changes in practices in schools. Finally, being involved directly with education policy-makers (provincial government, CSF, schools, etc.) could also be a way to facilitate changes.

Ultimately my research did not initiate a revolution. However, my experience shows that even at this early stage of an academic career, it is possible to conduct research that facilitates social change. I also believe that a creative research design can greatly improve potential for impact. Moreover, it is never too early – or too late – to reach out, in order for local stakeholders to be more involved. After all, they are the ones deciding if our research has value enough to motivate changes in their life.

Chapter transcription conventions

Transcription conventions based on Lamarre et al. (2015).

1) Respect orthography norms except to showcase talk variety.
2) No use of punctuation signs such as (.) (,) (;), (:); except (!) or (?) to mark intonation.
3) Words stressed orally marked by capital letters.
4) Slash bars indicate pause in speech:

/ short pause.
// slightly long pause (2–4 sec.).

5) Comments or additions such as indication of noise, laugh, etc., are between brackets.
6) Underscores mark simultaneous talk.

Acknowledgements

First and foremost, my gratitude goes to the twelve wonderful, bright, and amazing children who participated in this research. *J'ai un peu grandi moi aussi grâce à vous!* I am very grateful to all other stakeholders and participants, such as the CSF, Beaulieu school and its community, and *la Fédération des parents francophones de la Colombie-Britannique.* I warmly thank Patricia Lamarre and Dave Sayers for their out-of-this-world support, advice, and patience. Thank you also to my colleagues and friends for their advice, encouragement, and support: Ruth Kircher, Mathieu Cooke, Christian Dumais, and many more. My eternal gratitude goes to Gwennan Elin Higham for her much needed proofreading. Finally, I acknowledge the generous financial support of *le Fonds de recherche du Québec – Société et culture (FRQSC), le Centre canadien de recherche sur les francophonies en milieu minoritaires (CRFM) de l'Institut français de l'Université de Régina, le Centre d'études ethniques des universités montréalaises (CEETUM),* and *l'Université de Montréal.*

References

Anderson, Benedict. 2006. *Imagined Communities: Reflections on the Origin and Spread of Nationalism,* revised ed. London: Verso.

Arrighi, Laurence, and Annette Boudreau. 2013. "La construction discursive de l'identité francophone en Acadie ou 'comment être francophone à partir des marges'?" *Minorités Linguistiques et Société/Linguistic Minorities and Society* 3: 80–92.

Barth, Fredrik. 1969. "Introduction." In *Ethnic Groups and Boundaries: The Social Organization of Culture Difference,* ed. by Fredrik Barth, 9–38. Boston: Little, Brown and Company.

B.C. Ministry of Education. 2014. "Student statistics – 2013/14. Province – public and independent schools combined. Provincial reports." Accessed 12 March 2015. Available from: http://www.bced.gov.bc.ca/reporting/province.php.

Billiez, Jacqueline. 2007. "Etre plurilingue: Handicap ou atout?" *Ecarts d'identité* 111: 88–90.

Block, David. 2008. *Multilingual Identities in a Global City.* Basingstoke: Palgrave Macmillian.

Boutet, Josie, and Dominque Maingueneau. 2005. "Sociolinguistique et analyse de discours: Façons de dire, façons de faire." *Langage et Société* 4: 15.

Brubaker, Rodger, and Frédérique Junqua. 2001. "Au-delà de l'«identité»." *Actes de la Recherche en Sciences Sociales* 139 (2): 66–85.

Conseil scolaire francophone de la Colombie-Britannique. 2006. *Le Nouveau Guide de Francisation en Colombie-Britannique.* Richmond: CSF.

Conseil scolaire francophone de la Colombie-Britannique. 2010. *Rapport Annuel 2009–10.* Richmond: CSF.

Conseil scolaire francophone de la Colombie-Britannique. 2011. *Rapport Annuel 2010–11.* Richmond: CSF.

Conseil scolaire francophone de la Colombie-Britannique. 2014. "Historique du CSF." Accessed 20 August 2014. Available from: http://www.csf.bc.ca/a-propos-du-csf/historique-du-csf/.

Cormier, Marianne, and Anne Lowe. 2010. *Étude des Mesures D'accueil et D'accompagnement et de L'implantation de Différents Modèles D'intervention en Francisation.* Moncton: Centre de Recherche et Développement en Education.

Dagenais, Diane. 2003. "Accessing imagined communities through multilingualism and immersion education." *Journal of Language, Identity and Education* 2 (4): 269–283.

Fairclough, Norman. 1993. "Critical discourse analysis and the marketization of public discourse: The universities." *Discourse Society* 4 (2): 133–168.

Fontan, Jean-Marc, David Longtin, and Jean-Francois René. 2013. "La recherche participative à l'aune de la mobilisation citoyenne." *Nouvelles Pratiques Sociales* 25 (2): 125–140.

Funk, Anna, Natasha Van Borek, Darlene Taylor, Puneet Grewal, Despina Tzemis, and Jane Buxton. 2012. "Climbing the 'ladder of participation': Engaging experiential youth in a participatory research project." *Canadian Journal of Public Health* 103 (4): e288–e292.

Gerin-Lajoie, Diane. 2004. "La problématique identitaire et l'école de langue Française en Ontario." *Francophonies d'Amerique* 18 (1): 171–179.

Heller, Monica. 2001. "Legitimate language in a multilingual school." In *Voices of Authority: Education and Linguistic Difference*, ed. by Monica Heller and Marilyn Martin-Jones, 381–402. London: Ablex Publishing.

Heller, Monica. 2002. *Éléments d'une Sociolinguistique Critique*. Paris: Éditions Didier.

Heller, Monica. 2007. "'Langue', 'communauté' et 'identité': Le discours expert et la question du Français au Canada." *Anthropologie et Sociétés* 31 (1): 39–54.

Hengst, Heinz. 1997. "Negotiating 'us' and 'them' – Children's constructions of collective identity." *Childhood* 4 (1): 43–62.

Jacquet, Marianne. 2009. "La dimension marginale de l'inclusion de la diversité ethnique à l'école: L'exemple de la Colombie-Britannique." *Canadian Ethnic Studies* 41 (1–2): 95–113.

Jacquet, Marianne, Danièle Moore, Cécile Sabatier, and Mambo Masinda. 2008. *L'intégration des Jeunes Immigrants Francophones Africains dans les Écoles Francophones en Colombie Britannique*. Halifax: Centre Métropolis Atlantique.

Keller, Reiner. 2007. "L'analyse de discours comme sociologie de la connaissance." *Langage et Société* 120 (2): 55–76.

Lamarre, Patricia, Stéphanie Lamarre, Marina Lefranc, and Catherine Levasseur. 2015. *La socialisation langagière comme processus dynamique: suivi d'une cohorte de jeunes plurilingues intégrant le marché du travail*. Québec: Conseil supérieur de la langue française.

Landry, Rodrigue, Réal Allard, and Kenneth Deveau. 2008. "Un modèle macroscopique du développement psycholangagier en contexte intergroupe minoritaire." *Diversité Urbaine Numéro hors série*, 45–68.

Landry, Rodrigue, Réal Allard, and Kenneth Deveau. 2010. *École et Autonomie Culturelle: Enquête Pancanadienne en Milieu Scolaire Francophone Minoritaire, Nouvelles Perspectives Canadiennes*. Gatineau: Patrimoine Canadien.

Levasseur, Catherine. 2012. "'Moi, j'suis pas francophone!': Paroles d'élèves de Francisation à Vancouver." *Québec Français* 167: 55–57.

Levasseur, Catherine. Forthcoming. *'Moi j'suis pas francophone!': Discours, Pratiques Langagières et Représentations Identitaires d'élèves de Francisation à Vancouver*. PhD thesis, Université de Montréal.

Lynch-Cerullo, Kristen, and Kate Cooney. 2011. "Moving from outputs to outcomes: A review of the evolution of performance measurement in the human service nonprofit sector." *Administration in Social Work* 35 (4): 364–388.

Magnan, Marie-Odile, and Annie Pilote. 2007. "Multiculturalisme et francophonie(s): Enjeux pour l'école de la minorité linguistique." *Glottopol: Revue Internationale de Sociolinguistique* 9: 80–92.

Moore, Danièle. 2006. *Plurilinguismes et École*. Paris: Éditions Didier.

Morgan, Branwen. 2014. "Research impact: Income for outcome." *Nature* 511 (7510): s72–s75.

Pavlenko, Aneta. 2003. "'I never knew I was a bilingual': Reimagining teacher identities in TESOL." *Journal of Language, Identity and Education* 2 (4): 251–268.

Perregaux, Christiane. 2009. "Dans les dessins de jeunes enfants, les langues sont des images." In *Le Dessin Réflexif: Élément pour une Herméneutique du Sujet Plurilingue*, ed. by Muriel Molinié, 31–43. Cergy-Pontoise: Université de Cergy-Pontoise.

Pilote, Annie. 2004. *La Construction de l'identité Politique des Jeunes en Milieu Francophone Minoritaire: Le cas des élèves du Centre Scolaire Communautaire Sainte-Anne à Fredericton au Nouveau-Brunswick*. PhD thesis, Université Laval, Québec.

Pilote, Annie, and Marie-Odile Magnan. 2012. "La construction identitaire des jeunes francophones en situation minoritaire au Canada: Négociations des frontières linguistiques au fil du parcours universitaire et de la mobilité géographique." *Canadian Journal of Sociology/Cahiers Canadiens de Sociologie* 37 (2): 169–195.

Sabatier, Cécile. 2010. "Plurilinguismes, représentations et identités: Des pratiques des locuteurs aux définitions des linguistes." *Nouvelles Perspectives en Sciences Sociales: Revue Internationale de Systémique Complexe et d'études Relationnelles* 6 (1): 125–161.

Statistique Canada. 2011. "Population selon la langue maternelle, par province et territoire, à l'exclusion des résidents d'un établissement institutionnel." *Recensement de la Population de 2011*. Accessed 4 September 2014. Available from: http://www.statcan.gc.ca/tables-tableaux/sum-som/l02/cst01/demo11c-fra.htm.

Waller, Tim, and Angeliki Bitou. 2011. "Research with children: Three challenges for participatory research in early childhood." *European Early Childhood Education Research Journal* 19 (1): 5–20.

Chapter 4

Sociolinguistics in the museum

Enrichment, engagement, and education

Fiona Douglas, ORCID NUMBER 0000–0002–2641–7010

Introduction

This chapter describes the journey to impact of the *Language, History, Place* project, a sociolinguistic research, teaching, and public engagement venture between the university and museum sectors. By examining the strategies adopted in the project, most especially its use of 'enactive engagement' (Hooper-Greenhill 1994), I hope to show how sociolinguists can play a role in shaping the impact landscape and making it more habitable. We have massive potential to develop mutually beneficial partnerships with various agencies and the general public, which can be enriching for all concerned (cf. Wolfram, this volume). But in order to do so, we must think hard about how we approach these relationships, how we value the knowledge and expertise that others bring, and how we inhabit the complex interrelated roles of academic researcher, university teacher, and public ambassador for our subject. How fundamental and pervasive an influence should impact be on our research? To what extent should we be shaping our research to take account of impact, or should impact be reshaping our research? Arguably impact should challenge not only what we do with our research, but how we do it – our methodologies, our assumptions, our basic research practices, and even our discourses may all need to be reshaped if we are to negotiate this seismic shift in the research landscape and grasp the opportunities it presents. Lastly, I demonstrate the key role that university students can play in the impact journey – largely ignored by current institutional understandings of impact.

The impact landscape

The global rise of the 'impact agenda,' with Australian, European, New Zealand, US, and UK governments all requiring universities to measure 'impact' and to engage more with R&D and knowledge exchange (Watermeyer 2014), has transformed the landscape of research in Higher Education. In the United States, following the landmark recommendations of Boyer (1990) and the Kellogg Commission (2000), many institutions have developed 'public scholarship' policies, with potential repercussions for individual academics' promotion and tenure, as well as for universities' civic engagement profiles (Yapa 2006). In the UK, what began as encouragement to engage in *knowledge transfer* was followed by the more democratised dialogic discourse of *knowledge exchange*. Policies and funding strategies around *impact* and *public engagement* soon followed (Watermeyer 2014).

There has been some understandable anxiety in the academic community about what the impact agenda means for the future of research, and for research funding in particular. But on a pragmatic level, we in the UK have little alternative but to engage with the impact agenda. Our research councils now require the completion of 'pathways to impact' statements as an integral part of funding applications, asking applicants to predict how the proposed research will achieve impacts beyond the academy. And the national Research Excellence Framework (REF) requires universities to give an account of their research in terms of 'impact case studies', a system under which those achieving the highest rating have an estimated monetary value of as much as £720,000 over a five-year period (Dunleavy 2012).

Unsurprisingly, since the advent of the impact agenda, university researchers have increasingly sought to foster links beyond academe. Often, the primary motivation is to find 'impact-friendly' outlets that will disseminate the results of completed research endeavours and deliver them to public audiences, thereby satisfying the stipulations of the funding body and research auditors. These can sometimes be little more than symbiotic marriages of convenience, or worse still, parasitic. But despite the controversy, debates, and uncertainty surrounding the central tenets of impact – that academic research should be shared with a wider audience and ought to have social, economic, cultural, environmental, health, and quality-of-life benefits beyond academe (HEFCE 2010) – these are aspirations that, if sensitively and creatively implemented, have the potential to significantly enhance our research.

Sociolinguistics and the road less travelled

As sociolinguists, we are particularly well placed to respond to the impact challenge. The subject of our research, the language of individuals and groups within society, means that we have a built-in human dimension to most of the research we do. For sociolinguists, language is not divorceable from the people who use it. We are used to undertaking fieldwork that involves engaging with people as a fundamental part of the research methodology, and presumably those same people are likely to be interested in our research findings. We are, or should be, primed for impact.

Yet given sociolinguistics' inherent advantages, it has arguably been rather slow to respond to the impact agenda. As a discipline, we have not been especially good at articulating what we do in this regard, and why and how we do it. Even public engagement (a potential precursor or 'route to impact') is mentioned less often in the academic literature than might be expected. Most of the discussion tends to be concentrated in the United States, where 'service' rather than 'impact' has long been a metric used in tenure and promotion processes. Although some of the more recent handbooks and introductions include discussion of how public engagement might best be undertaken (e.g. Chambers and Schilling 2013; Mallinson 2013), few sociolinguistic journal articles explicitly address the impact question and our relationship with it. A comparison with human geography, a not unrelated field, shows a discipline much more actively involved in discussion of what the impact agenda means for its research (Pain et al. 2011).

Of course, there are linguists who are already engaging with non-academic audiences. Many researchers, perhaps most notably those working in the area of minority or endangered languages, have long sought to engage with the communities they study and have seen their research make a real, impactful difference (see Coleman, this volume; Purnell et al. 2013: 405). Some prominent sociolinguists have written persuasively about the need to recognise our responsibilities to the communities we study. As early as 1982, Labov wrote about the *principle of debt incurred*: "an investigator who has obtained linguistic data from members of a speech community has an obligation to use the knowledge based on that data for the benefit of the community, when it has need of it" (1982: 173). Wolfram has long been vociferous in encouraging researchers to give something back. His *principle of linguistic gratuity* argues that: "investigators who have obtained data from members of a speech community should actively pursue positive ways in which they can return linguistic favours to the community" (1993: 227), a call that he and other US scholars have repeated in recent times (e.g. Wolfram et al. 2008; Wolfram 2012, this volume; Purnell et al. 2013). However, as Wolfram et al. (2008: 1111) note, "constructs such as gratuity, collaboration, partnership, and benefit are ideologically laden notions that need to be examined critically."

Dialogue, collaboration, and co-produced knowledge

In academe, knowledge has often been seen as the preserve of the 'expert'. Even publicly engaged sociolinguistic research can be characterised by the deficit model, on the implicit assumption that the sociolinguists are the 'real language experts', and that the public are misinformed or ignorant about language matters (Johnson 2001). Under the deficit model, the dominant modes of public engagement are more likely to be focused on researchers sharing their findings with public audiences (i.e. dissemination) and giving something back to the community having taken something (e.g. sociolinguistic data) from it. Dissemination styles of impact generation are basically monologic: the 'experts' in the academy share their research findings with the public via a series of activities or events that are deemed appropriate. Valuable as these outreach activities are, as sociolinguists perhaps we ought to aim for more embedded engagement with public audiences that emphasises dialogism.

The UK National Co-ordinating Centre for Public Engagement (NCCPE) stipulates that "engagement is by definition a two-way process, involving interaction and listening, with the goal of generating mutual benefit" (NCCPE 2014a). Meanwhile the guidelines for REF impact submissions require evidence of "the distinctive contribution of the department's research" to the public engagement activity and "a case for the benefits arising from it, *which must go beyond dissemination*" (HEFCE 2010, my emphasis). But 'broadcast styles' of engagement are undoubtedly still prevalent (NCCPE 2014a), with dissemination rather than collaboration, co-creation, or co-production featuring heavily in REF impact case studies (NCCPE 2014b).

Yet whilst collaborative and co-creative approaches have received less attention and acceptance in academic settings than in other institutions, ideologies have shifted somewhat. The rather patronising term 'knowledge transfer' has been replaced with 'knowledge exchange' and the increasing emphasis on impact and public engagement may help to democratise research and encourage us to listen to others rather than assume that we have a monopoly on knowledge. In a now foundational piece, Cameron et al. (1992: 22–24) write that research should be *on, for,* and *with* the people studied, where *with* implies "interactive or dialogic research methods" as opposed to "distancing or objectifying strategies." They argue for more egalitarian and "empowering research." Pain et al. (2011: 185–186) contend that, by embracing the impact agenda, we can help to effect social justice and change, rather than merely playing an "audit game." They insist that although impact is often viewed as a one-way process, it should be thought of as two-way with an emphasis on co-production of knowledge, metrics that are "explicitly attentive to instances in which academics listen, not only talk, to the rest of society," and research that:

> pursues positive social change in partnership with non-academics, not just as research users whose knowledge and activities are to be 'impacted', but as collaborators who shape research agendas and play a role in directing research processes and outcomes. . . . Where knowledge is co-produced, impact is two-way: research may inform society, but its own agendas, design, conduct and outcomes are also profoundly informed and shaped by various users, publics and participants.
>
> (Pain et al. 2011: 185–186)

As Engelstad and Gerrard note, Haraway's (1988) notion of "situated knowledges" (note the plural) underlines the importance of "communication between different knowledge producers and different ways of producing knowledge" (Engelstad and Gerrard 2005: 10) and makes the boundaries between expert and lay knowledge "porous" (p. 11). An inclusive approach need not undervalue academic expertise. We may be used to seeing ourselves as the 'language experts' but we would be wise not to discount the knowledge and life experience that our 'data subjects' have about their own linguistic varieties and choices (Wolfram et al. 2008; Wolfram, this volume). As responsible and engaged sociolinguists, we should be engaging in dialogue and partnership *with* our non-academic audiences, rather than talking *at* them and seeing outreach as a one-way street.

The *Language, History, Place* project

The *Language, History, Place* project builds on a partnership between the University of Leeds (specifically the School of English and the Brotherton Library's Special Collections) and three Yorkshire folk museums: the Dales Countryside Museum in Hawes, the Shibden Hall Folk Museum outside Halifax, and the Ryedale Folk Museum in Hutton-le-Hole. Since 2010, we have been exploring different ways of working together that unite academic research, university teaching, museum collections, local communities, and engagement with museum visitors. There is still some distance to travel, and a major grant (in preparation) would allow us to realise many more of the project's aims; but in the interim we have learned a great deal about the opportunities and challenges of this type of work, which we hope will inspire others to explore the fertile landscape that lies beyond the ivory tower.

The University of Leeds has long been associated with sociolinguistics' elder sister discipline, dialectology. In the 1950s and '60s, Harold Orton and Eugen Dieth undertook the *Survey of English Dialects (SED)*, a complete survey of the dialects of England, and a monumental task. This was followed by the setting up of the *Institute of Dialect and Folk Life Studies (IDFLS)* in 1964, a research and teaching centre which flourished for nearly two decades until its closure in 1983. In 2002–5, under the guidance of Clive Upton and Oliver Pickering, the materials from the *SED* and the former *IDFLS* were brought together, housed in the Brotherton Library's Special Collections, and catalogued under a new umbrella – the *Leeds Archive of Vernacular Culture (LAVC)*. This important multimedia collection (composed of audio recordings, word maps, photographs, *SED* published and unpublished materials, folk life files, *IDFLS* research, etc.) gathers together dialect and folk life research carried out from the 1950s to the 1980s. Given that many of the *SED* respondents were advanced in years at the time of the Survey, and the subsequent work of the *IDFLS*, the *LAVC* offers valuable insights into the English language from the late nineteenth to the late twentieth centuries. But its location in the University Library means that access is largely restricted to academic researchers, and its rich resources remain untapped. Such a valuable cultural heritage and linguistic resource deserves to be shared more widely and especially with the communities from which its materials were collected.

Impact through partnership

The *Language, History, Place* project is premised on the firmly held conviction that academic research and archive collections should be shared and exchanged with a wider audience. After all, the language that people lend us for our research belongs to them; we are custodians of the merest echo of their voices. By working in partnership with local folk museums, the *Language, History, Place* project is making the *LAVC* materials publicly available to the communities from which they were collected via enrichment of the folk museums' collections and exhibitions, and a series of public engagement initiatives.

These museums are located in the communities from which the original dialect words, pronunciations, and recordings were taken, and the museums' artefact collections are considerably enriched by the addition of digitised complementary intangible heritage materials from the *LAVC*. UNESCO defines intangible cultural heritage as "the practices, representations, expressions, knowledge, skills – as well as the instruments, objects, artefacts and cultural spaces associated therewith – that communities, groups and, in some cases, individuals recognize as part of their cultural heritage," noting a "deep-seated interdependence between tangible and intangible cultural heritage" (UNESCO 2003). It characterises intangible cultural heritage as being "transmitted from generation to generation," "constantly recreated by communities and groups in response to their environment, their interaction with nature and their history," and providing them with "a sense of identity and continuity" (UNESCO 2003). "Intangible heritage is: traditional, contemporary and living at the same time," "does not only represent inherited traditions from the past but also contemporary urban and rural practices in which diverse cultural groups take part" (UNESCO 2014), and is manifested, among other things, through "oral traditions and expressions, including language as a vehicle of the intangible cultural heritage" (UNESCO 2003). Wolfram et al. (2008: 1114) found that the people they interviewed for the *Voices of North Carolina* project saw culture, history, and language as "inseparable" and perceived language as an integral part of their heritage (see also Wolfram, this volume).

It is this capacity for such intangible heritage, and especially language, to engage people with a sense of place, their past, their present, their communities, and traditions that the *Language, History, Place* project seeks to harness. The partner museums have collections of tangible heritage artefacts relating to trades, domestic, and rural and folk life such as agriculture, blacksmithing, dairying, coopering, wheelwrighting, games, and songs; the *LAVC* has the associated intangible heritage of language and dialect research materials. By reconnecting the voices, language, and other *LAVC* materials with the physical objects from the museums' collections, the past can be brought to life, and valuable new connections and meanings made. Giaccardi and Palen (2008: 281) remind us that "the living relationship between intangible and tangible forms of heritage, as well as natural and cultural heritage, is a situated one, always in place." By reuniting these different forms of cultural heritage, and crucially by doing so within their places of origin, we can help the museums enrich local cultural identities, strengthen "the storehouse of cultural memory," and promote archival materials from the *LAVC* that have "distinctive regional resonance" (NCCPE, 2011). These activities seek to deliver positive outcomes for all, and feed into our understanding and articulation of impact, as discussed in the following.

Impact across and throughout the research process

Embedding the *LAVC* materials in local museums is valuable, but it remains largely within the monologic dissemination model of impact activity. Pain et al. (2011: 186) note that:

> as currently [2010] conceived, definitions of impact assume that the results and outputs of research are the only, or at least primary, means by which research has impacts on wider society.

They argue that the *processes* associated with collaborative research can be impactful and empowering. McCormack (2011) advances a theory of 'engaged scholarship' where the doing and using of research are thoroughly integrated in practice. Feedback on the 2014 REF impact case studies queried whether the focus should be only on the impact of research outcomes, or whether the impact of the research *process* should also be taken into account (NCCPE 2014c). Achieving impact across the lifetime of a project is not without its challenges, however, and some argue that the current definitions impose unhelpful timeline restrictions (Watermeyer 2014).

Following Pain et al. (2011), the *Language, History, Place* project operates on the premise that impact can be embedded at all stages in the research process, and that research can and should engage with public audiences throughout a project's lifetime. This agrees with, and adds to, the aspirations of RCUK's pathways to impact (RCUK 2011), as discussed below. In addition to sharing the research with a wider public audience (the dissemination model), and involving partner organisations in the research design (the collaborative model), the *Language, History, Place* project aims to listen to, and engage in dialogue with, public audiences via a series of research-informed and research-informing collaborative activities (the engagement model). These form the basis of a new tranche of research data collection from the museum visitors themselves, where the data collection methodologies are designed to be inherently impactful.

Enactive public engagement in and beyond the museum

The discourse of collaboration has received more acceptance in the museum world in recent years than it has in academe, and the heritage sector seems to have found ways of coping with the challenges and opportunities presented by working in partnership with the public. Collaboration, co-creation, and co-curation with visitors have become increasingly popular approaches, with Simon's (2010) book, *The Participatory Museum*, a practical guide to how these can best be achieved. The activities she describes run the full gamut from basic interactive opportunities within the constraints of an individual exhibition to full-on participatory design, where members of the public shape exhibition and institutional priorities, and research agendas. All these approaches have applications for the sociolinguistic researcher.

Underpinning Simon's (2010) discussion is the belief that the museum space can and should be dynamic, dialogic, and transformative. Rather than being passive recipients of information, visitors can be proactive and bring their own knowledge and experience to bear, thereby enhancing their visit by making it more memorable and meaningful. One powerful means of achieving this is through enactive engagement (Hooper-Greenhill 1994). This is a familiar concept in the fields of museum studies, psychotherapy, educational pedagogy, and cognitive science, but hitherto much less well known in sociolinguistics. Enactive engagement in the museum can take a variety of forms, such as demonstrations, live interpretation, and re-enactments. These rely on museum interpreters and education officers, invited artisans, and volunteers to help bring both artefacts and history to life. However, other forms of enactive engagement rely on the visitors themselves to participate, perhaps by contributing their own stories and recollections. In the process, they become co-creators rather than simply consumers of knowledge. It is on these more active forms of engagement that the Language, History, Place project bases its methodologies.

Enactive engagement offers some impactful possibilities for sociolinguistic research throughout the process, not just at the endpoint. The Language, History, Place project uses a range of activities within the museum context, to collect language research data whilst simultaneously seeking to enrich the visitors' experience. We invite them to engage with museum displays, stimuli, and activities of various types (artefactual, visual, audio, audiovisual, textual, interactive), and to respond by sharing their own linguistic practice (their words, pronunciations, idiom, and dialect) with us. In this way, we seek to make the data collection phase (not just the dissemination of outputs) impactful.

As well as facilitating the collection of linguistic data, we want to empower and enlighten visitors. We aim to collect new materials within the museum environment in such a way that visitors become contributors, co-creators, and co-beneficiaries. By contributing, they take away something valuable and lasting from the experience. By putting existing research outputs from the LAVC into the museums and inviting people to engage with and contribute to our ongoing research, we seek not only to enhance the museums' collections, but also to offer ways for the visitors to encounter their own cultural and linguistic inheritance, and compare it with that of others. In this way, people interact with, and respond to, voices from the past; they explore their own linguistic and cultural heritage, and perhaps discover and reconnect with communities.

Funding permitting, a future aim is to collect data from people via a project website using online crowdsourcing methodologies. Such methods have proved effective for other sociolinguistic research projects (e.g. the collection of lexical data by the BBC Voices website – BBC 2014), and have the advantage that visitors can submit their own language data, and also browse and search through data provided by others. Simon (2010: 256) argues that the best collaborative cultural experiences have a "thin and permeable division between spectating and actively collaborating." Ideally then, the data collection and browse/search/display website functions would be closely integrated, perhaps using single pane user interface technology.

Simon (2010) also emphasises the importance of ensuring that visitors' contributions are valued and acknowledged, that goals are clearly defined, and that visitors receive clear information about how to contribute and how their contributions will be used. These are important considerations both for museum professionals and for sociolinguists. Mallinson (2013: 257) believes that "sociolinguists can do both research and outreach" but insists they should "plan carefully and strategically in advance," that they must "set clearly outlined goals" in which they consider "questions of ethics, ownership, relevancy, responsibility, and resources." A project website would give us a means of initiating follow-up activities, and the museums another way of publicising and democratising access to their collections. In addition to offering functionality in terms of language data collection and exploration, a website could also help the project initiate and maintain dialogue with museum visitors before and after their visits.

One of the challenges of traditional sociolinguistics vis-à-vis the impact agenda is that so often we collect data from people and then, having analysed it, publish the results in academic journals and squirrel the data away in research archives. Occasional public lectures or other dissemination events take us only part of the way towards impact. If we want to generate long-lasting dialogue with the public then we have to create an arena where such exchanges can take place. Setting up online visitor forums or similar areas that allow us to harness the potential of social media and online interaction may help to extend the dialogue beyond the single museum and/or website visit. This is likely to be welcomed by those who want a more sustained connection with the project. By giving people access to the ongoing research via a project website, allowing them to explore it and respond at leisure, to revisit and see their contributions, and those of others, valued and celebrated, the project could hopefully encourage a much more inclusive conversation. By collaborating with visitors (actual and virtual), rather than viewing them merely as 'data informants', we have the opportunity to make data collection enhancing and affirming for both them and us.

Museolinguistics: Opportunities and challenges

With the foregoing discussion in mind, the museum context offers enormous untapped possibilities for sociolinguists. The Arts Council for England notes "increasing numbers of people visiting museums over the past few years, and now just under half of the adult population, 46.3%, have visited a museum at least once in the past 12 months of 2010/11" (ACE 2011: 21). Properly harnessed, and with appropriate consideration for the needs and wishes of the visitors themselves, that offers us a huge public audience, and a great many people who may be willing to share their linguistic practices.

When it comes to engaging with public audiences, museums and their staff are usually more adept than even the most outwardly-focused academic, and by working with them we can benefit and learn from their experience and knowledge. They are much more practised than we are at 'translating' academic research for non-academic addressees, and they can advise on matters of presentation, interaction, and reaching target audiences. Museum professionals have a wealth of knowledge that extends beyond their collections into the local community, its heritage, and its people. They also tend to know their visitor profiles very well, something that can be very useful for the sociolinguistic researcher.

Many museums also have large groups of active volunteers, who tend to have local knowledge; they may be members of the local speech community, and can act as go-betweens or ambassadors, providing the researcher with unparalleled access into communities (c.f. Yamada 2007). Often, they can provide specialist local knowledge and input, especially in terms of named personal contacts, thus obviating the need for the researcher to try to 'break in' as an 'outsider' to a largely unknown discourse community. They are also often available, willing, keen and able to act as satellite fieldworkers, an experience that can be rewarding for them (e.g. skills development, supporting lifelong learning) as well as beneficial for the project. Between them, the *Language, History, Place* partner museums have several hundred volunteers, many with longstanding multi-generational links to the local area. They have been knowledgeable, committed, and enthusiastic about the aims of the project. We hope to extend volunteer involvement in the future by training project ambassadors who will act as project fieldworkers.

In addition, such a strategy may help to sustain the project in the longer term. The inevitability of short- to medium-term grant funding in both the academic and museum worlds is notorious and is something that should be considered as part of the project strategy from the outset. This is especially important in projects where we are encouraging the public to have significant intellectual and emotional investment in our research. Pulling the plug on partner communities after a period of three or five years is both ethically and academically questionable, so we need to find a way of making publicly engaged research sustainable. RCUK guidance recognises that "impacts can manifest at any stage in the research and project life cycle and beyond" (RCUK 2014). For the AHRC and the other research councils, sustainability generally refers to the requirement to ensure that project outputs such as websites or other resources are accessible and maintained for a minimum of three years beyond the life of the project. And whilst the AHRC's Follow-on Funding for Impact and Engagement recognises some of these issues, it rules out providing extended support for impact activities that featured in the original proposal (i.e. continuing existing activities), and requires that the funding be used to engage new user-communities and audiences (AHRC 2014: 25). So for the time being, individual researchers must grapple with some aspects of sustainability themselves. Embedding the research within the community, and training volunteers to carry it on without research-funded institutional support, is one way of tackling this thorny problem.

This wealth of knowledge, experience, and connections, coupled with the opportunity to share and collect research data in an accessible and stimulating environment with a constantly replenishing visitor base, makes the museum context – and hence what we might term 'museolinguistics' – a very attractive proposition. And some of the most potent possibilities are those generated by the visitors themselves.

Engaging with public audiences

From its earliest stages, the *Language, History, Place* project reaffirmed the fact that people really care about language. The so-called 'ordinary woman/man in the street' may not think of her/himself as a language expert; but enquire about their likes/dislikes or ask for examples of their own and others' linguistic practice, and we have found that lively and informative conversations usually ensue. Couple this with an interest in their local community and linguistic variety and many people are happy to engage in discussion at some length. Of course, this is something of which sociolinguists and dialectologists have long been aware (see Wolfram et al. 2008). Other sociolinguistic projects have found the public to be willing and eager participants. To return to BBC *Voices*, this project received over 700,000 responses from more than 75,000 respondents, and had over a million hits, with people still submitting data two years after the project had finished (Wieling et al. 2014). But nowadays the rigours and institutional priorities that accompany the pursuit and quantification of success in academic research and funding can sometimes mean that we lose sight of the enthusiasm and knowledge that 'ordinary' people bring.

Public engagement events designed to tell people about the *Language, History, Place* project have received a warm welcome, whether held in the local communities themselves or in other contexts. For example, early on, one of the museums gave the project central billing at their first ever AGM, held in the local village hall. It was a cold, dark, February night but the hall was packed with local people (the local landowner, farmers, teachers, labourers, those retired from full-time work, long-term residents, and more recent settlers) all keen to hear about the project's plans to put the LAVC's language resources into the museum, and to use this as a means of eliciting dialect from visitors. At a more recent lunchtime event in Leeds Town Hall, the audience demonstrated a similar level of enthusiasm and a healthy appetite for information and discussion about language and dialect. People were eager to share their own usages, as well as to ask questions about the project.

Museum visitors (as individuals or in groups) are usually relaxed and willing to engage with exhibits, activities, and staff. This offers opportunities for the sociolinguist to collect language data from people in an environment that is rewarding for both the visitor and the language researcher. Wolfram et al. (2008: 116), in their ongoing *North Carolina Language and Life* project, found that the "community-based museum exhibit" could be a "productive venue for collaboration" (see also Wolfram, this volume). On the *Language, History, Place* project, we believe there is a need to value and harness the knowledge that visitors bring with them to the museum. This requires the development of mutual trust and respect, and means that we stop regarding people merely as 'data subjects' or 'informants' and begin to see them as research collaborators. Mallinson (2013: 254) considers important ethical questions such as how we can best "initiate, foster, and sustain ethically sound collaborations with various communities" and "maximize our efforts for the public good." At the heart of these ethical considerations are the relationships fostered with the people whose language we study, and the power dynamics involved (Cameron et al. 1992; Wolfram et al. 2008). There is public appetite for sociolinguistic research; we just need to harness it, to learn how to listen as well as talk, and to reflect on our attitudes towards those whose language we study.

Attitudes, ideologies, discourse, and practice

One might be forgiven for thinking that in our pursuit of scientific rigour, the people we study have become theoretical abstractions rather than sentient beings who might be interested in their own language and what we say about it, and who may be able to contribute something valuable themselves. It is pleasing, therefore, to note that discourse practices may be changing, and under the influence of the impact and public engagement agendas, may continue to do so. Examination of all full-length research articles in the 2014 editions of the *Journal of Sociolinguistics* – an approximately 200,000-word corpus analysed using Wordsmith Tools (Scott 2012) – revealed that the most popular naming strategies for those whose language was being studied were: *people(s)* 383, *speaker(s)* 364, *participant(s)* 108, *individual(s)* 88, *interlocutor(s)* 84, *person(s)* 67, and *informant(s)* 66. *Interviewee(s)* occurred 16 times, *subject(s)* 5, and *data*, as a term for people, was reassuringly absent. It is interesting, however, to note that though *partner(s)* occurred three times, and *partnerships* once, these occurrences referred to personal or business relationships and not to mutually affirming partnerships between sociolinguistic researchers and those whose language was being studied. Though word frequency analysis gives only a somewhat superficial snapshot of current practice, it suggests that ideologically there is still some way to go.

The *Language, History, Place* project is trying to work in partnership with a range of stakeholders, and bringing different types of expertise together for the benefit of all. Since its inception, the project has been characterised by continuing dialogue and knowledge exchange between academic, museum, and library archive partners. While negotiating different priorities, funding mechanisms, and timelines, together we have been able to devise methodologies and outputs that work well for all; we recommend similar inclusive planning practices to other sociolinguists who are trying to integrate impact into their research.

But most importantly, we value the knowledge that visitors bring with them to the museum; it is their language that we seek to learn from, and they have their own insights to offer, which may complement, affirm, or challenge received academic wisdom. Thanks to their primary and testimonial knowledge, members of the public can bring first-hand insights into their own linguistic behaviour and that of others. As sociolinguists, we may have a more synoptic and comparative understanding of linguistic varieties and behaviour, and be able to offer summative and scholarly knowledge, but the visitors are the ones *doing* rather than merely *studying* language. By combining these differently situated knowledges through ongoing partnership and dialogue, we hope to enrich the understanding of all, and to achieve fresh insights into language use. We collaborate with visitors, museums, and local communities as full partners, instead of viewing them merely as 'informants,' 'routes to impact,' or 'dissemination outlets': impact *with* and *for*, not *on*.

Impactful encounters

Because language is so resonant for both individual and group identity, these museolinguistic encounters can be highly meaningful for visitors. They offer both opportunities and responsibilities for sociolinguistic research – opportunities to enhance people's understanding of their cultural heritage and linguistic practices; to raise issues such as social inclusion and cohesion – and responsibilities to make good on promises of true partnership. In collaboration with our visitors, we aim to create and interpret "cultural capital . . . enrich and expand the lives, imaginations and sensibilities of individuals and groups" and at the same time to collect valuable research data and advance research into "the languages and culture of minority linguistic . . . cultures and communities" (HEFCE 2012) that we can share with both public and academic audiences. In collaboration with the museums, our research aims to preserve, conserve, and present cultural heritage, and we hope that the resulting exhibitions and participatory enactive engagement activities will "contribute to the quality of the tourist experience" (HEFCE 2012) for those visiting the museums. By tapping into the interdependence of tangible and intangible heritage and their rootedness in place, we can encourage and enable communities and individuals to interact with their history and identity, and encourage dialogue between past and present.

We can also help visitors to be more informed and confident about their linguistic practices. Sociolinguistic theory tells us that people are often conflicted and self-conscious about the language varieties they use, especially if they are seen as non-standard or even sub-standard. Such linguistic insecurity is a well-attested phenomenon (c.f. Labov's (1966) Index of Linguistic Insecurity for New York City – Preston 2013). UNESCO frames its discussion of the reasons for safeguarding intangible heritage (including oral traditions and language) in terms of human rights and mutual respect for cultural diversity, a discourse that is reminiscent of well-trodden research and activism on regional and minority language rights (Phillipson 2000; May 2012). By asking visitors to contribute their own present-day linguistic practice in a non-judgemental context, we can celebrate the knowledge and language they bring. By juxtaposing past and present usage alongside regional variation, we can give visitors the opportunity to see their own linguistic practice as part of the bigger picture of language variation and change. At various project-related events, we have witnessed first-hand visitors' discovery of their linguistic 'pedigree.' We have seen disbelief and then pride when you tell them that what they had previously dismissed in their own or their family's usage as 'bad English' or 'slang' has a solid historical basis, and in some cases a much longer tradition than the so-called 'standard' forms. It is therefore possible, via quite modest methods, to effect real cultural impact; and sociolinguistic research that engages in this kind of public dialogue may even be able, in some small measure, to contribute to social inclusion and cohesion. Evidencing and measuring these types of impacts, of course, is much trickier.

Evidencing and measuring impact in the museum and the wider community

One of the biggest challenges facing individual researchers, universities, governments, and research funders is how to evidence, measure, and incentivise impact, public engagement, and public scholarship activities (NCCPE 2014b). Reporting strategies vary, but problems of evidencing, measuring, and 'proving' impact are widely shared:

> The pathway from research to impact is complex and more often realised through indirect routes than a linear path. There may be many players involved along the way, the time lag before a benefit is realised can be many years, and there is often more than one stage and level of impact. For these reasons, pinpointing a direct relationship between a specific piece of research and a specific outcome is one of the greatest challenges in understanding and assessing research.
>
> (Russell Group 2012: 11)

As a project team, we are aware of the need to develop robust impact measurement strategies and to ensure that visitor exit surveys or other types of feedback (e.g. via a project website) help to make such effects more quantifiable. Suggestions as to how impact can best be measured abound in the guidelines, but we have found that working with museums can have additional benefits as the sector has over many years (certainly within the UK) had to measure its impact on visitors, local communities, and the public. A museum's very survival is often contingent on such evidence. Museums are routinely required to demonstrate their effectiveness in outreach, social inclusion, and educational activities.

Generic Learning Outcomes (GLOs) are embedded in planning, funding, delivery, and evaluation models across the sector, with museums being encouraged to mix and match them in order to demonstrate impact. It is clear from the following five GLO headings just how useful these can be in measuring impact: "knowledge and understanding"; "skills"; "attitudes and values"; "enjoyment, inspiration, creativity"; "activity, behaviour and progression" (MLA 2008a). In addition, the former Museums, Libraries, and Archives Council (MLA) developed three Generic Social Outcomes (GSOs) which help museums "describe the wider impact of their work in communities" and relate to UK government policy priorities: "stronger and safer communities;" "health and well-being"; and "strengthening public life" (MLA 2008b). Even a cursory comparison with both UK REF and RCUK guidance and policy documents shows clear similarities; evidently we have much to learn from our colleagues in museums when it comes to demonstrating and measuring public impact. As a project, we are therefore working together to ensure that we develop measurement strategies that address both the impact agenda and the museums' reporting needs. We have already received excellent feedback as noted above, though not in quite this level of detail or structure. There is still much work to do, but by collaborating on these at all stages of the project, we are more confident of being able to find robust and reliable ways of evidencing the impact we achieve.

Impact, public engagement, or public scholarship?

So far, this chapter has argued that public engagement activities, carried out in partnership with the museum sector and members of the public, can be truly impactful, and that the impact can be dialogic rather than monologic, generated *for* and *with* rather than just *on*. However, one set of voices is notably absent even from this more inclusive conversation: the voices of our students. The UK's REF and RCUK policies explicitly exclude academic beneficiaries and students at the submitting institution from definitions of impact (HEFCE 2011), thereby divorcing research assessment from teaching. The US system of 'public scholarship' has a much more integrated approach, combining research, teaching, and 'service.' As Yapa (2006: 73–74) notes, it

> addresses issues of public interest; knowledge is generated in the community as well as in the university; agents producing the knowledge include community residents as well as teachers and students . . . the beneficiaries of new knowledge include the university as well as the community.

In many US institutions, students are involved in public or 'engaged' scholarship as part of their studies; in some cases it enhances their main programme but in others it forms a key credit-bearing component of their degree. Examples include the *Berkeley Public Service Centre*, the *Graduate Public Service (GPS) Fellowship* at Stanford, the above-mentioned *North Carolina Language and Life Project* at North Carolina State (see Wolfram, this volume), the *Public Engagement and Community Engagement Minor* at the University of Central Arkansas, and the *School Kids Investigating Language in Life and Society* (*SKILLS*) programme at the University of California, Santa Barbara (see Bucholtz et al., this volume).

The *Language, History, Place* project is well suited to this more inclusive vision of public scholarship, such as that described by Purnell et al. (2013), whereby outreach and teaching activities are integrated with research. The project's activities described above are complemented by undergraduate learning opportunities, where students benefit from the chance to help shape new research, and see their work published and celebrated in a public context. Students on the *Language, Identity and Community* module at the University of Leeds are directly involved as impact-creating apprentice researchers. This has benefits for them, the university, and the wider community. We have mounted special exhibitions and generated research-informed display materials and supplementary resources. The latter include children's activity packs, classroom materials (to support school visits and tie in with the national curriculum), and audio and film content. We have also taken part in museum event days where students have recorded face-to-face interviews with visitors in the 'dialect tent', yielding dialect material for the students' research as well as oral history recordings for the museums' collections. Last year students working with the Ryedale Folk Museum made an educational film on the local dialect to be shown in the schoolroom, which brought together their linguistic research and the museum's special focus on commemorating WWII. As part of their background research, they interviewed one of the museum's volunteers who gave them his personal account of child evacuees arriving in the village, living in his house, and attending school alongside him and his friends. Thus we were able to combine language, history, education, and personal reminiscence in one resource. Inspired by an early pre-release version of the film, the Dales Countryside museum asked the producer to create one for them on 'Language and Landscape.' We combined this with a tailor-made dissertation project for the student concerned.

Special museum events attended by staff and students, such as 'Tractor Day' at the Ryedale museum or the free May Day activities at Shibden Hall, have proved productive loci. Tractor Day is often held early in the year, before the main tourist season begins, drawing a largely local audience. Shibden Hall has several free open days each year, at which they mount craft demonstrations, children's activities, and cultural events like Pace Egg Plays. These open days tend to draw a more culturally diverse audience than the museum's regular opening hours; in 2010, about 60 families and 28 schoolchildren attended the event.

In all of our activities, we have invited the public to become involved with our research on the understanding that we will share our findings with them. For example, students have run mini-dialect surveys where visitors were invited to contribute their own dialect words via the museum's 'dialect post-box', and the analysed results were posted on the museum's blog, so that participants could access the research results afterwards. We undertake to share all of the students' project outputs with the museums, to enhance their collections and displays. In all of this, not only are the students using the *LAVC* materials to complement the museums' collections and bring our linguistic and other resources to a wider audience, they are using the resulting combination of tangible and intangible heritage as a stimulus to further data collection. Most importantly, they are learning a great deal from the process. There are obvious transferable skills and employability benefits, but the students are also experiencing at first-hand the challenge of undertaking and presenting sociolinguistic research with a public audience beyond the academy.

Elsewhere in the UK, the desire to involve students in publicly engaged scholarship can be seen in the University of Sheffield's innovative undergraduate modules *Storying Sheffield*, *Sense of Place*, and *Old English and Public Engagement*, and in its MA in *Public Humanities*. The University of East Anglia has a *History, Heritage and New Media* module run in collaboration with Norfolk museums, trusts, and heritage organisations. The NCCPE (2014c) has a Case Studies resource detailing some of these ventures, searchable by subject area. But clearly there is scope for many more 'engaged learning opportunities' within our universities. If we want to empower tomorrow's researchers to engage with impact, perhaps we should begin in the classroom – or better still – outside it. By restricting participation in impact and public engagement to academic researchers, and assessing separately the contributions made in research and teaching, the UK system is in danger of diluting the 'reach' and 'significance' of both (HEFCE 2011). Perhaps now is the time to rewrite our definitions of impact and to rethink the relationships between teaching and research, staff and students, academe and the outside world. Why not develop a more inclusive vision for impact: one that avoids academic schizophrenia, marries together research with teaching and outreach, and empowers our students to work alongside us as partners, achieving impact for themselves and for the wider community? With more effective integration, we could achieve more impactful, innovative, and inspiring universities.

Conclusion: A vision beyond impact

What does all of this mean for the future for sociolinguistics, or indeed, museolinguistics? Clearly we have the wherewithal to engage meaningfully with impact. The nature of our subject gives us a head start, but we need to adjust our practices, our methodologies, and our thinking. By employing dialogic and inclusive partnership approaches, we are more likely to engage and empower those who contribute to our research, whilst also enriching their sense of identity, and their cultural and linguistic heritage. By embracing the co-production of knowledge, we can gain richer research data, and may find ways of continuing productive conversations with communities beyond the lifetime of individual research projects.

As sociolinguists, we have the potential to lead the way in responding to the impact and public engagement agendas. Museolinguistics especially offers powerful opportunities to embed language research in local communities. Museums can be thought of as accessible gateways that are 'plugged in' to local communities in ways less immediately available to academic institutions. By working with museums and other external partners, we can contextualise and enhance research, make it more meaningful, and give it new life. If we embrace this kind of dialogic partnership, then we are better placed to achieve real impact, and to make a difference to the lives of those whose language we study.

But in addition to 'responding' to the requirements of impact, there is an opportunity for us to shape the impact landscape itself. We can encourage our research funders, institutions, and government bodies to have a bolder and more inclusive vision for impact, which integrates research, public engagement, and teaching. This should inspire us to map out the impact terrain more effectively and persuasively than we have to date. After all, now that we have set our feet firmly on the pathway to impact, who knows where it may lead?

Acknowledgements

I am grateful to my friend and colleague, Professor David Fairer, for his unstinting encouragement, incisive comments, and peerless copyediting. All errors remain my own. Thanks also to my museum partners, students, colleagues in Special Collections, and those members of the public who have contributed thus far; without you, there would be no project.

References

ACE (Arts Council England). 2011. "A review of research and literature on museums and libraries." Accessed 16 February 2015. Available from: http://www.artscouncil.org.uk/publication_archive/museums-and-libraries-research-review.

AHRC (Arts and Humanities Research Council). 2014. "Research Funding Guide." Accessed 16 February 2015. Available from: http://www.ahrc.ac.uk/SiteCollectionDocuments/Research-Funding-Guide.pdf.

BBC. 2014. "Voices." Accessed 18 November 2014. Available from: http://www.bbc.co.uk/voices/.

Boyer, Earnest L. 1990. *Scholarship Reconsidered: Priorities of the Professoriate*. Princeton, NJ: Carnegie Foundation for the Advancement of Teaching.

Cameron, Deborah, Elizabeth Fraser, Penelope Harvey, M.B.H. Rampton, and Kay Richardson. 1992. *Researching Language: Issues of Power and Method*. London: Routledge.

Chambers, J. K., and Natalie Schilling (eds.). 2013. *The Handbook of Language Variation and Change*, 2nd ed. Malden, MA: Wiley-Blackwell.

Dunleavy, Patrick. 2012. "REF Advice Note 1: Understanding HEFCE's definition of impact." Accessed 18 September 2014. Available from: http://blogs.lse.ac.uk/impactofsocialsciences/2012/10/22/dunleavy-ref-advice-1.

Engelstad, Ericka, and Siri Gerrard. 2005. "Challenging situatedness." In *Challenging Situatedness: Gender, Culture and the Production of Knowledge*, ed. by Ericka Engelstad and Siri Gerrard, 1–26. Delft: Eburon.

Giaccardi, Elisa, and Leysia Palen. 2008. "The social production of heritage through cross-media interaction: Making place for place-making." *International Journal of Heritage Studies* 14 (3): 281–297.

Haraway, Donna. 1988. "Situated knowledges: The science question in feminism and the privilege of the partial perspective." *Feminist Studies* 14 (3): 575–599.

HEFCE (Higher Education Funding Council England). 2010. "Research Excellence Framework impact pilot exercise: Findings of the expert panels, Annex J (71–77)." Accessed 18 November 2014. Available from: http://www.ref.ac.uk/media/ref/content/pub/researchexcellenceframeworkimpactpilotexercisefindingsoftheexpertpanels/re01_10f.pdf

HEFCE (Higher Education Funding Council England). 2011. "Decisions on assessing research impact." Accessed 18 November 2014. Available from: http://www.ref.ac.uk/media/ref/content/pub/assessmentframeworkandguidanceonsubmissions/GOS%20including%20addendum.pdf.

HEFCE (Higher Education Funding Council England). 2012. "Panel criteria and working methods." Accessed 18 November 2014. Available from: http://www.ref.ac.uk/media/ref/content/pub/panelcriteriaandworkingmethods/01_12.pdf.

Hooper-Greenhill, Eilean. 1994. *Museums and Their Visitors*. London: Routledge.

Johnson, Sally. 2001. "Who's misunderstanding whom? Sociolinguistics, public debate and the media." *Journal of Sociolinguistics* 5 (4): 591–610.

Kellogg Commission on the Future of State and Land-Grant Universities. 2000. *Renewing the Covenant: Learning, Discovery, and Engagement in a New Age and a Different World*. Washington, DC: National Association of State Universities and Land Grant Colleges. Accessed 14 October 2014. Available from: http://www.aplu.org/library/renewing-the-covenant-learning-discovery-and-engagement-in-a-new-age-and-different-world/file.

Labov, William. 1966. *The Social Stratification of English in New York City*. Arlington: The Center for Applied Linguistics.

Labov, William. 1982. "Objectivity and commitment in linguistic science: The case of the Black English trial in Ann Arbor." *Language in Society* 11 (2): 165–201.

Mallinson, Christine. 2013. "Sharing data and findings." In *Data Collection in Sociolinguistics: Methods and Applications*, ed. by Christine Mallinson, Becky Childs, and Gerard Van Herk, 253–257. Oxon: Routledge.

May, Stephen. 2012. *Language and Minority Rights: Ethnicity, Nationalism and the Politics of Language*, 2nd ed. Oxon: Routledge.

McCormack, Brendan. 2011. "Engaged scholarship and research impact: Integrating the doing and using of research in practice." *Journal of Research in Nursing* 16 (2): 111–127.

MLA (Museums, Libraries and Archives Council). 2008a. "Generic learning outcomes." Accessed 5 December 2014. Available from: http://www.artscouncil.org.uk/what-we-do/supporting-museums/ilfa/measuring-outcomes/generic-learning-outcomes/.

MLA (Museums, Libraries and Archives Council). 2008b. "Generic social outcomes." Accessed 5 December 2014. Available from: http://www.artscouncil.org.uk/what-we-do/supporting-museums/ilfa/measuring-outcomes/generic-social-outcomes/.

NCCPE (National Co-ordinating Centre for Public Engagement). 2011. "REF impact pilot: Background briefing." Accessed 1 November 2014. Available from: https://www.

publicengagement.ac.uk/sites/default/files/REF%20Impact%20Pilot%20background%20briefing.pdf.

NCCPE (National Co-ordinating Centre for Public Engagement). 2014a. "What is public engagement?" Accessed 1 November 2014. Available from: http://www.publicengagement.ac.uk/explore-it/what-public-engagement.

NCCPE (National Co-ordinating Centre for Public Engagement). 2014b. "After the REF – taking stock: Summary of feedback." Accessed 1 November 2014. Available from: http://www.publicengagement.ac.uk/sites/default/files/publication/nccpe_after_the_ref_write_up_final.pdf.

NCCPE (National Co-ordinating Centre for Public Engagement). 2014c. "Case studies." Accessed 22 February 2015. Available from: http://www.publicengagement.ac.uk/case-studies.

Pain, Rachel, Mike Kesby, and Kye Askins. 2011. "Geographies of impact: Power, participation and potential." *Area* 43 (2): 83–188.

Phillipson, Robert (ed.). 2000. *Rights to Language: Equity, Power, and Education*. Mahwah: Lawrence Erlbaum.

Preston, Dennis. 2013. "Linguistic insecurity forty years later." *Journal of English Linguistics* 41 (4): 304–331.

Purnell, Thomas, Eric Raimy, and Joseph Salmons. 2013. "Making linguistics matter: Building on the public's interest in language." *Language and Linguistics Compass* 7 (7): 398–407.

RCUK (Research Councils UK). 2011. "RCUK impact requirements: Frequently asked questions." Accessed 25 November 2014. Available from: http://www.rcuk.ac.uk/RCUK-prod/assets/documents/impacts/RCUKImpactFAQ.pdf.

RCUK (Research Councils UK). 2014. "Impact policies." Accessed 16 February 2015. Available from: http://www.rcuk.ac.uk/innovation/policies/.

Russell Group. 2012. "The social impact of research carried out in Russell Group universities." *Russell Group Papers* 3. Accessed 1 May 2015. Available from: https://www.russellgroup.ac.uk/media/5235/socialimpactofresearch.pdf.

Scott, Mike. 2012. *WordSmith Tools Version 6*. Liverpool: Lexical Analysis Software.

Simon, Nina. 2010. "The Participatory Museum." Accessed 14 August 2014. Available from: http://www.participatorymuseum.org/read/.

UNESCO. 2003. "Intangible heritage: Text of the convention." Accessed 12 November 2014. Available from: http://www.unesco.org/culture/ich/en/convention.

UNESCO. 2014. "What is intangible cultural heritage?" Accessed 12 November 2014. Available from: http://www.unesco.org/culture/ich/en/what-is-intangible-heritage-00003.

Watermeyer, Richard. 2014. "Impact in the REF: Issues and obstacles." *Studies in Higher Education*. Accessed 15 October 2014. Available from: http://www.tandfonline.com/doi/full/10.1080/03075079.2014.915303.

Wieling, Martijn, Clive Upton, and Ann Thompson. 2014. "Analyzing the BBC *Voices* data: Contemporary English dialect areas and their characteristic lexical variants." *Literary and Linguistic Computing* 29 (1): 107–117.

Wolfram, Walt. 1993. "Ethical considerations in language awareness programmes." *Issues in Applied Linguistics* 4 (2): 225–255.

Wolfram, Walt. 2012. "In the profession: Connecting with the public." *Journal of English Linguistics* 40 (1): 111–117.

Wolfram, Walt, Jeffery Reaser, and Charlotte Vaughn. 2008. "Operationalizing linguistic gratuity: From principle to practice." *Language and Linguistic Compass* 2 (6): 1109–1134.

Yamada, Racquel-María. 2007. "Collaborative linguistic fieldwork: Practical application of the empowerment model." *Language Documentation and Conservation* 1 (2): 257–282.

Yapa, Lakshman. 2006. "Public scholarship in the postmodern university." *New Directions for Teaching and Learning* 105: 73–83.

Chapter 5

Public sociolinguistic education in the United States

A proactive, comprehensive program

Walt Wolfram, ORCID NUMBER 0000–0002–5386–7754

Introduction

Every research proposal submitted to the National Science Foundation in the United States requires a narrative section titled "Statement of Broader Impacts." Under this heading, the principal investigator is obliged to address the project's "potential to benefit society . . . or advance desired societal outcomes." To be honest, this section is typically viewed as a boilerplate sidebar rather than an opportunity for genuine reflection on the social, educational, and political implications of the proposed research. This is unfortunate, because the broader social consequences of sociolinguistic research are not insignificant afterthoughts. In fact, thoughtful consideration and strategic planning related to outreach engagement should be integral to any research project, particularly those related to the role of language in society.

As Cameron et al. (1992: 24) observe: "if knowledge is worth having, it is worth sharing" – not only with our colleagues in the academy, but with others who might benefit from it, including the communities who provide us with our data and other public communities. As Rickford (1999: 315) puts it, "The fundamental rationale for getting involved in application, advocacy, and empowerment is that we owe it to the people whose data fuel our theories and descriptions." Perhaps more fundamentally, we are committed to a search for fundamental truths about matter, nature, behavior, and society. When it comes to language diversity and variation, however, there is a social tolerance for misinformation that is matched in few subject areas (e.g. Bauer and Trudgill 1998; Lippi-Green 2012). And the factual misinformation is not all innocent folklore; it actively reproduces relationships of social inequality, prejudice, and discrimination based on language differences. At the very least, then, our research should assume responsibility for replacing misguided notions and erroneous beliefs about language diversity with information about the authentic nature of language variation.

In this chapter, I consider the impact of research derived from a range of sociolinguistic research projects in the Southeastern United States, particularly within the state of North Carolina. A state-based model for engagement and outreach activities (cf. *West Virginia Dialect Project* [West Virginia University 2014]; *Voices of California Project* [Stanford Linguistics 2012]) offers obvious

advantages for addressing political systems, educational systems, and civic organizations which are all state-based in the United States, as well as tapping into a
natural focus on "state pride" exhibited in many states, including North Carolina
where we conduct our primary research (Wolfram and Reaser 2014; cf. Douglas,
this volume, on a similar approach to dialects in the north of England).

The current level of sociolinguistic outreach and engagement involves a comprehensive set of activities and programs, from formal curricular programs on language
in the public schools to the dissemination of rapid, anonymous informal education
to casual strollers at a state fair or television viewers browsing program channels
during a leisure hour. In the following sections, I discuss a number of levels of, and
venues for, formal and informal education and engagement efforts derived from our
research, and consider some ways of evaluating the impact of particular programs
and activities. Finally, I offer a set of guidelines for sociolinguistic researchers who
desire to see outcomes from their research extend beyond the highly restricted set of
professional colleagues in specialized fields of sociolinguistic inquiry.

Impact on whom?

Audiences for sociolinguistics do not fall into neatly compartmentalized, generic
categories such as "professional" and "public." Baumgardt (2012), in his discussion of SCIENCE ACCOMMODATION – the adapting of technical, scientific knowledge for presentation to those outside of a field of expertise – observes that the
impact of sociolinguistics has to be considered in terms of a wide array of diverse
audiences and encounters. We need to consider those that range from the immediate and direct audiences to the mediated and indirect audiences, starting with
our professional linguistic colleagues and extending outward.

Modern sociolinguistics in the United States rose in the 1960s from the natural
evolution of linguistic description within the tradition of cultural anthropology
(e.g. Hymes 1962; Gumperz and Hymes 1964; Hymes 1964, etc.) and an attempt
to account for the nature of language variation (e.g. Labov 1966, 1969). In part,
this development was a natural outgrowth of a longstanding progression of inclusive linguistic description and, in part, it was a reaction to the developing abstract
formalism of Chomskyan generative linguistics which gave primacy to intuitively
based linguistic "competence" vis-à-vis the "performance" of language in everyday life. The debate about the proper object of linguistic description continues
to this day, notwithstanding Labov's early and persistent claim (1966, 2001) that
the study of language variation is central to the solution of fundamental problems
in linguistic theory. Over time, sociolinguistics became an established track or
"subfield" within linguistics, and it is safe to say that all linguists, regardless of
their opinion of the inherent (in)significance of sociolinguistics in constructing
a model of language, at least support the foundational tenets of language diversity
embodied within the field. The fact that the most widely adopted introductory
linguistic textbooks (e.g. *Language Files* [Linguistics Department, the Ohio State
University 2011]; *Contemporary Linguistics* [O'Grady et al. 2009]; *An Introduction*

to Linguistics [Fromkin et al. 2013]) all include chapters on the social dimensions of language variation, and the fact that students of linguistics are now routinely offered courses in sociolinguistics ratifies its institutional standing within the discipline. The establishment of language variation and sociolinguistics as a field within the broader field of linguistics is a story deserving of its own narrative (see Tagliamonte 2016), but it is important not to dismiss the impact of sociolinguistics within its home discipline.

In some respects, allied professional audiences such as speech and language pathology, education, foreign language study, English studies, and human development, constitute a much more populated audience for the consumption of sociolinguistic knowledge than the small, relatively restricted specialization of linguistics. For example, more than 175,000 speech and language pathologists (certified by the American Speech-Language-Hearing Association) reside in the United States, and there are more than 17,000 programs that utilize the expertise of speech and language clinicians, including every public school in the United States. Speech and language pathology is therefore a vast, allied professional audience for sociolinguistic knowledge and application, since the distinction between natural language "difference" and "disorder" is foundational to the diagnosis and remediation process. When sociolinguists first encountered the field of speech and language pathology in the late 1960s, legitimate language differences were classified and treated as "disorders" (Baratz 1968; Labov 1969; Wolfram 1970). Through sociolinguistic education (Labov 1970; Williams and Wolfram 1977; Wolfram 1979), policy statements (e.g. ASHA 1983; Cole 1983), and the revision of existing standardized assessment measures to include vernacular dialect responses as appropriate norms for language development, the influence of sociolinguistics advanced. The applications now even include assessment instruments developed specifically for vernacular dialect speakers (e.g. Seymour et al. 2003). Standards, policies, and procedures in the field of speech and language pathology have been transformed over the decades, notwithstanding some persistent ideological conflicts that continue to impede the practical application of sociolinguistics within the field (Wolfram 1993a). Other allied professional groups (e.g. the National Council of Teachers of English [NCTE], Teaching English as a Second or Other Language [TESOL], the International Reading Association [IRA]) also have been affected by fundamental principles of sociolinguistics in policy positions, standards, and training that are comparable to those noted for the allied field of speech and language pathology.

Professional, allied groups represent one level for sociolinguistic transmission and diffusion, but these professional groups are, of course, intermediary to the students and clients they serve. It also is possible to target clients and students directly rather than through those who teach and serve them. Unfortunately, the public education of students in the schools rarely has been undertaken in sociolinguistics, and is still relatively novel (Bucholtz et al., this volume; Reaser 2006; Sweetland 2006). The examination of language variation as a topic of inquiry for students from kindergarten through secondary school (K–12) offers great opportunity for students in public education to investigate linguistic and social diversity grounded in geography, history, and cultural beliefs and practices. In the context of public schooling, of course, sociolinguistic study needs to accommodate standard courses and objectives currently in place at the state-wide level, so that the *Voices of North Carolina* curriculum developed by Reaser and Wolfram (2007) is designed specifically to fit the mandated standard course of study for the state of North Carolina for Grade 8 (13–14-year-old students) social studies (http://www.ncsu.edu/linguistics/research_dialecteducation.php).

The effect of sociolinguistic research may extend considerably beyond professional disciplinary domains and formal public education, from sharing information with the members of the communities who provide data for our research and other targeted communities to a variety of levels of informal education. Following Labov's (1982) well-known *principle of error correction* and *principle of debt incurred*, and Wolfram's (1993b) *principle of linguistic gratuity*, sociolinguists need to foster an understanding of the linguistic validity of all language varieties, particularly the vernacular-speaking communities that have been subjected to the principle of linguistic subordination (Lippi-Green 2012), as well as an understanding of the significance of language variation in society.

Audiences of local community members where we conduct our research (and those interested in these communities) have become increasingly available for sharing sociolinguistic knowledge, and presentations to civic organizations, cultural preservation and historical societies, and other special-interest groups are now often expected and requested by communities. Barbara Johnstone (2013), who has conducted extensive research on Pittsburghese over the last decade, reports that she has given about 50 presentations to civic and community group organizations in the Pittsburgh area since the onset of her research there, demonstrating how communities can become intrigued and engaged in the role of language in a community's sense of place, culture, and history reflected in language variation.

One of the obvious but often-overlooked communities for the transmission of sociolinguistic knowledge and application is the broader university community in which we participate as researchers and teachers. Notwithstanding the reputation of universities for promoting progressive social and political viewpoints, campus communities are often sites where ideologies of linguistic subordination may still be evident. A study of university students representing a rural Appalachian dialect region of North Carolina at North Carolina State University located in a metropolitan area in North Carolina showed that these students often feel marginalized and devalued within the context of the campus community because of their highland Southern US dialect (Dunstan 2013; Dunstan and Jaeger forthcoming). Dunstan's (2013) study showed that a range of behaviors could be affected based on these language differences, including class participation, perceptions of intelligence by professors and other students, and a sense of belonging on campus. Furthermore, the study indicated that these behaviors did not necessarily align with traditional sociopolitical ideologies found in different disciplinary fields; the social sciences and humanities, in fact, were perceived by students as less tolerant of language variation than the natural and physical sciences. In response to these findings, a collaborative team initiated an institutional program on language diversity targeted at the entire campus community, including students, staff, and faculty (Dunstan et al. 2015). Although institutional diversity efforts at most North American universities now extend to a range of groups and behaviors such as race/ethnicity, sex/gender, sexual orientation, religious affiliation, and so forth, they rarely are targeted for language diversity, which can index all of those characteristics. Our goals for the encompassing program are: (a) to raise awareness about language as a form of diversity on college campuses; (b) to educate a full range of members of the campus community about language variation and diversity; and (c) to provide multifaceted resources and strategies for the campus community to facilitate the inclusion of language in diversity programming. A CAMPUS-INFUSION IMPLEMENTATION MODEL was designed for a community of more than 40,000 faculty, staff, and students as we work with key university organizational units across campus. Ultimately, our goal is to ensure that language variation takes its rightful place within the institutional diversity canon.

Of course, more non-specific public audiences may be targeted, such as those who attend public exhibits, visit museums, watch television programs, interact on social media sites, and read books about history, culture, and, we hope, language. All of these are potential audiences for sharing and applying sociolinguistic knowledge. The representative kinds of communities we have discussed above are shown in Figure 5.1.

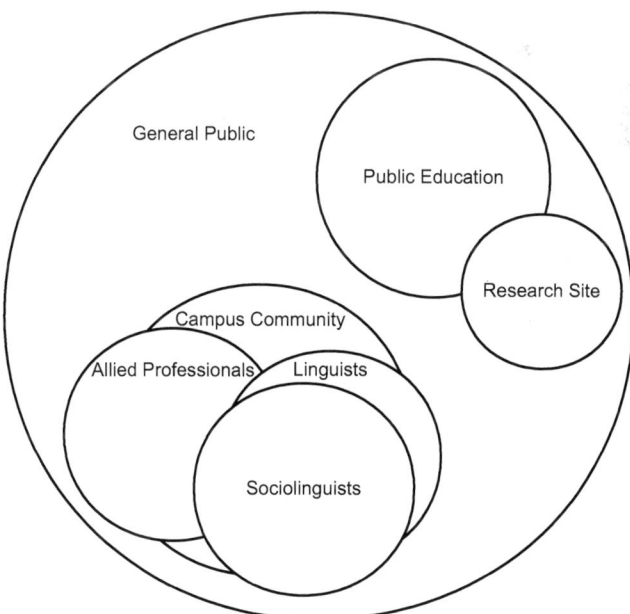

Figure 5.1 Audiences in the transmission of sociolinguistics information

Figure 5.1 is only intended to provide an illustrative sample of engagement audiences, indicating the overlapping and embedded nature of the communities targeted for sociolinguistic application. It is not intended to be exclusive, and other researchers may target different constellations of audiences in their outreach and extension programs. Furthermore, it cannot be assumed that engagement is a unilateral process that extends from sociolinguistics outward. There are many instances where the process is bilateral, as sociolinguists are influenced by other fields and audiences in their understanding of language variation.

Resources for sociolinguistic transmission

Sociolinguists have typically used venues and genres conventionally available to professionals for presenting their findings and perspectives on language diversity. These include journal articles, textbooks, websites, occasional invited media interviews, and editorial opinion articles in newspapers and popular magazines. According to Baumgardt's (2012) interviews with prominent sociolinguists in the United States, most do not feel successful in conveying their knowledge to audiences beyond the academy using such venues, though Baumgardt notes that the cascading, diffusional effect of sociolinguistic knowledge through allied professions and students may not warrant the pessimism of sociolinguists' self-evaluations.

At the same time, the potential venues for sharing information about language differences seem limited only by our imagination and creativity. In fact, Joshua Katz, a graduate student in statistics at North Carolina State University at the time, applied a relatively straightforward heat map visualization based on the 2003 Harvard Dialect Survey conducted by Bert Vaux and Scott Golder (see http://www.tekstlab.uio.no/cambridge_survey for current survey) to present data on lexical distribution in American English and to create a popular quiz based on these data that pinpoints the regional identity of speakers throughout the United States. The results, published in the *New York Times* in December 2013 (Katz and Andrews 2013, http://www.nytimes.com/interactive/2013/12/20/sunday-review/dialect-quiz-map.html), received more than 38 million hits, becoming the *New York Times* article with the highest number of hits for the entire year. The social media trending created an instant sensation, and sociolinguists could only envy the buzz created by Katz's adaptation and presentation of data that had been accessible to professionals and the general public for almost a decade. Perhaps more importantly in retrospect, the generated interest illustrated the natural curiosity that just about everyone has in language differences, and the potential for disseminating sociolinguistic information in a media world far different from the one in which sociolinguistics developed historically. Venues for sharing sociolinguistics obviously need to extend beyond the traditional parameters of academic disciplines, and many of these necessarily involve technical and creative expertise and alliances rather than simple cross-disciplinary, academic collaboration (cf. Lawson, this volume).

One of most the popular venues we have developed for public and educational audiences over the past couple of decades is video productions, ranging from vignettes posted on a YouTube channel (NCCLP 2014a) to the regular production of television broadcasts. The audiences for these "language and life" productions range from national audiences (e.g. *Mountain Talk* [Hutcheson 2004]; *First Language: The Race to Save Cherokee* [2015]), to regional (*Voices of North Carolina* [Hutcheson 2005]; *Spanish Voices* [Cullinan 2011]), to those produced primarily for community organizations (e.g. *The Ocracoke Brogue* [Blanton and Waters 1996]), though these are not mutually exclusive. Fortunately, high-quality video recording equipment and user-friendly editing software are now available, making video documentary production more feasible for students and faculty. Though our success in documentary production has now convinced the administration at our university to employ a talented, full-time videographer as an integral part of our research-engagement program, it is important to understand our modest beginning. Our first documentary was, in fact, produced by a couple of undergraduate students in a linguistics class who were more interested in documentary film production than linguistic analysis. They had no prior experience in filmmaking and production, no equipment, and no budget to carry out the project. We set up an independent study the next semester, borrowed equipment from a generous Communication Department, and operated on a shoe-string budget of less than $1,500 used exclusively for travel and supplies. Almost two decades later, their production of *The Ocracoke Brogue* (Blanton and Waters 1996) remains one of the most successful documentaries we have distributed. It has become a staple component of an exhibit on local dialect at the Ocracoke Preservation Society's museum where it still runs all day long on a loop in the "Dialect Room." Current editing software technology available at most Western universities makes these types of projects quite accessible at modest cost.

The compilation of oral histories on CDs and/or online is yet another convenient and straightforward way that we can share the diverse voices of communities where we have conducted sociolinguistic research. Based on sociolinguistic interviews, and with the assistance of community members, we have compiled a number of collections of stories that reminisce, celebrate, and entertain both community residents and outsiders. We have partnered with the Ocracoke Preservation Society to produce two such compilations a decade apart (Childs et al. 2001; Reaser et al. 2011), and a similar project was compiled with community members in a small, isolated African American community in the Smoky Mountains (Mallinson et al. 2006) based on the data extracted from interviews used for sociolinguistic research and repurposed with explicit permission from the participants for oral-history compilations.

The museum exhibit, both in physical and digital format, is another productive venue for significant sociolinguistic presentation and engagement (cf. Douglas, this volume). With community-based preservation societies and museums, it is possible to construct permanent and limited-time exhibits that highlight language variation. For example, an exhibit we conducted titled *Freedom's Voice: Celebrating the*

Black Experience on the Outer Banks (Vaughn and Grimes 2006) included images, a documentary, interactive audiovisuals, artifacts, and audio clips first recorded for sociolinguistic interviews and re-appropriated for oral histories to complement informational panels that highlighted African Americans' involvement in the history of coastal North Carolina. This exhibition brought together history, culture, and language through narrating the story of the previously overlooked contributions of African Americans at the island site of the so-called "Lost Colony" of Roanoke Island in coastal Carolina at the same time that we conducted research on this enclave sociolinguistic community.

One of the most successful exhibits we have used to present sociolinguistic research in a public forum is an annual booth at the North Carolina State Fair that has a yearly attendance exceeding one million people. Video vignettes and free dialect buttons celebrating dialect use (e.g. "bless your heart," "dingbatter," "I speak North Cackalacky" [a folk term for the State of North Carolina], etc.) are very popular with attendees. In addition, an interactive touch screen monitor allows visitors to guess the regional voices of speakers from the archival recordings. The 10-day fair is staffed largely by more than 100 student volunteers as part of a service-learning endeavor in which students interact about language in North Carolina with fair attendees.

Writing about sociolinguistics for non-specialized audiences is often difficult for linguists, and most do not have the journalistic expertise to write general books and articles for broad-based audiences, though there are a few notable exceptions (e.g. Tannen 1990; Rickford and Rickford 2000; Pinker 2007). With varying degrees of success, we have authored trade books aimed at these non-linguistic audiences. For example, Wolfram and Schilling-Estes' (1997) *Hoi Toide on the Outer Banks: The Story of the Ocracoke Brogue* remains available to tourists who visit the Outer Banks almost two decades after it was written, and Wolfram et al.'s (2002) *Fine in the World: Lumbee Language in Time and Place* is useful for residents of the community, educators, and others curious about the language variety of the Lumbee American Indians, the largest group of American Indians East of the Mississippi River (population circa 55,000). Translating highly specialized technical knowledge about science into accessible descriptions for lay people has proven to be a rhetorical challenge for those attempting to extend their descriptions beyond the academy (Reaser and Myrick 2015), but we have also found that the incorporation of digital enhancements can reinforce print data and make descriptions come to life for readers.

A recent trade book aimed at residents of and visitors to North Carolina, *Talkin' Tar Heel: How Our Voices Tell the Story of North Carolina* (2014), relies on more than 130 audiovisual enhancements where readers get to experience the language as they read, through the extensive use of Quick Response Codes (QRs), along with more than 60 images of people and places. Figure 5.2 includes a copy of a page with quotes from a long-time, elderly resident of the city of Charlotte about traditional attitudes towards Northerners who move to the South. Instead of simply reading the quote in orthographically altered script for the effect of

FIGURE 4.4. Author Martha Pearl Villas discusses the rapid changes she has seen in Charlotte. (Photograph by Neal Hutcheson)

southern dialect: "And these No'thuhnuhs come down heuh, and we take 'em in. And befo' you know it, it ain't the same. It's really not. They don't think and ac' like we do. Well they shu' don't tawk like us. They have a shahpness to theuh speech, don't you think so? Most South-uhnuhs and all, ah mean ah feel like we have kahna a soft, me-lodious voice. Of cou'se, whah shouldn't ah think it; ah don't know any different."[22] Notice that her speech, as an elderly, upper-class resident of the city born in 1916, is characterized by r-lessness and i ungliding. And the content is permeated with the undercurrent of tension between the old and the new.

To view the video of this quote, visit http://www.talkintarheel .com/chapter/4/video4-6.php

Figure 5.2 **Page image of trade book with QR enhancement** Copyright © 2014 by the University of North Carolina Press.

dialect, readers can scan the QR using any portable internet device like a smart-phone or tablet to go directly to the quote and see and hear the speakers.

Many of the audio and video enhancements are extracted from our archive of audio and video footage gathered as a part of our various research projects. Though the integration of QRs is somewhat novel in the field of linguistics, *Talkin' Tar Heel* is, to our knowledge, the first book to do so. The general reader experiences language and dialect rather than imagining it, and all the reader has to do is navigate any web browser to the provided URL, or use a smartphone or any device with a QR reader to snap a picture of the QR code to access the media directly. In the enhanced e-Reader version of the book, these enhancements are embedded within the text itself so a reader simply has to click on the icon.

The kinds of venues described above can be utilized and integrated into an array of informal and formal education programs, with broad-based and specific goals. Each of the programs utilizes different strategies and venues tailored for targeted audiences. For example, the *Educating the Educated Program* (Dunstan et al. 2015) implemented on the campus of North Carolina State for students, faculty, and staff ranges from the production of a language diversity training video to a branding campaign related to language differences. Using a campus-infusion model, the leadership team facilitated connections across campus in a variety of divisions and began sharing language diversity awareness materials in a variety of forms. We produced a six-minute vignette on dialect diversity at the university (NCLLP 2014b) filmed on campus that included spontaneous student responses to questions about their speech and about language diversity on campus. It also included interviews with staff, faculty, and key administrators, including an endorsement about language diversity from the head officer of the university, the Chancellor. This vignette has become a key component of presentations, and now serves as a resource for others on campus in diversity training/programming. We also created materials for distribution on campus to raise awareness, such as buttons and posters (see Figure 5.3) highlighting the NC State Wolfpack mascot, placing them across campus in locations such as in residence halls, on busses, and in digital format on digital campus monitors and bulletin boards.

Figure 5.3 "Howl with an accent" button and campus posters

Source: North Caroline State University language diversity program, led by Stephany Dunstan, Walt Wolfram and Audrey Jaeger

In addition to workshops conducted by the staff with all levels of students and employees, a student ambassador program was established in which graduate students in sociolinguistics engaged in peer education in the form of workshop delivery and the development of resource materials. The campus-infusion model targets the major administrative units – Student Affairs, Academic Affairs, Human Resources, and Faculty Affairs, as well as the Office of Institutional Equity and Diversity – strategically selecting units and programs in each of these areas in an effort to fully address the entire campus community.

Probably the most ambitious – and in many ways, the most essential – program for sustained sociolinguistic impact involves formal education about language variation beyond the university level. As noted earlier, school-based programs have still not progressed beyond a pilot stage, though the dialect awareness curriculum developed by Reaser and Wolfram (2007) fits in with the standard course of study for the state of North Carolina for Grade 8 social studies. It is also the first program endorsed by a state Department of Public Instruction in the United States, showing the current lack of progress. This language and dialect awareness program aligns with the curricular themes of "cultures and diversity," "historic perspectives," and "geographical relationships" as they relate to North Carolina. In addition, the dialect awareness curriculum helps fulfill social studies competency goals such as "Describe the roles and contributions of diverse groups, such as American Indians, African Americans, European immigrants, landed gentry, tradesmen, and small farmers to everyday life in colonial North Carolina" (Competency Goal 1.07) or "Assess the importance of regional diversity on the development of economic, social, and political institutions in North Carolina" (Competency Goal 8.04). Students are not the only ones who profit from the study of dialect diversity.

The kinds of venues described in this section underscore both the range and the potential of sociolinguistic education and impact. It also emphasizes the role of collaboration beyond the academy in maximizing effectiveness. Our most productive alliances, in fact, have been with creative and technical professionals, working with graphic designers, artists, programmers, producers, and marketing experts who help facilitate our attempts to infuse a wide variety of audiences and populations with an understanding of language variation and the role of language in society. This is the current reality, potential, and challenge of sociolinguistic engagement.

Assessing impact

The "scholarship of engagement," which challenges narrow definitions of academic research, is gradually edging its way into the canon of intitutionally recognized "research," though it hardly has equal standing with discovery-based inquiry in the academic meritocracy (e.g. Fish 2003). By scholarship of engagement, I am refrerring to "the collaborative generation, refinement, conservation, and exchange of mutually beneficial and societally relevant knowledge that is communicated to and validated by peers in academe and the community" (Report of the Scholarship of Engagement Task Force 2010: 3). This type of scholarship aims to develop ethical and practical solutions to social, health, economic, and environmental issues, and may involve institutions of higher learning and off-campus comunities in partnerships of shared resources and expertise. Naturally, the development of evaluation metrics for such programs is an essential part of the activity (National Review Board for the Scholarship of Engagement 2002), but the measures call for a variety of quantitative and qualitative methods.

The assessment of the effects of formal instructional programs for targeted populations is more straightforward than informal education programs with indeterminate audiences, though theoretical and practical issues of validity and reliability arise in interpreting the outcomes of sociolinguistics application, as they do in any metric measuring treatment effects. Nonetheless, some of the results from pre- and post-testing of sociolinguistic knowledge and attitudes have provided strong support for the efficacy of these programs. Reaser (2006), in piloting the Grade 8 curriclum on language awareness in the public schools, constructed a 20-item pre- and post-test survey on a 4-point Likert scale with questions that addressed knowledge (e.g. *Dialects do not have patterns; There are people who do not speak a dialect*) and attitudes (e.g. *Some people are too lazy to learn Standard English; Dialects are sloppy forms of English*). The pre- and post-test results showed significant positive gains in both content knowledge and attitudes, with the highest gains in questions such as "Dialects do not have patterns" and "There is never a good reason to use a dialect." Figure 5.4 summarizes Reaser's (2006) results on the pre- and post-test results, with the vertical axis showing change in the mean results and the horizontal axis showing standard deviation.

In addition, Reaser asked free-response questions about the curriculum (e.g. *What was the most surprising thing you learned? Do you think it is important to study dialects? Why or why not?*) that supported some of responses from the pre- and post-test. 98% of students (N = 129) said that they learned something that would change the way they think about dialects, and 87% of the students

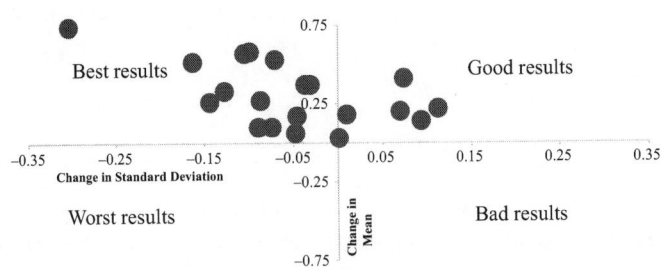

Figure 5.4 **Pre- and post-test results for experimental dialect curriculum (from Reaser 2006: 126)**

thought that studying dialects is important for all students. The most frequently mentioned discovery cited by students was the fact that dialects had patterns; this aligned with the quantitative results that showed this question to have the most significant pre- and post-test differences. Furthermore, some of the student comments in their open-ended questions offered support for the need for and effectiveness of the program, including the following types of comments by students.

> I learned that a dialect doesn't tell anyone if the person is smart or dumb or anything along those lines.

> There are tons of stereotypes, which are almost always wrong. People should be more informed about dialects, so they would know that dialects represent people's culture and past.

> I was surprised at how much racism exists against people with certain dialects.

On an anonymous survey at the end of the year, students were asked to respond to three free questions (*What's the most interesting thing we did this year? What's the most important thing we did this year? What will you remember most about this year?*), and over 90% of the students responded, "the dialect unit." These results offered justification not only for the significance of the program but a rationale to the administrators at the State Department of Public Instruction when presenting the curriculum for adoption throughout the state.

Similarly, the program on dialect diversity targeting the university community has been subjected to quantitative pre- and post-testing using a 5-point Likert scale and summative comments of participants related to goals for workshops (e.g. *Language standards are social constructs; Dialect difference is inevitable and natural; Dialects are systematic and patterned*). The responses were overwhelmingly positive and significant statistically, and the assessment indicated that workshop attendees were interested in the material covered and met the learning outcomes of the workshop (Dunstan et al. 2015). 97% of the participants (N = 144) agreed or strongly agreed that the workshop was interesting and that they learned something new about dialects; and the majority (75%) noted that the workshop changed the way in which they view their own and the speech of others (see Dunstan et al. 2015 for more details).

Measuring the effectiveness of outreach and engagement naturally needs to extend beyond traditional kinds of measures. For example, traditional measures applied to museum exhibits (visitor lists, timed-length of visit, time at each exhibition, etc.) can be applied to exhibits, and the number of "hits" on social media posts (cf. Lawson, this volume). Audience ratings for TV broadcasts compared with regular programs in the day and time slots are also critical for programs targeting more general public audiences. Our documentaries are also routinely entered in a variety of film festivals and have won national and regional awards, including an Emmy Award for one of the films produced by our videographer (Hutcheson 2008). Another (Hutcheson and Cullinan 2015) is currently nominated for an Emmy. One of our most valued accolades was the selection of one of our documentaries as an incentive gift for "generous support" in a fundraising campaign (Hutcheson's [2005] *Voices of North Carolina*) by a state-wide public television station.

These types of acclaim may be difficult to quantify in an evaluation metric but they are highly symbolic of the raised visibility of language variation as a part of the state landscape. Happily, a by-product of these public tributes is the increased and continued support from the institutional administration and information services program at the university. These agencies seize on successful programs recognized by the public to promote the university's status as a land-grant institution that serves the public in unique ways.

Guidelines for optimizing impact

In this final section, I consider some of the principles that should guide a research agenda committed to engagement and outreach beyond the narrowly defined domains of a research inquiry for our field of professional specialization. These guidelines were presented originally in Wolfram (2012), with specific illustrations of how these principles have been instantiated in practice.

From the outset of a research project, consider how linguistic research might have a strategic public outreach dimension

Even before a research project begins, it is essential to plan how research might serve the community being researched and the broader public. In fact, the National Science Foundation's section on "Statement of Broader Impacts" would be better served if it actually required a strategic implementation plan for disseminating information about the "broader impacts" of research rather than a general account of the possible effect on society and human welfare.

During the first week of our initial visit to conduct sociolinguistic interviews on the island of Ocracoke in 1993, we sought out leaders in the community including the president of the Ocracoke Preservation Society (OPS) and the principal of the school to explain our study and to offer ways in which we might work collaboratively with these institutions as we gathered information. The offer to talk to the students at the school was accepted, and parlayed the next year into the development of a week-long curriculum on dialect awareness that has now been taught annually in the school for more than two decades, becoming the springboard for our state-wide curriculum for Grade 8 students. These contacts turned into an enduring collaborative relationship that led to the compilation of two oral-history CDs for the public and the community, three video documentaries for local and regional TV broadcast, two permanent exhibits in the museum, and a trade book on the language variation on the Outer Banks distributed at stores and tourist sites all over the coast of North Carolina. For the record, all of these outreach activities coincided with detailed, technical analysis of language change and recession in dialect enclaves published in highly competitive, refereed journals and in scholarly books. And it started simply with proactive offers to inform the community, to work with them, and to merge some of our research activity with the concerns of community residents.

Be proactive with institutional programs in disseminating information

Information and media services at research institutions and universities are always looking for good stories. We need to contact them and propose stories of public interest related to language. It is also important to be responsive to inquiries from external journalists, media, and others who might be interested in following up on a story or soliciting our opinion as linguistic experts (cf. Coleman, this volume; Levasseur, this volume). I know colleagues who don't respond to media inquiries for one reason or another. Admittedly, the press doesn't always "get it right" (Lawson, this volume) but they're not the only ones – as we know quite well from our students' exams and papers, and some of our professional colleagues' interpretations of our research. We have an obligation to share our research with the public and to work with those who can help tell our story.

Brand the program

Branding a program – in both symbolic visual representation and cultural ethos – is not a trivial concern if we care about sharing our research information beyond our narrow subfield. In fact, in the initial class of my first research seminar at NC State in 1993, the students and I decided on a name for our public extension program and, over the years, we have worked with graphic artists on logos and images. We are more than a random group of professors and students from the university doing research. Hours of deliberation went into the selection of the title, the objectives, and the design of a logo for our products and different programs. The brand helps identify us; it instantiates our public presence, and presents a collective unity for different types of productions and venues that include both research and engagement. Comments like, "You're the ones who do those TV shows" or "Oh, I know about your work" certainly are inspired by the public's association with the brand and the logo that appears on our products and presentations.

Utilize complementary technical and creative skills
of professional associates and students

Linguists generally do not have expertise in design, production, and marketing that is necessary for the presentation of professional programs and products for audiences beyond the academy. Happily, such expertise is often found among our colleagues, and often by the students in our classes. Such skills can readily be tapped in a collaborative production team effort. Most universities have highly talented and skilled staff with the kinds of skills needed for effective public communication, offering an essential creative resource for interdisciplinary professionalism, and talented students in other fields who are looking to build their professional portfolios provide an excellent, affordable resource.

Invest in long-term, sustainable projects

While one-time venues can be effective, sustainable programs need to be implemented to keep sociolinguistics in the public eye. Our documentary productions on language and life started as a one-time, exploratory venture on a shoe-string budget, but over the last 15 years, it has become an integral part of the Sociolinguistics Program now supported by core university funds and supplemented by external and internal funding. Public television viewers can expect a new documentary each year, which is then available as a DVD in our online bookstore (TalkingNC 2014). The college and university administration has been highly supportive because the programs bring high, positive visibility to the college and university. The products also can be used in promotional activities for boards of advisors, potential donors, alumni, and even state legislators who are interested in positive public presentations of university activities for their constituencies.

Develop curricular materials on language diversity
for public education, particularly K–12

One of the biggest oversights of public linguistics is its absence from the mandated primary and secondary education curriculum. Despite its vast potential, formal education about language variation has been omitted (cf. Bucholtz et al., this volume). Naturally, these programs have to fit the objectives of the standard courses of study for the regulating agency. And they also have to be readily teachable by non-linguists, one of the primary requisites in the program implemented by Reaser and Wolfram (2007). Students are not the only ones who profit from the study of dialect diversity; teachers also learn as they teach their students, and, in fact, some of our strongest support has been from teachers who taught the curriculum. One teacher summarized her experience:

> Thanks for such an edifying experience in teaching the dialect unit. I really think the students got a lot out of it (not the least of which was the

challenging of a lot of stereotypes they might have had that are tied to language). I know it was enlightening for me and I truly enjoyed it.

In the process of developing curricular materials, it is essential for linguists to collaborate with curriculum and instruction writers who can effectively design materials; it is not enough to have linguistic expertise.

Be visionary and entrepreneurial in promoting the applicability of research results

Linguists need to think creatively in their endeavors to connect with audiences beyond their professional specializations, exploring previously untapped venues for public and media presentation. New alliances of expertise and public communication strategies need to be embraced. In fact, a number of the examples of communicating to non-linguistic audiences presented here were without precedent. Our annual language exhibit at the North Carolina State Fair started with the simple comment, "Wouldn't it be cool to have an exhibit on dialects at the State Fair?" That led to an e-mail about whom we might contact, some social networking with fair administrators to circumvent the normal four-year wait for procuring scarce and valuable space, the rapid submission of a proposal to our college administration to obtain funding, finding an appropriate designer and constructor for the exhibit, and getting volunteers (service learning for students in classes) to staff the exhibit 12 hours a day for 10 days. It all worked out, resulting in thousands of visitors, television and newspaper coverage, and accolades from university administrators who were impressed with the unique exhibit.

Connecting with an inherent public curiosity about language is at the core of a public outreach program. Knowing how to package such information in a way that seizes on this opportunity, however, is a talent that is not usually within the skill set, job description, creative talents, and technical expertise of most linguists. But we do not have to do it alone. The kinds of alliances noted earlier are not intended to exclude the current trend of interdisciplinarity advocated in the academy, but simply to acknowledge the practical value of those with expertise in the dissemination of knowledge and information in a way that is appealing to the audiences we target vis-à-vis our academic peers.

Conclusion

Readers might feel that the luxury of envisioning and establishing public programs in language diversity is reserved for established, full professors and researchers who have "ranked-out" in the academic meritocracy. But it is quite possible for researchers and professors at any level to engage in such activities without compromising their professional research careers, to say nothing of the prospect of conducting research in the emerging scholarship of engagement. Personally, I think that it is a responsibility that we all must share if we desire to sustain and expand our discipline. My personal conviction is that linguistics is an "endangered discipline" and that part of the reason lies within the field itself. Linguistics is a highly specialized field of inquiry offered primarily on a graduate level, with a reputation as an esoteric, highly abstract field unrelated to the everyday world. Unlike math, chemistry, history, Spanish, and other fields of study, linguistics has no tradition of study in primary and secondary curricula and limited representation in undergraduate studies. It would not be difficult for it to quietly vanish as an autonomous discipline in the academy, notwithstanding those of us who cannot imagine life without linguistics. If linguists firmly believe that understanding the nature of language is a central theme in understanding human cognition and behavior, then we owe it to the profession to have more of a presence in public life. If the field of linguistics wishes to sustain itself and expand, it must do a more effective job of public presentation. In this regard, sociolinguistics can lead the way. Most topics of sociolinguistic inquiry are of interest to the community and the broader public if they are presented in a way that connects with the natural curiosity that people have about language as a type of social and human behavior. Knowing how to package such information in a way that seizes on this natural interest, however, is a specialized skill that does not align with the technical level of most linguistic presentations and academic registers. Working with journalists, designers, and producers, along with community partners and the broader public, can result in a highly productive, symbiotic relationship for researchers, community members, and creative artists in collaborative synergy.

Acknowledgements

I acknowledge the support of a number of grants from the National Science Foundation over the past two decades to carry out these initiatives, as well as funding from the William C. Friday Endowment, and the NC State Office of Institutional Equity and Diversity for funding programs reported here. Colleagues Jeffrey Reaser and Stephany Dunstan, and a host of graduate students were also instrumental in the carrying out these programs. The most recent cohort of graduate students includes Caroline Myrick, Kellam Barta, May Chung, and Amy Hemmeter, but graduate students have routinely supported these initiatives for decades. And they've all been great.

References

American Speech-Language-Hearing Association. 1983. "Social dialects." Accessed 1 September 2014. Available from: http://www.asha.org/policy/PS1983-00115.htm.

Baratz, Joan C. 1968. "Language in the economically disadvantaged child." *ASHA* (April): 143–144.

Bauer, Laurie, and Peter Trudgill (eds.). 1998. *Language Myths*. London: Penguin.

Baumgardt, Daniel Q. 2012. *A Historical View of Science Accommodation: The Case for Sociolinguistics and African American English*. PhD thesis, Carnegie Mellon University.

Blanton, Phyllis, and Karen Waters (producers). 1996. *The Ocracoke Brogue*. Raleigh, NC: North Carolina Language and Life Project.

Cameron, Deborah, Elizabeth Fraser, Penelope Harvey, M.B.H. Rampton, and Kay Richardson. 1992. *Researching Language: Issues of Power and Method*. London: Routledge.

Childs, Becky, Walt Wolfram, and Ellen Fulcher Cloud (producers). 2001. *Ocracoke Speaks*. CD. Raleigh: North Carolina Language and Life Project.

Cole, Lorraine. 1983. "Implications of the position statement on social dialects." Accessed 1 September 2014. Available from: http://www.asha.org/policy/PS1983-00115.htm#AP1.

Cullinan, Danica (producer). 2011. *Spanish Voices*. Raleigh: North Carolina Language and Life Project.

Dunstan, Stephany B. 2013. *The Influence of Speaking a Dialect of Appalachian English on the College Experience*. PhD thesis, North Carolina State University.

Dunstan, Stephany B., and Audrey J. Jaeger. Forthcoming. " 'They assume by the way you talk that you grew up on a farm and that you know everything about NASCAR, you know?' The role of language in interactions with others on campus for rural Appalachian college students."

Dunstan, Stephanie B., Walt Wolfram, Audrey J. Jaeger, and Rebecca E. Crandall. 2015. "Educating the educated: Language diversity in the university backyard." *American Speech* 90: 266–280.

Fish, Stanley. 2003 (May 6). "Aim low." *Chronicle of Higher Education* 49 (36): C5.

Fromkin, Victoria, Robert Rodman, and Nina Hyams. 2013. *An Introduction to Language*, 10th ed. Boston: Wadsworth.

Gumperz, John. J., and Dell Hymes. 1964. "The ethnography of communication." *American Anthropologist* 66 (6): 137–154.

Hutcheson, Neal (producer). 2004. *Mountain Talk*. Raleigh: North Carolina Language and Life Project.

Hutcheson, Neal (producer). 2005. *Voices of North Carolina*. Raleigh: North Carolina Language and Life Project.

Hutcheson, Neal (producer). 2008. *The Last One*. Raleigh: Sucker Punch.

Hutcheson, Neal, and Danica Cullinan (producers). 2015. *First Language: The Race to Save Cherokee*. Raleigh: North Carolina Language and Life Project.

Hymes, Dell H. 1962. "The ethnography of speaking." In *Anthropology and Human Behavior*, ed. by Thomas Gladwin and William Curtis Sturtevant, 13–53. Washington, DC: Anthropological Society of Washington.

Hymes, Dell H. 1964. *Language in Culture and Society: A Reader in Linguistics and Anthropology*. New York: Harper and Row.

Johnstone, Barbara. 2013. *Speaking Pittsburghese: The Story of a Dialect*. Oxford: Oxford University Press.

Katz, Josh, and Wilson Andrews. 2013. "How y'all, youse, and you guys talk." Accessed 1 September 2014. Available from: http://www.nytimes.com/interactive/2013/12/20/sunday-review/dialect-quiz-map.html?_r=1&.

Labov, William. 1966. *The Social Stratification of English in New York City*. Washington, DC: The Center for Applied Linguistics.

Labov, William. 1969. "Contraction, deletion and inherent variability of the English copula." *Language* 45 (4): 715–762.

Labov, William. 1970. "The logic of nonstandard grammar." In *Georgetown Monograph Series on Language and Linguistics No. 22*, ed. by James E. Alatis, 1–43. Washington, DC: Georgetown University Press.

Labov, William. 1982. "Objectivity and commitment in linguistic science." *Language in Society* 11 (2): 165–201.

Labov, William. 2001. *Principles of Linguistic Change: Social Factors*. Oxford: Blackwell.

Linguistics Department, the Ohio State University. 2001. *Language Files: Materials for and Introduction to Language and Linguistics*, 11th ed. Columbus: The Ohio State University Press.

Lippi-Green, Rosina. 2012. *English with an Accent: Language, Ideology, and Discrimination in the United States*, 2nd ed. London: Routledge.

Mallinson, Christine, Becky Childs, and Zula Cox. 2006. *Voices of Texana*. Texana, NC: Texana Committee on Community History and Preservation.

National Review Board for the Scholarship of Engagement. 2002. "Evaluation criteria for the scholarship of engagement." Accessed 1 September 2014. Available from: http://www.scholarshipofengagement.org/evaluation/evaluation_criteria.html.

North Carolina Language and Life YouTube Project (NCLLP). 2014a. "North Carolina Language and Life YouTube Channel." Accessed 1 September 2014. Available from: http://www.youtube.com/user/NCLLP.

North Carolina Language and Life Project (NCLLP). 2014b. "Language Diversity at NC State." Accessed 1 September 2014. Available from: https://www.youtube.com/watch?v=eQYNEHwDFhE.

O'Grady, William, John Archibald, Mark Aronoff, and Janie Rees-Miller. 2009. *Contemporary Linguistics: An Introduction*. New York: St Martin's Press.

Pinker, Steven. 2007. *The Language Instinct: How the Mind Creates Language*. New York: HarperCollins.

Reaser, Jeffrey L. 2006. *The Effect of Dialect Awareness on Adolescent Knowledge and Attitudes*. PhD thesis, Duke University.

Reaser, Jeffrey, Paula Dickerson Boddie, and Walt Wolfram (NCLLP) and DeAnna Locke, Chester Lynn, and Philip Howard (Ocracoke Preservation Society). 2011. *Ocracoke Still Speaks: Reflections Past and Present*. Raleigh: North Carolina Language and Life Project and the Ocracoke Preservation Society.

Reaser, Jeffrey, and Caroline Myrick. 2015. "Writing language-based trade books: Making linguistics accessible to lay audiences." *Language and Linguistics Compass* 9 (5): 198–208.

Reaser, Jeffrey, and Walt Wolfram. 2007. *Voices of North Carolina: Language and Life from the Atlantic to the Appalachians*. Raleigh: North Carolina Language and Life Project. Accessed 1 September 2014. Available from: http://www.ncsu.edu/linguistics/dialectcurriculum.php.

Report of the Scholarship of Engagement Task Force, North Carolina State University. 2010. *Integrating Learning, Discovery, and Engagement through the Scholarship of Engagement*. Raleigh: North Carolina State University.

Rickford, John R. 1999. *African American Vernacular English: Features, Evolution and Educational Implications*. Oxford: Blackwell.

Rickford, John R., and Russell J. Rickford. 2000. *Spoken Soul: The Story of Black English*. New York: John Wiley & Sons.

Seymour, Harry N., Thomas W. Roeper, and Jill de Villiers. 2003. *Diagnostic Evaluation of Language Variance (DELV)-Screening Test*. Chicago: Pearson.

Sweetland, Julie. 2006. *Teaching Writing in the African American Classroom: A Sociolinguistic Approach*. PhD thesis, Stanford University.

Tagliamonte, Sali. 2016. *Making Waves: The Story of Variationist Sociolinguistics*. Oxford: Wiley-Blackwell.

TalkingNC. 2014. "Educational Media from the North Carolina Language and Life Project." 2014. Accessed 1 September 2014. Available from: http://www.talkingnc.com.

Tannen, Deborah. 1990. *You Just Don't Understand: Women and Men in Conversation*. New York: Morrow.

Vaughn, Charlotte, and Drew Grimes (exhibiters). 2006. *Freedom's Voice: Celebrating the Black Experience on the Outer Banks*. An exhibit at the Outer Banks History Center. Roanoke Island, NC: North Carolina Language and Life Project and the Outer Banks History Center.

Vaux, Bert, and Scott Golder. 2003. "The Harvard Dialect Survey." Accessed 1 September 2014. Available from: http://www.tekstlab.uio.no/cambridge_survey.

Stanford Linguistics. 2012. "Voices of California Project." Accessed 1 September 2014. Available from: http://web.stanford.edu/dept/linguistics/VoCal.

West Virginia University. 2014. "West Virginia Dialect Project." Accessed 1 September 2014. Available from: http://dialects.english.wvu.edu/.

Williams, Ronald, and Walt Wolfram. 1977. "A linguistic description of social dialects." In *Social Dialects: Differences versus Disorders*, ed. by Irma K. Jeter, 1–31. Rockville, MD: American Speech-Language-Hearing Association.

Wolfram, Walt. 1970. "Linguistic premises and the nature of nonstandard dialects." *The Speech Teacher* (September): 176–186.

Wolfram, Walt. 1979. *Speech Pathology and Dialect Differences* (Dialect and Educational Equity Series). Washington, DC: Center for Applied Linguistics.

Wolfram, Walt. 1993a. "The sociolinguistic model in speech and language pathology." In *International Perspectives in Speech and Language Pathology*, ed. by Margaret M. Leafy and Jeffrey L. Kallen, 1–29. Dublin, Ireland: Trinity College.

Wolfram, Walt. 1993b. "Ethical considerations in Language Awareness Programs." *Issues in Applied Linguistics* 4 (2): 225–255.

Wolfram, Walt. 2012. "In the profession: Connecting with the public." *Journal of English Linguistics* 40 (1): 111–117.

Wolfram, Walt, Clare Dannenberg, Stanley Knick, and Linda Oxendine. 2002. *Fine in the World: Lumbee Language in Time and Place*. Raleigh: North Carolina State Humanities Extension/Publications.

Wolfram, Walt, and Jeffrey Reaser. 2014. *Talkin' Tar Heel: How Our Voices Tell the Story of North Carolina*. Chapel Hill: University of North Carolina Press.

Wolfram, Walt, and Natalie Schilling-Estes. 1997. *Hoi Toide on the Outer Banks: The Story of the Ocracoke Brogue*. Chapel Hill: University of North Carolina Press.

Part II

Impact in institutions

Chapter 6

The signed language interpreter's role in team meeting discourse

Jules Dickinson, ORCID NUMBER 0000–0002–4922–406X

Introduction

Picture yourself, as a hearing person, in a team meeting at work. The meeting is being chaired, but there is little formal structure and you and your colleagues frequently speak at the same time or across one another. There is a lot of banter and teasing and some side conversations are taking place. Much of what is discussed is implicit, i.e. you need some prior background knowledge to know what people are talking about. A lot of the language being used is particular to your team – abbreviations specific to your organisation, nicknames you have for different people and slang or jargon terms you use for certain processes. Discussions often stray from the agenda, with you and your colleagues engaging in talk distinctly separate from the business of the meeting, e.g. a recent television programme or the latest sports results.

Now imagine the same scenario from the perspective of a profoundly deaf employee. Your significant hearing loss means that you cannot hear what your colleagues are saying. All of your attention is, by necessity, directed to the signed language interpreter booked for the meeting. This makes it hard for you to see which of your colleagues is speaking at any one time. You think that sometimes the speaker has changed, but it is difficult to be certain and you are often confused about who has said what. Your access to the meeting is limited – you can see that the interpreter struggles to keep up when people talk at the same time. You continually ask people to take it in turns to speak, but after about five minutes the meeting reverts back to a free-for-all. You notice that team members often laugh at each other's comments but you are never really sure why. Sometimes the interpreter tries to explain a joke, but you don't really get it, and you laugh just to go along with everyone else.

Finally, slip in to the interpreter's shoes. This is the first time you have interpreted this meeting and you are unsure of the roles and responsibilities of team members. The discussion is largely of a technical nature, with jargon and abbreviated terminology being used, and you don't fully understand much of what is said. There are a lot of in-jokes, as well as teasing, gossip and banter related to incidents and people you have no previous knowledge of. People consistently talk over each other, and you. It is almost impossible to indicate who is saying what. The speed of the exchanges between participants means you have to try, moment by moment, to decide what to prioritise and what to omit from your translation. The team meeting is generally conducted as if neither you nor the deaf employee is present.

This scenario should give you some insight in to the challenges a deaf employee can face participating in workplace discourse, even with an interpreter. Many workplaces are not 'deaf-aware'; most hearing people think an interpreter simply "translates word for word" or "tells him/her what I said" (Dean and Pollard 2005), and, moreover, will solve any and all communication problems. Taking a closer look at an interpreted team meeting reveals a more complex picture. Many team meetings are characterised by a collaborative floor, i.e. participants cooperatively building on each other's comments, suggestions and jokes (Edelsky 1993). Signed language interpreters interpret an interlocutor's spoken or signed contribution at almost the same time it is produced. In meetings with multiple participants, with overlapping talk and rapid exchanges, this job is almost impossible, putting the deaf employee at a considerable disadvantage. The interpreter's management of interaction in a workplace meeting therefore directly affects the extent to which the deaf employee can become a full member of the team. This in turn affects their integration into the workplace, their job satisfaction, and their sense of wellbeing at work.

In this chapter I focus on the effect of the interpreter in workplace meetings, examining how they influence collegial interaction between deaf and hearing employees, and concentrating specifically on how the interpreter can ensure participation through the translation of humorous exchanges. The data is drawn from a sociolinguistic PhD study which examined the role of the signed language interpreter in workplace discourse in the United Kingdom.

I demonstrate that the findings of the research are not just of academic interest, but have practical implications for successful communication between deaf and hearing people in the workplace. From my perspective, 'impact' means bringing about change in the status quo, thus enabling individuals and organisations to reflect on transforming their current practice or behaviour – in other words, taking steps (sometimes small but always significant) towards achieving different outcomes. The notion of 'impact' is a fundamental strand of my research. Working as a signed language interpreter, I identified that workplace discourse, particularly team meeting interaction, presented a number of challenges. Most deaf people work in environments with hearing colleagues, where work practices are designed for (and by) hearing people, and are constrained by their norms (Turner et al. 2002). This means that deaf people are, in many instances, disadvantaged in comparison with their hearing peers. My goal from the outset was to identify ways of enabling parity of communication between deaf and hearing employees, and to achieve useful outcomes not only for interpreters, but also for deaf and hearing employees, and for employers. I was inspired by participatory research models, where the aim is to gather a rich range of data whilst at the same time allowing for the possibility of achieving positive and practical outcomes for both individuals and organisations (Stubbe 2001).

Methodology

I collected data through a variety of methods, including a questionnaire distributed to interpreters, practitioner journals, the filming of naturalistic workplace interpreted interaction, and video playback interviews. The video data was collected across five different workplaces; it consisted mainly of team meetings and constitutes the primary data for the research. Whilst the majority of the meetings were in public sector type settings (e.g. social services, education, supported living), one was from a more commercially driven institution. In this chapter I draw predominately on data from Livingwell, an organisation providing residential supported living services for adults with learning disabilities and additional physical disabilities. Pseudonyms are used for all participants and organisations throughout this chapter.

Video data collection

Negotiating access to film at the different workplaces was a lengthy and sensitive process. I had to first establish the willingness of the deaf employee to approach their employer. Once contact was made, I explained the purpose of the research and assured all participants that confidentiality was paramount. I had anticipated considerable resistance to my request to film so I was delighted when all the employers, bar one, agreed to take part in the study. I attribute this to the considerable preparatory work that I undertook prior to beginning the research process. All participants consented to being quoted under pseudonyms.

I was aware that my presence, armed with a video camera, could be inhibiting and intrusive, and could potentially affect the interaction outcomes (Roy 1989; Wadensjö 1992; Metzger 1995). Therefore, I used a small digital camera to try to minimise any disruption (cf. Innes, this volume; MacLeod and Haworth, this volume). The majority of the video material was of team meetings, ranging between 19 minutes and 54 minutes. The number of participants per meeting varied in size from three to ten, and in most of the meetings there was only one deaf employee. All of the meetings filmed were pre-planned, chaired, had an agenda for discussion, and could be characterised as semi-formal in nature. Despite these factors, all of the meetings were generally conducted without explicit direction from the Chair, with participants frequently engaging in overlapping talk, interruptions and humorous exchanges. This last aspect was an unexpected finding. I was aware that small talk and humour were features of workplace discourse; however, I had not anticipated the way in which humour, sometimes interwoven with small talk episodes, appears to be a consistent feature of workplace meetings.

Video data selection

The complex mix of spoken and signed language multi-party data led to my decision to transcribe the video data manually. I viewed and re-viewed the video tapes a number of times, which naturally brought to the surface 'points of interest.' Guided by Rampton's (2007) recommendations for investigating interactional data, I focused on how participants were interacting, whether they were doing what was expected of them, and how they managed their relationships. I selected excerpts where it appeared that the discourse process was not particularly smooth, or where the interpreter's management of the interaction suggested potential moments of cultural mismatch or discord. The process was also informed in part by my own experience of interpreting team meetings, as well as anecdotal evidence arising from discussions with colleagues.

Video data transcription

The workplace video-recordings and the video playback interviews were transcribed differently; this section outlines my transcription methods for both.

The goal of all transcription is to produce a permanent written record of communicative events which allows for analysis and re-analysis (Hoiting and Slobin 2002). However, transcriptions are not always 'user-friendly,' and employing conventional writing where possible can enhance readability (Wadensjö 1998). With signed language data, transcription is never easy. The visual nature of a signed language, where meaning is produced utilising the fingers, hands, arms, neck and all the components engaged in facial expression (Metzger 1999), makes rendering an adequate description of a deaf person's contribution highly challenging. It can only be truly captured by video; and reducing a signed message to a written form always runs the risk of losing some of the rich information inherent within the visual-gestural modality.

In my transcription of the workplace video data, the signs produced by participants have been 'glossed,' i.e. I have written a word in English for each BSL sign produced. Glossing is a technique used widely in transcription of signed languages, and I based my transcription on the work of Cokely (1992) and Metzger (1999). In BSL, meaning is not solely produced on the hands but is indicated in facial expression, head and body movement, eyebrow movement, mouth patterns, etc. Role-shift (a process whereby a signer takes on the role of a character, animal or object), placement within the signing space, and referencing are also used to indicate people, places and concepts. The speed and size of signing, together with the position and movement of the hands, also contain far more information than the representation of a word. A gloss of a sign can run the risk of making BSL appear simplistic and merely a signed production of English. To counter this I added, as far as possible, information to indicate facial expressions, and head and body movements that contribute to the meaning of the signed message.

In the introduction to this chapter I highlighted the simultaneous nature of signed language interpreting, i.e. the interpreter is working between two modalities (signing and speaking), as well as two languages. As a result, the interpreter's contributions almost always overlap with those of other participants. To show this I adapted Metzger's musical-score format of transcription to represent signed language interaction, as this allows for "the simultaneous and overlapping nature of interactive discourse" (Metzger 1999: 44). Representing participant overlap is also a prime consideration when attempting to adequately represent spoken language multi-party talk. Edelsky (1993), for example, discusses extensively the challenges in transcribing interaction within a collaborative floor. Following Coates (2007) the transcription format I have used is produced in stave notation, allowing all participants' contributions to be read simultaneously, like instruments in a musical stave. Words or portions of words that appear vertically above or below any other word in the stave should be read as occurring at the same time as that word. Relevant non-verbal behaviour is recorded in the line above the transcription.

Video playback interviews

As part of my study I met with the main participants from two team meetings filmed at Livingwell, to show them selected video excerpts of their meetings. I chose the excerpts on the basis that they showed the extent to which hearing team members engaged in a collaborative floor, and the challenge this presented the interpreter and the deaf employee. I showed the video extracts to Derek (deaf employee), Alex (team manager, hearing) and Stuart and Sandra, who are both BSL/English interpreters. I used semi-structured interview questions to guide their responses to the video clips they observed. Amongst other questions, I asked participants to comment on the extent to which they felt a part of the meeting, how much control they had and whether they were aware of the ways in which speaker/signer changes and turns were taking place. The responses of the participants are discussed in the final section of this chapter, where I look at impact achieved during and after the research.

All of the interviews were video-recorded. I produced full transcripts of the interviews but these were 'tidied up,' i.e. I did not include all the *ums, ahhs* and repetitions inherent in natural speech – whilst such aspects of discourse can undoubtedly "perform delicate interactional tasks" (Wooffitt 2005: 12), decisions about transcription style are driven by the purpose for which the data has been described. I made the decision to omit these items based on the fact that I would not be using the transcripts for a discourse analytical purpose, but rather to reproduce participant views and experiences (Arksey and Knight 1999).

'Do you want to hear the panic alarm?'

A common assumption of workplace communication is that it consists predominantly of transactional talk, i.e. that people are mostly engaged in task-oriented interaction, with their focus directed to the exchange of information (Holmes 2010). However, research has shown that workplace talk is in fact used for a variety of tasks, ranging from giving instructions and disagreeing with/challenging colleagues, to sharing jokes, avoiding miscommunication and maintaining good collegial relations (Holmes and Stubbe 2003; Mullany 2007; Koester 2010).

In interpreter-mediated communication between deaf and hearing people, the interpreter is tasked with translating all aspects of talk, including asides, small talk, jokes and banter. One aspect I identified as problematic for interpreters is that of translating humorous exchanges. Humour is a "high stakes game" (Bell 2006: 2), in that it is an important way for intimate relationships to be developed and maintained. However, if the linguistic and cultural resources used to construct humour are not shared or grasped by all participants, the extent to which they can engage in humorous play will be limited (Bell 2006: 2). The interpreter therefore has an important role when people who do not share a language or culture engage in humorous play.

The problem for the interpreter is that the translation of humour is a complex activity, and producing an adequate interpretation under the conditions and constraints of simultaneous interpreting is particularly challenging (Pavlicek and Pöchhaker 2002). There are a number of factors which affect the interpreters' ability to interpret humorous exchanges: their ability to pick up on signals (from the deaf or hearing participants) which indicate a shift from serious talk to play talk; their background knowledge of the event; and their understanding of team dynamics and relationships. Working simultaneously, the interpreter has a split second in which to absorb the source message, make sense of the meaning and identify the speaker/signer's intent before delivering the message in the target language (Humphrey 1997). The fact that the interpreter is inevitably working with a time-lag, i.e. they are a few seconds behind the speaker/signer, and are interpreting between a visual signed language and a spoken linear language, also adds to the pressure of rendering an adequate translation. Their difficulty is further compounded by the cultural dimension of the translation process. Research suggests that deaf humour is motivated by "the visual Deaf experience of the world" and often involves attacking the "out-group," i.e. hearing people (Sutton-Spence and Napoli 2012: 311–313). In translating humorous exchanges, the interpreter also has to make decisions about how to make the humour relevant or amusing to the intended recipients.

The following example provides a useful illustration of how an interpreter's translation of a humorous utterance can influence the interaction between deaf and hearing participants. The excerpt is from a team meeting at Livingwell. There are five participants, and Derek is the only deaf member of the team. The meeting is chaired by Alex and is interpreted by Stuart. Members of this group have known each other for some time, with meetings occurring on a fortnightly basis. The same interpreter is not present at all of the meetings. The team members have some understanding of deaf culture and sign language. They have developed a set of shared discursive and behavioural norms (Schnurr 2008), including the extent to which they engage in banter and humorous exchanges. The meetings are characterised by frequent episodes of teasing, and are generally of a highly interactive nature, with members talking over each other and competing for turns.

In recent weeks one of the tenants has been presenting with challenging behaviour of a physical nature and so a panic alarm has been fitted in the staff room of the complex where he lives. The alarm emits a loud, high-pitched sound. As most of the staff and tenants within the complex are profoundly deaf, the alarm, which is solely audible in nature (with no visual display), is only of benefit to hearing staff members.

In the discussion which takes place just before the excerpt begins, the usefulness of the alarm system has been debated, along with details about the procedures staff must follow. The team manager, Alex, has also given a fairly lengthy explanation as to why the alarm has been installed. His tone throughout the delivery has been serious, and all the responses from the deaf and hearing team members – mainly consisting of feedback signals such as head nods and 'mmhmm –' have matched the serious nature of the discussion. In Stave 1, the transcript begins with Alex, the chairperson, moving on to the next item on the agenda (see pages 185–186 for transcript conventions).

Excerpt: Do you want to hear the panic alarm?

1————————————————————————————————

Alex: it its could be a difficult morning so
Jason: Yep

2————————————————————————————————

Alex: we just need to be extra careful really
Stuart: DIFFICULT CAREFUL AWARE ALL OF US LET KNOW

3————————————————————————————————

Alex: we've also got to
Derek: YOU WANT

4————————————————————————————————

Alex: sorry?
Stuart: GO AHEAD

                                              [laughs]
Derek: WANT TEST PULL WANT HEAR? YOU?

5————————————————————————————————

Derek: [extended laughter]

                            [all participants laugh]

Stuart: *yeah err so shall we test the err panic alarm*

Alex: [sardonic, mock exasperated tone]

                        again?

6————————————————————————————————

Stuart: *AGAIN HEADACHE*

Derek: [looks around, innocent facial expression]

           WANT TRY ME PULL

7————————————————————————————————

Stuart: *y' know I'd like to try it . . . see what happens*

Derek: [innocent facial expression] [contorts face]   [shrugs]   [laughs]

           WHAT?   EARS HURT OH DEAF PUT BACK IN

8————————————————————————————————

Stuart: *it doesn't affect deaf people so*

9————————————————————————————————

Alex: the other thing we've looked at is Michael's windows just to update people

In Stave 3, as Alex starts a new sentence, Derek begins to sign, asking "YOU WANT." The other team members, including Alex, can see that Derek has made a contribution and so in Stave 4, even before Stuart (interpreter) has had the opportunity to translate Derek's signed comment into spoken English, Alex responds with "sorry." Stuart interprets Alex's "sorry" as an indication for Derek to "go ahead" and the floor is then open to Derek to ask the hearing team members if they would like him to test the panic alarm, a request that he concludes with laughter.

In Stave 5, Stuart translates Derek's signed contribution as "yeah err so shall we test the err panic alarm." He renders this in a somewhat monotone voice, but at the same time Derek continues to laugh, and by the end of Stuart's interpretation, all team members join in with the laughter.

Alex responds with "again" as this laughter dies down, which Stuart interprets in Stave 6 as "AGAIN," but adds the sign "HEADACHE." Derek then signs "WANT TRY ME PULL" and follows this with a comedic impression of someone appearing very innocent, wondering what all the fuss is about. In Stave 7, Stuart interprets this as "y' know I'd like to try it see what happens," whilst Derek is completing a 'mimed' version of pulling the alarm cord out, unleashing the sound on the hearing staff and then replacing it, to enquire what the problem was (WHAT? in Stave 7). Derek continues with "EARS HURT OH DEAF PUT BACK IN." Derek's signed contribution is almost akin to a mime which makes it relatively accessible to the hearing participants, enabling them to get the gist of what he is signing, even without the translation into spoken English. As the laughter begins to ebb and fade out, Stuart (Stave 8) interprets Derek's comment as "it doesn't affect deaf people so." Again, Stuart's interpretation is delivered with very little intonation, is factual in nature and contains little of the humorous intent suggested in Derek's visual delivery. In Stave 9, Alex brings the humorous frame to an end, moves back to the business of the meeting, and initiates a discussion regarding another tenant.

The example outlined above begins with a shift of frame, moving from a serious discussion (where staff safety is at issue) to the hearing staff team members being teased about the new alarm system. In spoken discourse the shift from serious or business talk to a 'play frame' is indicated in a variety of ways, including laughter, laughing or smiling voice, the speaker's tone of voice and sudden changes in pitch or rhythm (Coates 2007). In this example most of the signalling originates with Derek's laughter, beginning in Stave 4 and extending into Stave 5. Laughter is an important contextual cue that people are engaging in a play frame, often occurring at the point the play frame is invoked. All participants join in with the laughter at the end of Stuart's translated comment, demonstrating their "togetherness" with colleagues, thus sustaining the play frame (Coates 2007: 47).

In Stave 5, Alex appears to run with the change of frame, saying "again" in a somewhat sardonic, mock-exasperated tone, which Stuart renders by adding "HEADACHE" to the sign of "AGAIN," emphasising the humour. The play frame appears to become less sustainable in Staves 8 and 9. Derek's indication that he wants to inflict the noise on the hearing staff, and his apparent lack of concern, would have been reasonably clear to the hearing participants. However, the finer nuances of meaning appear to have been missed, possibly resulting in the 'quieter,' ebbing laughter. Stuart's voice-over, coming at the end of the 'mime' in Stave 9, is very factual. The visual nature of Derek's display may have influenced Stuart's decision to render a fairly literal interpretation with "it doesn't affect deaf people so" as he may have considered that anything else would have 'over-egged the pudding.' However, it should be noted that after Stuart's contribution, Alex brings the meeting back to a formal 'business' frame, without any rejoinder to Derek's teasing.

In this example Derek could be said to be teasing the hearing participants in the meeting about the 'agony' resulting from setting off the panic alarm, something which, as a profoundly deaf person, he is immune to. In doing so he portrays his lack of hearing (traditionally perceived by hearing people as a negative qual-ity) as an advantage that he has over the hearing members of the team.

Humour at one's own expense is not always indicative of a weak sense of self-respect but can sometimes demonstrate a very specific sense of self-respect (Kotthoff 2000). Humour can be used to build a community and promote group solidarity as well as being used by an oppressed group to poke fun at its oppressors (Tray 2005). Derek's use of humour in relation to his deafness suggests that he is reinforcing his deaf identity in this instance, positioning himself in the role of 'outsider,' as he is the only person in the team who is unaffected by the sound of the panic alarm.

Deaf humour can often be based on deaf people's shared experience, espe-cially in the case of miscommunication with hearing people and the oppres-sion that deaf people have faced in their contact with the hearing world (Sutton-Spence and Woll 1998). Personal experience and anecdotal evidence from interpreters support the view that deaf people often use sound, and the effects of sound, as a way of teasing hearing people. In terms of Boxer and Cortés-Conde's (1997) teasing continuum of *bonding–nipping–biting*, this example could sit somewhere on the *nipping–biting* end. Given the relationship of the participants as an established team, with some deaf awareness, Derek's com-ment seems more likely to represent a gentle humorous nip rather than a more aggressive bite. The teasing could also be considered to be directed at hearing people outside of the meeting, as the 'absent other,' and could function as a bonding activity with the more deaf-aware participants in the interaction (e.g. Alex and Stuart).

Successful humour requires joint construction, with complex interaction taking place between the person making the humorous contribution and those receiving it (Holmes and Hay 1997). Had Stuart produced a more detailed and explicit interpretation there may have been a less abrupt shift into serious talk. For example, an interpretation of 'Ooh, well, that's one of the benefits of being deaf you know' or 'you hearing people, always so sensitive to noise' may have offered the hearing employees the opportunity to extend the play frame, to collaborate in "playing together" (Coates 2007: 31) and thus respond to the 'gentle nip.'

This example demonstrates the effect that the interpreter can have on humor-ous exchanges, whereby their understanding of the shifts from serious to play frame and the context in which the humour is being played out is crucial to the success of the interaction.

Research impact

This section examines the impact of my research in three stages. First, I look at the impact the research had on the participants during the research process, including the video playback interviews. I then go on to detail the impact subse-quent to the research, followed by a discussion of ongoing impact.

Starting the conversation: Impact during the research process

The impact of the research began during the data collection stage. Negotiating access to the workplaces selected for the study involved contacting employers and deaf employees to discuss the aims of the research. This process raised awareness of the challenges facing the workplace interpreter and of the barriers deaf people experience. This evidently had an effect on the deaf participants. Deaf people have very little opportunity to give their views on the quality or effectiveness of interpreting provision. For some of the deaf participants it was the first time they had been given an opportunity to discuss the problems they face in the workplace, and this process validated and 'made real' their experiences. One respondent expressed his frustrations in an email, stating "the problem I have is the same as others: when the discussion is going fast and I'm using the interpreters, it's hard to interject appropriately due to time delay and processing (interpreters and me as the user!)." Just having the opportunity to express the frustrations with workplace communication, to actually be heard and to influence the direction of the research, is a step on the path to change.

Many of the employers who engaged in the research were aware of the difficulties experienced by their deaf employee, and were enthusiastic about the potential to make changes which could lead to improved working relationships. The discussion with employers centred on my commitment to provide information from the research which could contribute to a positive working relationship between deaf and hearing employees. Again, this was a small step towards achieving impact, in that employers were prepared to engage in research which would ultimately benefit their organisation and their employees.

Throughout the research process I was keen to engage with all of the research participants, especially with members of the Deaf community. Napier and Rohan (2007: 159) state that research should be "on, for, and with stakeholders" – in other words those affected by the research, or those who have a stake in the outcome. Historically, deaf participants have been the subjects of research without benefiting from any insights into the research findings. Whilst this is also often true of other (non-deaf) research subjects (see, e.g., Cameron 1992, on the unequal distribution of knowledge), deaf people's lack of access to traditional research feedback methods (English is a second language for many BSL users) constitutes in effect a double barrier.

In all my discussions with deaf employees, I demonstrated a desire to feed back the findings of the study, to contribute to changes in their work environment and to work with employees and employers to develop better working practices. This was a major undertaking, but I believe it to be an integral part of the research process and therefore worth the effort. It is an approach that I would highly recommend. To begin with, and before any such positive outcomes were realised, this commitment was a major factor in securing participant involvement. The importance of establishing an ongoing relationship with the participants, making sure that they are fully aware of what the research is, and are satisfied with the level of feedback that they will receive (Stubbe 2001), cannot be overestimated.

The initial impact of the research was clearly evidenced during the video playback interviews. As outlined previously, participants viewed video excerpts from the team meetings they had been involved in. Being able to observe in some detail what actually happened during a team meeting enabled these participants to identify the problems and to reflect on the challenges posed by team meeting talk.

Deaf people rarely get to see why it is so difficult for the interpreter to interject and take turns in meetings. After viewing the video excerpts, Derek became more aware of the way in which the turn-taking behaviour of the hearing team members affected the interpreter's ability to interrupt and contribute on his behalf. He stated he could see that there were "lots of people talking over each other," and noted the difficulty the interpreter had when they tried to take a turn. Derek felt the speed of the exchange produced difficulties for the interpreter, and this in turn had a detrimental effect on his ability to take a turn during meetings. When I asked him how this made him feel, he responded with a heavy sigh, stating much of his time was spent working out "what they were talking about, who said that, who said this." After watching the clips, Derek was able to discuss a number of turn-taking strategies with his regular interpreters and thus work towards a more equitable way of taking part in the team meeting.

For Alex, the team manager, the effect of watching the video evidence and realising the extent to which Derek was excluded was particularly striking. He noted that Derek's access was "limited, very limited . . . he was just sort of having a barrage of information." Alex stated "the speed and intensity" of the meeting talk meant the interpreter could only "keep up with what's being said." He felt this resulted in a loss of things such as the "wider language, and tone of the meeting," as well as the "stuff going on in the corner . . . is everybody agreeing or not?"

Both of the interpreters involved in the two team meetings noted the difficulties posed by the overlapping talk within the meetings, commenting on the problems with indicating speaker change and turn-taking. Stuart felt that the team's cultural norms – "mainly hearing norms" – added to the complexity of managing multi-party talk, and stated that it "puts deaf people at a disadvantage." Sandra noted that her inability to indicate speaker change meant that it often appeared as though one person was speaking, whereas the reality was that "it was loads of different people chipping in." Viewing evidence of interpreting practice is relatively common in interpreter training, but is rarely utilised by interpreters once they have qualified. For both interpreters in my study, watching their interpreting performance enabled them to identify where and why problems occurred. They affirmed that the process was a useful one, particularly as it helped them realise that many of the issues lay beyond their control, with behavioural change required by all participants in order for successful communication to take place.

Whilst all of these initial examples are of small-scale impact, they are nonetheless important stages in making all participants more aware of their roles within interpreted interaction, opening their minds as to what actions they can undertake to change the status quo.

Dissemination and distribution: Impact subsequent to the research

Napier (2005: 101) suggests that the purpose of "interpreter field work research" is to "contribute to the professionalization of interpreting," i.e. to provide interpreters with the information and the insights necessary to make them aware of the challenges that deaf and hearing consumers face in accessing interpreted discourse. The majority of impact from the research has therefore resulted from the dissemination of the research findings to the interpreting profession. This has predominantly been achieved through the delivery of presentations at interpreting conferences, and through training and workshops (cf. Innes, this volume; MacLeod and Haworth, this volume, on training delivery). The findings have been presented at national interpreting conferences (e.g. Association of Sign Language Interpreters [ASLI] 2008), as well as international interpreting and translation conferences (Supporting Deaf People Online Conference 2006 and 2011; Critical Link 2010).

The dissemination of the research has contributed to making interpreters more aware of the complexities in this domain, as evidenced by discussions on interpreter e-groups. During an online debate on the translation of humour, I contributed the following: "If the deaf client has got good English they will want it as is so that they can appreciate . . . most other deaf people will go 'oh, hearing joke, not bothered – deaf' after you have killed yourself trying to explain it (and killed whatever semblance of a joke was there in the first place!)." One interpreter subsequently sought permission to include my contribution in her university assignment, with the statement that "the experience of the majority of BSL/English interpreters when required to interpret English humour into BSL is rather nicely summed-up by Jules Dickinson" (Frances Coates, personal communication).

I have also had numerous requests for the research material from practitioners and interpreter trainers, in the United Kingdom and abroad. To date this has included the United States, Zimbabwe, and Australia. Material from my PhD has been utilised by students on the Post Graduate Diploma in BSL/English Interpreting at the University of Central Lancashire, who are required to write 'Critical Interpreting Awareness' (CIA) logs, reviewing their interpreting performance through the lenses of theoretical and conceptual models (see Turner 2005).

A number of MA students on Heriot-Watt University's EUMASLI course (www.eumasli.eu) have drawn on my PhD material in their theses. Additionally it has informed the work of other signed language researchers and practitioners in both Australia (Major 2013) and the United States (www.streetleverage.

com/2013/05/allies-sign-language-interpreters-and-a-bigger-picture-view/). My PhD thesis was requested as background material for the MA in Signed Language Interpreting at Queen's University Belfast, specifically in relation to the Interpreting in Employment Settings module. The course leader noted that not only was the work useful, it was also the most current she could find (Janet Beck, personal communication).

My research has added to the body of knowledge on interpreting, demonstrating that the complexity of the interpreter's task increases when managing events with multiple participants. I demonstrated that responsibility for effective communication does not lie solely with the interpreter, but requires a collaborative effort by all involved. Additionally, I highlighted the interpreter's influence on the interaction between deaf and hearing employees, particularly in relation to turn-taking in multi-party discourse, and accessing informal talk and humorous exchanges. This was noted in feedback from a workshop participant who, after the event, contacted me to say that she was going to do her best "to remember to make notes in my reflective diary of 'humour' moments in the workplace!" and that she would share the information at her local reflective practice group meeting (Monica Wyatt, personal communication). This is a good example of how training derived from research not only benefits individual workshop participants, but can be cascaded informally between practitioners.

In addition to the contributions the research has made to interpreting studies, it has also informed the work of a number of researchers. It further evidences the interactive nature of the interpreter's engagement in interpreted discourse events, and affirms the impossibility and unsuitability of maintaining an uninvolved, conduit-derived stance, particularly in the workplace domain. In doing so, it upholds the view of those working in the deaf professional/designated interpreter field (see Hauser et al. 2008). The research also substantiates the interpreter's tendency, when faced with multiple speakers and overlapping talk, to produce an un-attributed monologue (identified by van Herreweghe 2002, but extended in my research).

The research findings have formed the basis of training delivered to a number of UK interpreting services (Deaf Action in Edinburgh, Royal Association for Deaf People, Nottinghamshire Sign Language Interpreting Service, Deafinite Interpreters). This has involved practical role-plays of team meetings, encouraging interpreters to experiment with different strategies for managing overlapping speech, turn-taking, and interpreting humour. Feedback from the sessions suggests that participants' practice has been influenced by the training. One interpreter who took part in a 'humour' workshop said: "I have been thinking about all the things and my mind keeps making new connections – I had hoped to be able to pick up some new techniques and tools and think that I have a lot to contemplate over the next few months" (Clare Seal, personal communication). I would highly recommend utilising research findings in this manner to other researchers, as it makes a strong link between theory and practice.

Napier (2011) argues that unpublished research does not make an impact, and emphasises the merits of publishing interpreting research. As noted above, my PhD received a reasonable circulation and impact, but theses are not eminently accessible to practitioners, nor to research participants. I therefore created a more 'user-friendly' version of the findings in the form of an Executive Summary. This was widely disseminated amongst members of the interpreting profession, having been publicised via several interpreter e-group networks. In terms of employers, the Summary was made available to the workplaces participating in the research. I delivered a short training session to one of the participating workplaces, which focused on the extent to which the deaf employee was excluded from team meeting discourse. I illustrated this by providing the hearing team members with a 'back translation,' i.e. the message the deaf employee would have received from the interpreter's attempt to manage the overlapping contributions of the meeting participants. This enabled the hearing team members to grasp the exclusionary nature of overlapping speech, and they went on to discuss the various tactics and strategies they could employ to change their behaviour.

Copies of the Executive Summary were supplied to a number of deaf professionals. However, as I am conscious that a document in written English is not the most appropriate way of disseminating information to the Deaf community, I am currently working on producing a BSL version on video. Making the research findings available in BSL was always my aim, but funding has proved a stumbling block. Once completed, the video clip will be uploaded to YouTube and the link made available via social media and websites/e-groups relevant to the Deaf community.

A number of other publications have been produced, detailing the research findings (see e.g. Dickinson 2008, 2010, 2013, 2014; Dickinson and Turner 2008; Bristoll and Dickinson 2015). However, aware that it is often difficult to make connections with practitioners via academic journals, I also aimed to produce a book. This was published in 2014. Apart from making the research findings more widely available to practitioners, interpreter trainers and researchers, the volume has also proved useful to research participants. One of the deaf people who took part in the research stated: "There's so much in it that's relevant to any workplace (not just ones with deaf workers), all the things we know unconsciously but you spell out for us to acknowledge and use."

Again, some of the impact of the research was on a smaller, more local scale. Informal conversations about the research with deaf colleagues revealed the extent to which they were unaware of the importance of small talk and casual conversation. Deaf employees often fail to see the value of small talk for creating relationships with their hearing peers, dismissing non-work related talk as "inconsequential stuff" (Bristoll 2008: 24). In the video playback interviews Derek referred to small talk as being something that "wasn't worth it," that he would tell the interpreter "not to bother," and so there is undoubtedly a need for a wider awareness of its importance to and for deaf participants.

Ongoing impact

Findings from my research have recently been used in a report submitted by the Association of Sign Language Interpreters to the Department of Work and Pensions (ASLI 2014), challenging an Access to Work policy decision which is potentially detrimental to the interpreting profession. I was subsequently invited to give evidence at a Commons Select Committee Inquiry on 15th October 2014. I used data from my research to answer questions about the unsuitability of full-time 'staff' interpreters within the Access to Work scheme (Work and Pensions Committee 2014). The signed language interpreting profession is facing considerable pressures, with various government departments seeking to reduce costs through the utilisation of Communication Support Workers (i.e. individuals who generally hold no interpreting qualifications, and who have lower levels of skills in both spoken and signed languages). My research demonstrates that deaf employees in fact require highly skilled professionals to enable them to integrate into the workplace on a level with their hearing peers (see Bristoll and Dickinson 2015). I anticipate that the research will be used in future campaigns to challenge government policy.

These instances of impact, together with other examples not documented in this article, contributed to my being awarded a FASLI (Fellowship of Association of Sign Language Interpreters) for the contribution of my research to the interpreting profession and for developing "individual interpreters and the profession as a whole."

The research also has the potential to encourage future sociolinguistic research. It highlights the interpreter's complex role in multi-party interaction, opening the door for further research in this neglected area of interpreting studies. In terms of signed language linguistics, the research demonstrates the need for a more detailed examination of turn-taking, and the shifts between serious and humorous talk. This can then inform the teaching of interpreting, raising the standard of the interpreter's skillset and thus developing both the interpreter and the profession. Whilst the focus of the research has been on workplace discourse, the findings could be of value to interpreters working across different domains. The findings could be particularly relevant to spoken language interpreters working with multiple participants. The interpretation of humorous exchanges and relational talk during meetings is also of significance to spoken language interpreters, given their role in diplomatic and political domains.

Whilst the Executive Summary mentioned earlier was sent to the participating workplaces, offers of a follow-up visit to discuss the findings were not widely taken up. I suspect that the fine-grained details of the challenges facing the workplace interpreter are difficult for hearing employers and employees to take on board. The challenge is to make explicit the barriers that deaf employees face. Training sessions with practical role-exercises would be a good way of enabling hearing employees to comprehend the challenges and limitations of the interpreter's task in workplace meetings. Unfortunately this has implications in terms of cost and resources, making it a difficult 'sell' in the current UK economic climate. Still, it is part of my plan for future impact.

Conclusion

Much of the research impact detailed in this chapter has been on a small, local scale. Measuring the impact of sociolinguistic research can be challenging, particularly when it comes to bringing about change on a larger scale. In the current economic climate, employers and government policy makers have little time or interest to look beyond short-term gains, to the sort of fine-grained analyses of workplace talk which make recommendations for long-term improvements for access and equality. The challenge lies in making research findings relevant and accessible to all stakeholders, an issue which needs further exploration.

However, by making the research findings on aspects of small talk, humour and collegiate interaction available to interpreter educators, interpreting practitioners and service users (both deaf and hearing), the importance of these forms of communication for workplace participation has been, and will continue to be, highlighted. Interpreter training which focuses on these aspects, together with training for all employees on how to work with interpreters in team meetings, will lead to a more equitable experience for deaf employees. Furthermore, it will open the door for dialogue between interpreters and deaf people about how these elements can be translated and conveyed. Ultimately, this will directly influence deaf people's ability to access the workplace on an equal level with their hearing peers.

The importance of full workplace integration for deaf employees cannot be overestimated. The effect of continually being marginalised and excluded within the workplace is considerable (see Grant 2005). Overall, deaf people report negative emotions and feelings such as frustration, dissatisfaction, loneliness, and anger in relation to their workplace experiences. These mainly result from the communication barriers in this setting (Kyle and Dury 2005), reflecting deaf people's experiences of interacting with hearing people generally (Young et al. 2000). For me, it is therefore vital to continue to use the research findings to fully inform all participants engaging in workplace discourse.

Mullany (2007) describes our ultimate responsibility as sociolinguists as being able to show what people are achieving through discourse. Sociolinguistic research can be a valuable resource and 'impact-stimulating' tool across many disciplines, as demonstrated by the contributions to this volume. In an emerging discipline such as signed language interpreting research, there is a particular need for more research drawing on insights from 'mainstream' sociolinguistics. This will help challenge the prevailing ignorance about interpreting, and enable all participants – but particularly deaf people – to 'see both sides' of interpreted talk (Turner 2005). As Napier (2005: 103) notes, researchers, educators and practitioners alike "need to collaborate on identifying, conducting and disseminating research to ensure that local issues can be considered worldwide." For true impact to take place, this should be the underlying ethos of all sociolinguistic research, together with the researcher's commitment to engage with all stakeholders in the research process.

Transcription Conventions

Text   spoken contributions from hearing participants
Text   spoken contributions from signed language interpreter
TEXT   signed contributions from deaf participants
TEXT   signed contributions from signed language interpreter
[]   paralinguistic features, descriptive comments, e.g. [laughs]
?   rising or question intonation or facial expression

Acknowledgements

Thanks are due to the many people who have contributed to this chapter. First and foremost are the research participants. Members of the Deaf community allowed me to witness their everyday working lives. Interpreting colleagues willingly exposed themselves to the camera's gaze, and to my scrutiny and questioning. Organisations showed a commitment to improving deaf people's access to the workplace, as well as placing their trust in me as a practitioner-researcher. Thanks too to Professor Graham H. Turner, my PhD supervisor, for being an invaluable source of inspiration, ideas and energy throughout. Funding and other support were provided by Nottinghamshire Deaf Society, the University of Central Lancashire and Heriot-Watt University; it would have been impossible to complete my research without their contribution. Finally, thank you to Dave Sayers and Robert Lawson for their wise words and guidance in pulling this chapter together.

References

Arksey, Hilary, and Peter T. Knight. 1999. *Interviewing for Social Scientists: An Introductory Resource with Examples*. London: Sage.

ASLI. 2008. "'Did you have a good weekend?' The importance of interpreting small talk in workplace settings." Presentation given at the Association of Sign Language Interpreters Conference, London 6th April 2008.

ASLI. 2014. *Access to Work Survey*. Northampton: Association of Sign Language Interpreters.

Bell, Nancy D. 2006. "Interactional adjustments in humorous intercultural communication." *Intercultural Pragmatics* 3 (1): 1–28.

Boxer, Diane, and Florencia Cortés-Conde. 1997. "From bonding to biting: Conversational joking and identity display." *Journal of Pragmatics* 27 (3): 275–294.

Bristoll, Simon. 2008. *'But we booked an interpreter!': To What Extent Do Interpreting Practices and Practicalities Contribute to the Glass Ceiling for Deaf People?* MA dissertation, University of Leeds.

Bristoll, Simon, and Jules Dickinson. 2015. "Small talk, big results." *Newsli* 92: 6–13.

Cameron, Deborah. 1992. "'Respect please!': Investigating race, power and language." In *Researching Language: Issues of Power and Method*, ed. by Deborah Cameron, Elizabeth Frazer, Penelope Harvey, M.B.H. Rampton, and Kay Richardson, 113–130. London: Routledge.

Coates, Jennifer. 2007. "Talk in a play frame: More on laughter and intimacy." *Journal of Pragmatics* 39 (1): 29–49.

Cokely, Dennis. 1992. *Interpretation: A Sociolinguistic Model*. Burtonsville, MD: Linstok Press Inc.

Dean, Robyn K., and Robert Q. Pollard, Jr. 2005. "Consumers and service effectiveness in interpreting work: A practice profession perspective." In *Sign Language Interpreting and Interpreter Education: Directions for Research and Practice*, ed. by Marc Marschark, Rico Peterson, and Elizabeth Winston, 259–282. Oxford: Oxford University Press.

Dickinson, Jules. 2008. "'Pretty sandals': The importance of interpreting small talk in workplace settings." *Newsli* 65: 9–11.

Dickinson, Jules. 2010. "Access all areas: Identity issues and researcher responsibilities in workplace settings." *Text and Talk* 30 (2): 105–124.

Dickinson, Jules. 2013. "One job too many?" In *Interpreting in a Changing Landscape: Selected Papers from Critical Link 6*, ed. by Christina Schäffner, Krzysztof Kredens, and Yvonne Fowler, 133–148. Amsterdam: John Benjamins.

Dickinson, Jules. 2014. *Sign Language Interpreting in the Workplace*. Gloucestershire: Douglas McLean Publishing.

Dickinson, Jules, and Graham H. Turner. 2008. "Sign language interpreters and role conflict in the workplace." In *Crossing Borders in Community Interpreting: Definition and Dilemmas*, ed. by Carmen Valero-Garcés and Anne Martin, 231–244. Amsterdam: John Benjamins.

Edelsky, Carole. 1993. "Who's got the floor?" In *Gender and Conversational Interaction*, ed. by Deborah Tannen, 189–227. Oxford: Oxford University Press.

Grant, Susan. 2005. "Reaching deaf minds in the workplace." Accessed 7 April 2015. Available from: http://www.deafinfo.org.uk/policy/RDMITW_Report.pdf.

Hauser, Peter, Karen Finch, and Angela Hauser. 2008. *Deaf Professionals and Designated Interpreters: A New Paradigm*. Washington DC: Gallaudet University Press.

Hoiting, Nini, and Dan I. Slobin. 2002. "Transcription as a tool for understanding: The Berkeley Transcription System for sign language research (BTS)." In *Directions in Sign Language Acquisition*, ed. by Gary Morgan and Bencie Woll, 55–75. Amsterdam: John Benjamins.

Holmes, Janet. 2010. "Small talk at work: Potential problems for workers with an intellectual disability." *Research on Language and Social Interaction* 36 (1): 65–84.

Holmes, Janet, and Jennifer Hay. 1997. "Humour as an ethnic boundary marker in New Zealand interaction." *Journal of Intercultural Studies* 18 (2): 127–151.

Holmes, Janet, and Maria Stubbe. 2003. *Power and Politeness in the Workplace: A Sociolinguistic Analysis of Talk at Work*. Harlow: Pearson Education Limited.

Humphrey, Janice H. 1997. "Chopping down and reconstructing a tree." *Meta* 42 (3): 515–520.

Koester, Almut. 2010. *Workplace Discourse*. London: Continuum.

Kotthoff, Helga. 2000. "Gender and joking: On the complexities of women's image politics in humorous narratives." *Journal of Pragmatics* 32 (1): 55–80.

Kyle, Jim, and Alex Dury. 2005. "Sign of employment: Experiences and aspirations of deaf people in employment." In *A Valued Part of the Workforce? Final Report on the Sequal Project on Employment and Disabled People*, ed. by Debby Watson and Val Williams, 86–130. Guildford: SEQUAL Development Partnership.

Major, George. 2013. *Healthcare Interpreting as Relational Practice*. PhD thesis, Macquarie University.

Metzger, Melanie. 1995. *The Paradox of Neutrality: A Comparison of Interpreters' Goals with the Realities of Interactive Discourse*. PhD thesis, Georgetown University.

Metzger, Melanie. 1999. *Sign Language Interpreting: Deconstructing the Myth of Neutrality*. Washington, DC: Gallaudet University Press.

Mullany, Louise. 2007. *Gendered Discourse in the Professional Workplace*. Basingstoke: Palgrave Macmillan.

Napier, Jemina. 2005. "Linguistic features and strategies of interpreting: From research to education to practice." In *Sign Language Interpreting and Interpreter Education: Directions for Research and Practice*, ed. by Marc Marschark, Rico Peterson, and Elizabeth Winston, 84–111. Oxford: Oxford University Press.

Napier, Jemina. 2011. "If a tree falls in a forest and no one is there to hear it, does it make a noise? The merits of publishing interpreting research." In *Advances in Interpreting Research: Inquiry in Action*, ed. by Brenda Nicodemus and Laurie Swabey, 121–152. Amsterdam/Philadelphia: John Benjamins.

Napier, Jemina, and Meg J. Rohan. 2007. "An invitation to dance: Deaf consumers' perception of signed language interpreters and interpreting." In *Translation, Sociolinguistic, and Consumer Issues in Interpreting*, ed. by Melanie Metzger and Earl Fleetwood, 159–203. Washington, DC: Gallaudet University Press.

Pavlicek, Maria, and Franz Pöchhaker. 2002. "Humour in simultaneous conference interpreting." *The Translator* 8 (2): 385–400.

Rampton, Ben. 2007. "Questions and procedures for investigating interactional data." Lecture handout, *RDI- Ethnography, Language and Communication Course*.

Roy, Cynthia B. 1989. *A Sociolinguistic Analysis of the Interpreter's Role in the Turn Exchanges of an Interpreted Event*. PhD thesis, Georgetown University.

Schnurr, Stephanie. 2008. "Constructing leader identities through teasing at work." *Journal of Pragmatics* 41 (6): 1125–1138.

Stubbe, Maria. 2001. "From office to production line: Collecting data for the Wellington language in the workplace project." Accessed 16 February 2015. Available from: http://www.victoria.ac.nz/lals/centres-and-institutes/language-in-the-workplace/docs/ops/op2.pdf.

Sutton-Spence, Rachel, and Bencie Woll. 1998. *The Linguistics of British Sign Language: An Introduction*. Cambridge: Cambridge University Press.

Sutton-Spence, Rachel, and Donna Jo Napoli. 2012. "Deaf jokes and sign language humour." *Humor* 25 (3): 311–337.

Tray, Shaun. 2005. "What are you suggesting? Interpreting innuendo between ASL and English." In *Attitudes, Innuendo, and Regulators: Challenges of Interpretation*, ed. by Melanie Metzger and Earl Fleetwood, 95–135. Washington, DC: Gallaudet University Press.

Turner, Graham H. 2005. "Toward real interpreting." In *Sign Language Interpreting and Interpreter Education: Directions for Research and Practice*, ed. by Marc Marschark, Rico Peterson, and Elizabeth Winston, 29–56. Oxford: Oxford University Press.

Turner, Graham H., Jennifer K. Dodds, and Lisa A. Richardson. 2002. *Always the Last to Know: Institutionalised Audism and Linguistic Exclusion of Deaf People from Workplace Communities*. Preston: University of Central Lancashire.

Van Herreweghe, M. 2002. "Turn-taking mechanisms and active participation in meetings with deaf and hearing participants in Flanders." In *Turn-Taking, Fingerspelling and Contact in Signed Languages*, ed. by Ceil Lucas, 73–103. Washington, DC: Gallaudet University Press.

Wadensjö, Cecilia. 1992. *Interpreting as Interaction: On Dialogue-interpreting in Immigration Hearings and Medical Encounters.* PhD thesis, Linköping University.

Wadensjö, Cecilia. 1998. *Interpreting as Interaction.* Harlow: Addison Wesley Longman Ltd.

Wooffitt, Robin. 2005. *Conversation Analysis and Discourse Analysis: A Comparative and Critical Introduction.* London: Sage.

Work and Pensions Committee. 2014. "Improving access to work for disabled people." Accessed 2 April 2015. Available from: http://www.publications.parliament.uk/pa/cm201415/cmselect/cmworpen/481/481.pdf.

Young, Alys M., Jennifer Ackerman, and Jim G. Kyle. 2000. "On creating a workable signing environment: Deaf and hearing perspectives." *Journal of Deaf Studies and Deaf Education* 5 (2): 186–195.

Chapter 7

Summing up in jury trials as interactive discourse – one plank in the New Zealand judiciary's effort to improve communication with juries

Bronwen Innes, ORCID NUMBER 0000–0002–9464–694X

Introduction

In 2007 an ordinary New Zealander, who watched a trial throughout and was highly familiar with the facts of the case (murder), listened to the judge's summing-up and told me afterwards, "I didn't understand a word of it." This kind of anecdote, combined with research on juries carried out in New Zealand in the 1990s (Young et al. 1999; New Zealand Law Commission, 2001), and in Australia (Ogloff et al. 2006), suggests that judges' communication with juries needs some attention.

The issue is also recognised by the New Zealand judiciary (numerous personal communications). As part of addressing that, in 2005 the Chief Justice of New Zealand and the Chief High Court Judge asked me to do some research on the language used in judges' summings-up for juries. This chapter outlines the research process I used and some of my findings, as well as looking at the project's impact for judges to date and what might increase that in future.

New Zealand's population has been largely monolingual in English since the mid-twentieth century. It has been easy to assume, as many have done, that linguistic differences are minor in this speech community and that most if not all people would be able to understand and manage all that happens in a court. However, both the language situation and the relative homogeneity of New Zealand society are changing, making the issue of differences in accessibility to courtroom language perhaps more urgent.

Judges are used both to assessing highly complex information and to applying strict rules of objectivity for evidence. New Zealand's Court of Appeal exhorts judges to be more concerned with making things clearer to juries than having an eye to the appeal courts (a comment repeated frequently by the late Justice Sir Robert Chambers). However, it would be surprising if the possibility of appeal did not remain in judges' minds and inform their work to at least some extent (a fact confirmed many times personally to me). The techniques of sociolinguistics have the potential to appeal to judges' sense of intellectual rigour as well as to their clear acknowledgement that the crafting of language is a particular strength in their endeavours. The results of this project provide them with evidence and some tools to assist them in achieving the aim of improving communication with juries.

As part of attending to the way concepts are expressed, judges need to think about their audience, and to assess how far jurors are likely to have experience and knowledge of the legal framework and discourse. In New Zealand there is no *voir dire* for juries as in the American system. Judges here do not have the opportunity of hearing prospective jurors answer questions. The only information available to a New Zealand judge is the juror's place of residence and occupation, and the judge's observation of the juror's gender, age and demeanour. Therefore, aiming for clarity, understanding, and engagement through plain language is the only tool a judge has. Such an aim respects jurors' ability to understand relevant legal concepts and ensures they are not barred from doing so by unnecessary complexity (syntactic and lexical complication) in the language in which those concepts are expressed.

Earlier research

The earlier New Zealand juries research had found that, although jurors stated that they "generally" found summings-up clear, "fairly fundamental misunderstandings of the law" or uncertainty existed among them (Tinsley 2001: 1470). These misunderstandings concerned elements of charges, wording on indictments, the meaning of 'intent' and 'beyond reasonable doubt', and drawing inferences. Although the researchers concluded that those misunderstandings were resolved through jury discussions (although not without frequent disagreements), they did not appear to relate such resolution directly to their other findings on such matters as the influence of dominant jurors. (They found that dominant jurors affected the results in almost 50% of the cases in their study. However, they also found that misunderstandings occurred in more than 25% of the cases, but added that these did not affect verdicts. They did not appear to consider a possible relationship between that and the dominance of certain jurors.)

Much of the research on judicial trial directions has taken place in the USA (e.g. Charrow and Charrow 1979; Tiersma 2010). However, because those directions are rather different from summings-up in New Zealand, and the legal cultures differ (both facts noted by Young et al. 1999), they will not be canvassed here. On the other hand, the situation in Australia and Britain is similar to that in New Zealand, with the three legal systems sharing philosophies, approaches and practices in large part. The Law Reform Commission of New South Wales' 2012 *Report on Jury Directions* points to the "growing awareness that jury directions are not always working well in guiding jurors in their task" (2012: 13), noting that this awareness is "long-standing" (2012: 34). A pertinent study by Heffer (2005) looks more specifically at language in English jury trials. It works from the premise that there is a "strategic tension between two markedly different ways of viewing the trial: as crime narrative or legal argument" (2005: xv), both essential to understanding the genre. Heffer accordingly classes the summing-up a "hybrid genre" (2005: 34). He called for more real-life courtroom studies, and the current project responds to that call. While two such linguistic studies have been done in New Zealand (Lane 1988; Innes 2001), neither dealt with summings-up, being concerned instead with the examination phases of the trials. On the other hand, as noted, the summing-up process has been receiving attention from legal researchers in New Zealand for some time now (Young et al. 1999). Currently the same group has a study in progress assessing the written question trail method proposed for summings-up and championed by Justice Chambers. (Question trails are a written series of yes/no questions provided to the jury and intended to guide them through their deliberations.)

Background

In New Zealand only the most serious criminal matters must be heard by juries. There is, in addition, a range of less serious crimes for which the accused person may choose whether to have the case heard by a judge and jury or a judge alone. In 2012, 113 jury trials were heard in the New Zealand High Court; for the year ending 30 June 2012 there were 3,091 in the District Court. (It is expected that these numbers will decrease as the New Zealand Bill of Rights Amendment Act 2011 has raised the threshold for electing jury trials.) New Zealand juries comprise twelve adults; there are no education or property requirements or requirements for a gender or ethnic mix. Being a non-fluent speaker of English as a second or foreign language, however, is considered a disqualification (determined on the basis of self-assessment and discussion with the court registrar or the judge).

Jury trials in New Zealand begin with a brief statement by the judge, setting out basic tenets for the jury, explaining the trial process and their respective roles. The question of role is important, for the judge and the jury have different tasks: the judge is in charge of matters of law and procedure, while the jury's task is to decide on matters of fact, in effect whose story they believe. The second step is for the prosecution lawyer to outline the prosecution case and what evidence he or she intends to present to the court. That is often (but not always) followed by a short statement by the defence. The evidence for the prosecution is then presented to the judge and jury. That for the defence follows (unless the defence decides not to call evidence), beginning with an outline as the prosecution has done. Both proceed through evidence-in-chief (in which the lawyer takes a witness through his or her 'story'), cross-examination (in which the lawyer for the other side questions aspects of that story), and re-examination (by the first lawyer). Finally, the judge has an opportunity to ask questions. The lawyers for each side then complete their task by presenting closing statements. By this stage the jurors may have already been exposed to important concepts a number of times. The judge's summing-up follows, in which traditionally the judge discusses relevant law and how the jury might apply it to the facts, as well as outlining the main planks of the prosecution and defence cases. With the introduction of question trails, discussion of the law is expected to decrease substantially. Judges take care to avoid presenting a view on what the jury's decision should be as to which evidence they believe. At the conclusion of the summing-up the jury retires to consider its verdict.

Employing an ethnography of speaking framework (Hymes 1972) leads to some additional comments. The direct participants in summings-up are the judge and the jury and the communicative norms of this speech event are closely circumscribed. The judge has the only speaking role; the jury may not respond, although they may submit questions in writing during their deliberations. Others are involved at this stage purely as hearers: the defendant; lawyers, who attend to the summing-up very closely and critically; and (possibly) witnesses. Police or security guards, members of the media and the public may be present but have no active spoken participation at any point (they must remain silent). However, the jury is expected to listen closely, as are the lawyers present. Other than the judge, lawyers, jury and the press, no one may make notes (except with the permission of the judge) or record what the judge is saying.

A trial contains a number of sub-genres, of which the summing-up is one. The discourse occurs within a legal framework and the linguistic context is professional legal language. As noted above, the goals of the summing-up are to outline the jury's task (and sometimes ideas on addressing it), to delineate the main planks of prosecution and defence, and to explain relevant and necessary law to the jury. It is the only point in a trial (apart from the judge's opening statement) where the speaker's advocacy does not play a part: the judge's role is to be neutral and objective (despite summarising the prosecution and defence positions). The tone of the summing-up is serious, considered and formal, albeit that judges occasionally attempt to engage juries through jokes and laughter. Heffer notes it as part of the "adjudicative" phase of a trial (2005: 67) and characterises it as "deliberative" in nature. While the summing-up is always a spoken monologue, all of those in this corpus were drafted first in writing. Most judges in the study also provided the jury with some material in writing, often titled 'issues sheets.' These contained a variety of information (including definitions and questions juries needed to resolve), and were most often given out at a relevant point during the summing-up. While not the same as the question trails now encouraged, they could be seen as precursors to those and were certainly attempts to improve juries' understanding.

Approaching the research task

The judiciary asked me to investigate clarity in summings-up. How could I do this? The obvious and desirable method (from a linguist's point of view) would be to record real-life deliberations and ask the juries themselves, by way of exit interviews. However, such recording is impossible at present in New Zealand. There is no judicial interest in exposing the detail of what goes on in jury rooms to this degree, and there are potent reasons for this. Jurors who do so may be charged with contempt of court and journalists may not approach them for specific comment. However, the results of this study may provide a useful basis for questions if exit interviews were to be used in future studies. Other options could be public questionnaires (suggested by the judiciary) and mock trials (an expensive and time-consuming exercise). But the general public is simply not in the same situation as real jurors; the gravity of the situation and its consequences would not reflect the situation real jurors are in. On the other hand, complexity can be investigated comparatively easily and directly. It is incontrovertible that complex legal language and the legal discourse framework can be difficult for people who do not deal with it every day and are not familiar with it (Stygall 1994); therefore complexity seemed to me to be the most useful and measurable factor to assess in this project.

What do sociolinguistics and corpus linguistics have to offer here, other than in an academic sense of expanding our knowledge of language genres? Judges are at the pinnacle of their professional tree, and that tree is largely built on the craft of words. Judges see words perhaps from a legal point of view, a sense of what is included and excluded. For them it is crucial to achieve as much precision as possible, to get the legal niceties right. Judges, including those who took part in this study, see the need to explain any necessary legal aspects with great care to ensure that juries are making their decisions on proper bases. Just as juries bring their own stories to the task of being jurors, as pointed out by Stygall (1994), so too do judges have a distinctive framework within which they work. I see the task of this research as providing them with tools to build a bridge between the two. A linguistic approach, used in conjunction with an understanding of language in the law, can provide a different perspective which might help judges in their endeavours to create that bridge.

Several things arose as a result of these considerations. First and foremost was the need to involve the judges at all stages in the research process. Without this, the project would be destined to be merely an academic exercise to languish, soon forgotten, in bottom drawers.

Second, judges might be more prepared to countenance any suggestions which arise from the study if they were more than "just a plain English exercise" (as one judge put it). My experience in this field leads me to believe that many lawyers and judges consider plain language a useful concept and have participated in training seminars accordingly. However, they do not necessarily see it as fitting in with the rigour of the law. For such training to be effective, recipients must be able to see it as relevant; therefore it must be based on their language practices. Accordingly, a linguistic description of the language used in summings-up, crafted from the angle of complexity and empirically based, would be an essential platform for that training.

Third, as noted above, judges are used to dealing with evidence. Providing judges with empirical linguistic evidence on where complexity lies in their language use would perhaps be rather more appealing to judges than intuitive or subjective comments. Obtaining such evidence requires both sociolinguistic genre description and corpus linguistics. The latter, by providing a quantitative analysis, can demonstrate both patterns and the degree to which analysed phenomena occur. Such demonstration may well be attractive to judges, who spend so much of their time hearing and assessing evidence.

Collecting the data

The first step was to meet with the Chief High Court Judge and another senior member of the judiciary. The purpose of this meeting was to work together to devise a research plan which would work both from both judicial and research perspectives. We made various decisions which set up the data-gathering process.

First, we decided that work would be conducted mainly in the Auckland High Court for this stage of the project, given that the research request came through that court. However, the District Court and courts outside Auckland tend to be rather different in character. At a later point I would consider and discuss with the judiciary whether and how far to extend the project to those courts. This decision would depend on a number of factors, including funding and practicality.

We agreed to seek volunteer participants. The process would be to send an outline of the project under cover of an explanatory and supportive letter from the Chief High Court Judge. Willing judges would then contact me directly to give their consent (having the option to call or email me with any queries) and to make arrangements for the data collection. At that time there were twenty judges in the Auckland Court, and in the end twelve agreed to take part. This response is a mark of the judiciary's willingness to involve itself actively and openly in the improvements they are seeking. In all cases, the judges presiding over the hearings contacted legal counsel beforehand in order to check whether they were happy for the hearing to be part of the project.

Another decision was that I would attend trials in person wherever possible. I would be entitled to take notes throughout (not generally permitted) and would sit within the court hearing area. The judges and I agreed that it was important for me to hear and see the summings-up. Although court transcripts are relatively accurate, they do not include features of delivery and production (e.g. gaze, gesture, speech rate, repetition, pausing, repair, intonation, etc.). Relying on transcripts would have allowed only a limited view and may have led to misinterpretation of the data. Note-taking would allow a record of gaze and gesture.

The reasons for observing hearings in their entirety were twofold. First, an accurate analysis would require full knowledge of the contexts for the summings-up. Second, the degree to which judges explained concepts and issues in summing up may have been affected by whether and how such matters were explored earlier in the trials.

This all meant that I would spend a large amount of time in court (the hearings ranged from three days to seven weeks) and data collection would take some time. On the other hand, these decisions meant that others in the court process could see overt signs that the project had the imprimatur of both the judiciary and of the individual judges taking part. Scheduling issues meant that the data collection took rather more time than had been anticipated initially as suitable hearings (defended criminal jury trials) did not arise frequently for the participating judges. Inevitably, the flow of data collection became intermittent and spread over a long period. These problems may not occur in the District Court where many more (and shorter) trials take place.

It was also agreed that I would be given audio recordings of the summings-up (recording them is standard practice for the High Court). The recordings would be reliable and of good quality. Further, most of the judges offered me their own typed versions, which formed the basis for my more detailed transcripts; this saved much time and effort. I had hoped that video-recording would be possible, but while two judges agreed to this there were technical difficulties (to do with compatibility of systems in the court) which prevented it. These could perhaps have been resolved by my taking independent recordings. However, the court administration appeared uncomfortable with this and it seemed better to take up their offer. In the end I took notes of gaze, body stance and gesture during each summing-up (cf. Dickinson, this volume; MacLeod and Haworth, this volume), made easier by those judges who gave me copies of their drafts in advance.

In addition to these arrangements, informal discussions occurred with each of the participating judges before, during, and after the hearings and in a variety of contexts. These initially concerned the trials themselves and more latterly the results and presentation of the findings, with an emphasis on how to make them useful. I have been in the fortunate position of having had personal and professional contact with many of the judges, which came about in a number of ways. First, I am married to a lawyer who later became a judge, resulting in many personal contacts over many years. Second, I have provided plain language training and editing, including for the legal fraternity, for almost as many years. Third, my PhD research (completed more than a decade ago) involved observing and analysing hearings in the Auckland District Court. Last, I have taken a role as an expert witness in a number of legal matters. The fact that I was known by and had personal and/or professional contact with a number of judges (previously and throughout the project) perhaps expedited the establishment of trust and the openness of these discussions. While not having such contacts does not preclude the possibility or effectiveness of research work in the courts, a prospective researcher would need to establish their credibility and understand and accept the courts' constraints.

I coded the data manually for use with concordancing software (an enormous task; using the efficient taggers now available would be a better option). I chose to use MonoConcPro (Barlow 2003), which has the particular advantage that it is applied to material in text format without that material needing any further treatment, and Nation's (2002) Range BNC. These allowed searching, for example, for the most common words and their concordances. Further searches provided information on all the features which I had coded. Given the task of the study, I hoped to produce something of practical value within a relatively short time; the use of this software enabled that.

Fourteen summings-up form the data for the project so far. I observed ten hearings. Four more judges provided their own transcripts for hearings where direct observation was not possible, but the judges were keen to have their summings-up included. Two judges provided two summings-up each. Eight male judges and four females took part. In total the corpus contains 174,182 words. The trials, which took place in 2007–2009, involved murder/manslaughter, methamphetamine issues (manufacture, supply, conspiracy to supply, importation), money laundering, procuring a miscarriage, sexual violation, bribery, corruption, and attempting to pervert the course of justice.

The empirical evidence

A corpus approach is quantitative. However, as Schegloff (1993) points out, a quantitative approach must begin with an analysis of every single instance, so necessarily begins with the qualitative. Further, wider functional analysis is needed if we are to provide a full picture.

The first task was to decide how to code the data, which necessarily involved a number of analytical and theoretical decisions. The elements of legal language are well known (Mellinkoff 1963); aside from the legal and factual complexity of the material being dealt with, they can be summarised as involving sentence length, embedding (including multiple subordination), nominalisations, the passive voice, negation, cleft constructions, hypotheticals, and vocabulary choice (including technical language and complex derivational morphology). Douglas Biber's (1988) framework of axes for spoken/written language and informational/involved style is based on frequency of linguistic elements in a range of genres. It provides a non-legal structure which also points to features which could participate in the analysis. I chose codings which would also reflect the kind of information likely to be recognisable and useful for the recipients of this research, i.e. judges. The codings were, therefore, based to a considerable extent on the features of legal language as well as on more general issues.

Second, I needed to make decisions on how to assess linguistic complexity in an overall sense. Widely used measures I chose for the study included type-token ratio (the number of different words divided by the total number of words), lexical density (the ratio of content words to function words), word length (three syllables or more), and word frequency. I also assessed syntactic complexity and other features of legal language.

Selected brief notes follow on the results obtained from these measures.

- The overall lexical density of the corpus is 44%, just above the lower level in the range Stubbs (1996) found for written language. Stubbs also found a higher lexical density for spoken language where the audience is not present and no recipient feedback is possible (such as radio commentary) than for that where the audience is present and feedback is possible. Summings-up exist between these two stools (i.e. the audience is present but no feedback is possible), but fall just within the range which includes the possibility of feedback.

- The overall type-token ratio of 7.67 falls midway between the ratios found for conversation and newspaper reporting in the *Longman Grammar of Spoken and Written English* (LWSE; Biber et al. 1999). Given the often academic nature of language in the law, this result is encouraging.

- Spontaneous spoken language, with its involved style, has been found to contain more verbs than more informational written styles, which have more nouns. I found a narrower difference in the numbers of nouns and verbs in the summings-up than Biber et al. (1999) found between spoken and written language in LWSE. This suggests that summings-up are "more nouny" (Brown and Levinson 1987: 213) and more informational in style, perhaps reflecting the fact that they were all drafted in writing first. Another possibility is that judicial style is inherently informational, whether spoken or written. Brown and Levinson comment that "the more nouny an expression, the more removed an actor is from doing or feeling something" (ibid.). This is consistent with the judicial aim of neutrality which is so important in summing up.

In summary, the results show that the language of the summings-up is markedly more complex and informational than everyday conversational language, but much less complex and more involved than academic prose (cf. Stubbs 1996).

I also assessed specific features of legal language, with the findings including the following.

- More passive verbs were used than are found in conversation, but fewer than in academic prose, suggesting what may be a conscious effort by judges to reduce their use of this construction when summing up. Certainly the judges in the study often mentioned the passive to me when talking about the difficulty of legal language, signalling that they are aware of this issue.

- A wider range was found in the number of nominalisations than with other features considered in the study. This suggests that this is another area where judges can and do exercise more choice in their mode of expression, although judges did not mention this so may not have been aware of it in an explicit way.

- Embedded clauses (relative clauses, adverbial clauses, complement clauses, infinitive clauses, participial clauses) occurred remarkably more often than co-ordinate clauses in the data, further evidence of a more informational style. Multiple embedding was also frequent. The highest score here came from the judge with the highest score for lexical density; perhaps the two go hand in hand.

Noun phrases (NPs) provide one instance of features engendering complexity, arising from the inclusion of adjectives, prepositional phrases and modifying clauses, and again show variation in these data. As Miller and Weinert (2009) note, spontaneous spoken language simply does not contain this kind of complexity as it does not have the same kind of lexical precision that more informational styles do, including legal language. They also report that the numbers of words in NPs are important. Written English, particularly that which is more formal, has a higher proportion of longer NPs, which are inevitably more complex. The longest NP in the summings-up contains sixty-eight words. Both after presentations and during personal discussions with me, judges have expressed shock that this could be possible. While 80% of the NPs in the data are simple in structure (either single elements or containing determiners and/or adjectives), almost 20% are characterised as complex (containing one or more prepositional phrase and/ or embedded clause). The analysis of NPs demonstrates both complexity and informational style, backing up the conclusion that summings-up, with their high processing load, may be difficult for jurors. It also points clearly to an area in which complexity can be reduced – judges can make choices here.

The results clearly reflect the fact that the summings-up were drafted in writing and read to the jury. This has the corollary that more planning time was available for crafting them than is available during spontaneous spoken language (Miller and Weinert 2009). However, while the judges have that planning time, juries have to process this complex spoken material on the fly (although possibly aided by having heard all the evidence already and any written material provided in advance). Perhaps an awareness of this is why the summings-up also include some sense of interaction. In other words, the judges (some more than others) made conscious efforts to engage the juries; part of their technique for doing so appears to be to introduce elements of spoken and interpersonal language.

One way in which a sense of interaction is evident in the data is in the use of first and second person pronouns, which are more frequent in spoken language (involved style) than in formal written language. Judges have two options when talking to the jury: they can use the third person (*judges, the court, the jury, they, one*), or they can use first and second person pronouns (*I, we, you*, etc.). Using the latter may be designed to create a sense of personal interaction and less formality. It may place the judge and jury together in the courtroom endeavour (perhaps even including jurors as temporary members of the court community). It may reduce a sense of holding them at arm's length.

Example I

> As judges **our** task, when I have **your** job and **your** task toda:y, is to view the facts, putting aside the emotions that the case will inevitably give rise to. The great American Judge Justice Cardozo, u- once said **all of us** have passions, emotions, there's no point pretending **we** don't but **a Judge** must identify those passions and emotions and put them aside.

Here *our task* places the judge and jury in one (the same), ordinary person framework; the judge then opposes *we* (and *all of us*) to *a Judge*. During his summing-up this judge leaned back well in his chair, turning it (and his body) towards the jury and maintained a high level of eye contact with the jury. He used a measured speech rate with good pausing. He also smiled at them and used gestures. All these factors were likely to add to the interactive effect of these pronouns in his summing-up.

Judges chose *you* substantially more often (29.96:1000 words) than first person pronouns and it generally has a plural referent in the summings-up. Including *your* brings the rate to 33.41:1000. There is a wide range in these pronouns' frequency of use by individual judges (21.3–65.9:1000 words). Surprisingly, the judge with the highest rate uses more complex informational language according to the other measures used in this study. It may be that some judges are simply attempting to reduce formality. Alternatively, these pronouns may emphasise distance between judge and jury, which would not be surprising given the different roles carried out by the two groups. This usage may then need to be explained in terms of judges' individual goals.

Judges may choose first person plural pronouns (*we, us, our*) to establish common ground between the judge and the jury, thereby perhaps increasing the degree of engagement as well as reducing formality. However, these plural pronouns are used the least often (1.52:1000) of the first and second person pronouns, which suggests that these functions are not considered highly relevant by the judges as a group. Further analysing them according to inclusive use (the judge referring to himself or herself, the court, the lawyers, the jury or New Zealand society) or exclusive use (the judge referring to himself or herself, lawyers and 'the law') proved interesting in that inclusive *we* was more frequent, occurring in all but one summing-up.

A second interactive technique is to use discourse markers more commonly found in spoken language. Some discourse markers include a pragmatic sense of relating to the wider context. Here that context includes the juror audience and the judges' perceptions of both their need to have jurors engaged in their task and jurors' desire to understand the material they are dealing with. All judges used discourse markers with such pragmatic functions, again showing wide variation. This variation suggests that some judges are prepared to introduce spoken language elements, making their summings-up appear more interactive and involved in style.

Three single-word discourse markers common in the data are *and, now,* and *well.* In brief, *and* appears to be used for extra co-ordination for the benefit of the listening audience, to draw their attention to something which may be achieved in writing simply by adjacency.

Example 2

> If you're *not* sure of that your answer will be no: **and** I also remi:nd you **and** I am
> going to remind you again *later* that you must be unanimous in your answers
> to each question.

Now, according to Schiffrin (1987), is used to indicate either reference time, "the deictic relationship between a proposition and its speaking time" (1987: 228), or discourse time, where it looks "forward [to an upcoming proposition] in discourse time" (1987: 229). In spoken language it is often used during explanation. In these data, it often occurs with disputable material. As with *and*, the judges may use *now* for the benefit of the juror audience, marking the point about to come. Additionally, it may signal comparison or recognition of disputability, "displaying the speaker's recognition of interpersonal differences about that topic" (Schiffrin 1987: 235), a typical example being "Now that may b- s:ound complicated but it's not."

Example 3

> It is for you to weigh up, see what you think of the witnesses and how much of the evidence you view as reliable. **Now** it's not my job to express any view on a witness or any particular part of the evidence.

This is not referencing time, but rather signalling that an important aspect of the judge's role is perhaps contrary to the jury's expectations.

Well, also much more common in spoken than written language, is generally characterised as a response marker (Schiffrin 1987). This would be an unlikely analysis here, where audience response is not possible. However, its use in the examination phases of trials and ordinary conversation (Innes 2010) suggests it has other functions in addition, including signalling a departure from what the hearer might expect, both structurally and attitudinally. Its use in summings-up falls into this category, and is therefore interactive in nature.

Example 4

> **Well** now you *are* um of course faced with something of a stark choice. If L's account is *correct* then Mr T is plainly guilty on each of the four counts in the indictment? On the other hand if Mr T's explanation is broadly correct, ah the Crown case *must* fail and he must be acquitted.

Jurors have been presented with two convincing but opposed cases; perhaps against their expectations it is not going to be straightforward for them to make a decision.

In summary, despite the prevalence of precedent in the common law, the judges show variation in their language use in summings-up, that variation occurring both within and between summings-up (echoing Heffer's 2005 findings). Second, the same judges do not always turn out to be the most (or least) complex on all measures, again demonstrating individual choice in approach. Third, the summings-up show clear signs of straddling the spoken–written continuum, with judges appearing at various points along it. One explanation for this may be the degree to which judges attempt to tailor their summings-up to the perceived needs of their jury audience (as well as the lawyer audience and the potential appeal court audience), working to engage the jurors in an interactive way.

All these findings are demonstrated through the combination of classic sociolinguistic ethnography of speaking and the description of variation in the summings-up, illuminated by the application of corpus linguistic techniques. In turn, this provides a different perspective from that which judges are accustomed to when looking at judicial language. Its novelty and rigour have the potential to appeal to judges who may wish for more than "just a plain English exercise."

Using the findings

Heffer (2005) suggests that jury comprehension of summings-up might be increased through linguistic (speech) accommodation (Giles and Powesland 1975) rather than simplifying per se. This kind of awareness is clearly demonstrated by some of the judges. Such an explanation is one of the ways in which sociolinguistics can provide a fresh and potentially productive approach. However, speech accommodation tends to be an unconscious rather than overt phenomenon; further, it occurs during dialogue and is a response to the language of the other interactant(s). On the other hand, judges' summings-up are monologues in terms of their production (despite the approach taken here that they are interactive in some sense). What is happening here is rather better described as a conscious effort; in other words, audience design (Bell 1984). It is suggested that this is distinctly difficult to do in anything other than a general way in summings-up, given that the judges have so little information about juries and, of course, do not hear them talk. It is most likely based on judges' perceptions of jurors (including any stereotypes), and a perceived aim of consciously simplifying complex legal issues as well as complex language, contrary to Heffer's suggestion. The challenge here is to encourage judges to see that as a positive exercise, rather than some kind of 'dumbing down', and as a way they can contribute positively to better outcomes for justice. Providing them with empirical evidence, showing them just how their language is complex and yet interactive, gives them a pertinent basis for their audience design as opposed to material aimed at a more general audience.

I have produced two reports for the judiciary, the participating judges, and the New Zealand Law Foundation. The first provides an overview, considering complexity, the measures used and tables of results, as well as providing detailed discussion of, and some plain language alternatives for, common legal concepts (including those mentioned in the New Zealand juries' research). The plain language alternatives further increase the potential impact of the research by providing specific relevance for judges. The second report considers complexity in noun phrases. It takes on board comments by judges that they would like "lots" of examples and again provides detailed analysis of examples and plain language alternatives for those. I have also provided the judiciary with summary outlines of 'pointers' and the numerical results, again prepared on the suggestion of judges. To anyone researching judicial language and wanting their work to have the possibility of greater impact, I recommend producing reports which combine analytical detail with numerous examples from professional practice.

The way I have presented the results allows the participating judges to gain a picture of complexity in their own language as well as to see where they fit in relation to others in the study (although no identifying details are present). It also allows others to gain an overall picture and to see how and where variation occurs within that. All of the judges involved have commented that they found the reports, approach used, and recommendations interesting and useful. Some were delighted (for example, the judge who used the word *job* instead of *onus of proof*). Some were horrified to see where they stood on particular aspects (one judge, seeing his level of complex NPs, commented jokingly that perhaps he should retire!).

I have received comments informally from a range of judges at various times. I have been in the fortunate position of interacting with judges on many different occasions at all stages of the project. This has meant that I have been able to keep it in their consciousness; my presence at various occasions has often acted as a spur for enquiry and comment, not only from the participating judges but also from others. I have been asked for copies of the reports a number of times (which suggests that simply placing such material on an intranet, as happened with this project, does not ensure that they are accessed by as many readers as one might hope). I recommend responding promptly to such requests so as to strike while the iron is hot.

Taking up another opportunity to create impact for the project, I have presented two talks for New Zealand judges as part of training seminars provided by the Institute of Judicial Studies and run by judges. Comments were made immediately after my talks (and at other times), both by participating judges and those running the workshop. The participating judges appeared receptive and enthusiastic both to the information presented and to the somewhat more (socio) linguistic/academic approach than plain language talks often present. For example, I presented instances of complex noun phrases as part of presentations. In doing so, I was careful not to choose the most extreme in terms of length and complexity, in order to avoid the comment, "But I would never do that." I presented these instances in three ways: first, the examples themselves; second, with the coding employed in the project; third, as phrase structure diagrams (noting that the most complex ones simply could not be presented readably on a single slide – this created amusement and seemed to make a constructive point in itself). This approach might seem out of context. In fact, it allowed the audience to gain a practical look at and appreciation of how it is that complex language becomes difficult to process, and demonstrated how complex even apparently quite simple language can be.

These talks were unfortunately all too short, being 45 minutes only. They were part of an intense whole-day workshop where judges worked on preparing a summing-up for a particular scenario and had their efforts critiqued. I would like to see an increase in the time for the plain language component for such workshops. In preparing for such talks, I again suggest combining analytical material with real-life examples. A light-handed approach is also helpful, as the recipients of such talks are, after all, experts in using language.

Some judges have asked me if I would be open to providing them with individual training as a follow-up. My answer of "certainly" had to be tempered with the need for them to seek approval for this. To date, this has not progressed further, likely due to funding and perceived workload constraints. I intend to approach the judiciary and the Institute of Judicial Studies (responsible for much training of judges in New Zealand) in the near future with an offer to undertake such individual training. I would be prepared to offer group workshops as well, although I have found one-to-one training more effective.

I presented a further paper at the Australasian Institute of Judicial Studies Conference in 2012. The participants at this conference included judges from various courts in both Australia and New Zealand. The responses I received were similar in tone to those I received at other points. I have also presented papers at linguistics conferences, thus continuing cross-disciplinary interaction.

One of the aims of the research is to bridge the gap between legal and academic linguistic discourse. I have, therefore, made every attempt to present the results in ways accessible to the judiciary while providing them with the detail necessary for them to gain the greatest benefit. Despite the comparatively complex and linguistically academic material, judges have responded positively. Judicial readers of the reports and summaries have said that they found the approach interesting and that they enjoyed both the detail and the relevance to their own situations. I recommend couching any reports and talks in language accessible to readers other than academic linguists.

One senior judge who has read both reports carefully has expressed the view within the judiciary that the reports ought to be made required reading for all trial judges. While gratified, I also understand that judges' workloads are heavy. Accordingly, I have begun work on a book and a handbook, so that judges and interested others have the option of reading in more or less depth, while yet obtaining something of practical value for them. Again, I recommend including a combination of empirical analytical detail and examples chosen from real-life data, although the extent of each would need to vary for the two different purposes of a book and handbook. Determining the audience for each, which may be different, would need to be done at the beginning of the writing.

The research has been academic in nature in order to provide the necessary rigour and formal basis to underpin the sociolinguistic description of this subgenre of trial discourse. There is significant challenge in making the work accessible to judges. It must not appear to add too much to their workloads, yet it needs to provide a good level of detail. Judges need to be able to see that this work is not just what a (District Court) judge claimed, in a trial in which I was an expert witness, to be the linguist's purview: "they just ask people what they think." The field of linguistics is not yet widely known, at least in New Zealand (cf. Wolfram, this volume, on popular awareness of linguistics in the USA), and respect has to be earned through demonstration of its attention to detail and a proper theoretical basis.

Some may comment that the reports present a high level of linguistic detail (as indeed some judges have remarked). I have done this partly to encourage judges to see and respect the linguistic rigour of the exercise which has been carried out and which linguistics can offer. However, it has also served to include a positive perspective. I considered it important to show judges where they have made constructive and productive efforts to ensure that juries understand and are engaged in what they have to say and how they achieved that. The existing reports include both complex examples and examples where judges have provided a simpler, more straightforward mode of expression, whether in the use of vocabulary or in syntactic structure. My provision of plainer alternatives is intended to give judges more ideas on how to achieve a better balance. It also lets them know that there are usually a number of straightforward ways of expressing what they have to say to juries; plain language is no straitjacket (contrary to the perceptions expressed by some in the legal fraternity).

As a further benefit, I have pointed out to judges that they can apply the results of the study to other areas of judicial communication, such as writing judgments and question trails. While the most likely audience for judgments is lawyers (and other judges), who we can assume would not have difficulty with legal discourse, these documents are also presumably intended to be read by participants in the disputes they concern. A great many of the discussions, points and recommendations made in the reports can equally well be applied to those kinds of documents. A useful technique for increasing the impact of any research project would be to suggest how research results could be applied more widely.

The combination of approaches used in this project provides a useful perspective for judges, with the aim of assisting them in their goal of improving communication with juries. It elucidates a range of techniques used and provides judges with very specific information about linguistic complexity. The fact that judges have been involved at all stages, through both formal and informal discussions, has perhaps encouraged them in finding the approach interesting and useful. The project illustrates a practical application of sociolinguistics in a situation which is everyday for judges but highly unusual and significant for the accused and for juries. The extent to which the project will lead to lasting behaviour changes remains to be seen, but the signs are encouraging.

Conclusion

When entering another sphere and community of practice as a researcher from a different field, there are a number of challenges. First and foremost, we must always respect the members of that community and their endeavours. It is all too easy to come in with a generalised notion of how a particular endeavour can be improved. With my approach in this project, I made every effort to avoid falling into that trap. I achieved this through two directions. First, the project began and has continued with engagement with the participating judges and the judiciary in general. I hope this will continue, and various judges have expressed the same sentiment to me. The involvement of judges at all stages has been crucial in ensuring that the study was welcomed, and proceeded in a productive manner. I have encouraged feedback throughout and acted upon it in terms of the format for presenting findings and how to make them more useful for the judiciary.

The second way of avoiding the generality trap and making the findings relevant has been through the use of rigorous linguistic analysis of pertinent data presented so as to be accessible for the end users of the work (i.e. judges). One of my continuing efforts in this regard will be to work on encouraging judges to operate under the notion of working together with jurors. One aspect of this will be to show judges how they can alter their language in such a way as to help jurors understand the legal discourse framework that prevails in court.

Even though the use of question trails is expected to reduce the discussion of legal concepts in summings-up, judges still talk to juries. Further, the extent to which individual judges use question trails is variable. Complex language, therefore, remains an issue. This project is recognised as providing a constructive and useful addition to the work done in New Zealand on the improvement of judges' communication to juries. At this stage its impact has been noted, but confined to a relatively small sphere. I expect that my producing a handbook will extend the number of judges likely to read the material and act on the recommendations.

This project remains a work in progress, in terms of both data analysis (and collection) and making practical use of the findings. Much more can be done with the data, in particular extending the corpus linguistic arm of the analysis. At some point, I intend to approach the judiciary again with the aim of extending the research to other courts, recognising judges' comments that those other courts are rather different from the Auckland High Court. One way to do this, so as to achieve results relatively quickly, would be to work on the court transcripts of the summings-up rather than personally observing entire cases. I will continue discussion with the judiciary on how to encourage judges to take up the opportunities offered, both in terms of group training possibilities and individual (one-on-one) training. Part of this will be further efforts to encourage judges to recognise that the legal discourse framework is foreign to most lay participants as well as being a matter of complex language.

Lawyers involved in the hearings were, without exception, comfortable with the process and keen to discuss anything with me (both during and after the hearings). A number of them asked for copies of any material published on the project. This means that it may be possible for the results and recommendations to be useful for a wider legal audience as well as the judiciary. This direction will be followed up, and has begun with my presenting a well-received webinar on plain language for practising lawyers run by the Auckland District Law Society. Another possibility under discussion is for me to participate in continuing legal education to be provided by another organisation.

Finally, the possibility of applying the findings to other areas of judicial and legal written language use means that its impact has the potential to be wider still. The book and handbook may well appeal to such a wider audience.

What useful tips arise from this project? Practical matters have been mentioned in the discussion in this chapter. In summary, researchers will need respect for the other stakeholders in the research, persistence and patience, attention to detail and flexibility. Working with groups whose perspectives and needs differ from the researcher's requires an understanding of those factors. Being prepared to take time establishing relationships before beginning research is likely to help both in establishing credibility and in shaping the research so that it will be relevant for stakeholder needs. Open-minded listening to those stakeholders is helpful at all stages, including when trying to achieve positive impact for the research.

The project has been a productive and enjoyable exercise for both me and the judges involved. This has partly been so because of its content, but also because of the involvement, active participation of and positive responses from those in the judiciary who have allowed me to observe and comment on their language in a very direct manner. Last, it has been due to a further group who have taken time from their busy schedules to read the reports or attend the workshops or conferences where the results have been presented. The biggest challenge now is to keep the momentum going; this is challenging because the New Zealand legal system faces many issues in its endeavours to improve access to justice, and inevitably choices must be made amongst them. However, it is a worthwhile exercise and deserves on-going effort.

Acknowledgements

I wish to thank Dame Sian Elias, the Chief Justice of New Zealand, The Hon. Justice Randerson (the former Chief High Court Judge of New Zealand), The Hon. Justice Helen Winkelmann (the present Chief High Court Judge) and the participating judges for their support of and involvement in the project. I have also been most grateful for the helpful comments of Professor Jim Miller during the project, and the editors and reviewers of this chapter. Finally, I thank the Law Foundation of New Zealand for its generous financial support for the project. This was greatly appreciated. The Law Foundation, an independent body, "develops legal expertise on major and emerging public policy issues", providing "grants for legal research, public education on legal matters and legal training" (www.lawfoundation.org.nz, accessed 21 October 2013). In the main, this organisation's grants go to those working in the law and, to my knowledge, this is the first time that it has supported a linguistics project. The grant for this project also supports the notion that sociolinguistics can provide useful insights in the law, and that legal professionals are open to this idea.

References

Barlow, Michael. 2003. *MonoConc Pro 2.2*. Houston: Athelstan.

Bell, Allan. 1984. "Language style as audience design." *Language in Society* 13 (2): 145–204.

Biber, Douglas. 1988. *Variation across Speech and Writing*. Cambridge: Cambridge University Press.

Biber, Douglas, Stig Johansson, Geoffrey Leech, Susan Conrad, and Edward Finegan. 1999. *Longman Grammar of Spoken and Written English*. Harlow, Essex: Pearson Education.

Brown, Penelope, and Stephen Levinson. 1987. *Politeness: Some Universals in Language Usage*. Cambridge: Cambridge University Press.

Charrow, Robert, P., and Veda R. Charrow. 1979. "Making legal language understandable: A psycholinguistic study of jury instruction." *Columbia Law Review* 79 (5): 1306–1374.

Giles, Howard, and Peter Powesland. 1975. "A social psychology of speech diversity." In *Speech Style and Social Development*, ed. by Howard Giles and Peter Powesland, 154–170. New York: Harcourt.

Heffer, Chris. 2005. *The Language of the Jury Trial*. Basingstoke: Palgrave MacMillan.

Hymes, Dell. 1972. "Models of the interaction of language and social life." In *Directions in Sociolinguistics: The Ethnography of Communication*, ed. by John Gumperz and Dell Hymes, 35–71. New York: Holt, Rinehart and Winston.

Innes, Bronwen. 2001. *Speaking up in Court: Repair and Powerless Language in New Zealand Courtrooms*. PhD thesis, University of Auckland.

Innes, Bronwen. 2010. "'Well, that's why I asked the question sir': *Well* as a discourse marker in court." *Language in Society* 39 (1): 95–117.

Lane, Chris. 1988. *Language on Trial*. PhD thesis, University of Auckland.

The Law Reform Commission of New South Wales. 2012. *Report on Jury Directions*.

Mellinkoff, David. 1963. *The Language of the Law*. Boston, MA: Little, Brown.

Miller, Jim, and Regina Weinert. 2009. *Spontaneous Spoken Language*. Oxford: Oxford University Press.

Nation, Paul. 2002. *Range and Frequency: Programs for Windows based PCs*. Wellington: Victoria University of Wellington.

New Zealand Law Commission Report. 2001. *Jury Trials in New Zealand – A Survey of Jurors*. 69.

Ogloff, James R. P., Jonathan Clough, Jane Goodman-Delahunty, and Warren Young. 2006. *The Jury Project: Stage 1 – A Survey of Australian and New Zealand Judges*. Melbourne: Australian Institute of Judicial Administration.

Schegloff, Emmanuel. 1993. "Reflections on quantification in the study of conversation." *Research on Language and Social Interaction* 26 (1): 99–128.

Schiffrin, Deborah. 1987. *Discourse Markers*. Cambridge: Cambridge University Press.

Stubbs, Michael. 1996. *Text and Corpus Analysis*. Oxford: Blackwell.

Stygall, Gail. 1994. *Trial Language*. Amsterdam: John Benjamins.

Tiersma, Peter. 2010. "Redrafting California's jury instructions." In *The Routledge Handbook of Forensic Linguistics*, ed. by Malcolm Coulthard and Alison Johnston, 251–264. London: Routledge.

Tinsley, Yvette. 2001. "Juror decision-making: A look inside the jury room." In *British Society of Criminology Conference: Selected Proceedings*, Vol. 4, ed. by Roger Tarling, 1464–1488. London: British Society of Criminology.

Young, Warren, Neil Cameron, and Yvette Tinsley. 1999. *Juries in Criminal Trials – Part Two – A Summary of the Research Findings*. New Zealand Law Commission preliminary paper 37, vol. 2. Wellington: The Law Commission.

Chapter 8

Developing a linguistically informed approach to police interviewing

Nicci MacLeod, ORCID NUMBER 0000–0002–6642–5509
Kate Haworth, ORCID NUMBER 0000–0002–3446–8838

Introduction

This chapter focuses on discursive patterns in interactions between police inter-viewers (hereafter IRs) and interviewees (hereafter IEs), be the latter victims, witnesses or suspects. We describe a novel police interviewer training course we have developed and piloted under the British Association of Applied Linguistics (BAAL)'s 'Applying Linguistics' fund. We took the training package, grounded firmly in sociolinguistic theory, on the road to three English police forces. Our innovative activity takes as its point of departure the observation that the appli-cation of social scientific research has "traditionally been characterised in terms of the authority of social scientists' definitions, where the researcher possesses the expertise . . . and judges the adequacy of participants' knowledge against that expertise" (Wiggins and Hepburn 2007: 290). In contrast to this, our activity focuses firstly on explicating the knowledge and skills of practitioners for the benefit of their own professional practice, highlighting areas of good practice as well as instigating a general awareness of the effects of particular discursive choices. Further to this, we involve the participants – practicing police IRs – at every stage of the process. Since language is the primary medium through which the daily working activities of organisations are conducted (Drew and Heritage 1992), it is clear that sociolinguistic research has an important role to play in the development of best practice. We hope that our efforts will encourage other sociolinguistic researchers to view the police service and similar organisations as potential sites for meaningful collaboration and engagement.

If we take *impact* to mean the demonstrable outcomes of the *application* of social research to social problems, it is a fairly straightforward matter to categorise the activity described here as achieving impact. However, it is worth keeping in mind that many definitions of what constitutes a 'social problem' are guided by politi-cal and governmental objectives (Willig 1999), rather than genuine concern for human wellbeing. In our original research projects on which this activity is based (Haworth 2009; MacLeod 2010), we were both firmly guided by a commit-ment to raising awareness of sociolinguistic issues among legal and police practi-tioners, and, in turn, positive change in professional practices. The production of meaningful outcomes for police IRs, consequently leading to improved conditions for individuals who encounter the police, has thus been high on the agenda from the outset. Through engaging with police officers and allowing the research to be guided and adapted according to their professional requirements, our activity represents, we hope, the best method for attempts at securing human wellbeing.

It should be noted that the relationship between critical analysis and progressive practice is fraught with difficulties. As highlighted by Willig (1999), even scientific observations cannot be detached and uninvolved, and having originally taken a distinctively Critical Discourse Analytical approach to the research, it was necessary for us to adapt this approach in order to engage in a meaningful two-way process with practitioners. Thus, the approach we take here is in line with Roberts (2003), who argues that applied linguists can and should intervene, but that "we need to do it collaboratively and reflexively working with other professionals from the initial design stage through to mutual critique and evaluation" (Roberts 2003: 147).

In this chapter, we discuss the relevance of various theories of language and communication to the police interview context, but more importantly the application and impact of this knowledge within the context of collaboratively designed IR training materials. We collected feedback from all our participants, and this forms an integral part of the activities.

Identifying the problem, and the role of sociolinguistics

In England and Wales it has been claimed that the Police and Criminal Evidence Act (PACE) 1984, and the associated implementation of the PEACE[1] interviewing model, led to a significant decrease in miscarriages of justice occurring as a result of poorly conducted suspect interviews. However, it is further claimed that PACE had little impact on the interviewing of victims and witnesses, which remained flawed on the grounds that many officers assumed that the interviewing of a co-operative and competent adult witness required little specialist skill (Savage and Milne 2007). The interviewing of suspects is now guided by the Conversation Management model (Shepherd and Griffiths 2013), while the interviewing of significant witnesses is guided by the Enhanced Cognitive Interview (ECI) model (Milne and Bull 1999; Milne 2004). These approaches to investigative interviewing differ vastly from the Reid technique, favoured in the US and a number of other countries, which is characterised by the encouragement of coercive interrogation, and lacks the evidence base from which the methods discussed here have been developed. However, some of the techniques recommended within the UK models do have some equivalence with what is termed the 'information gathering' phase of the Reid interview.

While all attempts at improving the process are to be welcomed, there is a notable absence of linguistic research drawn on in the current training programmes. Furthermore, it has been pointed out that there exists a general lack of consistency amongst academics and practitioners about relevant categories for analysing police interview discourse (see, for example, Oxburgh et al. 2010). Current training programmes have neglected to address some of the issues surrounding the conflict that arises when IRs attempt to engage in the recommended 'personalised' interaction, which must simultaneously fulfil its institutional role of gathering potential criminal evidence. Furthermore, there has been little acknowledgement that IRs accomplish a far more diverse set of tasks in the interview room than simply 'questioning.' The approaches informing the current training programmes might also be criticised on the grounds of their assumption of a subjective/objective distinction. The emphasis on adopting strategies which minimise the introduction of 'biased' information implies that the task of isolating one version of events as neutral and objective can be carried out relatively easily. This is not a perspective shared by the majority of researchers working within a discourse-analytic paradigm (see Auburn et al. 1999).

It could be argued that our activity risks further empowering the dominant group in a context which has been widely noted to have significant potential for disempowering IEs. Why are we not reaching out to IEs and empowering *them* to develop awareness and resistance strategies for dealing with potentially coercive questioning? The answer is that a comparable, accessible group of witnesses, victims or suspects is simply not available, and the process of assembling such a group – for example through police contact – is fraught with ethical and practical difficulties. At any rate, as maintained by Wodak (1996), there are a number of domains in which changes to discursive practices have the potential to advance the interests of the powerless. Thus, we take up the credible counter-argument that the most effective way of assisting vulnerable IEs is to ensure that interviews are conducted in the most informed manner and that their voices are heard. Working with practitioners is the most effective method of ensuring that the insights arising from the sociolinguistic research – issues of power, dominance, negotiation and so on – are put to meaningful use in improving the police interview process. This is in line with the position set out by Wiggins and Hepburn (2007) that discursive intervention can be used to provide practitioners with a more analytically informed set of resources, using real-life examples to highlight features of good practice as well as the complexities of how IRs' goals are achieved. Of course, as Willig (1999) points out, the effectiveness of this kind of engagement depends upon the willingness of the relevant professionals to co-operate: "reform . . . must be acceptable to those whose power is grounded in the status quo" (Willig 1999: 17).

It has been noted in the past that discourse analysts have generally been reluctant to move beyond critical commentary to active engagement with social and institutional practices, owing in part to an "acute awareness of the dangers associated with a clear commitment to particular policies and practices" (Willig 1999: 1). Few discourse analysts have addressed the issue of application, and even fewer have tackled the formulation of concrete proposals for social interventions (but see, e.g., Roberts 2003). The approach we originally took was committed to exposing the ideologically laden nature of discourse and its role in maintaining unequal power relations – that is to say, a critical approach. But we wondered: how could we go about reconciling this agenda with our aspiration to instigate positive change in institutional practices? It was clear that remaining 'critical' while maintaining close engagement with practitioners was a significant challenge. In this chapter we discuss how we overcame these challenges, and we encourage other researchers to consider tackling these obstacles as well.

Like many types of institutional talk, police interview discourse can be characterised as goal-oriented, with restrictions on the turn-taking patterns and allowable contributions of participants, and as being structured and asymmetrical (Drew and Heritage 1992). Police interview interaction has attracted the attention of discourse analysts primarily interested in the effects on discursive patterns of this obviously asymmetrical distribution of power and the goal-oriented nature of institutional talk. Research has also focused on ways in which such relationships and purposes are managed, negotiated, and resisted at the local level (see, e.g., Haworth 2006; Newbury and Johnson 2006). In interviews with both suspects and witnesses, it is generally the IR who controls the interaction, possessing as they do the authority, invested in them by the institution they represent, to constrain IEs' type and length of turn, and to control the topics discussed. Recently in England and Wales, however, there has been a move towards a more IE-led style of interviewing, in which IRs are encouraged to "transfer control" (Milne and Bull 1999), ask fewer questions, and allow IEs more space to give their account of events. The police interview is thus a site of tension between the traditional institutional goals of such an interaction, and these more recent recommendations for personalisation. A further clash arises from the mismatch of agendas between participants – in carrying out familiar day-to-day work, professional IRs display awareness and orientation to institutional practices and priorities, while IEs do not generally possess such awareness and bring conflicting sets of expectations to the interaction (see Stokoe and Edwards 2008; Haworth 2013).

Previous linguistic research in the area of police interviews has commented on the discursive effects of the interaction's dual role and context, and explored numerous aspects of IRs' talk as they pursue their institutional goal of fixing the 'facts' of the case 'on the record' for the benefit of the future 'overhearing' audience (i.e. the Court) (e.g. Heydon 2005; Johnson 2008; Stokoe and Edwards 2008; Haworth 2013). There has also been interest in the processes by which a 'police preferred' version of events is produced as an alternative to the suspect's version, with the observation that this broadly corresponds to fitting reported events into the legal framework of an offence (e.g. Auburn et al. 1999; Heydon 2003; Benneworth 2010; Haworth 2010).

Overview of the research

The original research on which the current activity is based relied upon England and Wales police archive interview data – video recordings of interviews with women reporting rape (MacLeod 2010), and audio recordings of interviews with suspects (Haworth 2009), recorded as a routine part of police investigations (cf. Dickinson, this volume; Innes, this volume, on the use of audio-visual recording methods). We felt that the investigative interview was a site that had the potential to yield rich insights into the relevant professional practices, and provided a strong springboard for effective attempts at influencing these practices.

MacLeod's (2010) study investigated the discursive patterns of interactions between police IRs and women reporting rape in significant witness interviews. Data in the form of video-recorded interviews were obtained from an English police force for the purposes of the study. The data were analysed using a multi-method approach, in line with Heydon (2005), incorporating tools from a number of approaches to discourse to reveal patterns of interactional control, negotiation, and interpretation. The study adopted a critical approach, which is to say that as well as describing discursive patterns, it explained them in light of the discourse processes involved in the production and consumption of police interview talk, and commented on the relationship between these discourse processes and the social context in which they occur. A central focus of the study was how IRs draw on specific interactional resources to shape IEs' accounts in particular ways, and this was discussed in relation to the institutional role of the significant witness interview.

The research established that IRs have access to an array of linguistic resources, which they potentially draw on in order to (re)construct the events that are reported, and to exert their influence over the final account. Far from fully and accurately representing the IEs' stated position, 'final versions' often report only on those elements of the account deemed significant by the police. Since what is treated as significant in the treatment of rape cases has repeatedly been shown to rely heavily on unsupported cultural assumptions about rape and its causes (Moore 2009; Antaki et al. 2015; Haworth 2015), these practices have serious implications for both the quality of the evidence and for victim care. The findings of the study indicated that there are a number of issues to be addressed in terms of the training currently provided to officers at Level 2 of the Professionalising Investigation Programme (PIP) (NPIA 2009) who intend to conduct significant witness interviews. Furthermore, a need was identified to bring the linguistic and discursive processes of negotiation and transformation identified by the study to the attention of the justice system as a whole.

The training materials are also based on Haworth's (2009) study (see also Haworth 2010, 2013), in which she analysed the current role of police-suspect interview discourse in the England and Wales criminal justice system, with a focus on its use as evidence. A central premise is that the interview should be viewed not as an isolated and self-contained discursive event, but as one link in a chain of events which together constitute the criminal justice process. The research examined two aspects: first, the format changes undergone by interview data after the interview has taken place; and second, how the other links in the chain – both before and after the interview – affect the interview-room interaction itself. It thus examined the police interview as a multi-format, multi-purpose, and multi-audience mode of discourse. An interdisciplinary and multi-method discourse-analytic approach was taken to a corpus of police-suspect interviews. The analysis revealed several causes for concern, both in aspects of the interaction in the interview room and in the subsequent treatment of interview material as evidence. Overall, the study demonstrated the need for increased awareness within the criminal justice system of the many linguistic factors affecting interview evidence.

While we acknowledge that the many and varied approaches taken to the data within these two different studies represent differing philosophical frameworks, our concern here is what each of them can offer to practitioners seeking to evaluate their own professional performance. We therefore present the concepts and categories to the end user much like an analytical toolkit.

A sample analysis: Footing and audience design

By way of example, we present here a snapshot of the types of analyses undertaken in these studies which provided important insight into the strategies adopted by interviewing officers in order to achieve the intended goals of the investigative interview.

The concepts of audience design (Bell 1984) and footing (Goffman 1981) relate to participants' alignment to a message, and orientation to particular roles, either as receivers or producers of talk. As producers, participants can present themselves as the Principal, or the person responsible for the content of the utterance; as the Author, or the creator of the utterance, "the agent who scripts the lines" (Goffman 1981: 226); or as the Animator, or the physical producer of the utterance. MacLeod (2010) noted that an examination of the roles occupied by participants in the police interview provided a sound basis for identifying the phases of the interview, but that more importantly it had implications for ensuring the interaction is both IE-led and adequately personalised, as per ECI guidance.

The effect of the intended *recipient* of talk has been a concern of sociolinguists for some time, and Bell's (1984) model, accounting for various categories of audience, remains influential. Haworth (2013) demonstrates that the police interview is a poor fit for the model, and that the IR and IE often orientate to different audiences, with potentially serious consequences. Extract 1 demonstrates the significance of these models for police interview discourse.

Extract 1

1	IR:	[°right°] (.) and where do you live Angela?=
	IE:	=eleven Clearmount Road.
	IR:	okay • hh (2.5) so this intervie:w is commenced at ten thirty four
	IE:	• shih
5	IR:	(3) last night about (.) seven o'clock (.7) e:rm which'll've been the: (.7) eighteenth of May (.) two thousand and seven >you were at your home address< weren't you.=
	IE:	=yeah.
	IR:	and what happe:ned? after that did you go out that night?
10	IE:	yeah (.) I was getting ready (.7) and I went to my friend's house at Field Park (.) and then we went to the town. • shih

The extract begins as the IR is eliciting a list of personal details from the IE. This in itself reveals the IR's orientation to the institutional context – it seems safe to assume that she is not recording these details for her own purposes, but rather due to institutional requirements. On line 3, the IR uses a metalinguistic comment to begin the 'interview proper,' a clear indication that what has gone before is not considered to belong in this category. The passive construction – use of the word "commenced" – and the specificity of the time reference are all typical of "policespeak" (see, e.g., Fox 1993), indicating that the IR is merely animating a message authored by the police institution. On lines 6–7, the IR appears to shift her audience orientation part way through the utterance, repairing "last night" – adequate only for those positioned within the same temporal frame – to "the eighteenth of May (.) two thousand and seven" – demonstrating an orientation to an absent addressee. The IR misrepresents her knowledge state with the questions on line 9 – it seems safe to assume that she is already aware that the evening began at the IE's home address, and that she then went out. Rather than seeking unknown information, these questions are designed to elicit confirmation on the record from the IE (see Stokoe and Edwards 2008 for more on "silly questions" in police interviews). There are obvious reasons for these discursive strategies when one considers the institutional role of the interview, and these reasons are familiar to practitioners, as evidenced by trainees' responses to our examples (see below). However, we encourage our trainees to question the extent to which the purpose of such utterances is made clear to IEs, and to consider the potential effects of these discursive peculiarities on IEs' experiences of the investigative interview.

What we achieved

From the findings of the projects described above, we designed a one-day training course with the aim of explicating a wide range of discursive practices relevant to the police interview context. The process of transforming our research findings into useful training materials was rather a daunting one, and required us first to identify the key theoretical concepts that offered demonstrable insight into interview interaction. These included audience design and footing as discussed above. We then identified extracts from our own police interview data that exemplified these concepts. Our focus was on encouraging IRs to reflect on their own linguistic behaviour in the interview room – we did *not* intend to deliver a 'how to' guide for best practice interviewing. We began the day with a brief overview of the discipline of Forensic Linguistics, where we explained our areas of interest and the kinds of input forensic linguists have had into the investigative process. We find this provides a good grounding for our subsequent discussion of how linguists' input can be put to meaningful use in the interview room. As well as the broad area of police interviewing, linguists have assisted the police with a wide array of tasks, including training online undercover investigators and offering expertise in cases of disputed authorship of forensic texts. These types of input might prove fruitful avenues to pursue for linguistic researchers seeking to engage with the police in achieving impact.

This session was followed by input on suspect interviewing delivered by Dr Haworth. This session introduced the basics of certain concepts emerging from approaches to discourse that have provided useful insight into police interview interactions, including turn-taking, speech act theory, and audience design. Crucially, each theory and analytical concept was illustrated with reference to real police-suspect interview data, including audio recordings. Dr MacLeod provided the next session of input, which introduced concepts including footing and formulations – again illustrated with real examples, this time from significant witness interviews. We delivered content through a number of methods – lecture-style sessions were supplemented with group discussions and hands-on practical data analysis tasks. Attendees were encouraged to participate at will, either with questions, comments or examples from their own professional practice. The final session of the day was devoted to gathering feedback from the course attendees on our training. They were asked to provide this through two methods: an individual written feedback form; and a one-hour focus group (in quoted feedback below we refer to these as FF and FG respectively).

Most importantly, the input from attendees on the first course guided our design of the second course, and the feedback provided in response to the second course guided our design of the third. Feedback collected at the third course will be pivotal to the design of the next research project, and perhaps more crucially to the development and adaptation of the training to ensure that it is as relevant and useful as possible to practitioners. It is in this way that we can ensure the continuing active involvement of our participants.

At the time of writing, we have completed this activity with three English police forces – South Yorkshire, Sussex, and Greater Manchester – with a total of fifty-two participants. These course attendees were mainly Detective Constable or Detective Sergeant in rank, performing a wide range of roles including on the Adult Protection Team, the Public Protection Unit, the Serious Organised Crime Unit, the Major Investigations Team, and a number of Investigative Trainers. Participants' experience of investigative interviewing ranged from two to thirteen years. All participants were trained to at least the "core functions" section of PIP Level 2 (formerly known as Tier 2), meaning they were qualified to interview victims/witnesses and/or suspects "in relation to serious and complex investigations." Many were trained to the "specialist roles" section of PIP Level 2 (formerly known as Tier 3), meaning they were qualified to conduct "specialist interviews" with victims/witnesses and/or suspects (ACPO 2009: 8). At one force, the one-day input was incorporated into a three-week Advanced Interviewing course, while at the others it served as a standalone session for Advanced suspect and witness IRs, who self-selected to attend.

Impact achieved during the process

First, we wish to emphasise that all feedback has been anonymised and we obtained consent from participants to use their contributions in published work. Please note that we have transcribed the focus groups in such a manner as to make the *content* as clear as possible for readers. They are therefore not transcribed to the same CA standards as the police interview extracts described above. Meanwhile, written feedback has been transcribed exactly as it appeared on the handwritten forms.

Overall, the input from participants painted a picture suggesting that sociolinguistic research had a number of important contributions to make to interview training models. While a small number of participants commented that they perceived some overlap between what we presented and previous standard training delivered by psychologists, many more indicated that the input had enabled a fresh and novel insight into their own interviewing practices, and had alerted them to new areas that might warrant their attention in future. For example:

> It has provided a different perspective, provided new concepts, and an improved understanding. . . . It was also an excellent mix of academic and practitioner based knowledge and experience.
>
> [Course Attendee, Force 2, FF]

> More than anything, it is nice to know what a linguist makes of it, rather than training written by police officers.
>
> [Course Attendee, Force 3, FF]

These responses bode well for sociolinguistic researchers who are considering engaging with the police service or similar – there is clear potential for achieving impact in this area.

One clear theme that emerged from the feedback was that we had succeeded in pitching our input as being more concerned with explicating the processes at work than with making recommendations for best practice:

> I think it's an awareness and an understanding that you need to know earlier in your career that this could have an influence on what you're doing. I don't think you need to know in great detail but you need to have an awareness of it is what I'm trying to say.
>
> [Course attendee, Force 1, FG]

While this was wholly in line with our intentions, a number of participants indicated that in fact what they sought was indeed recommendations for good interviewing practice. Asked for their suggestions, many responses reflected a concern for more concrete guidance:

> More . . . good and bad practice comparisons.
>
> [DC, CID, Force 1, FF]

> Outlining different styles of interviewing and what potentially has gone wrong and what was particularly good.
>
> [DC, SOCU, Force 2, FF]

It is important to note that we do not intend to translate this feedback into a course geared towards offering interviewing guidance, as this is simply not in line with how we position ourselves as linguistic researchers in the field. Rather, the aim is to continue developing the materials with these participants' concerns in mind. We will endeavour to continually challenge attendees to consider the effects of alternative choices.

In terms of the methods of delivery, there was near-consensus at the first force in requesting more practical examples at the expense of some of the more theoretical input (cf. Innes, this volume, on preferences among judges for practical examples):

> Much as I found the theory interesting I think a half day front loaded approach is not long enough to fully grasp ideas. Some practical work would help cement theories into practice.
>
> [DC, PPU, Force 1, FF]

With this in mind, we endeavoured to incorporate more practical examples into the materials, although compromising on theoretical content while maintaining the necessary focus on describing IR behaviour in sociolinguistic terms was understandably challenging. There are obvious benefits in participants observing what actually happens in interviews (even though it has not thus far been possible to have them observing their own behaviour – this is discussed later). Feedback from the second course, designed to incorporate feedback from the first, indicated that we had gone some way to redressing the balance, with suggestions for *how* the practical examples could be used, as opposed to requests for more of them:

> Would be useful to hear more interviews, i.e. tone and pauses, rather than see transcripts.
>
> [DC, CID, Force 2, FF]

> Get actors to read out your interviews – adds bit of variety.
>
> [DC, MCT, Force 2, FF]

The following sections detail how participants responded to particular areas of our sociolinguistic input, and how this input has had a demonstrable impact on participants' professional practice.

Professional language

The peculiarity of IRs speaking on behalf of the police institution, and addressing future audiences not present in the interview room, appeared to be a new consideration for the participants, including trainers:

> We say things like 'at some point this interview may be listened to,' but we don't actually analyse it – it takes academics to come in and say let's analyse

that process what's happening and what yo- what you're doing in the interview to think through those cheap words that you say to people like you know 'this interview at some point might be listened to, so for the purpose of the tape, bla bla bla bla bla.

[Trainer, Force 1, FG]

The idea of the interview as a complex beast trying to communicate to the potentially vulnerable ill-educated and to the courts at the same time is a useful concept.

[DC, SOCU, Force 2, FF]

These participants, and others, indicated to us that our explication of the processes at work when IRs orient to absent audiences is highly valuable for them as they seek to understand their own behaviour. Both the extracts above demonstrate that our input on Audience Design had a strong and immediate impact on how these professionals view their role and practices. There are clearly important practical implications in taking established sociolinguistic theories outside the realm of academia.

Similarly, the seemingly obvious (to an outsider) negative effects of over-use of professional vocabulary for the process of building rapport had apparently only become clear to some participants following our input:

One of the biggest learning points that's come up for me is to talk like a normal person. And I think that's more important and I think if you had that basic understanding earlier on it wouldn't be such a big issue at either level that you could be trained at later on.

[Course Attendee, Force 1, FG]

The other point to emerge from the above extract is the level at which we should be offering sociolinguistic training. There appeared to be agreement that practitioners would benefit from engaging with the material at an earlier stage of their careers than that at which we were involved:

If at Tier 2 we'd've been doing things in more plain English we wouldn't have had the week 1 we've had, which we spent all of week 1 trying to undo all the really bad habits that we've got into from years of practice at Tier 2 so perhaps that would have been a more natural progression.

[Course Attendee, Force 1, FG]

We revisit this concern later in the chapter. The areas discussed here have clearly emerged as salient for participants' own practices. Our input increased awareness of unfamiliar sociolinguistic phenomena, which has had an obvious impact not only on how these professionals view their own role, but also on the way in which they view the training process as a whole.

Speech act theory, or what is said versus what is meant

As mentioned earlier, the standard training currently offered makes clear distinctions between *types* of questions, with the distinction being based in the main on grammatical form. Our training highlights utterance function, foregrounding the prolificacy of indirectness and reinforcing the matter of locution not necessarily mapping straightforwardly onto illocution. Or, as we presented it to the course attendees, 'form' versus 'function.'

Once more, exploring this theory allowed for fresh insight into strategies routinely adopted by IRs and equipped participants to reflect critically on existing training models that they had previously followed. In response to the question, "What parts of today's training will be most useful for your own interviewing practice?", one participant specified:

> Use of pragmatics – that different forms of an expression can have a common function, and that 5WH is not necessarily the be all and end all.
> [DC, Advanced Suspect Interviewer, FF, Force 2]

'5WH' refers to a category of question delineated in the current ECI training, which neglects to acknowledge the wide range of interactional tasks a question beginning with 'Wh-' might potentially accomplish.

> I think when you talked as well about the three different questions that are actually all the same question. I think that's really relevant, because you can quite easi- before coming here I didn't really give any real thought to how I phrased a question, or really even think about what I was getting from that question in many ways, and I think that- the way you demonstrated that with three things was quite- made sense to me.
> [Course Attendee, FG, Force 1]

Discourse markers and formulations, or what is said versus how it's said

Discourse markers, or "non obligatory utterance-initial items that function in relation to ongoing talk" (Schiffrin 2003: 57), particularly as prefaces to questions, can be highly revealing of IRs' orientations to the ongoing talk in a police interview context. For example, while prefacing a question with 'and . . .' links it to a preceding question-answer pair and gives the question a routine character (Heritage and Sorjonen 1994), prefacing with 'but . . .' indicates something problematic in the preceding answer and invites a second attempt. Thus, this is a feature which can be highly revealing of IRs' attitudes towards what they have heard; but this had not been explicated to these trainees before our input.

Now, I'll give real consideration to whether I say 'and' or 'but'.

> [Course Attendee, Force 1, FG]

The significance of these choices was evidently not as clear to all participants, with one attendee characterising them as idiolectal rather than strategic or revealing of a particular orientation. In response to the question of what had been *least* useful about the content, s/he responded:

> Discourse markers as we already learnt about power and control of inter-viewer and these can be mannerisms.

> [Course Attendee, Force 2, FF]

Thus, it seems there may still be some way to go in terms of providing input in this area that is meaningful to all participants.

On a related note, the marker *so* is often indicative of what has been labelled *formulation*, i.e. utterances that display which interpretation of a prior utterance is being taken up by the recipient, that *can* then be confirmed or disconfirmed by the original speaker (although given the asymmetry inherent in the police interview setting, it is questionable how far the possibility for disconfirmation is taken up). The preferred response is a confirmation and this is compounded by the fact that formulations are an effective means of preserving the original speaker's principalship for the utterance – to disconfirm a formulation is thus akin to disagreeing with oneself. Many formulations are structurally identifiable by their third turn position, but also by a recurrent syntactic form [(so) + you + verbal/mental process token] (Thornborrow 2002: 97).

Formulations, as explained by Heydon (2003), are an interactional resource frequently drawn on by police officers as a means of negotiating a 'preferred version,' and have a particularly controlling function since they are "a way of leading participants into accepting one's own version of what has transpired" (Heritage and Watson 1979: 136). Formulating necessarily involves the foregrounding of particular aspects of the narrative at the expense of others. Furthermore, it has been shown that formulations can and often do include aspects of narrative which were not introduced by the IE (Heydon 2003: 90). Asked what parts of the input will be most useful for their own interviewing practice, one participant responded:

> Formulating as inaccurate formulations are dangerous.

> [Course Attendee, Force 2, FF]

If we assume that this respondent has the same idea of what constitutes 'danger' in this context, i.e. undue IR influence, then the impact of our input is self-evident. It is encouraging to see that participants have not only been made aware of new concepts and new ways of viewing their interviewing behaviour, but that they have grasped the idea that this is not simply a case of distinguishing between 'good' and 'bad' strategies to adopt – formulating is not poor practice *per se,* and has many advantages – but an understanding of the risks as well as the benefits can surely only lead to enhancing the skill of the IR.

Subsequent impact, accessibility and dissemination

In future, we plan to return to the three forces at which the training was delivered in order to follow up on the extent to which our input has truly influenced professional practice. However, the feedback gathered through written questionnaires and focus groups indicates a high level of enthusiasm and intention to consider linguistic and discursive matters more carefully in the future, both in relation to their own practices and, for the more senior participants, when feeding back on others' interviews:

> Pragmatics and police interviews, impact on witness/suspect – **can now consider this further in planning stage**. Being made aware that consideration for forensic linguistics can continually improve your interview **and I will consider this when I evaluate any future interviews**.
> [DC MIT, Force 1, FF] (our emphasis)

As well as disseminating the findings of this research to numerous academic conferences, we have been involved with the International Investigative Interviewing Research Group (iIIRG) since its inception in 2007. The iIIRG's membership consists of academics and practitioners at varying levels, including specialist interview advisors, members of the College of Policing, and members of the Association of Chief Police Officers interview steering group, which is responsible for national interviewing policy. It is through involvement with this organisation that we were able to foster the strong working relationships and gain the support that allowed for the training activities to take place; and it is through continued involvement that we hope to design and deliver our revised training as an ongoing venture. We would strongly encourage sociolinguistic researchers with an interest in institutional language to seek connections with this iIIRG, which offers unparalleled opportunities for collaboration and the achievement of impact.

At iIIRG annual conferences we have presented on: narrative transformation (2009); footing in the police interview (2010); audience design (2012); and the treatment of IEs' excuses and justifications (2012). We have also raised awareness through contribution to a four-day course entitled *Linguistic and Psychological Techniques for Sexual Crime Investigation,* co-hosted by the University of Birmingham and Aston University in April 2012, the majority of whose delegates were senior police officers involved in training. Several CPD training events for police IRs have taken place at Aston University, with more events scheduled for the near future. Related publications have also appeared in practitioner journals such as *The British Journal of Forensic Practice* (e.g. MacLeod 2011).

While the ethos and activities of iIIRG represent a unique opportunity for academics and practitioners to engage with each other in a mutually beneficial and genuinely productive relationship, the practitioner membership is largely restricted to relatively senior policing representatives. Dissemination to iIIRG in no way ensures dissemination to professionals at the front line of policing. Likewise, as we discussed above, the sociolinguistic training has so far been restricted to advanced IRs. How should we broaden the scope of our activity to reach the lower ranks? It is clear that this is a concern shared by many of our participants:

I think it would be better delivered at Tier 2 interviewers, increase awareness and teach good practise from start.

[DC, MCT, Force 2, FF]

It's alright saying we're at the higher level now but in our force certainly Tier 2s can quite happily interview rapes, and a lot of other serious top end offences on a regular basis. It's not the Tier 3s that would be doing it.

[Course Attendee, Force 1, FG]

The Apollo units that predominantly deal with sexual offences but rapes in particular that the lead interviewers are PCs and they tend to be at the moment young in service . . . so if it was my job as a Tier 3 I would go and I would sit as second interviewer, which doesn't really sit well with me and we've got a lead interviewer that's got no knowledge and that is crucial evidence it's- and we're not getting the best evidence and- I think we're failing before we're even starting really.

[Course Attendee, Force 1, FG]

There were also suggestions for targeting the training even further down the line, to officers interviewing at Level 1 of the Professionalising Investigation Programme (formerly Tier 1); that is, officers who interview victims and witnesses and/or suspects in relation to "priority and volume investigations" (ACPO 2009: 8). On the other hand, others expressed concern that, pitched at its current level of detail, our training risked posing difficulties for IRs at a lower level:

Maybe it's a bit more of a cultural thing early on I think the input we've had today is relevant at this level and I don't think- if you tried giving a probationer that it would just blow their mind cos they're trying to learn too much.

[Trainer, Force 1, FG]

It is clear, then, that given our plans for the future (as outlined in the next section), something that will require careful consideration is how – and indeed whether – we adapt the material to suit a less advanced audience. This will be impossible to accomplish without the sustained input of our police colleagues.

Future impact

In line with Roberts' suggestion that applied linguists are "more likely to have an impact by trying to change practice with practitioners rather than through grand attempts at engineering policy change" (2003: 135), the activity reported here is geared towards engaging closely with interviewing practitioners in a bottom-up process of improving practice. However, there is also the potential, through our ties with iIIRG, to have a much larger impact on national training in the future, just as psychology has done with national police IR training models. One participant commented that the content should be:

> Rolled out in some form in general interview training to police.
>
> [DS, APT, Force 2, FF]

Comments such as this suggest that practitioners see great potential in the contribution of linguistics to nationwide interviewing training models. According to this participant and a number of others, our input is required at a more basic level than that at which we delivered – the level of 'general interview training,' i.e. fairly recent recruits to the police service, involved in interviewing in volume crime investigations. If this were to come to fruition, it would constitute further tangible impact of our research. Police work has, in recent times, become more amenable to the input of academics, so it would seem timely for more sociolinguists to become involved in contributing to good practice through mutually beneficial engagement such as that described in this chapter. On this basis, we have plans underway to produce a bid for further research funding in order to develop and extend the activities undertaken so far.

We cannot have a clear idea of how the materials are likely to be developed until we commence research collaboration with police partners (nor indeed until the analysis of the research reported here has been finalised). We can, however, glean some potential developments from the contributions of participants in the current activity.

> To come on this course everyone's got to do an assessment interview and you've all got to assess it yourselves and you all hand in an interview and a transcript mostly so it's like- we'll assess you to bring you on cos- everybody here's been assessed so they all come on the course assessed but why can't we not then just send you that transcript I mean you don't have to use a whole lot of it you'd just be looking at a bit of it and then it sort of personalises what you've then done.
>
> [Trainer, Force 1, FG]

This comment, and the general consensus that subsequently unfolded in the room, suggest that participants are keen to observe and reflect on *their own* use of particular discursive strategies. The feeling seems to be that this would enhance the impact of merely seeing these strategies in action in the interview rooms of other police colleagues remote in time and space. The suggestion in this extract is that transcripts from genuine interviews that course attendees had previously conducted be forwarded to us in advance of the session. We could then analyse these and incorporate extracts into the course materials. This suggestion was made several times and it seems fairly intuitive that this will allow for a deeper understanding of the relationship between sociolinguistic theory and individual professional development. The question of whether this is a realistic course of action for us, given the time constraints and the unpredictability of the data that we would actually receive, is the subject of ongoing debate, and we continue to consider ways in which this idea could be incorporated. One possibility is that attendees look at their own historical interviews as a hands-on analysis task, identifying how the various theories are relevant to their practice and reporting back to the group. In any case, our future training will always be guided by the participants and their own experiences.

Conclusion

In this chapter we have demonstrated the potential for sociolinguistic research to achieve wide-reaching and meaningful impact for professional practice. We repackaged findings from our discourse analytical research into interaction in police interviews as training materials, by using real examples from police interviews to exemplify key analytical points. Our aim from the outset was to explicate for IRs the strategies they adopt during interviews and to demonstrate the effects of these choices. We elicited input from the course participants and have used this in an ongoing process of evaluation and development.

One important issue to note is that our activities have been on a very small scale; the challenge of making the findings both accessible and relevant to all professionals undertaking investigative interviews cannot be overestimated. It is one thing to engage a handful of enthusiastic training co-ordinators – who by their very involvement with iIIRG are obviously accommodating to the potential for academic research to inform investigative practice. It is quite another to penetrate those areas of the police service that have yet to acknowledge the mutually beneficial potential of such collaboration. The 43 territorial police forces of England and Wales are each responsible for their own training provision, and thus a highly productive relationship with Greater Manchester Police is no predictor of success with other forces. It may be too much to expect that the resounding success of our collaborative efforts will either trickle down to the lower ranks, or spread out to colleagues in less progressive forces.

That said, we have identified a clear requirement both for more sociolinguistic research in the area of police interviewing and for more widespread engagement with police practitioners in general. Within the scope of forensic linguistics, there are myriad opportunities for engagement between sociolinguistic researchers and the police. As Roberts (2003: 132) notes:

> [I]t is not easy to work out what difference our research has made to those outside our world, but at least we should be asking ourselves the question and contemplating the conditions which might produce a satisfying answer for both the professional groups we work with and ourselves.

We hope that we can build on these first steps and these initial questions and work towards valuable outcomes for all parties.

Acknowledgements

We would like to thank the British Association of Applied Linguistics' 'Applying Linguistics' fund for recognising the potential of this project and providing us with the funding required to carry it out. We would also like to thank Sussex Police, South Yorkshire Police and Greater Manchester Police for their continuing enthusiasm, and for the attention and active engagement of the trainees and trainers at all three forces. We look forward to being involved with these organisations for many years to come. Lastly we would like to express our gratitude to the editors, and the two anonymous reviewers, for all their work in helping us to refine this chapter.

Note

1 A mnemonic for the recommended structure of any interview, PEACE stands for *Plan and Prepare, Engage and Explain, obtain an Account, Closure* and *Evaluation*.

References

ACPO (Association of Chief Police Officers). 2009. "National investigative interviewing strategy." Accessed 26 March 2015. Available from: http://wayback.archive.org/web/20140701170443/http://www.acpo.police.uk/documents/crime/2009/200901CRINSI01.pdf.

Antaki, Charles, Emma Richardson, Elizabeth Stokoe, and Sara Willott. 2015. "Police interviews with vulnerable people alleging sexual assault: Probing inconsistency and questioning conduct." *Journal of Sociolinguistics* 19 (3): 328–350.

Auburn, Timothy, Susan Lea, and Susan Drake. 1999. "'It's your opportunity to be truthful': Disbelief, mundane reasoning and the investigation of crime." In *Applied Discourse Analysis: Social and Psychological Interventions*, ed. by Carla Willig, 44–65. Buckingham: Open University Press.

Bell, Allan. 1984. "Language style as audience design." *Language in Society* 13 (2): 145–204.

Benneworth, Kelly. 2010. "Negotiating paedophilia in the investigative interview: The construction of sexual offences against children." In *The Routledge Handbook of Forensic Linguistics*, ed. by Malcolm Couthard and Alison Johnson, 139–154. Oxon: Routledge.

Drew, Paul, and John Heritage (eds.). 1992. *Talk at Work: Interaction in Institutional Settings*. Cambridge: Cambridge University Press.

Fox, Gwyneth. 1993. "A comparison of 'policespeak' and 'normalspeak': A preliminary study." In *Techniques of Description: Spoken and Written Discourse*, ed. by John M. Sinclair, Michael Hoey, and Gwyneth Fox, 183–195. Oxon: Routledge.

Goffman, Erving. 1981. *Forms of Talk*. Philadelphia: University of Pennsylvania Press.

Haworth, Kate. 2006. "The dynamics of power and resistance in police interview discourse." *Discourse and Society* 17 (6): 739–759.

Haworth, Kate. 2009. *An Analysis of Police Interview Discourse and Its Role(s) in the Judicial Process*. PhD thesis, University of Nottingham.

Haworth, Kate. 2010. "Police interviews in the judicial process: Police interviews as evidence." In *The Routledge Handbook of Forensic Linguistics*, ed. by Malcolm Coulthard and Alison Johnson, 169–184. Oxon: Routledge.

Haworth, Kate. 2013. "Audience design in the police interview: The interactional and judicial consequences of audience orientation." *Language in Society* 42 (1): 45–69.

Heritage, John, and Marja-Leena Sorjonen. 1994. "Constituting and maintaining activities across sequences: *And*-prefacing as a feature of question design." *Language in Society* 23 (1): 1–29.

Heritage, John, and D. Rodney Watson. 1979. "Formulations as conversational objects." In *Everyday Language: Studies in Ethnomethodology*, ed. by George Psathas, 123–162. New York: Irvington.

Heydon, Georgina. 2003. "'Now I didn't mean to break his teeth': Applying topic management to problems of power asymmetry and voluntary confessions." In *Applied Linguistics and Communities of Practice*, ed. by Srikant Sarangi and Theo van Leeuwen, 81–149. London: Continuum.

Heydon, Georgina. 2005. *The Language of Police Interviewing: A Critical Analysis*. Basingstoke: Palgrave Macmillan.

Johnson, Alison. 2008. "'From where we're sat . . .': Negotiating narrative transformation through interaction in police interviews with suspects." *Text and Talk* 28 (3): 327–349.

MacLeod, Nicci. 2010. *Police Interviews with Women Reporting Rape: A Critical Discourse Analysis*. PhD thesis, Aston University.

MacLeod, Nicci. 2011. "Risks and benefits of selective (re)presentation of interviewees' talk: Some insights from discourse analysis." *British Journal of Forensic Practice* 13 (2): 95–102.

Milne, Rebecca. 2004. "The enhanced cognitive interview." Accessed 26 March 2015. Available from: http://preview.tinyurl.com/z7yxxlu.

Milne, Rebecca, and Ray Bull. 1999. *Investigative Interviewing: Psychology and Practice*. Chichester: Wiley.

Moore, Sarah. 2009. "Cautionary tales: Drug facilitated sexual assault in the British Media." *Crime, Media, Culture* 5 (3): 305–320.

Newbury, Phillip, and Alison Johnson. 2006. "Suspects' resistance to constraining and coercive questioning strategies in the police interview." *International Journal of Speech, Language and the Law* 13 (2): 213–240.

NPIA (National Policing Improvement Agency). 2009. "Professionalising investigation programme (PIP)." Accessed 26 March 2015. Available from: http://webarchive.nationalarchives.gov.uk/20081230144213/http://www.npia.police.uk/en/10093.htm.

Oxburgh, Gavin, Trond Myklebust, and Tim Grant. 2010. "The question of question types in police interviews: A review of the literature from a psychological and linguistic perspective." *International Journal of Speech, Language and the Law* 17 (1): 45–66.

Roberts, Celia. 2003. "Applied linguistics applied." In *Applied Linguistics and Communities of Practice*, ed. by Srikant Sarangi and Theo van Leeuwen, 132–149. London: Continuum.

Savage, Stephen P., and Rebecca Milne. 2007. "Miscarriages of justice." In *Handbook of Criminal Investigation*, ed. by Tim Newburn, Tom Williamson, and Alan Wright, 610–627. Cullompton: Willan.

Schiffrin, Deborah. 2003. "Discourse markers: Language, meaning, and context." In *The Handbook of Discourse Analysis*, ed. by Deborah Schiffrin, Deborah Tannen, and Heidi E. Hamilton, 54–76. Oxford: Blackwell Publishing Ltd.

Shepherd, Eric, and Andy Griffiths. 2013. *Investigative Interviewing: The Conversation Management Approach*, 2nd ed. Oxford: Oxford University Press.

Stokoe, Elizabeth, and Derek Edwards. 2008. "'Did you have permission to smash your neighbour's door?': Silly questions and their answers in police suspect interrogations." *Discourse Studies* 10 (1): 89–111.

Thornborrow, Joanna. 2002. *Power Talk: Language and Interaction in Institutional Discourse*. London: Longman.

Wiggins, Sally, and Alexa Hepburn. 2007. "Discursive research: Applications and implications." In *Discursive Research in Practice: New Approaches to Psychology in Interaction*, ed. by Alexa Hepburn and Sally Wiggins, 281–291. Cambridge: Cambridge University Press.

Willig, Celia (ed.). 1999. *Applied Discourse Analysis: Social and Psychological Interventions*. Buckingham: Open University Press.

Wodak, Ruth. 1996. *Disorders of Discourse*. Harlow: Longman.

Chapter 9

A different drum

Social media and the communication of sociolinguistic research

Robert Lawson, ORCID NUMBER 0000–0003–1415–517X

Introduction

A key responsibility in academia is not only developing knowledge, but also sharing it with others (Cameron et al. 1992: 24). Generally though, dissemination is narrowly constrained to scholarly publications like journal articles with principally academic audiences (Watermeyer 2016: 369). Supplementing this has conventionally meant turning to print media, radio and television. In recent years, however, there has been a shift towards other forms of outreach, particularly Twitter, Facebook, research blogs, and other social media platforms. Researchers are taking ever more seriously the role social media plays in their research footprint (cf. Powell et al. 2012: 272). For example, Walker (2006: 6) notes how a list she had compiled of academic blogs in 2002 became impossible to keep up-to-date due to the number of new blogs being introduced. Fast forward to 2015 and the website www.academicblogs.org lists approximately 2,000 blogs across a variety of disciplines. Even more academics regularly use Twitter, Facebook, LinkedIn, Academia.edu, and other platforms to share research and to monitor the effectiveness of their outreach efforts.

My co-editor and I have both used our editorial privilege to discuss issues we felt were important but not based on impact demonstrably achieved in our own work (cf. Sayers, this volume). As such, this chapter examines how dissemination practices can help set up the right conditions for impact, particularly in the context of stimulating and informing public debate. In doing so, I discuss how researchers can use a variety of media outlets to augment their outreach efforts, and how social media more generally can be integrated into their research profiles.

In the first part of the chapter, I briefly discuss research dissemination and situate this discussion within the broader theme of language in the public eye. I also consider the extent to which traditional mass media constructs specific language ideologies, focusing on media coverage of "vocal fry" in the United States (more commonly known as "creaky voice" in the phonetics literature, although some [cf. Liberman 2014] distinguish between the two).

In the second part, I outline different methods of research dissemination, focusing on traditional mass media and social media (Of course, traditional media companies also utilise a range of social media in their outputs, including blogs, reader comments, Twitter feeds and so on. As such, the dividing line between 'old' and 'new' or 'traditional' and 'social' has become increasingly blurred). I also examine how social media enables the development of counter-narratives which run contrary to established ideologies of language use, and how the effective use of social media can help disrupt the "language news cycle" (cf. Cham 2009).

In the final part, I discuss how sociolinguists can use social media in their own research, and I offer some general points about the utility of social media within sociolinguistic research. These comments are guided by my practice of maintaining an academic blog (https://thesociallinguist.wordpress.com). I also posted a questionnaire on the Variationist List (https://www.jiscmail.ac.uk/var-l) and conducted a series of short email interviews with key scholars whom I know to be active on social media. All respondents consented to have their name, affiliation and comments used in this chapter.

Impact and dissemination in academia

For the purposes of the UK's Research Excellence Framework in 2014 (see Lawson and Sayers, this volume, for more details), dissemination did not fall within overarching institutional definitions of research impact (cf. HEFCE 2011: 4; Stilgoe 2011; Watermeyer 2016: 262). In more concrete terms, this prevented researchers from simply publishing a book or a journal article and counting this as "impact." In the official REF guidance, impact was more specifically taken to mean "an effect on, change or benefit to the economy, society, culture, public policy or services, health, the environment or quality of life, beyond academia as the result of excellent research" (HEFCE 2012: 26).

As part of this guidance, a range of different impact criteria were set out, including one criterion particularly pertinent to this present chapter – "public debate has been stimulated or informed by research" (HEFCE 2012: 28). Since it is impossible to contribute to public debate if one's ideas are not published to a wider audience, it goes without saying that this form of impact has dissemination at its centre. The key in terms of impact is to demonstrate that your message has stirred debate beyond the groves of academe.

Indeed, we have seen in recent years growing attention paid to how research dissemination happens, and the role dissemination plays in what might be termed the "impact chain" (cf. Brandtzæg 2011; Gruzd and Goertzen 2013). Examining how dissemination happens is key, especially since the traditional model of publishing inhibits access to research findings by policy makers, key stakeholders, and members of the general public (Watermeyer 2016: 369), usually by locking articles behind pay walls (Mounce 2013). The Open Access movement has certainly made some progress in making research available to a wider audience (Gargouri et al. 2010), but many publishers remain wedded to the pay-for-access model (see Collister 2015 for an overview of Open Access in linguistics). As such, there is a need to look at alternative methods of both formal and informal research dissemination. This is where social media has particular power.

As Pettigrew (2011) highlights, though, dissemination is about more than just getting research out to a wider readership. It can also help build networks with a variety of stakeholders and end users, making it easier to contribute to ongoing debates about policy, for example (cf. Coleman, this volume, on participation in media debates on language policy). The nuts and bolts of how this might be achieved, however, have been seldom discussed. Before covering these issues in more detail, I first outline the position of language issues in the public eye. I then present a case study on creaky voice which sheds light on how sociolinguistic knowledge is (or is not) used in language-related news stories.

Language in the public eye

In recent years, there have been a number of language issues in the mainstream media which have had very little input from professional academic sociolinguists (see, e.g., Patrick, this volume, on media discussion of language in cases of asylum applications). Even when sociolinguists *are* involved, their comments can be overlooked, ignored or edited out. John Rickford's retrospective on his involvement in the Ebonics debate in the mid-1990s is particularly instructive.

> Although the New York Times published several editorials and Op-Ed pieces critical either of Ebonics or the Oakland resolutions, linguists' attempts to get them to present a different viewpoint were all unsuccessful. I know of at least four Op-Ed submissions which they summarily rejected, and there were undoubtedly others. Similarly, other linguists had experiences similar to mine, in which leading television stations would do one and two hour interviews with us on the Ebonics issue, but never use any of it in their broadcasts. Linguists should not avoid these leading media sources, but be aware that breaking into them can be difficult if the views you represent do not correspond to the mainstream view. In matters of language, they often do not.
>
> (Rickford 1999: 270–271)

It is, of course, problematic to consider "the media" as a homogenous (and somewhat sinister) entity which controls the kind of news that is broadcast (cf. Baron 2010: 35). Rickford nevertheless raises the important point that parties within the media may be unwilling to include expert knowledge simply because this knowledge challenges mainstream views about language use (see also Wolfram and Reaser 2008: 3).

As Herman and Chomsky (2002) comment, this notion of picking and choosing news deemed worthy of covering is at the heart of what they call the "propaganda model." This model "trace[s] the routes by which money and power are able to filter out the news fit to print, marginalise dissent, and allow the government and dominant private interests to get their messages across to the public." Similarly, Rickford (1999: 270–271) highlights the problem of manufacturing consent in his dealings with the mainstream press and how far "dissenting information" is prevented from reaching public view (see also Blackledge [2005: 67] and Milani [2007: 114] for a discussion of how mainstream media outlets influence people's understanding of the wider social world). As such, it is important to examine how linguistic ideologies are promoted in the mainstream media and how narratives of linguistic exclusion and stigmatisation are constructed.

In the next section, I present a case study of exactly this. In doing so, I discuss how mainstream media shapes and constrains the discursive content of these stories and how sociolinguistic expertise is marginalised in favour of promoting a narrow discourse of language shaming.

"I'm burned out on the fry": Vocal fry, gender and language shaming

The piece of media coverage I discuss is the supposed increase in the use of "vocal fry" (I use the more linguistically accurate "creaky voice" for the remainder of the chapter). In phonetic terms, creaky voice is a non-modal voice quality where "the subglottal pressure is lower than that of modal voice, the airflow is lower, and the fundamental frequency is also lower, estimated at between 30 and 120 Hz" (Mendoza-Denton 2011: 264). This causes a series of irregular glottal pulses which are variously described as "a series of rapid taps, like a stick being run along a railing" (Catford 1964: 32) or "an old door creaking open" (Collins and Mees 2013: 34). Creaky voice has been described in phonetic descriptions of Received Pronunciation (cf. Catford 1964; Wells 1982) and is well-attested in a number of varieties (see Mendoza-Denton 2011 for a review of the literature on creaky voice).

The feature was catapulted to international consciousness following the publication of Wolk et al. (2012, although an online version was made available in 2011), which presented the findings of a project on creaky voice among female American college students. The association between creaky voice and young American women is so prevalent that an article in *Le Monde* called creaky voice "la voix de l'Amérique" (Chayet 2014). A brief search through YouTube for either "creaky voice" or "vocal fry" will yield illustrative, if not caricatured, examples.

The research by Wolk and her colleagues was picked up by major media outlets, including MSNBC (Dahl 2011), *The Independent* (Armstrong 2012), *The New York Times* (Quenqua 2012), CBS (Salie 2013), *Slate* (Vuolo 2013), and National Public Radio (Martin 2014). As I examined the coverage, three claims emerged: that it is a new phenomenon used by young speakers; that its use is highest among female speakers; and that it is spread by popular media figures. Since these claims were based on the research presented in Wolk et al. (2012), it is worthwhile briefly examining each one in turn.

First, Wolk et al. (2012) collected data from only one age group: 18–25. With no data from older speakers and the fact that previous research suggests that creaky voice has been around for some time (see above), it is difficult to say with any degree of confidence that it is a new phenomenon. Second, although more recent work presents the results for male speakers (Abdelli-Beruh et al. 2014), these results were unavailable at the time the original research was being covered. As such, claiming that creaky voice is a female speech feature is problematic in the absence of data from male speakers. Last, in discussing the possible influence of media figures, Wolk et al. (2012: 4) argue that "it is possible that these college students have either practiced or observed this vocal register and modeled it to match popular figures." That's it. While the influence of televised media on the acquisition and spread of sociolinguistic variation has been postulated (see, e.g., Stuart-Smith et al. 2007; Sayers 2014), Wolk et al. (2012) do not offer any evidence to substantiate their assertion of a possible media or popular culture influence.

Despite problems with the original article, these claims made their way into the public eye. For example, publications like the *Huffington Post* ran stories with headlines like "Vocal fry and young women: Are they trying to sound like Ke$ha and Britney?" (Chan 2011). Other media outlets framed the issue in terms of what Cameron (1995) calls "verbal hygiene." More specifically, the stories in which creaky voice was framed as a feature of young women's speech also contained an explicit discourse of language shaming. As Fruehwald (2011a) points out, "the *Today Show* clip described vocal fry as 'animal-like' and buffered the piece with iconic images of female frivolity: shopping, gossiping, talking about boys, and watching *Sex and the City*." The negative discourse of creaky voice is a continuation of the long-attested trope of women's language as somehow deviant and deficient in comparison to men's language. This becomes embedded as yet another way of denigrating the linguistic behaviour of young women, in much the same way as up-talk (that is, completing all phrases with high rising terminals) did in the 1990s. The media treatment here ties in with more general ideologies of the status of women's language and the prevalent social policing of how women (should) act. This is part of the "language news cycle" (cf. Cham 2009), where linguistic research becomes distorted as a way of supporting specific language ideologies promoted in the media.

This discourse of language shaming came to the fore once again following the publication of Anderson et al. (2014), a study which examined reactions to male and female creaky voice. Like Wolk et al. (2012), the research design was problematic. First, speakers in this study mimicked the feature rather than being natural producers of it. It could be argued, then, that the voices sounded unnatural to listeners. Second, the stimulus was only one sentence ("Thank you for considering me for this opportunity"). Research has shown that listeners make very quick judgements on the basis of limited speech data (cf. Baugh 2003). Creaky voice, however, typically does not occur over the course of an entire sentence, but rather at "prosodically significant locations such as phrase boundaries, utterance boundaries and pitch accents" (Redi and Shattuck-Hufnagel 2001: 408). Of course, the use of creaky voice is not always constrained by phonological effects, but can also be used for affective and pragmatic functions (see also Mendoza-Denton 2011: 269; Abdelli-Beruh et al. 2014: 185–186; Lee 2015). Nevertheless, the way the speakers mimicked creaky voice could have been at variance with natural productions at pragmatically and prosodically important boundaries. The authors, however, do not point out any controls put in place to mitigate against this kind of interfering influence.

Despite these flaws in the research design, Anderson et al. (2014) present their results as evidence that creaky voice is negatively evaluated across a range of personal characteristics, including competency, education and attractiveness. This effect occurs regardless of speaker sex and was found to be much stronger when the feature was used by female speakers, and stronger still when the listeners were also female. Of perhaps more concern, particularly in relation to language equality issues, the authors use the findings as a way of further policing acceptable language behaviour of women. They advise that "collectively, these results suggest young American women should avoid vocal fry in order to maximize labor market perceptions, particularly when being interviewed by another woman" (Anderson et al. 2014: 5). As with Wolk et al. (2012), this advice made its way into a number of news stories, including National Public Radio (Munoz 2014), *Time Magazine* (Rhodan 2014), and *The Washington Post* (Sullivan 2014). These stories all further the discourse that young women should actively monitor their behaviour, particularly for societal approval, ultimately reinforcing ideologies of linguistic inequality and discrimination.

The uni-directional nature of traditional media reporting though means that alternative viewpoints which run contrary to mainstream media perspectives are difficult to get heard. Even when there are opportunities to offer alternative viewpoints, it is not necessarily guaranteed that these viewpoints will be given any credence. For example, MSNBC invited Janet Pierrehumbert to discuss creaky voice on *The Today Show* (2011), where she argued that the feature had been around for some time and that celebrities were not the cause for its spread. Rather than engaging with these points, however, the story pursued the narrative that creaky voice is an endemic speech feature among young women and that the principal vector for this speech feature spreading was celebrities.

However, alternative perspectives appeared on social media quite quickly (I discuss this aspect of social media in more detail later). For example, Fruehwald (2011b) critiqued in a blog post the way the expert commentary was sidelined by the media. Similarly, Liberman (2011) posted several entries to *Language Log* (one of the most popular and longest running blogs written by professional linguists) discussing the coverage of creaky voice in the mainstream media, arguing that examples could be found among speakers born in the 1950s.

As should be clear from the discussion above, many mainstream media outlets constrain opportunities to present opposing views, as well as ignoring or overlooking views which do make it into the public domain, in favour of a narrative which fits in with prevailing views on language. Nevertheless, a great deal of research relies on disseminating the results and findings through mainstream media. As such, it seems a fair question to ask why sociolinguists should utilise mainstream media at all. In the next section, I discuss some key advantages and disadvantages of outreach via traditional forms of mainstream media.

Traditional media: The good and the bad

Traditional mass media formats have significant advantages, perhaps chief of which is an established audience base. For example, taken together, the BBC website, BBC World Service and BBC World News reach approximately 256 million people per week (Horrocks 2013), and the online version of the *New York Times* has approximately 7.5 million unique visitors every week (New York Times 2014). Having research covered in these outlets means that findings can be disseminated far more widely than through other more specialised means such as journal articles (cf. Baron 2010: 77).

Reaching such large audiences is possible due to the fact that traditional media outlets enjoy unparalleled levels of breadth, depth, and reach, primarily through their strategy of media diversification. To take just one example in the UK, the BBC not only has its regional and national televised news programmes, but also regional and national radio stations and a comprehensive international website. As such, a story reported online will likely also be covered on radio and television. Moreover, these media outlets (particularly broadsheet newspapers such as *The Telegraph* and *The Guardian* and well-known broadcasters like the BBC) have cultural and social prestige. This can influence perceptions regarding the quality of research presented in these outlets, in addition to boosting the public exposure of the researcher and their university or department.

Lastly, when research is reported via traditional media, it is packed up in a story, contextualising the research in real life (Baron 2010: 30). This links theory with practice and demonstrates the "real-world impact" of research, alleviating the barriers between the two domains and making research more accessible to the non-specialist. One result of this is that the usual caveats which characterise the vast majority of academic writing are omitted in favour of a straightforward storytelling frame (Radford 2009: 148).

In spite of the potential reach of traditional media outlets, there remain considerable barriers to their use. As noted previously, issues surrounding framing are among the most serious. So while an academic might put together a press release outlining the major points of a project, it is down to the journalist the extent to which he or she follows these guidelines. Indeed, there are regular complaints by academics that their work has been misquoted, misrepresented or otherwise reported inaccurately (Baron 2010: 36–38). Such misrepresentation can do a great deal of damage to the intended message. One example of this within sociolinguistics concerns media coverage of the British Sign Language Corpus Project, a multi-year ESRC-funded project hosted at University College London. The aim of the project was to create a corpus of BSL signs and to examine how BSL is changing over time, both lexically and grammatically. The *Guardian* article which covered the research (Hill 2012) claimed that the signs used for particular social groups, including homosexuals and minorities, were changing due to users of BSL becoming more culturally sensitive. For example, the article claimed that the signs for *homosexual, Jew* and other lexical items are different for deaf people age 16–30 compared to older deaf people:

> For deaf people aged between 16 and 30, the only culturally sensitive way to indicate China is to draw the right hand from the signer's heart horizontally across their chest, then down towards the hip, indicating the shape of a Mao jacket. Their sign for a Jewish man or woman is a hand resting against the chin and making a short movement down, in the shape of a beard. A gay person is indicated with an upright thumb on one hand in the palm of the other, wobbling from side to side.
>
> (Hill 2012)

It is certainly clear from the data gathered for the project that BSL is changing (see Schembri et al. 2013 for details), but crucially, signs about Jewish people or gay people were not collected. Much of what was included in the *Guardian* article was not substantiated by the original research, and it is not at all clear where the signs mentioned above come from. To this end, several investigators on the project (Bencie Woll, Kearsy Cormier, and Adam Schembri) published an open letter to the editor, highlighting their concern "about the misrepresentation of academic research to create another 'story' about political correctness" (Woll et al. 2012).

The Guardian then published a clarification explaining that "the British Sign Language Corpus Project did not collect data about or document changes in signs referring to Jewish and gay people, nor did it provide any evidence of claims made about changes in signs for countries including India, Germany, France and Ireland" (Hill 2012). It is a positive sign that this clarification was posted, demonstrating that negotiations between journalists and researchers can occasionally be productive. That said, a number of errors remain in the revised version of the article. For example, the tag line immediately under the headline reads as follows: "First major study of how British sign language has evolved shows younger users are more reluctant to use 'offensive' signs," a claim challenged by the researchers themselves. Moreover, the article continues to include the signs supposedly used by the younger Deaf community, suggesting that the substance of the article itself has not been changed (it was not possible to view the older version of the article).

I should take a moment to point out that the news is not all bad. There is other survey evidence of generally positive and consensual relationships between sociolinguists and journalists (Kerswill 2015), but the counter-points in the above discussion demonstrate that troublesome frictions remain. Without oversight of the writing process and continual back and forth between academic and journalist to ensure accuracy (usually impossible because of time pressures), it is difficult to see how to resolve these tensions while still retaining the benefits offered by mainstream media. So how far can social media represent a feasible alternative? In the next section of the chapter, I consider the extent to which social media is a useful addition to our toolbox of outreach and dissemination strategies, how the shift towards social media also entails a shift of authorial power, and the implications of all this for how we engage with end users of our research.

An alternative approach? Social media in sociolinguistics

In recent years, there have been various efforts to examine the role of social media in academic research in the UK. For example, the Impact of Social Sciences Project at the London School of Economics makes significant use of social media, including a Twitter feed and a Facebook site. The website also includes links to blog posts and podcasts about research outreach and dissemination. Last, the project team has authored a series of guides on using social media in research (available from http://blogs.lse.ac.uk/impactofsocialsciences/resources).

To date, however, there have been no concerted efforts to discuss the role of social media in communicating and disseminating sociolinguistic research. This is surprising given the number of (socio)linguistics/language blogs available online, some with especially large readerships. To give just one example, *Language Log* (mentioned earlier) has approximately 100,000 page views per month. Moreover, there now exists a range of social media platforms which help connect people with academic research. In the first part of this section, my comments focus primarily on academic blogging. In the second part, I discuss other social media platforms like Twitter.

As Batts et al. (2008) point out, "blogs represent a means of information dispersal with unprecedented power." Similarly, Dunleavy and Gilson (2012) claim that "in research terms, blogging is quite simply, one of the most important things that an academic should be doing right now." These authors argue that not only does blogging allow academics to share research with a wider audience, it also helps publicise research far more quickly and efficiently than the current academic publishing model. The lengthy process of submitting an article to a peer-reviewed journal means that findings can be out-of-date by the time they are published. In contrast, even tentative research can be published on a blog in a relatively short timeframe, usually with some form of public peer review. For example, Batts et al. (2008) discuss a number of processes that can be implemented for the purposes of blog quality control. These include review by moderators, editorial review or committee peer review, while websites like www.researchblogging.org aggregate posts that only discuss peer-reviewed research and allow bloggers to add an icon to show that they are discussing peer-reviewed work. Batts et al. (2008) end their discussion with the following point: "with a bit of technical savvy, a few guidelines, and an involved readership, the self-regulating style of the blogosphere can be harnessed in new ways that could prove useful for institutional science outreach." Of course, both approaches can be used together, with preliminary results shared for public review before the finished product is submitted for formal peer review in an academic journal. As such, blogs can be seen as complementary to traditional forms of academic dissemination, rather than as a replacement.

Blogging provides other tangible benefits. In particular, the author of an academic blog has unparalleled control of content. The author decides what content is made available and how the findings are presented, which elements of the research to foreground, and the overall tone of the post. Blogs such as *Dialect Blog, Language Hat, Language Log, Language on the Move, Lexicon Valley, On Language, Separated by a Common Language, Vocalised* and my own academic blog, *The Social Linguist* (discussed in more detail below) all have regularly updated content and provide in-depth commentary on language stories covered by the mainstream press. Such blogs offer a counter-point to mainstream media treatment of language issues, and help linguists get their point of view across without it being skewed by an editor. Given some of the issues surrounding misrepresentation and the lack of academic rigour outlined previously, this is an important intervention (see also Soon and Kluver 2014: 509).

Blogs can also help make research more transparent to non-academics. For example, the research process (e.g. the particular methodology used in a study) is typically reserved for journal articles and monographs. In work published by the mainstream media, though, the nuts and bolts of research are usually over-simplified in haste to reach the conclusion. Blogs do not suffer from such restrictions, allowing a researcher to outline the day-to-day practice of research. This transparency can help develop an understanding of the processes surrounding research. Moreover, social media facilitates direct engagement with end users and consumers of the research (Draper and Turnage 2008). This can occur through, for example, the use of comments in blog posts or more directly through Twitter or Facebook. However it is done, engagement with readers can help develop a positive feedback loop which encourages dialogue with external stakeholders, end users and the general public. As such, research dissemination becomes a proactive practice.

Perhaps one of the most distinguishing features of social media is that content can be picked up and shared by multiple users across multiple sites. On the odd occasion, content can even become "viral" and reach thousands of readers in a very short space of time (cf. Wolfram, this volume, on the results of Joshua Katz's lexical dialect quiz published in the *New York Times*). The emergence of long-form writing platforms such as Beacon, Medium and Contributoria means that there are now places where content can be cross-posted and reach larger audiences. Larger blogs can link to less well-read blogs. Articles can be posted to websites like Academia.edu or ResearchGate.net and shared with new readers (e.g. Coleman, this volume, relates an example of work he put on Academia.edu being fortuitously discovered and used to support a court case). Platforms like Twitter and Facebook can be used to discuss ongoing research, share conference content, and make connections with audiences beyond academia. It is in this sphere where social media shines, as a network where people share, link and bookmark content (Mounce 2013: 16).

This aspect of social media also means that how (and by whom) research is being shared and linked (via blog posts, open access repositories or sites like Academia.edu) can be monitored through the use of altmetrics. Altmetrics are a relatively new addition to academic citation measures (Priem et al. 2010). They go beyond a basic count of the citations in academic sources, to include citations in web sources like Wikipedia, as well as the number of views online, mentions in journal comments and forum posts, additions to social bibliographies like Mendely and Zotero, and shares via Twitter or Facebook. Using altmetrics through websites like Altmetric, Scopus, Impactstory and Plum Analytics can help highlight not only where one's research is reaching, but also where it is not (although see Colquhoun 2014 for an overview of some criticisms of altmetrics).

Unfortunately, a widely held view within academia is that platforms like Twitter, Facebook and other social media services dumb down knowledge and (re-) produce insubstantial chit-chat (Kolowich 2012). The responses I received from scholars active on social media, however, revealed a more positive take; and I was surprised by the extent to which social media formed an integral part of people's outreach efforts. Responses to my questionnaire (distributed using social media) from Lauren Collister (University of Pittsburgh), Fawn Draucker (University of Pittsburgh), Michaël Gauthier (Lumière University Lyon 2), and Damien Hall (University of Newcastle) all highlighted a range of benefits.

First and foremost, many of the responses focused on using social media to keep up-to-date with upcoming conferences and the publication of new papers. Other benefits were related to networking and building connections with other researchers. For example, Michaël Gauthier pointed out that using platforms like Twitter and Facebook is a way of finding out about new work and promoting his own research beyond his immediate academic circle:

> Social media is a way for me to be contacted by people who came across previous studies of mine and who wanted to know more about certain aspects of my research. So it has been a way for me to get to know more people and to discuss my findings.

This benefit was also echoed by Fawn Draucker:

> I also met a lot of other researchers on Twitter through conference hashtags and other such discussions. Twitter is . . . great for use at conferences, where you can connect with people that you might not already know in a more open forum. Facebook, again, is good for discussion with closer connections.

Other notable advantages of social media included using it to more effectively canvas academic opinion, as noted by Damien Hall:

> I joined [Twitter] exactly in order to ask a specific research question. . . . There wasn't any other way to have a quick conversation with a number of people

across the world (especially in N. America) who I knew would be online at the time, and have them all see each other's responses, with also the option of other interested parties weighing in.

Perhaps the most celebratory comments about social media came from Lauren Collister (University of Pittsburgh), who used social media approaches extensively in her doctoral research:

> I used Twitter to share a survey link for a project I was doing, using hashtags to get to the appropriate audiences. I also use Twitter to network and connect with folks in all of my fields of study; through knowing me on Twitter I got invited to do two talks at other Universities while still a graduate student, and have since managed to get in on two major projects in my new position. I also use Twitter at conferences to catalogue my impressions of the talks I'm attending, and now I use Storify to collect those thoughts afterwards like a notebook and share that with others who attended. Finally, through both Twitter and blog networks, I've discovered scholars and others doing studies that have informed my own research and whose work I've included in my literature review. . . . Whether it's blogging the research process or sharing links to (publicly accessible versions of) your papers, [social media] is really a great way to open and democratize science.

All of the above highlight the more concrete ways in which Pettigrew's (2011: 351) call for scholars to cultivate "complementary, social and reputational capital" can be answered. But perhaps more important is that these scholars use social media platforms not only to facilitate the dissemination of ideas, and thus the potential avenues for impact, but also for a host of other purposes. This includes sharing survey links with potential respondents, making connections with researchers at other universities, keeping up-to-date with research in the field, sharing emerging findings with colleagues and so on. All of this is to say that social media platforms are about more than just getting research out there.

Despite its advantages, social media has some clear problems. First, and perhaps most serious, is that an academic who puts her or himself into the public eye may encounter abusive behaviour from a variety of anonymous commentators, particularly in cases where online content becomes viral and reaches a large audience. For example, University of Cambridge classicist Professor Mary Beard suffered a period of prolonged online abuse (also known as "trolling") following an appearance on the BBC 1 programme *Question Time* (Day 2013). More pertinent to sociolinguistics, there have been instances where scholars have been attacked online for publishing articles which, for example, challenge prescriptivist language ideologies and tackle linguistic discrimination (cf. the case of Heike Wiese and her discussion of Kiezdeutsch is a good illustration of this, among many other examples; Kerswill 2016). While online abuse is one of the more unsavoury sides of the Web, governments and law enforcement agencies are becoming more proactive in addressing the problem. Updated legislation in the UK has recently criminalised online abuse (Owen 2014) and there has been a rise in media campaigns against online anti-social behaviour. Such strategies are in their infancy, but they are at least a step in the right direction in making online abuse a social taboo.

Another (far less serious) problem blogs face is that they generally reach much smaller audiences than mainstream media outlets. This may be alleviated by content being picked up by others and shared across sites, as outlined above. Nevertheless, blogs and other forms of social media typically require the cultivation of a following. Establishing this can be time-consuming. Moreover, it can be difficult to justify blogging and other social media activities in light of the ever-increasing demands placed on academics, in terms of teaching, research, publishing, administration, entrepreneurship and so on. However, using altmetrics can be useful for quantifying the impact of a blog and the reach of one's work for the purposes of, for example, a tenure review portfolio or a job application. Naturally, individual departments will view social media in different ways and will afford such activities different levels of support. In my own job, I have not faced pressure to focus on publishing at the expense of social media activities. Instead, I have been able to show that activities of this kind are part of my broader set of social responsibilities as an academic.

Establishing a research footprint also means carving out a niche where your content is sufficiently distinctive from other researchers to keep people visiting your site. In the competitive world of online readership, there is a danger of research blogs being drowned out by other online content. One question worth thinking about is whether social media is a disruptive technology or simply noise in the signal. In their updated introduction to *Manufacturing Consent*, Herman and Chomsky (2002: xi) argue that

> [t]he beauty of [the propaganda model] . . . is that . . . dissent and inconvenient information [via specific Internet outlets] is kept within bounds and at the margins, so that while their presence shows that the system is not monolithic, they are not large enough to interfere unduly with the domination of the official agenda.

This argument certainly made sense in the context of the late 1990s and Web 1.0 technology, where content was relatively static and non-participatory for end users, and widespread access to the Web was still in its infancy. In the Web 2.0 era, however, the landscape has changed dramatically. Now, social media and other Web 2.0 technologies are commonplace. Blogs and other social media platforms are no longer at the margins of society, and online civic participation and cyberactivism have grown in recent years (see Sandoval-Almazan and Gil-Garcia 2014 for an overview). One of the primary strengths of social media appears to be in generating grass-roots support and raising public awareness about a particular topic or concern. Of course, the extent to which this leads to concrete change should not be overstated, but as Soon and Kluver (2014: 500) highlight, cyberactivism "challenges the boundaries of accepted norms in society."

More specific to sociolinguistics, there is the problem that a great deal of mainstream media coverage is unconcerned with accuracy and rigour when it comes to language and linguistics. Some researchers have argued that this has to do with the lack of public engagement work carried out by linguists, while others argue that linguists' views are actively unwanted (Fruehwald 2011a discusses this debate in some detail). The difficulty in finding balanced commentary on the creaky voice coverage highlights this problem. Further examples could be cited where input from academic linguists is severely lacking, from the coverage of the Americanisation of British English (Engel 2011) to the story about the Essex primary school which hired an elocution specialist to teach pupils "correct" pronunciation (Lawson 2012). Part of this lack of informed commentary has to do with the extent to which sociolinguistic knowledge threatens the linguistic status quo. Tackling entrenched linguistic ideologies is often one of the biggest challenges linguists face when engaging with non-linguists (cf. Wolfram 2011; although see Baumgardt 2012 for a more positive take on the impact of sociolinguists beyond academia). The potential of social media to effect social change should be tempered by the understanding that it is not a silver bullet to the problems of linguistic inequality or discrimination. Nevertheless, if sociolinguists want to disrupt the language news cycle (cf. Cham 2009) in any meaningful way and be a more visible discipline, blogs and other forms of social media are a good starting point.

The social linguist: A personal retrospective of academic blogging

In the final section of the chapter, I outline some recommendations for sociolinguists to consider in their dissemination strategy. Much of what I discuss draws on my own experiences of starting an academic blog as a way of furthering connections beyond academia. My discussion here is also bolstered by comments and reflections solicited from sociolinguists who use social media in their own work. These recommendations are not intended to be exhaustive, but rather to signpost researchers wishing to engage more deeply with the processes underpinning research dissemination. I begin by discussing blogging and then move on to discuss other forms of social media that might also be helpful as part of an outreach strategy.

In July 2011, I decided to take the plunge into blog writing. My reason was summarised in my first ever blog post: "as academics, we have a responsibility to get our research out there into the public eye and to showcase the kind of cutting edge research that's happening in universities" (Lawson 2011). Blogging allowed me to share my writing (either personal reflections on language use or ongoing research work) far more quickly than other outlets for dissemination, and to a potentially wider audience. It was a way for me to engage with people who might not, for example, subscribe to the latest sociolinguistics journals, and to (potentially) demystify the inner workings of academia. To date I have written over 110 entries covering a variety of topics, from my PhD thesis on language and masculinity in Glasgow to sociolinguistic issues more generally. This is far more work than I would have been able to publish via traditional academic routes (admittedly, these are two very different forms of writing). Since its inception, the blog has had approximately 40,000 views; and although this is not a huge number in comparison to a blog like *Language Log,* it is still 40,000 more views than I would otherwise have had.

Perhaps one of the biggest problems I have faced in blog writing (and continue to face!) is the perennial question of "what do I write about?". In my case, I found that this can be alleviated, to some extent at least, by setting up a road map for the kind of content you might want to publish. This is easier when a blog is part of a larger research project, since clear goals, topics and targets can be identified at the planning stage. For example, at the beginning of a project, blog posts may be more useful at sketching out the broad details of the research, while towards the end of the project when findings are more substantial, utilising mainstream media outlets to publicise to a wider audience may be more appropriate. It may seem premature to consider how blogging fits into a research project before the research has even started, but adopting a proactive approach can help academics articulate, in funding bids for example, plans to communicate research beyond academia.

A secondary advantage of integrating a blog as part of a larger research project is that such projects will usually have more than one Principal Investigator and several Research Assistants. In such a scenario, it is possible to divide the responsibility for updating content across all collaborators. While not strictly a blog focused around one research project, *Language Log* adopts this strategy, with over 4,000 entries since 2003 submitted from multiple contributors. Similarly, *Language on the Move* publishes work from a variety of researchers across a range of topics. By adopting a peer-review model, the site editors maintain a high level of quality control while publishing work far more quickly than is possible with traditional journal outlets. It is perhaps less easy to do all of this when one is a lone blogger. In my case, media stories about language use (which is where the idea for this chapter originated), ongoing research and life as a university academic (usually) give me enough material.

The topics covered will also depend on the audience you expect to reach. By its nature, an academic blog is likely to have a variety of readers, from specialists to policy makers to the general public and many more besides. This not only has implications for the topics you might cover but also the writing style you might use. These considerations came up early in my own blog and I took the decision to adopt a more straightforward prose style in the hopes of better engaging readers. Again, it is worth repeating that blog writing is a very different form of academic communication to journal articles or book chapters, and it took me some time to find a voice that I felt worked effectively. Too technical and you risk turning away non-specialist readers. Too simplistic and you risk the impression that your posts lack critical insight or meaningful conclusions (cf. Wolfram, this volume, on similar concerns in writing books for public consumption based on academic research).

A related recommendation, especially to those starting out in blogging, is to update the blog on a regular basis. Blogs which have regularly updated content are likely to be more widely read in the long run. Readers who know that a blog is regularly updated are more likely to be repeat visitors and/or subscribers. This is certainly borne out by my own experience, simply by charting page hits per month against the number of updates I make. In periods where I regularly updated the blog, my page hits increased, and vice versa.

Getting readers to find your content, though, is another matter entirely. Word of mouth, being followed (and following others) on Twitter, and linking to work via Facebook and other platforms, go some way towards establishing a readership. But with the diversity of content available on the Web, making your work discoverable can be a challenge. The ubiquity of online searches now requires bloggers to think more carefully about how their pages are indexed and ranked on search websites like Google and Bing. For example, post titles, topic tags and other forms of search engine optimisation (SEO) are now ever more important in helping place content at the top of search results. Platforms like Buzzfeed are leading the way in creating SEO-friendly content by using long headlines and lists. Similarly, digital object identifiers (DOIs), uniform resource identifiers (URIs) and other forms of metadata can help anchor online content, a particularly important consideration in the rapidly changing landscape of the Internet (Kelly and Delasalle 2012). Effectively labelling and tagging one's outputs (and monitoring these outputs through the use of altmetrics) can help facilitate access to a wider readership, potentially opening up avenues for impact which might not have initially been intended.

To achieve the greatest benefit from the wide readership the Web offers, however, blogs should be augmented by other social media platforms. This could include, for example, Twitter, Facebook, Academia.edu, ResearchGate.net, various altmetrics resources and much more besides. In her response to my questionnaire, Lauren Collister made an observation which for me struck the heart of the matter: "You have to be following the right people and be savvy – you can't just put a link out there and expect it to work wonders." So not only is following the right people important, actively sharing, tweeting and otherwise broadcasting one's work is key.

In the four years since I started blogging and using other forms of social media like Twitter, much of what I have learned has been through trial and error. Starting my blog was very much a spur of the moment decision though and I have since come to realise that planning one's social media strategy, rather than it being bolted on as an afterthought, is an important step. This applies most particularly in cases where social media is included as part of a research project, but my comments also apply to academics looking to use social media in a more general way. Ultimately, a longer-term commitment to a social media outreach policy is likely to have a broader impact than a research project where a tokenistic one-day dissemination and impact event is organised (see Wolfram, this volume, on investing in sustainable long-term outreach activities).

Conclusion

The central message of this chapter is that traditional and social media should be seen as complementary (cf. Baron 2010: 6). By being aware of the different uses to which they can be put, be that research dissemination or contributing to ongoing discussions about language in the public eye, we can utilise the available range of strategies more effectively.

Just as this volume was going to press, creaky voice had once again generated substantial media interest due to an article by Naomi Wolf where she describes creaky voice as "that guttural growl at the back of the throat, as a Valley girl might sound if she had been shouting herself hoarse at a rave all night" (Wolf 2015). Wolf goes on to advocate that women should avoid using creaky voice at all costs, because it "undermine[s] women's authority in newly distinctive ways." Rather than examine the underlying discourses of verbal hygiene (cf. Cameron 1995), and the subsequent policing of women's verbal behaviour, Wolf patholo-gises creaky voice and sets up (white heterosexual) men's speech as the de facto norm against which the speech of everyone else is measured and evaluated. These are central concerns for scholars working in language and gender studies, and informed commentary which challenged Wolf's comments appeared relatively quickly on different forms of media. For example, Penny Eckert was a guest on National Public Radio's *Fresh Air* (Gross 2015), while Deborah Cameron contrib-uted to *The Current* (Tremonti 2015). Alternative perspectives on creaky voice also appeared on social media (e.g. Cameron 2015a, 2015b; Liberman 2015); and in an interesting application of crowd-sourcing, Paul de Decker created a Google Spreadsheets document where contributors submit media material about creaky voice to a navigable web timeline (de Decker 2015). These are all excellent illus-trations of how multifaceted our outreach efforts can be and how we can leverage different approaches for maximum effect.

As Walt Wolfram (this volume) points out, linguistics is at risk of becoming an endangered discipline; but by having a good media presence (either through traditional media, social media or both), linguists can keep the subject in the public eye and, as this chapter has demonstrated, contribute usefully to ongoing debates about language use. Taken together, traditional media and social media can help set up the right conditions for impact. How we use them in our work deserves careful attention.

Acknowledgements

My thanks go to Lauren Collister, Dave Hart, and Joan Beal for their helpful comments on various drafts of this chapter. Additional thanks go to audiences at Queen's University, Belfast, the University of Birmingham, the University of Leicester, the University of Tucson, and York St John University, where some of this work was initially presented. My final thanks go to Dave Sayers for his unstinting support and invaluable advice throughout.

References

Abdelli-Beruh, Nassima B., Lesley Wolk, and Dianne Slavin. 2014. "Prevalence of vocal fry in young adult male American English speakers." *Journal of Voice* 28 (2): 185–190.

Anderson, Rindy C., Casey A. Klofstad, William J. Mayew, and Mohan Venkatachalam. 2014. "Vocal fry may undermine the success of young women in the labor market." *PLoS One* 9 (5): e97506.

Armstrong, Rebecca. 2012. "Pronunciation: Make a speech purist cry – try vocal fry." Accessed 24 February 2015. Available from: http://www.independent.co.uk/news/science/pronunciation-make-a-speech-purist-cry-try-vocal-fry-7468950.html.

Baron, Nancy. 2010. *Escape from the Ivory Tower: A Guide to Making Your Science Matter.* Washington, DC: Island Press.

Batts, Shelley A., Nicholas J. Anthis, and Tara C. Smith. 2008. "Advancing science through conversations: Bridging the gap between blogs and the academy." *PLoS Biology* 6 (9): e240.

Baugh, John. 2003. "Linguistic profiling." In *Black Linguistics: Language, Society, and Politics in Africa and the Americas*, ed. by Sinfree Makoni, Geneva Smitherman, Arnetha F. Ball, and Arthur K. Spears, 115–168. London: Routledge.

Baumgardt, Daniel Q. 2012. *A Historical View of Science Accommodation: The Case for Sociolinguistics and African American English.* PhD thesis, Carnegie Mellon University.

Blackledge, Adrian. 2005. *Discourse and Power in a Multilingual World.* Amsterdam: John Benjamins.

Brandtzæg, Petter Bae. 2011. "Dissemination 2.0: The role of social media in research dissemination." Paper presented at the *Septentrio Conference Series*, University of Tromsø, Finland.

Cameron, Deborah. 1995. *Verbal Hygiene.* Oxon: Routledge.

Cameron, Deborah. 2015a. "A response to Naomi Wolf." Accessed 2 August 2015. Available from: https://debuk.wordpress.com/2015/07/26/a-response-to-naomi-wolf/.

Cameron, Deborah. 2015b. "How to write a bullshit article about women's language." Accessed 5 August 2015. Available from: https://debuk.wordpress.com/2015/08/03/how-to-write-a-bullshit-article-about-womens-language/.

Cameron, Deborah, Elizabeth Frazer, Penelope Harvey, M.B.H. Rampton, and Kay Richardson. 1992. *Researching Language: Issues of Power and Method.* London: Routledge.

Catford, John C. 1964. "Phonation types: The classification of some laryngeal components of speech production." In *In Honour of Daniel Jones: Papers Contributed on the Occasion of His Eightieth Birthday*, ed. by D. Abercrombie, D. B. Fry, P.A.D. MacCarthy, N. C. Scott, and J.L.M. Trim, 26–37. London: Longmans.

Cham, Jorge. 2009. "The science news cycle." Accessed 24 February 2015. Available from: http://www.phdcomics.com/comics/archive.php?comicid=1174.

Chan, Amanda. 2011. "Vocal fry and young women: Are they trying to sound like Ke\$ha and Britney?" Accessed 24 February 2015. Available from: http://www.huffingtonpost.com/2011/12/15/vocal-fry-raspy-voice-speech-trend-pattern-young-women_n_1151293.html.

Chayet, Stéphanie. 2014. "La voix de l'Amérique." Accessed 24 February 2015. Available from: http://www.lemonde.fr/m-actu/article/2014/07/11/la-voix-de-l-amerique_4454969_4497186.html.

Collins, Beverley S., and Inger M. Mees. 2013. *Practical Phonetics and Phonology: A Resource Book for Students.* Oxon: Routledge.

Collister, Lauren. 2015. "Elsevier up to their usual shenanigans." Accessed 11 March 2015. Available from: http://www.laurenbcollister.com/elsevier-up-to-their-usual-shenanigans-with-their-new-oa-linguistics-journal-ampersand/.

Colquhoun, David. 2014. "Why you should ignore altmetrics and other bibliometric nightmares." Accessed 11 March 2015. Available from: http://www.dcscience.net/2014/01/16/why-you-should-ignore-altmetrics-and-other-bibliometric-nightmares/.

Dahl, Melissa. 2011. "More college women speak in creaks, thanks to pop stars." Accessed 24 February 2015. Available from: http://bodyodd.nbcnews.com/_news/2011/12/12/9393348-more-college-women-speak-in-creaks-thanks-to-pop-stars.

Day, Elizabeth. 2013. "Mary Beard: I almost didn't feel such generic, violent misogyny was about me." Accessed 7 July 2015. Available from: http://www.theguardian.com/books/2013/jan/26/mary-beard-question-time-internet-trolls.

de Decker, Paul. 2015. "Vocal fry coverage 2010–2015." Accessed 5 August 2015. Available from: https://cdn.knightlab.com/libs/timeline/latest/embed/index.html?source=1VEQFYloSCrTm_rTDs65nZi4yqeukHMe979HymKWhdbU&font=Bevan-PotanoSans&maptype=toner&lang=en&height=650.

Draper, Lani, and Marthea Turnage. 2008. "Blogmania." *Internet Reference Services Quarterly* 13 (1): 15–55.

Dunleavy, Patrick, and Chris Gilson. 2012. "Five minutes with Patrick Dunleavy and Chris Gilson." Accessed 24 February 2015. Available from: http://blogs.lse.ac.uk/impactofsocialsciences/2012/02/24/five-minutes-patrick-dunleavy-chris-gilson/.

Engel, Matthew. 2011. "Viewpoint: Why do some Americanisms irritate people?" Accessed 24 February 2015. Available from: http://www.bbc.co.uk/news/14130942.

Fruehwald, Josef. 2011a. "I don't think it's linguists' fault." Accessed 24 February 2015. Available from: http://val-systems.blogspot.com/2011/12/i-dont-think-its-linguists-fault.html.

Fruehwald, Josef. 2011b. "On vocal fry." Accessed 24 February 2015. Available from: http://val-systems.blogspot.co.uk/2011/12/on-vocal-fry.html.

Gargouri, Yassine, Chawki Hajjem, Vincent Larivière, Yves Gingras, Les Carr, Tim Brody, and Stevan Harnad. 2010. "Self-selected or mandated, open access increases citation impact for higher quality research." *PLoS One* 5 (10): e13636.

Gross, Terry. 2015. "From upspeak to vocal fry: Are we 'policing' young women's voices?" Accessed 23 July 2015. Available from: http://www.npr.org/2015/07/23/425608745/from-upspeak-to-vocal-fry-are-we-policing-young-womens-voices.

Gruzd, Anatoliy, and Melissa Goertzen. 2013. "Wired academia: Why social science scholars are using social media." *46th Hawaii International Conference on System Sciences*. 3332–3341.

HEFCE (Higher Education Funding Council England). 2011. "Decisions on assessing research impact." Accessed 24 February 2015. Available from: http://www.ref.ac.uk/pubs/2011-01/.

HEFCE (Higher Education Funding Council England). 2012. "Panel criteria and working methods." Accessed 7 September 2015. Available from: http://www.ref.ac.uk/media/ref/content/pub/panelcriteriaandworkingmethods/01_12.pdf.

Herman, Edward S., and Noam Chomsky. 2002. *Manufacturing Consent: The Political Economy of the Mass Media*. New York: Pantheon Books.

Hill, Amanda. 2012. "Sign of the times: Deaf community minds its language." Accessed 24 February 2015. Available from: http://www.theguardian.com/society/2012/oct/07/british-sign-language-changing.

Horrocks, Peter. 2013. "A quarter of a billion people tuning in." Accessed 24 February 2015. Available from: http://www.bbc.co.uk/news/blogs-the-editors-23032145.

Kelly, Brian, and Jenny Delasalle. 2012. "Can LinkedIn and Academia.edu enhance access to open repositories?" OR2012: The 7th International Conference on Open Repositories. University of Bath.

Kerswill, Paul. 2015. "Sociolinguists in reactive mode." Paper presented at i-Mean 4, University of Warwick, UK.

Kerswill, Pail. 2016. "The media engaging linguists: A two-way street?" Paper presented at Humanities Research Centre, Sheffield Hallam University, UK.

Kolowich, Steve. 2012. "The academic Twitterazzi." Accessed 24 February 2015. Available from: https://www.insidehighered.com/news/2012/10/02/scholars-debate-etiquette-live-tweeting-academic-conferences.

Lawson, Peter. 2012. "Essex school gives pupils elocution lessons to lose their accents." Accessed 24 February 2015. Available from: http://www.telegraph.co.uk/education/educationnews/9044053/Essex-school-gives-pupils-elocution-lessons-to-lose-their-accents.html.

Lawson, Robert. 2011. "First foray into the world of blogging." Accessed 24 February 2015. Available from: https://thesociallinguist.wordpress.com/2011/06/25/first-foray/.

Lee, Sinae. 2015. "Creaky voice as a phonational device marking parenthetical segments in talk." Journal of Sociolinguistics 19 (3): 275–302.

Liberman, Mark. 2011. "Vocal fry: 'Creeping in' or 'still here'?" Accessed 24 February 2015. Available from: http://languagelog.ldc.upenn.edu/nll/?p=3626.

Liberman, Mark. 2014. "Real fry." Accessed 24 February 2015. Available from: http://languagelog.ldc.upenn.edu/nll/?p=13047#more-13047.

Liberman, Mark. 2015. "Cameron v. Wolf." Accessed 3 August 2015. Available from: http://languagelog.ldc.upenn.edu/nll/?p=20260.

Martin, Rachel. 2014. "Creativity, dirty eggs and vocal fry: The week in science." Accessed 24 February 2015. Available from: http://www.npr.org/2014/06/01/317843728/creativity-dirty-eggs-and-vocal-fry-the-week-in-science.

Mendoza-Denton, Norma. 2011. "The semiotic hitchhiker's guide to creaky voice: Circulation and gendered hardcore in a Chicana/o gang persona." Journal of Linguistic Anthropology 21 (2): 261–280.

Milani, Tommaso. 2007. "A language ideology in print: The case of Sweden." Language in the Media: Representations, Identities, Ideologies, ed. by Sally Johnson and Astrid Ensslin, 111–129. London: Continuum.

Mounce, Ross. 2013. "Open access and altmetrics: Distinct but complementary." Bulletin of the American Society for Information Science and Technology 39 (4): 14–17.

Munoz, Monica. 2014. "Is vocal fry hurting women's job prospects?" Accessed 24 February 2015. Available from: http://www.marketplace.org/2014/06/05/economy/vocal-fry-hurting-womens-job-prospects.

New York Times. 2014. "New York Times media kit." Accessed 24 February 2015. Available from: http://nytmediakit.com/online.

Owen, Glen. 2014. "Crackdown on the cyber-mobs poisoning Britain." Accessed 7 July 2015. Available from: http://www.dailymail.co.uk/news/article-2798573/crackdown-cyber-mobs-poisoning-britain-sentence-web-trolls-quadrupled-two-years-shocking-high-profile-online-abuse-cases.html.

Pettigrew, Andrew M. 2011. "Scholarship with impact." British Journal of Management 22 (3): 347–354.

Powell, Douglas, Casey Jacob, and Benjamin Chapman. 2012. "Using blogs and new media in academic practice: Potential roles in research, teaching, learning, and extension." *Innovate Higher Education* 37 (4): 271–282.

Priem, Jason, Dario Taraborelli, Paul Groth, and Cameron Neylon. 2010. "Altmetrics: A manifesto." Accessed 24 February 2015. Available from: http://altmetrics.org/manifesto/.

Quenqua, Daniel. 2012. "They're, like, way ahead of the linguistic currrrve." Accessed 24 February 2015. Available from: http://www.nytimes.com/2012/02/28/science/young-women-often-trendsetters-in-vocal-patterns.html?pagewanted=all&_r=1&.

Radford, Tim. 2009. "A workbench view of science communication and metaphor." In *Communicating Biological Sciences: Ethical and Metaphorical Dimensions*, ed. by Brigitte Nerlich, Richard Elliot, and Brendon Larson, 145–152. Farnham: Ashgate Publishing Limited.

Redi, Laura, and Stefanie Shattuck-Hufnagel. 2001. "Variation in the realization of glottalization in normal speakers." *Journal of Phonetics* 29 (4): 407–429.

Rhodan, Maya. 2014. "3 speech habits that are worse than vocal fry in job interviews." Accessed 24 February 2015. Available from: http://time.com/2820087/3-speech-habits-that-are-worse-than-vocal-fry-in-job-interviews/.

Rickford, John R. 1999. "The Ebonics controversy in my backyard: A sociolinguist's experience and reflections." *Journal of Sociolinguistics* 3 (2): 267–274.

Salie, Faith. 2013. "Burned out on the 'fry'." Accessed 24 February 2015. Available from: http://www.cbsnews.com/news/faith-salie-burned-out-on-the-fry/.

Sandoval-Almazan, Rodrigo, and J. Ramon Gil-Garcia. 2014. "Towards cyberactivism 2.0? Understanding the use of social media and other information technologies for political activism and social movements." *Government Information Quarterly* 31 (3): 365–378.

Sayers, Dave. 2014. "The mediated innovation model: A framework for researching media influence in language change." *Journal of Sociolinguistics* 18 (2): 185–212.

Schembri, Adam, Jordan Fenlon, Ramas Rentelis, Sally Reynolds, and Kearsy Cormier. 2013. "Building the British Sign Language corpus." *Language Documentation and Conservation* 7: 136–154.

Soon, Carol, and Randy Kluver. 2014. "Uniting political bloggers in diversity: Collective identity and web activism." *Journal of Computer-Mediated Communication* 19 (3): 500–515.

Stilgoe, Jack. 2011. "People, not papers: Rethinking 'impact'." Accessed 24 February 2015. Available from: https://jackstilgoe.wordpress.com/2011/06/13/people-not-papers-rethinking-impact/.

Stuart-Smith, Jane, Claire Timmins, and Fiona Tweedie. 2007. "'Talkin' Jockney'? Variation and change in Glaswegian accent." *Journal of Sociolinguistics* 11 (2): 221–260.

Sullivan, Gail. 2014. "Study: Women with creaky voices – also known as 'vocal fry' – deemed less hireable." Accessed 24 February 2015. Available from: https://www.washingtonpost.com/news/morning-mix/wp/2014/06/02/study-women-with-creaky-voices-also-known-as-vocal-fry-deemed-less-hireable/.

The Today Show. 2011. "New speech pattern of young women: 'Vocal fry'." Accessed 24 February 2015. Available from: http://www.today.com/video/today/45681253#45681253.

Tremonti, Anna Maria. 2015. "'Vocal fry' undermines empowered young women, says Naomi Wolf." Accessed 3 August 2015. Available from: http://www.cbc.ca/radio/thecurrent/the-current-for-july-28-2015-1.3170502/vocal-fry-undermines-empowered-young-women-says-naomi-wolf-1.3170511.

Vuolo, Mike. 2013. "Do you creak?" Accessed 24 February 2015. Available from: http://www.slate.com/articles/podcasts/lexicon_valley/2013/01/lexicon_valley_on_creaky_voice_or_vocal_fry_in_young_american_women.html.

Walker, Jill. 2006. "Blogging from inside the ivory tower." In *Uses of Blogs*, ed. by Axel Bruns and Joanne Jacobs, 127–138. New York: Peter Lang.

Watermeyer, Richard. 2016. "Impact in the REF: Issues and obstacles." *Studies in Higher Education* 41 (2): 199–214.

Wells, John. 1982. *Accents of English: Vol. 1: An Introduction*. Cambridge: Cambridge University Press.

Wolf, Naomi. 2015. "Young women, give up the vocal fry and reclaim your strong female voice." Accessed 3 August 2015. Available from: http://www.theguardian.com/commentisfree/2015/jul/24/vocal-fry-strong-female-voice.

Wolfram, Walt. 2011. "Sociolinguistic engagement: Principles and practices." Paper presented at Duke University.

Wolfram, Walt, Jeffery Reaser, and Charlotte Vaughn. 2008. "Operationalizing linguistic gratuity: From principle to practice." *Language and Linguistic Compass* 2 (6): 1109–1134.

Wolk, Lesley, Nassima B. Abdelli-Beruh, and Dianne Slavin. 2012. "Habitual use of vocal fry in young adult female speakers." *Journal of Voice* 26 (3): e111–e116.

Woll, Bencie, Kearsy Cormier, and Adam Schembri. 2012. "DCAL's response to *Guardian* article 'Signs of the times: Deaf community minds its language'." Accessed 24 February 2014. Available from: http://www.ucl.ac.uk/dcal/dcal-news/guardian.

Part III

Impact in language policy

Exploring the enigma of Welsh language policy (or, How to pursue impact on a shoestring)

Dave Sayers, ORCID NUMBER 0000–0003–1124–7132

Introduction

How can you pursue something as grand as 'impact' when you're out of work? Why would anyone listen to a researcher who isn't in charge of a funded project? And don't you need a research support office and other institutional backup to do impact properly? In this chapter I outline how impact can be pursued outside the groves of academe, given the right attitude to opportunities, some perseverance, and good temper.

The purpose of my chapter is not to lay claim to impact nearly as impressive as in the other chapters in this volume. But before you leave me to read them instead, let me explain. My co-editor and I have both used our editorial privilege to discuss issues we felt were important but not based on impact demonstrably achieved in our own work (cf. Lawson, this volume). This was a dilemma, but we felt that not discussing these topics would be too big a missed opportunity. I begin this chapter by detailing my own attempts to develop institutional connections during a period of employment (and unemployment) outside academia, and how this enabled me to present my work to senior policymakers in the Welsh Government.[1] Their reactions to my work suggested that they were moved to question certain assumptions within policy. Ultimately, this did not have particularly earth-shattering effects on policy, but, given my position at the time, even this modest stirring of reflection was quite an achievement. My aim here is to show how, despite finding myself professionally down and out, I still developed useful networks and pursued meaningful exposure for my research. This also helped set up the conditions for future impact as my academic career gradually re-materialised.

To mitigate a drift into navel-gazing autobiography, the chapter goes on to draw out generalisable routes to impact for trained sociolinguists, including those unemployed, semi-employed, or otherwise peripherally attached to academia. I also want to show how academic institutions can more effectively engage research-active sociolinguists who lack official affiliations – and how this could both help them and enrich the discipline. I offer this latter proposal very cautiously, fully aware of an ongoing heated debate about a shortfall of secure employment opportunities for PhD graduates, and the potential for exploitative working conditions. I discuss that tension towards the end.

The research in question focused on language policy in Wales, a field that has been significantly bolstered in strength and scope by political devolution within the UK. Decades of gradual devolution culminated in 1999 with the creation of the National Assembly for Wales, a combined legislature and executive. That devolution was bolstered in 2011 by a referendum which delivered primary law-making powers to the Assembly in areas including language policy. The very first piece of primary legislation passed by the newly empowered Assembly was the Welsh Language (Wales) Measure 2011, centring on promotion of Welsh in a range of domains. This pole position for language policy indicated the importance of the language; and although historically this issue had divided political parties, cross-party support had grown so strong by then that the 2011 Measure passed unanimously.

At the heart of this political and legislative thrust is "the active promotion of a bilingual Wales" (Welsh Government 2015) from a base of 19% Welsh-speaking in the 2011 census (Statistics for Wales 2012a). This is an immense ambition entailing a huge programme of social engineering. My research question arose here: what motivations propel this massive endeavour? What ideologies can be detected within the Welsh Government's language policies? There has been much debate on this – political, academic, and civic – but previously no detailed dissection of policy texts to weigh up those priorities.

Language policy in Wales over the last decade has been guided by major flagship policy documents – published in light of legislation – that set out what is to be done in practice. In my research I looked at four of these documents published between 2003 and 2012, to identify the priorities they set out and to examine similarities and differences in their ideological orientations. I discuss those in more detail later in the chapter.

Thinking about impact

What is impact anyway? For various reasons (not least co-editing this book), this question has occupied me quite a lot. Institutional understandings of the term, in the UK at least, tend to centre on how it is defined by funding bodies. That occupied much of our earlier essay (Lawson and Sayers, this volume) so here I focus on what the term means to me, and in particular what it can mean during a spell of under-employment.

The first question to ask is *whom* your research could influence. Since my research was about policy, the obvious route was to seek out policymakers. I describe that process below, and draw out how research in other fields could be applied by those with similarly limited means. As a general rule though, 'stakeholder mapping' is a useful initial technique to build a picture of possible interest groups; for an excellent free resource, see ODI (2009).

The second question, then, is *what* can be changed. As Otto von Bismarck put it (1895: 248), "politics is the art of the possible." A silver lining to the cloud of being an academic outsider is that nobody is pressuring you to achieve anything with your research (nobody in your professional life anyway). In this situation meaningful impact could seem small, relative to those with institutional backup and funding. My impact plan took the form of presenting my work to audiences of policymakers and going from there. As I set out below, having an outline plan and being flexible can lead in unexpected and fruitful directions.

Finally, *why* bother with impact? Without an academic career, the looming spectre of evaluation metrics (including impact) has little import. Naturally, it would help anyone seeking academic employment to demonstrate impact, but in the moment of research my motivation returned to some basic principles: my analysis had brought up some unexpected findings; I saw that my methodological approach had not really been applied to Welsh language policy before; and so I felt I could bring these new insights to the attention of policymakers and hopefully encourage new thinking, if only in a limited capacity.

It is worth emphasising that although the exposure I achieved was quite a coup given what little I brought to the task, nevertheless it was not quite 'impact' in the sense of effecting demonstrable change to professional practice. Unlike most chapters in this volume, my account is not really a full map to impact, but rather a construction kit for setting up the conditions to achieve impact in the longer term. Impact is not a linear process; it drifts back and forth, buffeted by the ebb and flow of shifting policy priorities and events. It is also maddeningly contingent, subject to chance occurrences and encounters (cf. Coleman, this volume; Levasseur, this volume; Patrick, this volume), being in the right place at the right time – or not. This chapter offers cartographic tools; drawing the map is down to you.

The research

When I set about this research I was coming to the end of a job as a Research Manager for a charity in Wales – a charity that helps a range of people experiencing different forms of social exclusion: mental ill health, homelessness, family breakdown, and so on. My PhD had previously looked into various aspects of Welsh language policy, and although this job was not about language policy, nevertheless I got to thinking about how the priorities of Welsh language policy might align with the lives of disadvantaged individuals in Wales. The idea for my research really began to take shape with an article by De Schutter (2007), which discusses three different ideologies at work in language policy generally (outlined below). From here I investigated how these three ideologies surfaced in the language policies of the Welsh Government.

First though, it is essential to stress that I was not – and am not – suggesting that the explicit wording of policies can be straightforwardly used to interpret the myriad rationales and justifications swirling around as policymakers put pen to paper. My aim was only to weigh up what the policies stated at face value. Gaining an understanding of how that relates to the actual motivations behind the policies was one of my hopes in presenting the research to policymakers, and remains an area for future investigation. I say a bit more about that towards the end. For now, let me outline De Schutter's three ideologies:

Constitutive ideology

> The constitutive view says that language constitutes who I am, that my language and my identity are inextricably intertwined, that I cannot have concepts or views for which I do not have language, and that language allows me to express or articulate things that I could not have without having language.
>
> (De Schutter 2007: 8)

In terms of Welsh language policies, for a text to reflect the constitutive ideology would be to assert that promoting Welsh would bolster Welsh identity.

Instrumental ideology

> Instrumentalists . . . typically defend the idea that languages should be primarily seen as tools to perform non-linguistically defined things [and] . . . that government interference in the domain of language is only legitimate in so far as it attempts to bring about these non-linguistic goals.
>
> (De Schutter 2007: 9)

According to this view, access to a language is not a self-evident benefit; it must deliver some increase in material wellbeing. To embody this ideology in the Welsh context would be to claim that increased Welsh provision would have such a benefit, for example in terms of health or prosperity.

Intrinsic ideology

De Schutter characterises this final view as the belief that

> languages are morally valuable in themselves, independently of the value their speakers attach to them. . . . This intrinsic argument stands opposed to instrumental accounts, which consider only the individual to be the bearer of rights.
>
> (De Schutter 2007: 10)

For Welsh language policy, articulating this ideology would mean planning to promote the language and increase its use, as an end in itself.

To assess the strength of each ideology in Welsh language policy, I needed a representative body of texts from the kinds of flagship policies I mentioned earlier. I selected the following, encompassing the most recent such policy as well as others from the preceding decade:

- Iaith Pawb: A National Action Plan for a Bilingual Wales (WAG 2003)
- Recruitment and the Welsh Language: Guidance under Section 3 of the Welsh Language Act 1993 (WLB 2009) (hereafter 'RWL')
- Iaith Fyw: Iaith Byw / A Living Language: A Language for Living – A Strategy for the Welsh Language. Public Consultation Draft (WAG 2010) (hereafter 'Iaith Fyw PCD')
- Iaith Fyw: Iaith Byw / A Living Language: A Language for Living – A Strategy for the Welsh Language 2012–2017. (Welsh Government 2012) (hereafter 'Iaith Fyw')

Iaith Pawb and Iaith Fyw were designed to guide a large range of actions over several years (the former was the predecessor to the latter). I analysed two versions of Iaith Fyw: a draft published in 2010 for public consultation; and the post-consultation finalised version published in 2012. These were both included in the analysis because they might represent interesting changes – not least the possible influence of the consultation process. The second of the four documents, RWL, is the most constrained in scope, relating only to recruitment practices mostly among public sector organisations – but this is still a very broad remit.

To weigh up the strength of De Schutter's three language ideologies in these texts I used a form of content analysis (Joffe and Yardley 2004; Silverman 2011: 65). This method is designed to get a value-neutral sense of where emphases lie in a text, by carefully trawling through and noting each time a given theme is mentioned. Codes are used to represent each theme and the text is annotated accordingly. In *inductive coding*, there are no expectations about what themes might arise; they are allowed to emerge from the text. This is commonly used in epidemiological research to generalise causative links from a body of semi-structured interviews – for example why people fail to follow a course of medication (Malta et al. 2005). In *deductive coding*, the researcher decides beforehand what the codes will be, usually based on prior research. I opted for deductive coding since I knew what codes I was looking for, namely De Schutter's three ideologies. A very similar approach was taken by Björkman (2014) in analysing the language policies of a number of Swedish universities, by developing codes based on Spolsky's (2004) framework of language policy.

The focus of my chapter is more about pursuing impact than the details of the research, so I will skip over further details of the methodology and analysis – pretending that the method was developed with no false starts, and that the data fell into place with musical ease. (For more detail see Sayers, in prep.) The findings – tallying up the occurrences of De Schutter's three ideologies across the four texts – showed interesting patterns. I begin with some short quotes to illustrate what I mean by 'occurrences' of each ideology, and then present the overall data in its broadest form. First of all, some indicative occurrences of the *constitutive ideology*:

> The Welsh language is an important element in our national culture and identity.
> (Iaith Pawb, p. 50)

> The Welsh language is an essential part of the cultural identity and character of Wales.
>
> (Iaith Fyw PCD, Foreword)

In these cases, as per De Schutter's definition, identity is explicitly linked to language – the corollary being that a plan to increase the use of Welsh would bolster identity.

Second, some indicative occurrences of the *instrumental ideology*:

> Research undertaken by Consumer Focus Wales showed that 73% of respondents were more likely to buy again from a business . . . if it provided them with a Welsh language service.
>
> (RWL, p. 22)

> Strengthening Welsh language services in health and social care . . . for many . . . is a matter of need . . . for instance, people with dementia or people who have had a stroke often lose their second language.
>
> (Iaith Fyw PCD, p. 16)

Here, demonstrable material benefits are explicitly foregrounded. Also worth noting, these two examples come from two quite distinct contexts: business and professional care.

Third, some occurrences of the *intrinsic ideology*:

> The Assembly Government is clear about the crucial importance of maintaining Welsh as a living community language if the language is to thrive and flourish.
>
> (Iaith Pawb, p. 21)

> All of the policies and projects discussed in this document have been included with a specific desired outcome: to increase the use of Welsh.
>
> (Iaith Fyw, p. 50)

Here, the goal to increase the use of Welsh is self-sufficient. Welsh is to be maintained, so that Welsh flourishes. These examples articulate a singular importance for promoting the language and its use, not explicitly as a means to increasing material wellbeing.

Figure 10.1 shows the overall tallies for all the occurrences of each ideology across the four texts. Two main caveats should be highlighted: first, since these are bare totals, they are somewhat skewed by the different sizes of the documents (RWL in particular is comparatively short); second, my limited means and even more limited data-crunching skills prevented measurement of statistical significance. Nevertheless, these data were enough to pursue impact as described below.

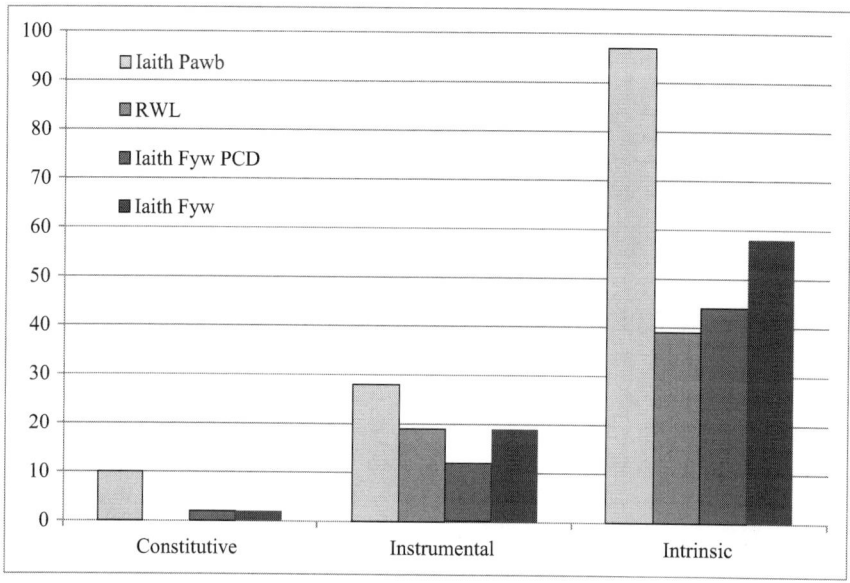

Figure 10.1 Total occurrences of each of De Schutter's (2007) three ideologies of language in four Welsh language policy texts

At this broadest level, then, a pattern appears. The intrinsic ideology seems to dominate. The findings for the constitutive ideology were surprising, namely that Welsh identity appears so downplayed. Without wanting to speculate about motivations (as caveated above), this may be intentional, in order to avoid conflating Welsh-speaking with Welsh identity, cognizant of the non-Welsh-speaking majority in Wales who nevertheless feel a strong sense of Welsh identity. For example in the 2011 census in Wales, although only 19% reported as Welsh-speaking (Statistics for Wales 2012a), fully 66% gave 'Welsh' as their national identity (Statistics for Wales 2012b).

Returning to the overall picture, the dominance of the intrinsic ideology suggests relative priorities, at least at the explicit level of what is stated in the wording of the texts. Consistently across the four texts is a predominant assertion of the importance of increasing the use of Welsh for no other stated reason than to increase the use of Welsh. And this bolstering of the language, as an independent entity in need of protection, is consistently articulated more frequently than concerns of human wellbeing and Welsh identity.

This all seemed rather remarkable. But perhaps I had missed some introductory statements in each document with words to the effect of 'when we say we want to increase the use of Welsh, of course this is just shorthand for a wider programme to raise human wellbeing' – statements to which those apparently self-justifying plans could be referring back (thanks to Nik Coupland for mooting this possibility).

Checking back though, there were no such provisos, only these repeated plans to increase Welsh proficiency as an end in itself. This was a puzzling emphasis to find cropping up across a body of social policy. Surely governments ultimately work in the interests of people, not abstract ideas. And so if growing the Welsh language is a priority, then surely it is because people will benefit. But that was not the dominant theme of the policy texts.

At least, this was how it looked from a dry reading of the text, going only on what was explicitly written. That would later turn out to be just the surface of a deeper enigma, which I discuss later in the next section.

Building credibility, pursuing impact

My data seemed to suggest something intriguing about government policy. But where could I go from here? My professional position went from unusual to invisible when the chasm of a global economic downturn began to arc out and my post of Research Manager became an unjustifiable decadence for a medium-sized regional charity. How we laughed as we realised that the charity's strained budget could be balanced by removing my salary. So I began eking out a living from bits of freelance copy-editing (the one thing I had in common with employed academics was that research occupied much of my free time), but that was hardly a useful title for networking. And despite a PhD, I had a publication record that would have taken some work to look meagre. From this diminutive position I was hardly well placed to make pronouncements about government policy.

Some things worked in my favour though. The first came about two years beforehand, straight after my PhD when I had just taken up my doomed job. The job was based in Swansea, and I made gentle overtures to Swansea University – specifically to the Head of the relevant School – to allow me some sort of unpaid affiliation. I had no prior connection to the university, but I was writing up my own research in my spare time, and my day job was about research as well. For these two reasons, after some deliberation and paperwork, they kindly awarded me an Honorary Research Fellowship: no salary, no formal responsibilities, just a title, library access, and an academic email address. This turned out to be a great help with research, as well as with networking and making contact with government. (I hope in turn to have represented the university well and contributed to its research profile.) This was the first big step to gaining a measure of credibility for pursuing impact.

At this time, unswerving in my stubborn determination to eventually get an academic career or die trying, I was attending conferences to present various ideas. These events helped to finesse my research focus. Also, when the time came, this helped me to find a way into policy circles to present my work, en route to impact.

In my charity research job I made some useful contacts in Welsh Government research circles, and when I felt I was finally ready to present something to policymakers I made use of one of these. Now, this chapter is about how anyone could pursue impact, so I hasten to add that I could have reached this particular person by inquiring through any normal public-facing email address and being referred on to him. Alternatively I could have contacted my new 'colleagues' at Swansea University for suggestions, where I'm sure I would have had a helpful response. Anyway, my contact actually referred me on to someone else with a more relevant role. The person in question was in charge of social research for the Welsh Government, and I felt things were getting a bit serious at this point. I explained, unassumingly and without burdensome detail, that I had some research about Welsh language policy which had been presented at academic conferences and which I thought may be of interest. Emphasising my flexibility, I asked if there might be opportunities to present my work. I was asked to send a summary, after which I was invited to give a presentation to a small group of civil servants in Cardiff. The group turned out to be very small, but quality outweighed quantity: they were among the most senior Welsh language policymakers. If there had been any doubt, things were certainly getting serious now.

As I said earlier, impact need not be all-singing and all-dancing (I attempted neither). It can be relatively modest, detectable only on slow-motion replay. So let me walk through my first germinal moment of impact, then rewind and play it again slowly.

As I presented the chart in Figure 9.1 – alongside various other charts, excerpts and analysis – it became clear that these senior policymakers were not overwhelmingly pleased. My findings did not reflect the point of their policies at all; I was misguided. "Your research misses the mark spectacularly" was one remark that almost caused me to lose consciousness. Why had I got myself into this situation? I had strolled into a den of foxes wearing a chicken costume. Thankfully the mood gradually improved and this chicken remained uneaten. In fact, as the presentation went on, we all came to more of an understanding (they were after all perfectly reasonable people). Nobody enjoys a direct challenge to their work, but I repeated a number of times that this was a passive and disinterested analysis of the texts. As we talked through our different positions, the enigma at the heart of these policies began to unravel.

The "mark" I had missed, as it was further put to me, was an underlying goal to support "fragile Welsh language communities," "in a way they want to live their lives." This rationale was a fundamental tenet of the whole policy enterprise. This was such a blindingly obvious premise to them that it essentially went without saying, and the reaction I provoked was due to this mismatch. As my presentation went on, and as I kept reiterating meekly that my research had no agenda – simply a passive reflection of codes tallied up from the texts – I reached a closer understanding with my audience, and vice versa. They saw the disjuncture between what was explicitly written and what they implicitly understood.

As my slides ended and we talked further, one policymaker pointed to my graph, with its imbalance between the different ideologies, and said pensively that he would keep it in mind as he was writing policy in future. Let me play that back again slowly: a senior policymaker told me that my research would inform his practice. There it was: my first moment of germinal impact. I was not in a position to follow this up and show changes to professional practice, but from where I was sitting I had still achieved something quite special. Of course, compare this to the kinds of sustained and substantial impact reported in the other chapters in this volume and you may wonder why you are still reading this one. But my point is that I was an absolute nobody, yet I had managed to get a senior policymaker to consider, even for a moment, a mismatch between his rationales and the policy texts he helped create. Controlling for relative capacity for impact, I think I did pretty well.

After this close encounter was over, my host recommended me and my charts to the convenors of a seminar series run by Social Research Association Cymru (the Welsh arm of a UK-wide body). Three months later I found myself in another government building in Cardiff, this time presenting an evening seminar to around twenty people, among them some similarly heavy-hitting policy officials. As it turned out I achieved a very similar reaction to my last presentation and a very similar form of germinal impact: a somewhat scratchy question from one particularly high-profile civil servant (whose language policy reports I knew well) followed by a robust and engaging debate. His question in fact provoked a countervailing response from another audience member. The whole thing was civil but lively. Even though this was another relatively brief encounter, nevertheless given my professional circumstances – and considering the calibre of the audience – I felt justified in chalking this up as another good day's work.

My story ends there, somewhat abruptly – or at least, the part about being a down-and-out academic does. At the same time as all this was happening I was furiously applying for academic jobs, with eventual success – just four short years after finishing my PhD. A few days after my second presentation I was on a ferry, with all my worldly possessions, preparing for a year's lectureship in Finland. So began the delightful but frenetic flurry of my early academic career. I was at long last coming in from the cold (ironically in sub-zero temperatures) and for the next couple of years I hardly had time to tie my shoelaces, let alone pursue impact. I have since returned to pursuing impact as my academic career has balanced out, building on the foundations I laid during my time at the peripheries of academia. I have also worked out ways that others could do the same, which is the subject of the next section.

Routes to impact for sociolinguists outside academia

Impact is a feather of many hues. In what follows, I look at quite specific routes to impact, namely influencing policymakers in the UK. In pursuit of other hues, a down-and-out academic could organise or contribute to campaigns, advocacy networks, or social movements (local, national, or international). There are opportunities for private consultancy, for example in language-in-education (see Coleman, this volume). One could write for public consumption, and then on the back of that pursue mass media exposure (see Lawson, this volume). David Crystal is an example of such an author in linguistics (and, foreshadowing my advice below, both Crystal and Coleman have honorary affiliations with universities). Moreover, I hope not to suggest that impact is only suited to those pursuing an academic career. Achieving impact with one's research is possible from a range of professional backgrounds, or from none. The basic kernel of my advice, which should match any hue of the feather, and any professional circumstance, is this: *don't ask, don't get*. Asking politely and patiently is a powerful tool, which can gradually open many doors.

Gaining an academic affiliation

It might not be important whom you work for day-to-day, but being affiliated to a university makes a difference when trying to pitch your ideas to policymakers and to other academics. Even if you have a doctorate, if you don't have a stall currently set out on the groves of academe it can be hard to be seen as more than a dilettante or hobbyist. At a basic level, academics tend to remember each other along the lines of *Dr. Jo Bloggs at Poppleton University*. By contrast, *Dr. Jo Bloggs of No Fixed Academic Abode* will not slot so easily into the academic mental Filofax. Meanwhile, among policymakers and government officials, an academic affiliation infers credibility (my own experience was backed up by personal communication from others whom I mention more later on). Lastly, without an academic title, bidding for research funding (even as part of a team) can be difficult, ruled out entirely by some funders.

So, step number one: how can a down-and-out academic gain a university affiliation? I described earlier Swansea University's kind award to me of an Honorary Research Fellowship. These titles are often poorly publicised and scarcely known, even among faculty. The use of honorary titles is perhaps best known for high-profile individuals outside academia undertaking prestigious work that is somehow relevant to the university. And these awards are made for mutual benefit: the awardee gains from a prestigious academic affiliation; the university gains from high-profile endorsement. But they can also be awarded to less high-falutin individuals (case in point) who happen to work outside academia and are publishing academic research.

The title of Honorary Research Fellow might not be well known, but it – or something like it – is a routine entry in the suite of ornate titles available at most universities. To get a sense of this in the UK context, try the following Google search:

site:ac.uk honorary research fellowship application

To explain what is going on here, the Google function 'site:ac.uk' refines the results to sites ending in 'ac.uk,' i.e. academic institutions in the UK. Running that search now, out of the first 100 results almost all are for the policies and procedures at various UK universities for appointing honorary personnel. So these positions are commonplace, but their relative obscurity is reaffirmed by the esoteric procedural language and the tucked-away location within each website. Reading through these application procedures, they tend to focus on two broad areas for eligibility: the quality of the research being conducted; and the benefit to the university. They also pinpoint (more or less specifically) who should authorise this application: usually the Head of School, Pro-Vice-Chancellor for Research, or other supra-departmental senior hat.

In the years since my own award I have encouraged many post-PhD acquaintances working outside academia to seek an honorary affiliation, and with some pleasing successes. For the purposes of this chapter I looked further at how different universities provide honorary affiliations. I emailed some of my academic contacts in decision-making positions at different universities, and sent a similar generic request for information to some academic email lists. I received many promising replies from various countries. Honorary affiliations do seem widely available, though usually focused on people who completed doctoral or post-doctoral research at that university (that is, apart from the high-profile individuals noted above). Below I report in more detail on the responses I received. Those respondents who are named have given consent to be named; others remain anonymous.

Awarding honorary affiliations to peripheral aspiring academics is usually done with the implicit understanding that this will have value to the awardees. I heard from Urszula Clark, Professor of English and Linguistics and Director of the Aston University research centre *InterLanD: Diversity, Equality and Inclusion*. She explained that Aston often awards Honorary Research or Visiting Fellowships to people who are not high-profile, and occasionally even who do not have a PhD. She explained that, in the case of InterLanD, such Fellows are usually appointed after a period of funded research, "primarily so they can continue with the publication projects ongoing since the end of funding and also to help them with their own bids for funding." She completes a form, which is then signed by the Head of School and Vice-Chancellor. I also heard from Paul Kerswill, Professor at the Department of Linguistics at the University of York, who explained that a limited number of non-stipendiary positions are awarded on a competitive basis to PhD graduates, allowing a year's access to the library, IT services, and a study space.

Some universities have formally routinised the award of honorary affiliations. Nicola Puckey, Lecturer in English Language at the University of Winchester, related to me the recent launch of an Early Career Researcher Visiting Fellowships scheme, for which all PhD graduates are eligible, and with no limitations on numbers. Ghada Khattab, Senior Lecturer in Speech and Language Sciences at Newcastle University, explained plans being considered there to award one-year non-stipendiary Fellowships to international graduates who maintain collaborations with staff – providing library resources, and facilitating collaborative research and grant applications.

At the University at Albany/State University of New York I heard from James Collins, Professor in the Department of Anthropology about Honorary Research Affiliates. These include former students, and employees of businesses or state agencies who have research interests relevant to existing faculty – for example at the NYS Department of Health or the NYS Museum. They go through a vetting procedure regarding their research interests, and are then granted various faculty/staff benefits, including library access, an email address, and parking privileges. Their administrative HR classification is 'voluntary,' to clarify the unsalaried nature of the post.

I received a similar response from David Britain, Professor and former Head of the English Department at the University of Bern, Switzerland. He explained that honorary affiliations may be awarded on a discretionary basis by agreement of the Department's Professors, but usually only if there were some pre-existing research connection with a current staff member.

On a less positive note, one respondent at an Australian university – who requested anonymity – outlined a constraint which they felt applied nationwide. Due to the way their research is assessed nationally, "honoraries count towards our head-count of research-active academics – so if they're not producing at the same level as full-time staff they're going to drag us down." Nevertheless, even with this constraint, they had given a number of their PhD graduates honorary affiliations, owing to their continued outputs.

I received a number of further replies from people who also wished to remain anonymous, and here lie some interesting lessons (some positive, some more cautionary). The Director of one major research centre in a northern European university explained to me that the university overall discourages honorary affiliations, but that he "fully exploits the grey zones in which 'institutes' or 'centers' usually reside within academic organisations," by awarding Fellow status to the centre's PhD graduates without explicit university approval. He added: "It's a matter, as you know, of being able to write a line under your name different from 'unemployed.' We are very pragmatic in this."

Meanwhile, an anonymous respondent at a UK university told me of a past attempt to routinise such awards, and its bleak unintended consequence. The awards had been advertised nationally, principally aiming to reach their PhD graduate diaspora, but this roused the scepticism of the local union branch – who suspected solicitation of free labour. The scheme quietly folded. I received another anonymous caution, from York University (Canada) that honorary affiliations are regularly awarded there but that this has caused similar union friction. These sorts of institutional politics are worth anticipating.

Still, despite important cautionary tales, the responses I received were positive in the main. And although most suggested that such honorary affiliations were principally for graduates or former employees of that university, there were exceptions (including, of course, me).

As an addendum, apart from affiliations, an increasing number of universities provide all their alumni with lifelong library access (including access to online journal services like JSTOR). I have such alumni access myself from both Essex and Cambridge. I was also informed by Oliver Stegen of the same provision at the University of Edinburgh, and by Nancy Frishberg of similar provisions at UC Berkeley and UC San Diego. Although not providing a title for networking, this nevertheless can help a lot with research. Many universities also run alumni email services. These do not tend to be run on the main '@university. edu' domain; they are more typically run through a subdomain (e.g. Columbia University's @caa.columbia.edu) or through an entirely different domain (e.g. Cambridge University's @cantab.net). Still, these at least have a bit more academic cachet than joebloggs1337@hotmail.com. I have long used my cantab.net address for academic networking, for this reason and also because it has always stayed the same despite my changing day jobs (I could easily just include that information in my email signature). I have noticed other itinerant academics doing much the same.

Achieving impact

Step two, then: you have your honorary affiliation; now how can you step up and make a difference? I begin here from my own context of experience, Wales, and then move outwards to the UK generally. The Welsh Government and the National Assembly for Wales have a range of structures to encourage external dialogue. For example, the Petitions Committee of the Assembly is set up to formally consider and respond to more or less any request for action: see www. assembly.wales/en/gethome/e-petitions/Pages/e-petitions.aspx. This sense of openness seems contagious to other areas, including research offices. The welcome I received, even with somewhat contentious findings, bore this out. For any PhD graduates conducting research in the Welsh context, I could confidently recommend approaching the Assembly and asking (politely, unassumingly) for contact with relevant research staff. At time of writing, the gateway email address for this purpose listed by the UK Economic and Social Research Council is research. evaluation@wales.gsi.gov.uk. Meanwhile, for research related to the third sector in Wales, there is the excellent Wales Council for Voluntary Action (www.wcva. org.uk), who could help facilitate dialogue. My experience working in a Welsh charity confirmed that they are perfectly approachable and helpful.

I now move on to the UK more broadly, and consider how someone with a PhD and a good idea, but not much else, could pursue something as grand as impact. There is a glut of excellent guides out there on how academics can win friends and influence people (e.g. Doig 2011; Flinders 2013; Goodwin 2013; ESRC n.d.). These contain useful general advice on a range of issues, for example how to deliver research presentations in a way that prevents non-academic attendees from napping, or just leaving. There are also whole organisations dedicated to connecting academics and policymakers, such as Policy Direct (www.policy-direct.org). But despite their wealth of good advice, these guides and organisations tend to begin from a presumption of secure academic employment, a stable professional base from which to pursue impact. For the aspiring and unsecured academic, some different approaches are needed.

For the purposes of this chapter, I contacted fourteen departments of the UK Government, plus the Social Science Research Group at the Scottish Government. When I started writing this chapter, the ESRC had a convenient 'Contact government organisations' webpage. That page has since been taken down because contacts were so frequently changing (personal communication, ESRC web support), but the Internet Archive has the page permanently backed up at http://web.archive.org/web/20131115015636/http://www.esrc.ac.uk/collaboration/public-sector/contact-government.aspx, and many of those email addresses still work. While there is still some truth in the old saying, 'It's not what you know, but who you know,' the internet has done a lot to erode that nepotistic glass ceiling. I wrote to all of those email addresses to ask, in hypothetical terms, whether someone with a PhD and some useful research findings (but little else) could engage meaningfully with that government department in some ad hoc manner (e.g. giving a presentation, contributing to a panel discussion, etc.). I kept the scope of my question broad, for maximum breadth of response. For the sake of a fair test to compare them, I sent only one email to each address, and resisted the temptation to search online for individuals within these government departments. Seven of my fifteen emails received responses, all from senior civil servants, and all very positive. One particularly informative reply from a senior analytical lead at the Home Office, outlining their approach, went as follows:

> From my perspective (and I think most of the other analytical leads adopt a similar approach), when contacted we make an assessment of policy relevance (having a good feel for current and future policy interests), methodological rigour (I tend to ask for a summary of methodology for new research), and inherent bias. Then make a judgement on how best to proceed. For some, we invite the academic in to either meet policy [sic], do a seminar or talk through their work with the analysts. With others, we'll ask for summaries of their work or ask for papers. And, if not relevant or methodologically robust, we will suggest they develop their methodology or think through policy relevance of their work.
>
> Also, a sizeable part of our role is proactively developing our networks of external researchers, so we know what research is being done in our respective policy areas. This is things like attending conferences, keeping an eye on the web and inviting people to policy workshops. Indeed, we've facilitated a number of these policy / academic / third sector round tables recently – with another in a few weeks time.

In a subsequent email, he added: "whilst I can't speak for OGDs [other government departments], that's basically just what happens across most departments I deal with."

In the central analysis team of another government department, I was given a long and informative phone call by a principal analyst. The team has built a database comprising around 200 academics and other research experts. Some had previously been commissioned by the department to conduct research; others had prior contact with ministers or policy officials; but the database was open to anyone with relevant expertise. That database is used to send out ideas, calls for proposals, and so on. I asked about routes into these sorts of circles, particularly for those without current academic credentials. The key theme that emerged was relevance, and if the research in question spoke to a particular policy priority, then there could be opportunities for engagement. It was impressed upon me the importance of working out this relevance before getting in touch, not to expect a patient exploratory dialogue about possible usefulness. It would also be crucial to get through to the right policy lead, which I was told could be tricky; but then, I thought, here I was talking to a senior analytical official who could have pointed me in the right direction, and I had no prior knowledge of whom to contact, so this seemed a surmountable obstacle. Above all, I was told, be tenacious. Keep pestering, and if your work is relevant then someone will pay attention eventually. The final gem in this phone call was mention of a 2013 briefing paper aimed at policymakers, *Engaging with Academics: How to Further Strengthen Open Policy Making* (Government Office for Science 2013). If my chapter is written for Romeo, then that briefing paper is for Juliet. Since this paper is available online, I simply point you towards it for insights on engagement from the policymaking perspective.

The responses I received from the five other government departments were similarly promising, outlining various ways that sociolinguists outside academia could engage with them. There are opportunities, for example, to sit on a number of panels and committees in the National Institute for Health Research, and to engage in an ad hoc manner at the Department for Environment, Food and Rural Affairs. The Department of Work and Pensions encourages engagement with academically qualified people regardless of their employment status (a suitable ethos for the DWP). Another senior official urged the importance of getting work published for it to be of interest. This is perennially good advice. Moreover, these discussions across government departments moved me to imagine different types of sociolinguists who might find an audience: linguistic ethnographers uncovering aspects of educational discourse; conversation analysts revealing tangles in professional-lay talk; communication specialists working on the public understanding of complex messages; and so on. It was exciting to get a sense of just how many kinds of sociolinguistic research could find a welcome reception, and open ears, across different parts of government.

A few cautionary notes can be added to all this, the first given to me by Donald Houston, Professor in Urban Studies at the University of Glasgow, in reply to one of my aforementioned emails to academic email lists: "Policy makers don't want to be told about a specific new piece of research by one individual . . . – they want to get a sense of a body of knowledge." Of note, policymakers can be contrasted with practitioners on this point, who may instead prefer specific practical examples over academic research (Innes, this volume; MacLeod and Haworth, this volume). I received further advice about policymakers from Barbara Doig, a freelance consultant and former senior civil servant, who emphasised two crucial points: impartiality (primarily to avoid suspicion of a political agenda); and adaptability (to keep up with a rapidly shifting policy landscape). Reflecting on my impact journey described earlier, my research into Welsh language policy probably benefited from being impartial – simply reflecting the content of policy texts – and adaptable in the sense that it applied across years' worth of policies in this area (and could be used to analyse future policy).

I gleaned one final major caution from various emails – particularly from academics – and from other readings. I sensed a palpable raising of eyebrows in the direction of the 'impact agenda.' Lawson & Sayers (this volume) covered that scepticism from other angles. The concerns I encountered in these emails went both ways: academics can be rather tokenistic in ticking the 'impact box,' e.g. by staging a perfunctory one-off seminar (Goodwin 2013), while funders, in assessing impact, can "assume a rather rational linear policy making process, which bears little if any resemblance to reality" (personal communication, Donald Houston). Without wishing to overlook such concerns, these need not be a major worry for down-and-out academics. If your goal is to enter academia, then even apparently superficial impact can show an understanding of contemporary priorities in the sector, which can be built upon. For those sensible individuals not aspiring to an academic career post-PhD, but who wish to have some influence with their research as matter of civic activism, even more latitude is available, with blissfully little pressure to dress one's impact in a particular colour.

Other concerns expressed to me would apply to a wider range of professional contexts. In an email thread I started on the Social Policy list (https://www.jiscmail. ac.uk/social-policy), various respondents raised concerns about prejudices – only based on anecdote, I should add, but worth noting. Gender and age were raised especially, namely that men may be listened to more than women, and that older researchers are taken more seriously. These are of course lamentably familiar prejudices in society at large. To these vectors of disadvantage one might speculatively add class, ethnicity, linguistic proficiency, and so on. On reflection, perhaps being white, male, British, and a native English speaker could have greased the wheels of my own impact. Meanwhile, perhaps youth went against me, and the discord I provoked was partly a sort of intergenerational balking at a contrarian Young Turk. Would I have got under people's skin so much as a wizened professor with a salt-and-pepper comb-over? I hope in time to find out. And I emphatically hasten to add that these reflective ponderings of mine are dangling at the extreme end of speculation, with no remote intention to accuse. In my dealings with government officials I sensed no trace of either prejudice or undue favour. I am simply reflecting on these salutary cautions from others, and offering them to you as food for thought. On balance I think anyone could make a good go of pursuing impact, with a good idea, a bit of tenacity, and the right attitude to chance. Don't ask, don't get.

Conclusion

Perhaps it is a little disingenuous of me to write at such length about being a down-and-out academic when I am nowadays a fully paid up, card-carrying denizen of the ivory tower. In some ways this chapter is a memoir, but the memories feel both close enough and distant enough for decent reflection. Hopefully this won't stick in the craw of anyone currently scratching around the periphery of academia.

A late addition to my list of caveats would be that my work involved rather unadventurous (and cheap) desk-based methods. Try organising something like systemic action research whilst unemployed. For anyone managing that I would like to create an international award. Another thematic limitation in my account is that I have focused on quite a specific area of influence, namely government policymaking, using fairly traditional forms of academic research, and mostly in the UK. But in all these blind spots of mine, I would simply take my ignorance and swing it around as an invitation and a challenge, to go forth and try. The only certainty is that nothing will happen if you don't. Eric Clapton once sang "nobody knows you when you're down and out," but I hope to have shown that even if you are down and out you can still make yourself known. With patience, perseverance, and a belief that nobody will simply reject you out of hand, it is perfectly possible for under-employed PhDs to be taken seriously and listened to. That little pep talk of mine doesn't really fit the meter of Clapton's song, but then I suppose my overall point here is that you can whistle your own tune. Find a new rhythm. Dance to the beat of a different drum.

As a final overture to universities, I believe it is well worth them investing time and energy in granting honorary affiliations to PhD holders who plan to continue their research outside academia – whether or not they aspire to an academic career. With an affiliation they can access research materials, and they can network in academia and beyond, for mutual benefit. And as I mentioned at the outset, I propose all this fully aware of disquiet about a shortfall of secure paid employment in academia. I feel no antagonism here. There is no suggestion of exploiting honorary faculty for unpaid teaching work, and these affiliations are a big enabler for developing an academic CV (I speak from direct experience). The contributions of research-active sociolinguists outside academia could significantly enrich the discipline. Meanwhile, the application of their research could lead to new and exciting forms of impact.

Acknowledgements

During the lowest ebb of my post-PhD professional destitution, I created the online community *Linguists Outside Academia* to help likeminded scholarly drifters share advice, cautions, and consolations. From its many creative and professionally agile members, I have learned about myriad ways to apply linguistic knowledge. I hope I have offered some useful advice to them here, but their combined expertise in reaching out beyond academia far outstrips mine. I hope one day to publish something about their disparate successes, but for now I dedicate this chapter to them.

I was supported in writing this chapter by the research allocations of lectureships at Åbo Akademi University, Finland, the University of Turku, Finland, and Sheffield Hallam University, UK.

For providing details of their university's provision of honorary affiliations and other facilities, my thanks go to David Britain, Urszula Clark, Paul Kerswill, Ghada Khattab, Nicola Puckey, James Collins, Nancy Frishberg, Oliver Stegen, and others who wished to remain anonymous. For broad-ranging advice in relation to achieving impact (in addition to the points directly attributed to them earlier), I am indebted to Barbara Doig and Donald Houston. For information about practices in the UK Government, I am grateful to senior officials at six government departments who opted to remain anonymous. For peer-reviewing this chapter, special thanks go to Nik Coupland and Joan Beal; they have spared me many blushes. Final editorial tweaks came courtesy of my endlessly amiable co-editor Robert Lawson. Remaining mistakes are mine . . . all mine.

Note

1 The name *Welsh Assembly Government* was changed to *Welsh Government* in March 2011; I use the latter except in pre-2011 references.

References

Björkman, Beyza. 2014. "Language ideology or language practice? An analysis of language policy documents at Swedish universities." *Multilingua* 33 (3–4): 335–363.

De Schutter, H. 2007. "Language policy and political philosophy: On the emerging linguistic justice debate." *Language Problems and Language Planning* 31 (1): 1–23.

Doig, Barbara. 2011. "Getting social science research into the evidence base in Government: A summary of Barbara Doig's 'Pathway to Impact to Central Government – A Route Map.'" Accessed 21 April 2014. Available from: https://www2.warwick.ac.uk/fac/cross_fac/ias/activities/ace/resources/impact_-_miles_2.pdf.

ESRC. n.d. "Public affairs." Accessed 21 April 2014. Available from: http://www.esrc.ac.uk/research/impact-toolkit/public-affairs/.

Flinders, Matthew. 2013. "Impact, engagement and dangerous liaisons." Accessed 21 April 2014. Available from: https://www2.warwick.ac.uk/fac/cross_fac/ias/activities/ace/resources/impact_-_miles_3.pdf.

Goodwin, Michael. 2013. "How academics can engage with policy: 10 tips for a better conversation." Accessed 21 April 2014. Available from: http://www.theguardian.com/higher-education-network/blog/2013/mar/25/academics-policy-engagement-ten-tips.

Government Office for Science. 2013. "Engaging with academics: How to further strengthen open policy making." Accessed 21 April 2014. Available from: https://www.gov.uk/government/uploads/system/uploads/attachment_data/file/283129/13-581-engaging-with-academics-open-policy-making.pdf.

Joffe, Hélène, and Lucy Yardley. 2004. "Content and content analysis." In *Research Methods for Clinical and Health Psychology*, ed. by David F. Marks and Lucy Yardley, 56–68. London: Sage.

Malta, Monica, Maya L. Petersen, Scott Clair, Fernando Freitas, and Francisco I. Bastos. 2005. "Adherence to antiretroviral therapy: A qualitative study with physicians from Rio de Janeiro, Brazil." *Cadernos de Saúde Pública* 21 (5): 1424–1432.

ODI (Overseas Development Institute). 2009. "Planning tools: Stakeholder analysis." Accessed 28 April 2014. Available from: http://www.odi.org/publications/5257-stakeholder-analysis.

Sayers, Dave. In prep. "Ideological directions in Welsh language policy: A content analysis."

Silverman, David. 2011. *Interpreting Qualitative Data*, 4th ed. London: Sage.

Spolsky, Bernard. 2004. *Language Policy*. Cambridge: Cambridge University Press.

Statistics for Wales. 2012a. "2011 Census: First results on the Welsh language." Accessed 10 April 2014. Available from: http://gov.wales/docs/statistics/2012/121217sb126201 2en.pdf.

Statistics for Wales. 2012b. "2011 Census: First results for ethnicity, national identity, and religion for Wales." Accessed 10 April 2014. Available from: http://gov.wales/docs/stati stics/2012/121217sb1262012en.pdf.

von Bismarck, Otto. 1895. *Fürst Bismarck: Neue Tischgespräche und Interviews*, Vol. 1. Stuttgart: Deutsche Verlags-Anstalt.

WAG (Welsh Assembly Government) (2003). Iaith Pawb: A National Action Plan for a Bilingual Wales. Accessed 14 February 2016. Available from: http://gov.wales/topics/welshlanguage/publications/iaithpawb/?lang=en.

WAG (Welsh Assembly Govenrment) (2010). A living language: A language for living – A strategy for the Welsh Language [Iaith Fyw: Iaith Byw]: Public consultation draft. Accessed 14 February 2016. Available from: http://gov.wales/docs/drah/consultation/20 101213alivinglanguageeng.pdf.

Welsh Government (2012). Iaith Fyw: Iaith Byw / A Living Language: A Language for Living – A Strategy. Accessed 14 February 2016. Available from: http://gov.wales/topics/welshlanguage/publications/wlstrategy2012/?lang=en.

Welsh Government (2015). Our Welsh Language Scheme. Accessed 14 February 2016. Available from: http://gov.wales/topics/welshlanguage/policy/wls/?lang=en.

WLB (Welsh Language Board) (2009). Recruitment and the Welsh Language: Guidance under Section 3 of the Welsh Language Act 1993. Accessed 14 February 2016. Available from: https://archive.org/details/RecruitmentAndTheWelshLanguageGuidance UnderSection3OfTheWelshLanguageAct1993.

Chapter 11

'To be consulted, to encourage and to warn'

The impact and the limits of language-in-education research in the developing world

Hywel Coleman, ORCID NUMBER 0000–0003–3996–1514

Introduction

This chapter discusses research studies on the educational role of the English language in developing countries, commissioned by the British Council (BC). The core of the chapter explores three case studies, from Indonesia in Southeast Asia, Gabon in Central Africa and Pakistan in South Asia. The BC's motivations for commissioning the studies, the methods employed and the findings are discussed briefly. Importantly, each research report was required to include recommendations. Stakeholders' reactions to the recommendations form the starting point for a more detailed discussion of 'impact.' The chapter concludes with observations on why impact varies from one context to another. Throughout, I provide some tentative guidance and suggestions to others working in similar contexts.

Over the years I have been asked by the BC to undertake research in nearly twenty developing countries in Asia and Africa. In some cases, the reports resulting from these studies have been published in print and on the BC website, while in others they have had only limited distribution within the countries concerned. In yet other cases, I have not been informed about what, if anything, has happened to the reports.

In every case, the BC's motivation for commissioning the research was to understand more about the use of the English language in the education system, usually in line with the aim expressed in its Charter to "develop a wider knowledge of the English language" around the world (British Council 2011). (It is important to note that the Charter also obliges the BC to "promote the advancement of education.") In some countries the initial prompt is that a country's government has recently introduced an innovation in English Language Teaching (ELT). As we will see, Ministries of Education sometimes believe that introducing ELT at a younger age will solve educational problems. If so, part of the research task is to critically evaluate the innovation and judge its chances of success. There is, after all, a long history of ambitious, expensive and largely unsuccessful ELT projects (Wedell 2009).

In exploring the sociolinguistic context in a given country, I typically need to find out what other languages are used. What roles do these languages play? Are any of these languages given official roles by the state? What are people's perceptions of their own languages, the national language and English? Do speakers of certain languages enjoy privileges unavailable to others? How does English fit into the overall language ecology? Is English threatening the existence of indigenous languages? (For a relevant discussion, see Rapatahana and Bunce 2012.) Consideration of the educational context will reveal the total number of teachers, their qualifications, how much time they spend in school, whether their numbers suffice for the number of learners, what proportion of children finish school, whether girls drop out more or less than boys, and how parents perceive education.

Coming to English, we need to see what role English *as a subject* has in the curriculum. How many hours are allocated? Is it a high-stakes examinable subject? Are English teachers confident in the language? Is there appropriate pre-service and in-service training? Are there inspectors of English, who actually visit schools? Where do the teaching materials come from? Last but not least, why is English being taught? If the teaching of English does have a clear purpose, are stakeholders aware of it?

Of particular interest is the question of which language is the *medium of instruction*. Are children's home languages used, is it the national language (unfamiliar to many), or the former colonial language (English or French, for example)? To what extent are official policies actually implemented in the classroom? If teachers are expected to teach using English, are they sufficiently proficient? Do teachers and pupils even share the same language (Lin and Martin 2005)?

Answers to these questions are important. There is overwhelming evidence of negative consequences from efforts to teach children through the medium of an unfamiliar language. Put simply, if children do not understand the language of the classroom, they do not learn. If they cannot communicate freely with the teacher, they become passive. Such children will be more likely to drop out of school. If the mother tongue is not recognised – or even forbidden – in school, then children's sense of identity is challenged. If parents are unfamiliar or uncomfortable with the language of school, then they cannot support the child's learning. Over time, whole communities may become alienated from education and – ultimately – from the state which marginalises them (see Pinnock 2009; Ouane and Glanz 2010).

If it is still considered essential that English (or any other second language) should be used as a medium of education, then it is generally recognised that: a) the transfer away from the mother tongue should be delayed as long as possible; b) the transfer should take place gradually; c) children should learn the other language as a subject to fluency, before it is used as a medium; and d) after the transfer, study and use of the mother tongue should continue (Kosonen and Young 2009). This is the approach known as Mother Tongue Based Multilingual Education (MTB MLE). A typical – though rather idealised – model is mother-tongue-medium initial primary education, with English taught as a subject for several years at this level, then English as the medium in secondary school with continued mother-tongue instruction. The hope is to create balanced bilinguals, fluent and positively-oriented towards both their first language and the international language.

Examination of the economic context is also important, because the mantra 'English is important for national development' is almost ubiquitous. Rigorous research in this area is still limited, but what research exists has struggled to cor-relate English proficiency and national economic vitality (Erling and Seargeant 2013), although there may be a correlation on the individual level in certain specific circumstances.

Adopting Amartya Sen's definition of "development" as "freedom" (1999: 3), we need to be aware of the importance of language for participation in civil society. Are speakers of minority languages free to seek justice in the law courts even if they do not know the national language? Are they free to seek hospital treatment? Can they apply for a driving licence? Are they consulted in their own language about development of their communities? If not, then these people are "reduced to silent objects of development" (Idris et al. 2007: 34). The research discussed here, therefore, is located at a disciplinary and professional junction. This is sociolinguistic work to be sure, but it is also development policy and educa-tion policy work.

A risk in this work – particularly commissioned by an organisation whose *raison d'être* includes promotion of English – is that, if one discourages English teaching, then one may be perceived as antagonistic towards English. This is not the case, at least for me. It is clear that English plays important roles in some developing countries (Coleman 2010a). But English cannot solve all the ills of the developing world, and, inappropriately used, it can be dangerous.

Impact

The Terms of Reference for the research I undertake always include a requirement for explicit recommendations in the final report. To that extent, then, 'impact' is central. My work is intended to influence language-in-education policy and practice. A straightforward way of gauging my impact might be to measure how far the report's recommendations are implemented. But this is over-simplistic and needs breaking down further.

First, impact may be felt at three different levels:

- at the level of awareness or conceptualisation of language issues in society, broadly speaking, and in education specifically;
- at the level of policy or planning;
- at the level of practice.

Identifying official policy is generally straightforward: for example, what do gov-ernment regulations say about language in education? Observing practice – finding out which languages are actually used in the privacy of the classroom, for instance – may be straightforward to arrange, but difficulties may arise in practice. The 'observer's paradox' weighs in here: participants may switch from their normal language to the language they think they ought to use if they are knowingly observed. But the most difficult level to describe and measure is stakeholders' awareness and understanding of language issues. Nevertheless, without changes in awareness, changes in practice are unlikely.

A further complication is that the kinds of research I am commissioned to produce, and the recommendations coming from it, may be read by different audiences, not only the BC (as sponsor) but possibly also the education authorities and even members of the public in the country concerned.

With all this in mind, there are multiple ways in which research impact might be gauged, including whether:

- the research findings and recommendations are understood by the sponsor (the BC), found to be acceptable/interesting/useful, and published and made available for comment;
- the sponsor takes on board the report's recommendations and incorporates them into its own policy and planning;
- the sponsor implements its own policy;
- the research findings and recommendations are understood by the end users (the in-country education authorities) and are disseminated;
- the education authorities adapt their policies in line with the report's recommendations;
- language-in-education practice changes.

I return to these measures later in the chapter.

Case studies: Gabon, Pakistan and Indonesia

To explore the above issues, I refer to research projects I have undertaken in three developing countries: Gabon (Central Africa), Pakistan (South Asia) and Indonesia (Southeast Asia). These projects were carried out in 2013, 2010 and 2009 respectively, in each case prompted by government initiatives – proposed or recently implemented – regarding the teaching of English in schools.

The three nations contrast demographically, in terms of human development and in language policy. Gabon has a small population, whereas both Pakistan and Indonesia have extremely large populations. On the Human Development Index (produced by the United Nations Development Programme), Gabon and Indonesia are ranked as having medium human development, whilst Pakistan is considered to have low human development (see United Nations 2013).

In terms of language planning, Gabon and Pakistan have inherited their former colonial languages (French and English respectively) and given them privileged status. Indonesia, on the other hand, rejected Dutch at independence and has developed its own national language, Bahasa Indonesia.

The three cases also contrast in terms of the impact I achieved, and this is the main reason for their ordering. As will become apparent, the Gabon study seems to have had zero impact; in Pakistan, some modest short-term impact can be identified; and in Indonesia, the research contributed to a significant change in educational policy and practice at the national level, although for reasons I could not really have foreseen.

Each case study falls into five parts: background (demography, human development, and sociolinguistic profile); research process; findings; recommendations; and impact (what changed and what stayed the same after the research had been completed).

Case study 1: Gabon

Gabon is very small, with a population of just 1.7 million. It was ranked 112th from 187 countries in the United Nations' 2013 Human Development Index. Although the country is oil-rich, 4.4% of its population were in severe poverty in 2012. The country was colonised by France between 1839 and 1960. At independence it adopted French as its national language. Estimates of the number of African languages vary between 10 and 42, but these languages have no role in education or in any official context. French is the only language permitted for instruction in schools. English has never had formal status, but is taught as a foreign language in secondary schools.

The government's *Strategic Plan for an Emerging Gabon* (Gouvernement du Gabon 2012) included among its ambitious aims that by 2015 English would be taught as a subject in pre-primary and primary schools. The stated rationale was to help to "prepare young Gabonese for working in companies." However, it is widely believed that the inspiration for this innovation was the attempt by the Government of Rwanda to replace French with English as the medium of instruction in schools (Samuelson and Freedman 2010; Steflja 2012), following accession to the Commonwealth in 2009.

My study was commissioned by BC Francophone West Africa (BC FWA), in response to a request for advice from the Gabon Ministry of Education. The Terms of Reference stated that the purpose of the study was "to examine the government's proposal to introduce the teaching of English in state primary schools and to make recommendations relating to that proposal."

My study aimed to create a profile of language use and language attitudes in primary and secondary schools, to identify whether English teachers were available at primary level, and to assess the economic rationale for the proposal. I visited fifteen schools and four teacher training institutions in four regions of the country: Libreville (the capital), Oyem in the north, Franceville in the southeast, and Port-Gentil on the Atlantic coast. I observed twelve lessons (French, English and other subjects) and interviewed fifty-four people, including pupils, teachers, head teachers, teacher trainers, local government officials, central government personnel, and the Minister of Education himself. I also interviewed several employers, since their presumed hiring practices were a major plank of the policy. I made use of central government documents as well as reports published by UNESCO, the African Development Bank, the World Bank, and the World Economic Forum. I also consulted published research on the African languages of Gabon and Gabonese French. As a means to discover the sociolinguistic position of English I would recommend this methodology; but as a means to influence policy, challenges were to follow.

At the level of the classroom I found that large numbers of pupils were unable to understand the lesson. Teachers in one school told me: "We try to use French when teaching, but we often have to use Fang vocabulary." They also said that even those whose home language is French speak "not real French." In another school the deputy head said that most pupils speak Ndasa Indal, Bakaningi, or Baumbu at home. Therefore, teachers often use these languages (unofficially) rather than French, especially for mathematics. However, the deputy head added, not all teachers know the local languages, having moved from other parts of the country. They have to ask above-average pupils from higher classes to interpret for them.

It also became apparent that huge numbers repeat school years, partly because they learn so little through the medium of French and partly because of inappropriate assessment practices. As a result, there are adolescents in the same classes as much younger children in primary schools and people in their mid-twenties still in secondary school. This explains why, according to UNESCO statistics, Gabon's education system is the most inefficient in the world.

The economic rationale for introducing English in primary schools – "to prepare young people to work in companies" – was not supported by large employers I interviewed, such as petroleum companies and sugar plantations. They told me they look for a solid basic education and ability to express oneself clearly in French, as well as soft skills of working independently and cooperating with others. These have important implications for what education should be doing. In any case, the formal sector provides employment for only a very small percentage of the workforce. People working in the informal sector require basic entrepreneurial skills and the ability to function in a range of African languages as well as French, but not English. As for the inspiration from Rwanda for English in primary education, I discovered that the Rwanda experiment had been a disaster and that the Rwandan government had had to reverse this policy.

My report recommended against introducing English in primary schools, because "if English is introduced . . . it will become yet another conceptual burden for children who, in many cases, are already struggling to understand what is happening in their classrooms" (Coleman 2013: 89). Employers did not consider English an urgent need and, in any case, nobody was qualified to teach English to young learners, or eager to be trained as specialists in teaching English to young learners. Instead I suggested, first, directing resources and energy towards introducing mother tongues as the languages of instruction and, second, addressing other major problems facing primary schools.

However, I also recommended that if the government was still determined to have English taught in primary schools, then a series of actions would need to be taken to create a cadre of appropriately skilled personnel. I predicted at least seven years would be needed to complete the necessary groundwork before English could be introduced in primary schools. I hoped that the Ministry of Education would realise how impractical their proposed scheme was.

A draft version of my report was shown by BC FWA to several senior members of the Government of Gabon and foreign ambassadors to the country. They identified a 'factual error' regarding French and African languages because in their opinion French is "the mother tongue of 80% of the population" and "Gabon is held up as one of the countries with the best French in Africa because of its mother tongue status." (By "best French in Africa" they meant closest to the Standard French of France.) This did not match my findings, and I soon found that the "80%" figure derived from an unsubstantiated Wikipedia article. I was also able to make use of substantial research from the University of Nice Sophia Antipolis, showing that Gabonese French has its own distinctive lexical and syntactical characteristics. Consequently, I revised my report, strengthened its original observations, and attempted to dispel the "80%" myth.

At first, BC's response to the final version of my report was enthusiastic. One message called it "a great, hard-hitting document." Another said: "The news from Gabon is that there is a real buzz about the report." Confusingly, it gradually became apparent that the report had not actually been presented to the Ministry of Education. The timing was not considered appropriate as the Minister of Education was about to visit the UK. Instead, a summary was prepared by BC FWA as the basis for a programme of activities which the BC was to offer to the Government of Gabon. I was able to look at the summary briefly but was not given a copy to keep. Disappointingly, the summary omitted all my analysis of sociolinguistic and language-in-education issues, and other matters relating to the primary education system in general (where my research suggested the most urgent needs were). It included only those elements which directly related to the teaching of English (which I had advised against). All my recommendations concerning the use of the mother tongue, reforming assessment procedures and creating conducive learning environments had disappeared, leaving only a rump of suggestions about preparing a cadre of English teachers for primary schools.

Since then nothing has happened. To complicate matters, the Minister of Education has been replaced and there have been changes in personnel at BC FWA. Few people have seen my report; the primary education system continues to face serious problems; children still repeat classes year after year; and teachers continue to teach in a language which most children do not understand. Meanwhile, the country's African languages continue to be ignored by the education system. At the same time, the proposal to introduce English in primary schools seems to have been forgotten. BC FWA did later support a conference presentation which discussed the survey's findings (Coleman and Mouanambatsi 2015), but in essence the research report and its recommendations have disappeared without trace.

A further message sent to me, after leaving Gabon, was that one of the government's reasons for pursuing English in primary education was the communication difficulties they had faced in negotiations with Chinese government officials. All this further illustrates the 'earlier the better' myth (Phillipson 1992: 199–209), the assumption that there is a link between teaching English in primary school and long-term competence in the language.

What lessons can be learnt from my experience in Gabon, by me and by anyone planning this type of research? First, it is clear that the sponsor and the researcher need to share the principle of linguistic equity, acknowledge the importance of MTB MLE, and recognise the danger of incompatible principles. Next, I should perhaps have seen that there were overarching political imperatives driving forward the use of English in education which nullified the likelihood of success or failure on the ground. I may also have been wise to recognise that part of the business of the BC is to maintain good relations; in certain circumstances this may override purely professional or academic considerations. I return later to compare this to my other case studies.

More recently an alternative interpretation has been suggested to me. It is possible individuals within BC FWA realised, after reading the report, that the Gabon government's plans were unrealistic and that the most diplomatic way forward was simply not to pursue the matter further. The fact that nothing happened, therefore, may constitute evidence that the report did have impact on its readers within the sponsoring organisation. I cannot judge how accurate this interpretation is.

Case study 2: Pakistan

Pakistan has a population over one hundred times that of Gabon, at 182 million. It is categorised as having low human development: 146th in the 2013 Human Development Index; 26.5% of its people experienced severe poverty in 2012.

Upon independence from British rule in 1947, Pakistan adopted Urdu as its national language. English was also given official status, in the expectation that it would be replaced by Urdu over time. This has not happened. Urdu today is widely used but is the mother tongue of only about 7% of the population. Meanwhile, English continues to play important roles in government and society. It is the principal home language of the upper class, the army, higher education, elite private schools, and (nominally at least) non-elite private schools. It is also taught as a foreign language in non-elite state secondary schools. But for most of the population, especially in rural areas, English is an alien language. As one interviewee from an educational charity put it: "These kids will never in their lives need English." Another said: "The common people don't use English."

There are between 61 and 72 indigenous languages in Pakistan. At the time of my study, Sindhi was the medium of instruction in primary education in the Province of Sindh. Pashto was used in some schools in Khyber Pakhtunkhwa, but the other indigenous languages had no role. Even in Sindh, the language-in-education policy is regional-language-based, not mother-tongue-based. Thus, Saraiki-speaking children in the north of the province have to learn through Sindhi, not Saraiki.

The National Education Policy (NEP) of 2009 (Ministry of Education 2009) stated that provincial ministries of education could opt to use English as the medium of instruction for certain subjects from that year and would be obliged to do so from 2014. Specifically, science and mathematics were to be taught through English from Year 4 of primary school. Shortly afterwards, the 18th Amendment to the Constitution was enacted (Government of Pakistan 2010), providing (among other measures) significant provincial autonomy, freeing provincial education authorities to determine their own language-in-education policies.

The NEP's stated aim in encouraging the use of English as a medium of education was to reduce social stratification by bringing the state schools into line (to a very modest extent) with the prestigious English-medium private schools. Meanwhile, the objective of the 18th Amendment was to strengthen local autonomy.

In response to these developments, BC Pakistan commissioned a study from me upon which to develop a three-year English language strategy. One of the study's aims was to describe the context of English language teaching – including sociolinguistic, language-in-education, and demographic parameters. Another aim was to look closely at the NEP and the consequences of current and proposed language-in-education policies. I visited state and private schools, colleges, madrasahs, universities, local and central government bodies, local education charities, international development agencies, a media organisation, and a teachers' association. I carried out observations, focus group discussions, and interviews, in Islamabad, Rawalpindi, Lahore, Okara, and Karachi. For security reasons, I was unable to visit Peshawar and rural Khyber Pakhtunkhwa and so respondents from those areas came to Islamabad to meet me. I interviewed approximately 120 people in total. I also consulted reports published by the Government of Pakistan, the UN and its agencies, international development organisations, and non-government organisations. As in Gabon, I found my methodological approach adequate to the inquiry.

I found that in most contexts primary education was provided in Urdu, not home languages (except, as noted above, in Sindh and Khyber Pakhtunkhwa). Indigenous languages were perceived by many as a constraint on children's development. A senior Pakistani educationist working for an American development agency complained that "in Sindh they're very attached to their local language so it's very difficult [for us to work there]." A teacher told me that the "intellectual level" of children who speak Punjabi at home is lower than those with English as a home language, making it difficult to teach Punjabi speakers. A primary school teacher declared that children should learn to speak English at nursery so she and her colleagues would face fewer problems. Other informants saw local languages as a threat to national unity.

English, on the other hand, was believed to facilitate access to higher education and employment in the civil service. Many respondents felt English-medium education would bring immense benefits to the nation, but they did not specify what these benefits might be.

My report (Coleman 2010b) noted various adverse outcomes arising from negative attitudes towards indigenous languages and from using Urdu and English as languages of instruction. These included high dropout rates, poor educational achievements, ethnic marginalisation and, longer term, a risk of language death. Furthermore, English language teaching in state schools is frequently unsuccessful.

The report concluded that there was an urgent need for awareness-raising about the importance of the mother tongue in the early years of education. It recommended that the ELT profession and the BC should contribute to the development of a National Language-in-Education Policy and to a National Plan of Action for English, and that attention should be given to ethical issues associated with the privileged status of English speakers in Pakistan.

My suggestion for further awareness-raising was accepted by the BC and a second stage of activity was instituted, aimed at disseminating the findings of the first report and encouraging public debate about the issues raised. To provide guidance an Advisory Panel was formed, comprising fifteen eminent Pakistani linguists, educationists, academics, and others. The report was published online; policy consultations were held in three different parts of the country; and a series of radio phone-in programmes was organised. Altogether, around 300 people made contributions to the public debates. Several press articles appeared, including a two-page special report in *Dawn*, the English-medium national newspaper, on 28 November 2010, and a later article, "Stupid in English" by Anjum Altaf, an economist, also in *Dawn* on 3 December 2010. Altaf argued that "prejudiced policies on language" (i.e. using English as medium and ignoring mother tongues) had "perpetuated poverty" in Pakistan. I was subsequently invited to participate in a television panel discussion. Then the journalist Zubeida Mustafa was inspired to write a book about language in education in Pakistan, *Tyranny of Language in Education: The Problem and Its Solution* (2011). Mustafa's book and the press articles were all sympathetic to the idea of initial mother-tongue instruction in primary school.

From the public consultation stage, it was concluded that the hierarchical and discriminatory nature of education in Pakistan is rigid and will not change easily. Language policy in schools is one contributing factor. Also apparent were widespread misunderstandings about language learning, about the role of language in education and specifically the role of English. An example is the 'earlier the better' myth noted earlier: that teaching English ever earlier in life will improve competence. In reality, second language learning is more effective if learners have already achieved "a high level of both oracy and literacy in their first language" and if the learning context "confers status on both their first and second languages" (Ellis 2007: 23).

My co-authored report on the second stage of activity (Coleman and Capstick 2012) recommended that every child should have an equal opportunity to access high-quality education, regardless of socio-economic status, gender, or home language. It was recommended that Urdu and English should be introduced as languages of learning only when children were ready.

However, the ubiquity and strength of the 'earlier the better' myth – and other misunderstandings – make it unlikely that policies will change soon. It was clear that perceptions and apprehensions were so deeply entrenched that change would require much patience, hard work, and time.

My involvement in Pakistan ended with the launch of the second report. At the same time, changes in BC personnel took place. Not long thereafter, BC Pakistan established a new project with the Ministry of Education of the Province of Punjab: the Punjab Education and English Language Initiative (PEELI). PEELI's website explains that the project aims to support the provincial government's desire for English to be used "to teach English and other subjects" in primary and middle schools (www.britishcouncil.pk/programmes/education/peeli).

I was disheartened that although the document describing the work of this project quotes one of the findings of my first report – that English teaching in state schools tends to be ritualised and delivered through the medium of Urdu – it then reiterates the 'earlier the better' myth: "Implementing a policy of English medium at a primary school level supports the education system as Higher Education and the majority of worldwide research and academic knowledge is in English" (British Council Pakistan 2013: 1).

The two stages of research and awareness-raising in Pakistan generated extensive discussion in academic settings and in newspapers and other media across the country. To that extent, they made a contribution to public understanding of issues relating to the importance of mother tongues and the role of English in education. But substantial longer term impact seems more elusive, with the BC itself – at least in the Province of Punjab – apparently promoting English as the language of instruction in primary schools barely a year after it had published a report in which this practice was condemned. On the other hand, in 2015 I was assured that in practice the BC's involvement in Punjab has helped to "curb the zeal for English" there. The use of English as the medium at the primary level has been quietly dropped and the project focuses only on the teaching of mathematics, science, and IT in upper secondary schools. Whether and to what extent my work contributed to this "curbing the zeal for English" is difficult to say.

My experience in Pakistan is in some ways a similarly salutary lesson to Gabon. But I was heartened to have contributed to such lively and engaged civic debate on the matter. As discussed in Lawson and Sayers (this volume), such contributions have been recognised by funding bodies as a valid form of impact, even without evidence of influence on actual policy. And, funding bodies aside, my work also helped advance the public understanding of language issues in Pakistan, if only modestly. A piece of advice emanating from this case study, then, would be to pursue contributions in the public sphere, even if not directly connected to lobbying in the halls of power. This can have positive outcomes in its own right.

Case study 3: Indonesia

Indonesia has the fourth highest population in the world, at 250 million. Ranked 108th in the 2013 Human Development Index, and with 1.1% of its people in severe poverty in 2012, it falls into the category of medium human development. Parts of Indonesia were colonised by the Dutch for 350 years, others for a much shorter period. Upon independence in 1945, the country rejected Dutch and adopted Bahasa Indonesia as its national language. The most recent census indicates Bahasa Indonesia as "known" by 92% of the population and the mother tongue of about 11%. There are at least 706 local languages, several of which have tens of millions of speakers. These languages have no official role but in a few areas are taught as subjects in school. English is the "first foreign language," taught as a subject in secondary schools. Other than that, English has no official function (Coleman forthcoming).

Legislation passed in 2003 required the establishment of one International Standard School (ISS) at each level of education (primary, junior secondary, senior secondary, and senior vocational) in each of the country's 500 districts. By 2011, approximately 1,300 such schools were in operation, representing under 1% of all state schools.

The ISS programme obliged schools to adopt elements of the curriculum of an "advanced" OECD member country and to use English as the medium for teaching science and mathematics from Year 4. The ISSs were given lavish government grants and, unlike other state schools, were also permitted to charge fees. The ostensible rationale was to help Indonesia compete internationally.

In 2009, BC East Asia invited me to undertake a study on English language education in East Asia to find out "what experience, critical success factors and potential" there was for Content and Language Integrated Learning (CLIL) – where English is used as a medium for teaching other subjects, popular in some European countries (see, e.g., Johnstone 2010). My aim was to find out how the ISSs interpreted their brief to mould young people to 'compete internationally,' how they viewed English, Bahasa Indonesia and the local languages, and how ready teachers were to teach their subjects through English.

I visited seven primary, junior, and senior secondary ISSs in five urban areas in Indonesia (Banda Aceh, Jakarta, Makassar, Tangerang, and Yogyakarta). I observed English lessons and other subjects being taught through English and I interviewed head teachers, teachers and pupils. I also made use of OECD data on the reading, science, and mathematics competence of Indonesian fifteen-year-olds. These data showed very low levels of competence, with Indonesia coming 64th of 65 countries in science and mathematics and 60th of 65 countries in reading. With almost 90% of children not being native speakers of the language used to teach them, it seemed likely that the medium of instruction was a contributing factor.

In my observations and interviews I found that the heavily subsidised ISSs had become the elite schools in their respective districts, largely the preserve of the wealthiest families. The ISSs had rapidly become discriminatory, fostering attitudes of superiority. At the same time – unsurprisingly – pupils and teachers in mainstream schools resented the privileges enjoyed by the ISSs.

Although the ISS scheme intended English as the medium of education only from Year 4, in reality many schools were attempting its use from Year 1, even before children had become literate in Bahasa Indonesia. My classroom observations clearly showed that this constrained pupils' ability to process information and interact with the teacher.

Local languages were not even taught as subjects in the ISSs; head teachers viewed them as an irrelevance, and Bahasa Indonesia as lacking prestige. The long-term implications were serious: if ISSs prioritised English while mainstream schools continued to use Bahasa Indonesia, then it was likely that an English-speaking upper class would emerge and that communication between them and the rest of the population would become increasingly difficult. Meanwhile, the decline of the local languages – already evident – would be hastened.

My consultancy report (Coleman 2009a) recommended that the BC should not support the ISS programme. Instead, I recommended that the BC encourage debate regarding the risks and benefits of teaching other subjects through English. The role of the BC should include not only capacity development (for example, developing teachers' skills) but also awareness-raising among parents, the public, and policy makers.

This was apparently not a message that BC East Asia wanted to hear. The report was given only very limited circulation and was not made available to the Indonesian education authorities. Another consultant was rapidly commissioned to undertake a further study, presumably in the hope that they would produce more congenial findings and recommendations.

Feeling that my research had identified important issues which deserved wider discussion, I presented a paper based on the report at the Eighth Language and Development Conference in Dhaka (Coleman 2009b), and I uploaded it to Academia.edu, where it can still be seen.

Fortuitously, responsibility for the project was transferred from BC East Asia to BC Indonesia. Here there were newly appointed people who shared my concerns about the ISS scheme. In 2010, a one-day seminar was held in Jakarta in which both the author of the follow-up research and I presented our findings and recommendations. The seminar was attended by representatives from the Ministry of Education, teachers, head teachers, and the press. It became even clearer from this event that there was widespread public concern about the scheme. This led in 2011 to the organisation of a more ambitious two-day symposium, 'The ISS System in Indonesia: Policy and Practice,' at which the Deputy Minister of

Education was the opening speaker. There was extensive press reporting (mostly critical of the scheme). My active involvement in investigating and commenting on the ISS scheme ended here, but my work went on to achieve unforeseen impact, under some chance circumstances.

In 2012, a group of concerned parents submitted a case to the Constitutional Court, arguing that the legislation which had led to the establishment of the ISSs was unconstitutional, for two reasons: because it was socially divisive; and because it marginalised the national language. Hearings took place, expert witnesses were called, and various items of documentary evidence were submitted. Unbeknownst to me, one of the Indonesian expert witnesses submitted documentary evidence, including my Dhaka conference paper (downloaded from Academia.edu). In 2013, the Constitutional Court published its ruling. It decided in favour of the parents and it specifically referred to my paper as one of the items of evidence which had aided its conclusions.

The government was bound to accept the Court's decision and consequently the ISS schools were converted back to normal schools at the end of the 2012–2013 school year. At least in state schools, English is no longer used as a medium for teaching science, mathematics, or any other subject (apart from the English language itself). To some extent, then, my research made a contribution to the achievement of change in national education policy. It should not be forgotten that the majority of children are still unable to study through their mother tongue; nevertheless, this was a positive development.

In terms of my route to impact and lessons to be learnt by other researchers, I benefited from putting my work in the public domain online, and from the chance discovery of my work by an expert witness. As noted at the outset, my impact was also facilitated by my report going with the flow of a wider argument, in this case a body of evidence denouncing the ISSs. On its own, my report would likely have had no such impact.

To summarise, then, in each of the three case studies the government had already introduced – or was about to introduce – the teaching of English to young children (Gabon) or the use of English for teaching other subjects (Indonesia, Pakistan). These innovations, though similar, had different motivations. In Indonesia and Gabon the principal objective was economic, whilst in Pakistan the reason given was to increase social cohesion. In each case, the BC's response was to commission research into the implications of the innovation. In Gabon this was done at the invitation of the government, while in Pakistan and Indonesia it was carried out under the British Council's own initiative. The research was expected to generate recommendations which would feed into BC policy and practice in the countries concerned. That did not consistently come to pass, though there were demonstrable impacts of sorts, albeit in unforeseen ways.

In the final section of this chapter I look briefly at the factors that contributed to both the failures and modest successes in these three case studies and the lessons which can be learnt from them.

Discussion

In the three case studies above, the proposals to give English new roles in education shared several problematic features:

1   Unrealistic assumptions about what English can do, e.g. in Pakistan seeing it as a panacea for wider social inequalities.
2   Overlooking negative consequences for other languages, e.g. in Indonesia displacing indigenous languages from the curriculum (Coleman forthcoming).
3   Neglect of potential damage to children's conceptual development, e.g. across the three case studies, mother tongues are given no role in education despite overwhelming evidence that this is better developmentally. Further, if parents lack proficiency in the school language, they cannot support the child's learning (Pinnock 2009; Ouane and Glanz 2010).
4   Inattention to children's social development. As Pinnock (2009) shows, exclusion of mother tongues from schools may lead to whole communities becoming alienated from education and – ultimately – from the state which marginalises them.
5   Prevalence of myths about language in society and language learning, e.g. the 'earlier the better' myth.
6   Insufficient planning for the availability of human resources, e.g. Indonesian Ministry of Education research showing teachers in the ISSs ill-equipped to function in English.
7   Subordination of much more pressing problems in the countries' education systems, e.g. Gabon with the world's least efficient education system, or Pakistan's 10% secondary school completion rate. In these contexts, extending English is an expensive irrelevance.

These features create a dilemma for the sociolinguistic researcher. If a government or a sponsoring organisation commissions research with the expectation that it will receive advice on *how* to implement a language-in-education scheme, to what extent is it appropriate for the sociolinguist to question *why* that scheme should exist? A co-authored discussion of this dilemma in the Gabon case concluded that "advice for Ministries of Education must be principled and based on objective analysis, even if this means not supporting Ministry plans" (Coleman and Mouanambatsi 2015).

I had raised the same dilemma in the first Pakistan report (Coleman 2010b) and suggested that there were "ethical implications" which could not be ignored. In making my recommendations I decided I could resolve the dilemma only by prioritising the development needs of the country (as I saw them) if they were in conflict with the interests of the sponsor or other stakeholders. However, there are risks in this approach. In the Indonesian case it was clear that the sponsor disliked my recommendations, such that a replacement consultant was commissioned – whose report, unlike mine, was published. In Gabon, also, my report was apparently not made available to the Ministry of Education.

Possibly, also, my 'ethical approach' was too rigid. In Punjab, it has been argued, the BC was able to discourage the worst excesses of using English as the medium of education by going along with the government's proposals and then quietly redirecting efforts away from primary schools into the upper secondary level.

Earlier in the chapter I noted that impact may be felt at three different levels:

- at the level of awareness or conceptualisation of language issues in society, broadly speaking, and in education specifically;
- at the level of policy or planning;
- at the level of practice.

I also suggested that impact might be gauged in six different ways, namely whether:

- the research findings and recommendations are understood by the sponsors, are found to be acceptable/interesting/useful and are published and made available for comment;
- the sponsor takes on board the report's recommendations and incorporates them into its policy and planning;
- the sponsor implements its own policy;
- the research findings and recommendations are understood by end users (such as the in-country education authorities) and are disseminated;
- the education authorities adapt their policies in line with the report's recommendations;
- language-in-education practice changes.

The possibility of the research having impact may stall at the first stage. If the sponsor is unhappy with the report or indifferent to its recommendations then nothing will happen and the research will have zero impact – as seems to have occurred in Gabon. This almost happened in Indonesia as well, where the original report was never published but was eventually 'rescued' by new personnel.

Online publishing may be an effective way to pursue impact by other means (cf. Lawson, this volume). For example, by July 2015 three of my papers about the Indonesian ISS programme (Coleman 2009b, 2009c, 2010c) had been viewed 6,600 times in total on Academia.edu, and 53% of these views came from Indonesia. In contrast, mainstream academic journals and expensive academic books are largely inaccessible in Indonesia.

Another scenario is that impact may occur at the first stage but then not be visible at the third stage. For instance, the Pakistan reports were well received by the sponsor and were widely disseminated (first stage), but then the sponsor's later practice (a primary school English-medium project) seemed not to reflect the recommendations of the report.

Impact may be felt immediately, but in other circumstances delayed (Coleman 1995). The Indonesian case provides a good illustration. The original research took place in 2009, the report and recommendations were submitted in evidence to the Constitutional Court in 2012 and the ISS programme came to an end in mid-2013.

Over four years passed between the research being carried out and impact being felt in the classroom. Indeed, it is often difficult for the researcher to know whether they have had any impact, since sponsors do not routinely keep researchers informed.

So, what leads to impact being so varied? Three factors can be identified:

1   Consistency in the sponsor's standpoint. As noted earlier, one of the BC's tasks is to "develop a wider knowledge of the English language." In addition, in recent years the BC has argued – alongside other organisations such as the Summer Institute of Linguistics (SIL) and the African Academy of Languages (ACALAN) – that it is not appropriate to use English or any other non-mother tongue language as the medium of education for the first nine years of a child's education (McIlwraith 2013). However, my experience suggests that some individuals within the organisation perhaps do not share (or may not be fully aware of) the BC's principled position. This explains why attitudes to my research sometimes changed markedly when personnel were rotated or when responsibility for a project was handed to a different unit.

2   Consistency between the sponsor and the researcher. Factors 1 and 2 overlap with each other. If the sponsor and the researcher agree on the same principles of linguistic equity and MTB MLE, then impact may be forthcoming. But if there are incompatible principles at play then, unsurprisingly, the sponsor may be unenthusiastic about the researcher's proposals.

3   Timing. Even if our recommendations appear to be implemented, we will almost always be just one voice in a choir of advisors. In Indonesia, there was already growing public concern about the ISS programme. My report was used as additional evidence, going with the flow of a wider argument. In contrast, in the Pakistan case both the Stage 1 and Stage 2 reports were widely circulated and discussed in various forums, yet ultimately my recommendations were not implemented. Perhaps this is not surprising, bearing in mind the historical sensitivity of language issues generally in Pakistan and of English in particular. The time was just not ripe for the changes the report recommended.

A complicating issue is that my reports may have had impact on the BC (or on some of the individuals within the organisation) by curbing the promotion of English in circumstances where it is not appropriate, but the individuals concerned may be unwilling to admit as much. The absence of a systematic mechanism for keeping consultants informed about the fate of their findings and recommendations makes this more likely.

Benson (2005: 65) bemoans the gap often found between research findings and language-in-education policy: " . . . most countries experience a disconnect between experimentation and more widespread practice of bilingual schooling. Somehow the gap needs to be bridged." She concludes:

> [We] researchers [should] be aware of what we can do, wherever we are along the continuum between information disseminators and outspoken advocates,

to be socially as well as academically responsible for our actions and to recognise that we already play a role in the development process.

(Benson 2005: 74)

In the end, one has to recognise that there are limits to the impact one can achieve. Rather like the Queen of England, the researcher in language-in-education policy is ultimately powerless. As Bagehot famously said of the constitutional role of the British Monarch, s/he can only "be consulted . . . encourage and . . . warn" (1915: 111). S/he has no authority to act independently. Similarly, the researcher can be consulted, can encourage and can warn, but subsequent action is taken by the sponsors and/or the education authorities.

As researchers in language-in-education, our findings may not be what sponsors expect, and we may find it difficult to endorse Ministry of Education innovations. The impact of our work may not be felt immediately, and we may even be unaware of the impact that it does have. But we should not be disheartened; our work can make a modest evidence-based contribution to broader attempts to improve education in the developing world.

Acknowledgements

I am very grateful to the many British Council personnel who commissioned the three case studies discussed here, who understood what I was trying to do and who supported me. They include Tony Capstick (no longer with the organisation), Shirley Finlayter, Eric Lawrie, David Martin, Muhaimin Syamsuddin, and Danny Whitehead. Thanks also to John Knagg of the British Council for his thoughtful feedback on an earlier version of the chapter. I am grateful to the hundreds of people – school pupils, teachers, head teachers, teacher educators, local and central government officials, academics, ministers of education, business people and others – who contributed to the three studies. I would also like to thank the editors of this volume for their encouragement and detailed editing of the chapter.

References

Bagehot, Walter. 1915. *The English Constitution*, revised ed. (1st ed. 1867). London: Longmans.

Benson, Carol. 2005. "Bridging the experimentation-implementation gap in bilingual schooling: The role of the researcher." In *National Development, Education and Language in Central Asia and Beyond*, ed. by Hywel Coleman, Jamilya Gulyamova, and Andrew Thomas, 64–77. Tashkent: British Council.

British Council. 2011. *Royal Charter and Bye-laws 1993*. London: British Council.

British Council Pakistan. 2013. *Can English Medium Education Work in Pakistan? Lessons from Punjab*. Islamabad: Punjab Education and English Language Initiative (PEELI), British Council Pakistan.

Coleman, Hywel. 1995. "Problematising stakeholders: Who are the holders and what are the stakes?" In *Language and Development*, ed. by Tony Crooks and Geoffrey Crewes, 45–61. Denpasar: Indonesia Australia Language Foundation.

Coleman, Hywel. 2009a. "Teaching other subjects through English in three Asian nations: A review." Unpublished report for British Council East Asia.

Coleman, Hywel. 2009b. "Indonesia's 'International Standard Schools': What are they for?" Paper presented at the 8th Language and Development Conference, Dhaka.

Coleman, Hywel. 2009c. "Teaching other subjects through English in two Asian nations: Teachers' responses and implications for learners." In *Access English EBE Symposium: A Collection of Papers*, ed. by Philip Powell-Davies, 63–87. Kuala Lumpur: British Council East Asia.

Coleman, Hywel. 2010a. *The English Language and Development*. London: British Council.

Coleman, Hywel. 2010b. *Teaching and Learning in Pakistan: The Role of Language in Education*. Islamabad: British Council Pakistan.

Coleman, Hywel. 2010c. "Are 'international standard schools' really a response to globalisation?" In *Responding to Global Education Challenges: Proceeding International Seminar on Education*, ed. by Nury Supriyanti, 11–35. Yogyakarta: Universitas Negeri Yogyakarta.

Coleman, Hywel. 2013. *Proposal to Introduce the Teaching of English in the Primary Schools of Gabon: Analysis and Recommendations*. London: British Council.

Coleman, Hywel. Forthcoming. "The English language as *naga* in Indonesia." In *Why English? Confronting the Hydra*, ed. by Pauline Bunce, Vaughan Rapatahana, Robert Phillipson, and T. Ruanni Tupas. Bristol: Multilingual Matters.

Coleman, Hywel, and Tony Capstick. 2012. *Language in Education in Pakistan: Recommendations for Policy and Practice*. Islamabad: British Council.

Coleman, Hywel, and Yves Roger Mouanambatsi. 2015. "The dilemma of English in primary schools: The case of Gabon." In *IATEFL 2014: Harrogate Conference Selections*, ed. by Tania Pattison, 79–81. Faversham: IATEFL.

Ellis, Rod. 2007. "Educational settings and second language learning." *Asian EFL Journal* 9 (4): 11–27.

Erling, Elizabeth J., and Philip Seargeant (eds.). 2013. *English and Development: Policy, Pedagogy and Globalization*. Bristol: Multilingual Matters.

Gouvernement du Gabon. 2012. *Plan Stratégique Gabon Émergent*. Libreville.

Government of Pakistan. 2010. *Constitution (Eighteenth Amendment) Act, 2010*. Islamabad.

Idris, Hélène Fatima, Karsten Legère, and Tove Rosendal. 2007. "Language policy in selected African countries: Achievements and constraints." In *Language and Development: Africa and Beyond*, ed. by Hywel Coleman, 21–39. Addis Ababa: British Council.

Johnstone, Richard (ed.). 2010. *Learning through English: Policies, Challenges and Prospects: Insights from East Asia*. Kuala Lumpur: British Council East Asia.

Kosonen, Kimmo, and Catherine Young. 2009. *Mother Tongue as Bridge Language of Instruction: Policies and Experiences in Southeast Asia*. Bangkok: SEAMEO (Southeast Asia Ministers of Education Organisation).

Lin, Angel, and Peter Martin (eds.). 2005. *Decolonisation, Globalisation: Language-in-Education Policy and Practice*. Clevedon: Multilingual Matters.

McIlwraith, Hamish (ed.). 2013. *Multilingual Education in Africa: Lessons from the Juba Language-in-Education Conference*. London: British Council.

Ministry of Education. 2009. *National Education Policy 2009*. Islamabad: Government of Pakistan.

Mustafa, Zubeida. 2011. *Tyranny of Language in Education: The Problem and Its Solution.* Karachi: Ushba Publishing International.

Ouane, Adama, and Christine Glanz. 2010. *Why and How Africa Should Invest in African Languages and Multilingual Education: An Evidence- and Practice-based Policy Advocacy Brief.* Hamburg: UNESCO Institute for Lifelong Learning.

Phillipson, Robert. 1992. *Linguistic Imperialism.* Oxford: Oxford University Press.

Pinnock, Helen. 2009. *Language and Education: The Missing Link.* Reading: CfBT Education Trust and Save the Children.

Rapatahana, Vaughan, and Pauline Bunce (eds.). 2012. *English Language as Hydra: Its Impacts on Non-English Language Cultures.* Bristol: Multilingual Matters.

Samuelson, Beth Lewis, and Sarah Warshauer Freedman. 2010. "Language policy, multi-lingual education and power in Rwanda." *Language Policy* 9 (3): 191–215.

Sen, Amartya. 1999. *Development as Freedom.* Oxford: Oxford University Press.

Steflja, Izabela. 2012. "The high costs and consequences of Rwanda's shift in language policy from French to English." Accessed 20 March 2015. Available from: https://www.africaportal.org/dspace/articles/high-costs-and-consequences-rwandas-shift-language-policy-reform-french-english.

United Nations. 2013. *World Population Prospects: The 2012 Revision, Volume I: Comprehensive Tables.* (ST/ESA/SER.A/336.) New York: Population Division, Department of Economic and Social Affairs, United Nations.

Wedell, Martin. 2009. *Planning for Educational Change: Putting People and Their Contexts First.* London: Continuum.

Chapter 12

The impact of sociolinguistics on refugee status determination

Peter Patrick, ORCID NUMBER 0000–0003–3996–1514

Introduction

Since the mid-1990s, the speech of asylum seekers (ASs) has been analyzed at the request of some governments (a) as an aid to determining their country of origin, and/or (b) "to deter false claims of origin" (UKBA 2013: 3). This practice, called LADO (Language Analysis for Determination of Origin), was not originally performed by academically-trained linguists – the expertise required to perform it validly and reliably is still a matter of controversy – but has become increasingly visible as an arena for the application of linguistic science (Zwaan et al. 2010; Patrick 2012). Here I investigate the context, process and consequences of LADO from a sociolinguist's perspective, tracing the impact of our field's involvement, through my journey: from a creolist conference in Honolulu in 2003, where I was introduced to a new phenomenon, to a UK Supreme Court decision in 2014 in which I played a role in establishing new standards for linguistic evidence.

Language Analysis for Determination of Origin: The context of impact

The work described here did not originate as research, but rather as an attempt to mobilize established linguistic knowledge to directly influence LADO practice and policy by governments, commercial provision of LADO and legal interpretation of linguistic evidence. It thus differs from the relationship of research to impact assumed by UK research councils, but sits comfortably inside the tradition of sociolinguistic applications to existing social problems (Labov 1982; Rickford 1997).

Many people have helped cultivate critical thinking and practice regarding LADO. My involvement has been threefold: as a co-developer of basic guidelines (LNOG 2004); as a speaker and organizer in conference sessions and expert meetings, as co-convenor of an international network of researchers and practitioners (the Language and Asylum Research Group: www.essex.ac.uk/larg/); and as a forensic linguist, providing reports in UK asylum appeals. These roles shaped my understanding of LADO, as anyone's institutional base and stance both inform and constrain their views and practices.

In the case of LADO, the social problem is clear: the fate of people claiming asylum due to 'fear of persecution' is partly determined by 'language analysis' processes whose scientific basis is questioned by linguists. Justice for ASs, and the reputation of linguistics, necessitate rigorous application of linguistics. However, outside academia few people know what linguistics is, or which questions it can confidently address – much less how best to commission and interpret linguistic analysis. Thus an important aspect of impact rests on successfully representing linguistic knowledge to advocates and decision-makers whose eagerness, or scepticism, concerning its use is ill-informed (a problem familiar to forensic linguists – see Innes, this volume; MacLeod and Haworth, this volume). In this activity, which resembles respectful lectures to an unusually powerful first-year class, persuasiveness crucially affects impact, and understanding the pressures and context they bring to the 'lecture' is essential.

I interact as an independent academic with various LADO stakeholders: lawyers, judges, interpreters, staff in commercial analysis firms, bureaucrats, linguists, NGO representatives, and academics. These are the primary participants and intended beneficiaries of my work. They participate in the work, its design and the dissemination of findings, and certainly use the results to pursue their own goals.

As an expert giving evidence, I must provide "objective unbiased opinion" and "not assume the role of an advocate" (Tribunals Judiciary 2010: 10.4). (My expert witness interventions evaluate LADO reports submitted to the UK Government; I explicitly do not offer views as to the origin of ASs. My fees are paid via Legal Aid.) Indeed, I deliberately stay at arm's length from ASs whose lawyers retain me (I have only met one), though I hear their voices and study their testimony. ASs undergoing LADO – selected by governments, not experts or researchers – thus stand to benefit from work on LADO if it improves current practice, or causes its discontinuation (in jurisdictions where it is performed inadequately, and injustice results) or initiation (in jurisdiction where it is performed well and aids recognition of genuine claims). My relationships with ASs in LADO necessarily contrast strongly with those which sociolinguists develop with speakers of languages we conduct research on (e.g. Patrick 1999), regarding for whom advocacy or empowerment may be appropriate (Cameron et al. 1993; cf. Bucholtz et al., this volume; Levasseur, this volume; Dickinson, this volume).

The global(ized) nature of asylum gives LADO broad geographic and cultural range. My UK cases have involved claims by ASs to have originated in East, West and North Africa, and the Middle East, including the languages Amharic, Arabic (many dialects), Kibajuni, Kikuyu, Kirundi, Krio, Malinke, Somali (many varieties), Sorani, Swahili, Tigrinya, and West African Englishes (Ghana, Liberia). The practitioners, government bureaux and commercial firms came from Australia, Austria, Belgium, Canada, Denmark, Germany, Ireland, Italy, the Netherlands, Norway, Spain, Sweden, Switzerland, the UK, and the USA. LADO has been considered by representatives of the European Union and the Office of the UN High Commissioner for Refugees (UNHCR) and other (I)NGOs (e.g. Tax 2010).

The difficulties faced by a formalized LADO process have not been solved anywhere, but recognition of such difficulties represents progress of a sort, as questions of method and theory can be asked and refined, research performed, preliminary answers tested, and standards developed and applied. Some asylum advocates argue LADO is too immature for Refugee Status Determination (RSD), given the human stakes (ILPA 2009). But it is also true that LADO was per formed before linguists became involved, and likely still would be without us. It thus raises thorny ethical problems concerning the terms of participation (if any) by linguists.

The broadest level of possible impact involves contributing to fair national and international processes for granting asylum, and representing linguistics to decision-makers. An intermediate level concerns development and acceptance of standards for applying linguistics as LADO in the unique institutional contexts of RSD. The ground level looks at how linguistic scholarship (including but not limited to research) and application link to particular changes in regimes of commissioning, evaluating and interpreting LADO. Here I focus on the UK Government, its commercial agent and the courts in which appeals are heard, up to a May 2014 UK Supreme Court decision.

Sociolinguistics and LADO

Linguistic approaches to LADO include cross-cultural communication, dialectology, first- and second-language acquisition, language contact, language assessment, code-switching, linguistic variation and change, phonetics, and speaker profiling or identification. Sociolinguistic approaches to asylum include critical discourse analysis of media representation of ASs (Baker et al. 2011); study of speech, narrative and text in RSD contexts (Maryns 2006); and exploration of how language ideology and globalization processes frame views of ASs (Blommaert 2009). Below, I examine a narrower issue: how governments use analyses of ASs' speech to evaluate their claims to natively speak a language, as part of testing their claims to come from a certain nation, region or group.

In the early 2000s, sociolinguists (including myself) defined this question as crucially requiring our expert knowledge, since non-linguists are unaware that "nationality, national origin and citizenship are all political or bureaucratic characteristics, which have no necessary connection to language" (LNOG 2004: 262). The first step is to clarify for decision-makers that linguists can only link native-language features to the speech communities where people were socialized early in life. These communities may cross national borders or exist in diasporas, and frequently constitute a range of multilingual competences. This premise, first stated for LADO in the *Guidelines for the Use of Language Analysis in Relation to Questions of National Origin in Refugee Cases* (LNOG 2004), has become widely accepted by most commercial firms and government agencies providing LADO reports, including leading firms in Sweden and the Netherlands, and the Swiss and Norwegian bureaux (Patrick 2012). Subsequently sociolinguists, and linguists with other training (e.g. phonetics) but substantial sociolinguistic knowledge, have contributed research, experience and criticism linking the research bases and practices of LADO to such issues and areas as language attrition, narrative analysis, the competence of native speakers, multilingualism, perception of foreign accent, code choice and style-shifting, the nature of bureaucratic interviews, validity theory in language assessment, borrowing, and variation.

This fundamental focus (socialization within a speech community), and the sociolinguistic perspectives relevant to particular cases, do not preclude use of other established descriptive or theoretical linguistic approaches, assumptions, and methods as necessary. Anything less would be naïve in the unique bureaucratic context in which AS speech is elicited and evaluated.

The LADO process

Before discussing my work and its impact, I outline important aspects of the LADO process and its history. LADO begins when a government asylum bureau, doubting an AS's claimed origin, commissions analysis of a brief speech sample, specially collected in a formal, bureaucratic setting – typically a telephone interview conducted by a native speaker of the claimed language or a related language, but sometimes a monologue by the AS. Some bureaux, such as the UK Border Agency (cf. Campbell 2013), contract out the entire process, including quality control, while others keep significant control in-house, using qualified personnel (e.g. the Swiss Lingua bureau, Baltisberger and Hubbuch 2010; the Netherlands Bureau Land en Taal, Verrips 2010).

Elicitation and analysis may be conducted by one person, or different individuals; by employees of a government bureau, or a commercial firm, or by independent linguists. Interpreters may or may not be used in interviews. Analysis may be performed by recognized experts in the relevant language; or by persons with lesser credentials, often ill-informed about the language; or by persons with no formal linguistic study or qualifications, whose claim to competence rests on native speakership of the language. In this third case, it is maintained that the analysts work together with linguists (of the first or second sort) in a process internally regulated by the agency. The distinction between qualified linguistic experts, and non-expert native-speaker analysts, and the division of labor between them in LADO, is the field's sharpest controversy (Wilson and Foulkes 2014).

This collaborative method is defended as ideal by firms and bureaux that employ it (Cambier-Langeveld 2010, with responses by Fraser 2011; Verrips 2011; UKBA 2013; LADO reports by Språkab, and Verified AB). An alternative method seeks to employ native-speaking qualified linguists whenever possible; or if non-expert native-speaker informants are consulted, the linguistic analysis is restricted to the qualified expert (Lingua; the Dutch firm De Taalstudio). The history of LADO, however, shows that it evolved from early days when analysts were non-expert native speakers rather than qualified linguists. The linguistics profession became involved through criticism and contra-analysis (Eades and Arends 2004); linguists' increasing involvement in primary analysis for governments and private firms was driven by legal and commercial pressures. Baltisberger and Hubbuch (2010), heads of Lingua, argue this involvement raised the quality of LADO reports significantly. Because of these roots in non-expert analysis, low-quality reports remain common, but contra-analysis and expert evidence in legal challenges have impressed some judges and government bureaus, and commercial firms have responded by improving their practices to varying degrees – part of the impact described below.

The task of LADO is often presented as a straightforward linguistic one in reports, and interpreted simply as common sense by decision-makers or immigration judges. Reports typically note phonological, grammatical and lexical features, in separate sections. Speech is contrasted with what the analyst or linguist 'expected,' given the AS's claimed native language. Overall evaluation of the claimed origin is typically given according to verbal scales.

High-quality reports explicitly consider two mutually exclusive hypotheses of origin (Broeders 2010), evaluating contrasting predictions concerning features of speech, grounded in scientific literature which argues they are characteristic or distinctive of geographic, ethnic or social dialects. They specify several features at each level, correctly using linguistic terminology and phonetic transcriptions. Argumentation is explicit and of a standard typical of peer-reviewed linguistic publications. Variation is often noted, and a dozen examples may be given at each level, with time-index links to the digital recording. Instances where speech features corroborate the AS's claim are noted alongside unexpected ones. Influences from multilingualism in the family, language of schooling and mass media, and documented migration and language contact may be noted, alongside cases where the AS's speech follows and accommodates the interviewer's; power relations in the society of claimed origin and the interview context may be taken into account. Evaluation may use a carefully-worded scale and acknowledge the limits within which certainty can be asserted, as well as factors attenuating certainty. (There are no published error-rate data for LADO work, unlike other forensic linguistic areas, and the high level of disagreement among analysts is recognized as a concern by stakeholders from all positions, cf. Patrick 2010a; Verrips 2010.)

Lower-quality reports may have no explicit hypotheses, or only consider 'unexpected' features which could falsify a claim, sometimes ignoring corroborating features. They may not have access to, and fail to elicit, social or personal information which sociolinguists consider crucial. The UK Home Office passes almost no information from asylum interviews to their contracted LADO provider. Interviewers may thus be tempted to embark on a 'fishing expedition,' searching for inconsistencies or evidence to falsify claims, much like asylum bureaucrats often do (Bohmer and Shuman 2008), rather than as neutral professionals evaluating competing hypotheses. Features may be included which are not dialect- or language-specific, and thus not suitable for discriminating between claimed and suspected origins. They may merely list examples of very few features – sometimes only one feature, and only three or four single words of data, for a linguistic level – without using linguistic terminology. There is often no reference to scientific literature and no explicit analysis or argumentation. They may categorize the same feature as, e.g. both syntactic and lexical, flagrantly misuse phonetic transcriptions, over-generalize from single examples, and show ignorance of language variation or the complexities of language contact. Sometimes they contain transcription or analysis errors, or analyze the interviewer's or interpreter's utterances by mistake. They may fail to note 'unexpected' features of code-switching, pronunciation or borrowing resulting from accommodation to the interviewer or interpreter, who often employs a different dialect. They may claim that 'expected' elements do occur but in an 'unnatural' or 'unconvincing' manner, or may make unsupported statements about pauses or 'hesitations,' advancing authoritative-sounding but logically vacuous judgments about the speaker's intention to deceive through language. Evaluation may use spurious quantification, or assert very high levels of certainty, without acknowledging attenuating factors or methodological limitations.

On receipt of reports, asylum decisions are made by government asylum bureaux, in an administrative process; LADO reports are only one type of evidence considered. Administrative law courts or specialist tribunals hear appeals; this legal process occasionally goes further, to appeals courts (Bryce 2013) or supreme courts (e.g. Netherlands Council of State, Eades 2010). On appeal, some jurisdictions allow 'contra-analysis' (second-opinion analysis of the original or new speech data, Verrips 2010), or accept expert reports evaluating the quality of the original LADO report (such as I perform in the UK). It is sometimes argued that only at appeals levels do expert witness rules apply (see RB (*Linguistic evidence – Språkab*) *Somalia [2010] UKUT 329 (IAC)* – hereafter simply *RB* – para. 167). Under that view, authors of LADO reports commissioned by governments do not need to qualify as experts, while linguists challenging them do. In any case, analysts and linguists with lower qualifications might well fail to meet the standards required at this level, which are similar to standards required of expert witnesses under civil and criminal law in the same jurisdictions, e.g. the USA, UK or the Netherlands. Because of this double standard, linguists whose work challenges government decisions must observe a high standard of professionalism.

Outputs and outcomes I: The 2004 *Guidelines*

This section describes events that mobilized the linguistics profession to examine and engage with LADO practice. This was initially a matter of scholarly criticism, rather than new research generation. Since academic linguists became aware of LADO c.2000, monitoring and engagement with government and commercial practices and legal cases has regularly featured in conferences, expert meetings and networks involving sociolinguists and applied and forensic linguists, alongside people from many areas touching asylum and RSD, including lawyers, doctors, immigration judges, policy-makers, government asylum bureaux, police officers, human rights practitioners, forensic scientists, and academics from such fields as anthropology, genetics, interpreting, and psychoanalysis.

The catalyst was a report by Australian linguists (Eades et al. 2003) studying 58 asylum cases before the Australian Refugee Review Tribunal. The authors concluded that the language analysis performed was invalid in method, being based on folk views about language rather than sound linguistic principles. Following the first LADO conference session in 2003 at a creolist meeting in Honolulu, linguists formed a discussion group which eventually generated the 2,000-word *Guidelines for the Use of Language Analysis in Relation to Questions of National Origin in Refugee Cases* (LNOG 2004). This Language and National Origin Group contained 19 linguists from the UK, the USA, Europe, and Australia, half with direct LADO experience. Our brief document was intended to caution and guide governments in assessing the validity of LADO (an aim criticized by Eriksson 2008, who believes such guidelines should aim instead at practitioners). "[M]uch of what is contained in the *Guidelines* is at the level of introductory linguistics" (Eades 2010: 37), covering the complexity of language use and the nature of linguistic expertise. The *Guidelines* address core issues of speech community and nationality, argue that expertise should come from qualified experts, describe rights and responsibilities of experts and LADO practitioners, and touch on matters of language variation, acquisition, choice and contact. Months of intense email discussion led to a clear focus on these key issues. In retrospect, it was time well spent, yielding later consensus across the field of stakeholders. An issue we spent less time discussing – the best use of native-speaker competence in LADO – has proven persistently thorny and divisive.

These *Guidelines* were endorsed worldwide by national and international linguistic organizations, theoretical and applied, with membership numbering tens of thousands, and made available to refugee law practitioners via UNHCR's RefWorld library (www.essex.ac.uk/larg/resources/guidelines.aspx). Stygall (2009: 260–261) cited them as an exemplar of "codes of ethics for forensic settings." Their programme for improving the standard practice of LADO is cited by organizations including De Taalstudio, Språkab, and Verified language firms; the Swiss, Canadian, Norwegian, and Dutch government bureaux; and NGOs and legal organizations concerned with fair treatment of refugees.

The *Guidelines* stimulated criticism from some professionally involved in LADO. For example, Cambier-Langeveld (senior linguist, Netherlands Office for Country Information and Language Analysis, which employs the collaborative method of linguist plus non-expert native speaker) notes that "no linguist could possibly be opposed to the main message of the *Guidelines*, that linguistic expertise is essential in [LADO]" (2010: 70), but goes on to criticize them for downplaying the "expertise of native speakers," and for failing to note that academic expertise alone is insufficient for the performance of LADO in a forensic context. (The latter point is one all forensic linguists surely learn early in their courtroom careers.) Cambier-Langeveld chaired a working group for the International Association for Forensic Phonetics and Acoustics (IAFPA) to draft a resolution, passed in 2009. It notes: "IAFPA recognises the contribution to be made by . . . linguists with in-depth research knowledge of the language(s) in question . . . and trained native speakers, with the latter working under the guidance and supervision of the former." Cambier-Langeveld later argued, "the *Guidelines* are not an effective tool for quality control in LADO" (2012: 100), partly on the basis of beliefs she controversially imputes to their 19 co-authors, and partly because she believes they fail to anticipate and address problems arising in cases where her agency's LADO conclusions have been disputed (see Fraser 2011 and Verrips 2011 – both *Guidelines* co-authors; Verrips founded De Taalstudio, which has performed thousands of counter-analyses in the Netherlands).

The *Guidelines* are routinely cited in asylum appeals in European and other countries. In 2007 the Netherlands Council of State accepted the qualifications and independence of a contra-analysis expert from De Taalstudio, observing that the expert had been selected according to the *Guidelines* and worked according to them (Eades 2010: 39). In Scotland, the late Lord Macphail granted a form of judicial recognition to *Guidelines* #3 ("Language analysis must be done by qualified linguists"), #6 ("Linguists should provide specific evidence of professional training and expertise") and #7 ("the expertise of native speakers is not the same as the expertise of linguists"),[1] as noted in the 2014 UK Supreme Court decision discussed below.

The *Guidelines* are thus a curious example in which impact is overwhelmingly disproportionate to output. My 1/19th share of their 2,000 words would not count as much of an output in any arena, nor qualify as original research. However, guided by colleagues with great experience in applying academic linguistics to the legal sphere, the scores of hours the Language and National Origin Group members spent over ten months discussing the issues and crafting the *Guidelines* had an impact beyond my imagining.

Crucially, this was not achieved by publication alone (though the *Guidelines* were published in linguistics and asylum journals). We made persistent efforts over several years to bring them to the attention of institutional players within linguistics and in broader spheres of asylum activity – a process I recommend to others seeking impact. We spoke at meetings of linguistic organizations to gain endorsements; I corresponded with UNHCR to make the *Guidelines* available via RefWorld; and we explained them to government representatives at expert meetings. Others circulated them to refugee advocacy organizations and networks of asylum lawyers, and engaged with government calls for input to inform the contracting process.[2] When the Norwegian government initiated LADO in 2009, envisioning an annual contract worth 7 million kroner ($0.87m, €0.78m), it specified that reports and procedures should be conducted "according to principles and guidelines as established in *Guidelines* (2004), with the exceptions stated below . . ." (UDI 2009). Eric Baltisberger of the Swiss bureau Lingua called the *Guidelines* "a turning point . . . the very first time that academia acknowledged LADO as a serious field for research and showed its willingness to get involved" (Baltisberger 2013). He added that they "gave Lingua some basic theoretical framework which confirmed the methodology that had been applied for years by the Swiss unit which – in turn – heightened the acceptance of LADO in the administrative context" (ibid.).

Every report issued in the UK by Verified AB – the contractor which replaced Språkab in August 2014 as primary LADO supplier to the Home Office – discusses the *Guidelines*, their critics and supporters. Every report from De Taalstudio – which takes both appeal clients and government contract LADO work – is "based on independent standards for expert reports in the legal system, including the . . . *Guidelines*" (Verrips 2010: 282). Like other linguists who author expert reports, I quote them in every submission. They are thus referred to in hundreds, if not thousands, of asylum cases annually. Some organizations and actors do not agree with every point, or indeed strive to belittle and discount them (Lövgren 2009), but cannot ignore their influence. Like much expert legal testimony, the *Guidelines* stress consensus in the field of linguistics and are based on established findings, rather than new research (Wilson and Foulkes 2014). Cutting-edge or controversial work is not normally relied upon to convince non-specialist decision-makers; nor would forensic linguists wish for someone's fate to depend upon our latest innovation. Experts are representing their entire field to decision-makers unfamiliar with it, and must expect that their evidence or opinions will be scrutinized and challenged by even more capable and respected colleagues – a lesson I learned early (Patrick and Buell 2000).

Decision- and policy-makers rarely consult several experts in a single field, precisely for their specialism – they want a broad range of answers or viewpoints from just one or two people. Outside the courtroom I present a generalist view, in addition to my research specialism. This has increased my audience and impact, but it also brings dangers, tempting me to deliver opinions on matters for which I am less qualified, and arousing the ire of colleagues who are more qualified in them, but less willing to engage publicly.

Having entered an unfamiliar arena with high stakes (RSD involves government policy, contractors, the legal professions, and often-unsubtle mass media portrayals), I found myself subject to unwelcome personal attacks and interference (cf. Lawson, this volume). My experience with LADO includes threatened lawsuits, veiled and open attacks on my competence, and pressure on editors (nobly resisted) to influence my published opinions. I sought advice and support from colleagues, lawyers and university officers, but still experienced considerable stress and anxiety. I have struggled to continue articulating strong and clear views in publications, legal reports, and mass media (http://privatewww.essex.ac.uk/~patrickp/media.htm), knowing it will provoke further aggression from parties whose interests are threatened. Working as a senior local officer for the University and College Union has provided helpful context, illuminating how other academics are subject to reprisals and threats to academic freedom, and providing a feeling of community as we work to defend them.

Outputs and outcomes II: Networking and organizing

I have pursued a conventional type of output and impact alongside many colleagues over the last decade. I convened or participated in colloquia on LADO in Ireland, the Netherlands, Sweden, Switzerland, the USA, England, Scotland, and Wales. Delivering LADO seminars to various professionals and the general public helped establish the practitioner/researcher dialogue in this field. I was slow to develop contacts beyond linguistics, and I recommend attending to this from the start. Unlike developing a research project from scratch, however, such exchanges and alliances were partly contingent on the involvement of existing groups with LADO: doctors who assess torture cases, and whose reports appear alongside mine; geneticists approached by the Home Office to assist with RSD; interpreters experienced in asylum cases, etc. Within my university, becoming a Member of the Human Rights Centre helped create local space and acceptance for LADO work which did not fit my home department's research goals and thus did not qualify me for assistance (support to attend conferences, etc.).

I convened a research seminar series in 2011–12 (Patrick 2010a) which hosted over 75 participants from Africa, Australia, North America, and Europe, spanning the range of professions listed at the outset of the last section, including four commercial LADO firms and six government bureaux (Austrian, Belgian, Dutch, Norwegian, Swiss, UK). The seminars provided a platform to exchange expertise, and work towards acceptance of professional linguistic standards and best practice in the asylum sphere.

One commercial linguist evaluated the series, saying that due to "the preparation and conduct of the ESRC meetings, a highly polarised debate, characterised by processes of exclusion, has turned into a constructive dialogue involving all stakeholders" (Verrips 2013: 4). Eric Baltisberger of Lingua commented that the meetings served "to widen the perspective and get more input to further develop the still relatively young domain of LADO," and noted that such efforts have proven "very valuable for Lingua: while in the early years it was very difficult to find qualified linguists willing to work with us as linguistic experts, this task has become easier" (Baltisberger 2013).

I also co-convened the first LADO network, the Language and Asylum Research Group (LARG), with Diana Eades. Its mission is "to stimulate research, contribute to further development of guidelines, and promote best practice in the field of LADO, through exchange of informed views, in the spirit of and extending the scope of the 2004 *Guidelines*" (www.essex.ac.uk/larg).

The impact of such frequent and long-term organizing and disseminating work is diffuse in that no government policy, legal victory or research grant will appear simply because the right person was invited to listen or speak. However, I believe that in an adversarial arena where highly accomplished and motivated participants disagree in court, compete for contracts or fiercely critique one another's proposals and publications, only extended dialogue, including willingness to learn from one's adversaries, has any hope of developing or shift-ing consensus.

Outputs and outcomes III: Casework in the UK

Having helped author and promulgate the *Guidelines*, I imagined my active participation in LADO was over, but a chance meeting with a colleague in the Human Rights Centre at the University of Essex determined otherwise. After we explored LADO in the UK (Patrick and Oakeshott 2007), my name was passed to the UK Refugee Legal Group network. In 2008 lawyers began contacting me for expert reports in appeals cases involving LADO. Since then I have authored reports in over 70 cases for two dozen law firms and NGOs. In all cases the lan-guage report's quality warranted an appeal, the Tribunal granted permission, and the Legal Aid Agency approved funding, so these do not constitute a representa-tive sample of all LADO reports.

Understanding the asylum process, the rules governing expert reports, the intricacies of asylum law, and the way specialist tribunals operate, is a huge project which might daunt any linguist. It has certainly taken me years – time therefore not spent on research, teaching or administration – and there is much still to learn. This time has been unrecognized and unrewarded within the university's view of my activities: no sabbatical time, travel funding, reduced teaching load, etc., were available for impact-producing work per se at Essex. With the intro-duction of workload modelling and performance management to UK universities (not an unmixed blessing), I have recently received recognition of some hours which might have been devoted to research instead. Holding a senior rank has doubtless helped, in the highly-stratified British system, as has the linking of impact to funding by the UK research councils in 2014 (see Lawson and Sayers, this volume); but the absence of academic tenure in the UK since 1988 means there is no immunity from the increasing pressures to attract major funding.

I chose to take up LADO work after wondering for decades how to link lin-guistics actively with human rights. I accepted it might lower my research profile and have negative consequences for my career as well as positive ones, and this has been the case. It is also true that such efforts may be successful in attract-ing research funding; and that the more linguists are deeply involved in cross-disciplinary long-term work which produces significant social impact, the easier it may become to argue our profession should value it and our universities reward it – regardless of whether it produces traditional research outputs. Meanwhile, I advise scholars new to this arena to think hard about the trade-offs involved in undertaking such efforts without the guarantee of either success or recognition, and explore how satisfied they might be with different outcomes.

The almost complete lack of linguists performing a similar role in the UK asylum system when I began meant it took me a long time to master the formal require-ments for expert reports, and understand their treatment in the tribunal system – in retrospect I should have consulted comparable experts, e.g. anthropologists and medical specialists, earlier for advice. I consulted forensic linguists, but as they only give expert evidence in criminal courts in the UK, help was limited. I found most lawyers were too eager for instant reports to provide critical feedback – though I had to educate them about what a linguistic expert could and could not legitimately do. I have urged many colleagues to lend their specific language expertise to LADO reports over the years, but most have remained too busy with research, unwilling to enter the legal arena or too chary of such a politicized topic to take up the invitation. Where possible, though, I strongly recommend accessing previous reports (or the equivalent in other domains), and seeking an hour's face-to-face advice from an experienced participant (another expert witness, lawyer, policymaker, etc.).

The UK Home Office pilot programme of 2001 became a long-term contractual relationship with Språkab, who conducted LADO for them until August 2014. From 2007 to 2010, UKBA commissioned over 4,000 LADO analyses (Campbell 2013: 10); in 2010 alone, Språkab performed 4,000 worldwide, according to its General Manager, having conducted 40,000 since 2000. A survey of 1,456 applicants for five countries from 2007 to 2009 found that 63% were from their claimed country of origin (Campbell 2013: 11). Campbell's detailed analysis of Home Office statistics and reports argues that LADO is a "fundamentally political" process, that it "rel[ies] on subjective rather than objective criteria in deciding which individuals to test," "misstates the science behind language analysis" and rests on "very little empirical evidence"; indeed, for Campbell, "the entire exercise is flawed" (2013: 16). Not surprisingly, asylum applicants turned down partly on LADO grounds have not shied from legal action.

I draw on my own experience and research in reports: for example, data-collection and analysis of Creole speech (Patrick 1999), forensic speech analysis (Patrick and Buell 2000), the speech community (Patrick 2002), ethnicity in dialect acquisition (Straw and Patrick 2007), variability in contact languages (Patrick 2008) and the applicability of variationist research to LADO (Patrick 2010b). However, unlike such research, my evaluation in LADO reports is from a general linguistic standpoint, as cases nearly always concern languages I am not a specialist in. Even for specialists, there is often a severe lack of documentation on relevant varieties: there is some research on Somali, but little for the Af-Reer Hamar dialect; research on Arabic abounds, but almost nothing on Gaza. Relevant speech communities may be inaccessible to researchers for the very reasons they produce refugees (civil unrest, armed conflict). These can also cause dramatic demographic change (e.g. age/sex imbalances due to flight and conflict), exodus to refugee camps, change or interruption of education, abandonment of traditional ways of life and speaking, etc., making existing descriptions of language varieties dubious and further obfuscating LADO.

Consequently, I explicitly do not offer views as to the origin of ASs. Rather, the focus of my opinions is the quality of reports provided to the government: the data and methods of collection, transcription and presentation, analysis and argumentation (if any), the assumptions and reasoning displayed, knowledge of relevant scientific literature and practices, formulation and testing of hypotheses, and the validity and reliability of the conclusions drawn. As a general linguist, I draw on descriptive research literature to illustrate (socio-)linguistic complexity where it has been ignored or misrepresented in reports, but am careful not to claim specialist knowledge. I examine the credentials displayed and claims of expertise made by analysts and linguists performing LADO for governments. My thinking is simple: a proper expert report should demonstrate relevant expertise according to accepted standards – always, but especially when a person's safety and future are at stake. While I do not expect judges and decision-makers to evaluate a detailed linguistic analysis, the scientific basis of a report must be laid open for inspection or challenge by other qualified experts. Testimony must be the product of reliable and scientifically accepted principles and methods, attested via peer review and publication.

My consulting practice largely consists of explaining to tribunals what generally accepted linguistic standards are, why they are important, and pointing out where reports fail to meet them. I have repeatedly observed all the characteristics of lower-quality reports enumerated above in UK cases. I acknowledge elements of good practice as evidence of progress, but they are few.

After 70+ critical reports, what are the results for LADO? What is the impact of these outputs? One measure might be how often appeal decisions favor ASs versus the government, but this is difficult to assess. By law, LADO reports cannot be the sole determining factor: evidence must be considered 'in the round.' Asylum decisions are confidential; only a few are published (anonymized) as guidance cases of special significance (see Innes, this volume, on the challenges of gaining such access); determinations must be accessed via lawyers months or years after submitting one's expert report. For a period of three years (2008–11) and 53 cases, I managed to obtain 25 judgments by pestering lawyers:

- Two cases were not determined on language grounds; no view of either my or the government's reports was given.
- In two others, appeals were denied outright, with little or no weight placed by judges on either report. I count these cases, conservatively, as failing to have impact.
- In an additional three, appeals were denied; however, the claims about language and/or origin were accepted. Little or no weight was placed on government reports, which were found to be 'flawed' or to have failed to meet a high standard.
- In the remaining 18 cases, appeals were allowed; in many the judge commented on the language reports, accepting and giving weight to my opinion, and/or rejecting or giving lesser weight to government reports.

By this measure, my reports had significant impact on a case-by-case basis. Many cases involved a single Språkab non-expert native-speaker analyst, anonymized as Ea20, who shot to public prominence in 2014. Ea20 was exposed first in Swedish court, then in an hour-long investigative television report aired by Swedish public station SVT (*Uppdrag Granskning,* "Mission: Investigate") on 12 November 2014, followed by several stories in UK newspapers (prominently *The Independent*). Ea20 was charged with involvement in minor drug offenses, and more importantly for his LADO work, with falsifying academic credentials (which in any case included no linguistic training). Of the 18 reports I filed concerning Ea20's cases up to 2011, resolution was favorable to the AS in 16 (88%). In response to the media scrum, Språkab wrote to the Home Office claiming Ea20 as "one of the best analysts" whose work is "flawless" and "of the highest standard" (Norrbom 2014).

Another measure is whether changes to Språkab reports appear to address repeated criticisms, accumulated over time. Voices other than mine have criticized UKBA's LADO practices; other language experts have authored evaluative reports at appeal, and De Taalstudio has provided high-quality contra-analyses in UK cases, while some judges have consistently criticized the quality of Språkab reports as evidence. Again, not all positive changes represent the impact of my expert opinions. However, such changes have occurred. I divide them into changes relating to expertise/reports, and linguistic matters (my reports comment on both).

Regarding expertise:

- Evaluation scales are no longer spuriously quantified when expressing certainty (LNOG *Guideline #4*).
- The qualifications of analysts and linguists are presented separately. Formerly, they were often misleadingly combined, leading judges' determinations and caseworkers' letters of rejection to mistakenly attribute linguistics degrees to unqualified analysts. I noted pooling of credentials in 18 of 27 reports dated before September 2009, when Språkab changed their practice.
- A declaration of truth – long required of all expert evidence by the Tribunals Judiciary *Practice Directions* – began to appear in 2010.
- Språkab reports now routinely address the *Practice Directions* requirement (10.9(b)) to "give details of any literature or other material which the expert has relied on in making the report," by acknowledging: "Literature or other material which the expert has relied on in making the Report: NONE." Elsewhere, Språkab declare they rely on "long term, first-hand experience of empirical language data collected by Språkab analysts, and not on academic publications . . . lack of academic references is not relevant" to expertise (Lövgren 2009: 12).
- Reports now routinely make clear that analysts, not linguists, perform the primary analysis: "Examination/analysis [is] carried out by expert analysts working under the supervisory umbrella of expert linguists." However, "analytical ability according to Språkab standards cannot and never will be acquired through academic training" (Lövgren 2009: 15).
- Reports since 2012 separately assess the speaker's claimed linguistic background, using a "likelihood" scale, and the speaker's actual background in Språkab's opinion, here still using a scale of "certainty" (Broeders 2010).

- Reports now state: "Knowledge assessment is separate and forms no part of the language analysis." Knowledge assessment refers to non-linguistic material elicited, such as familiarity with currency, geography or customs of the claimed home country.

Such changes in form and practice are objectively verifiable and satisfy certain legal challenges, but there is no evidence that they actually improve the quality of *linguistic* method at the heart of reports. Clearly my criticisms played a role in making Språkab reports more explicit, careful and professional and less likely to mislead decision-makers; however, such gradual progress falls short of the desired result – reports which consistently and scrupulously observe both legal requirements and high linguistic standards for expert evidence.
   On the linguistics front:

- All Språkab reports now make *some* comment, and provide *some* data, on the linguistic levels of phonology, morphology/syntax and lexicon (earlier reports sometimes only used lexical data).
- Linguistic features, and even processes, are occasionally correctly labelled using standard linguistic terminology. However, Språkab's descriptive practices are idiosyncratic at best – e.g. instead of using brackets [..] for narrow phonetic and slashes /../ for phonemic transcription, as linguists do, they use brackets "to refer to a sound produced by the speaker" and slashes "to refer to a sound not produced by the speaker," as "this format is preferred by Språkab's clients" (Lövgren 2009: 9).
- Efforts and claims have been made to use accepted linguistic tools such as the International Phonetic Alphabet (LNOG *Guideline* #3), although this was often not done correctly. From 2012 Språkab reports changed format; the standard claim that "The IPA transcription has been used . . ." disappeared from their reports. In the three preceding years, I commented in 31 reports that the IPA was used incorrectly.

The quality levels of collecting and reporting data, analysis and argumentation, awareness of sociolinguistic issues, attention to variation and language contact, etc., have changed little over six years. Språkab have apparently not taken on the responsibility of educating UKBA about linguistic best practice with the joint goal of constantly improving the quality of reports. In short, there have been few changes improving linguistic quality, or demonstrating expertise. (The introduction of a new LADO supplier to the Home Office in mid-2014, Swedish firm Verified AB, may change this in time.) However, recurring criticisms have perhaps drawn the attention of judges, bureaucrats, lawyers and NGOs with a critical view of linguistic expert evidence, and supported their efforts to take proper account of LADO in improving the UK asylum process.
   Given that case-by-case pressure can be linked with few changes, the third measure considers whether appeals succeed in setting higher standards that apply

to future use of LADO. Once an evidential standard is accepted, courts are often slow to change or reluctant to review it. In 2010, LADO offered this opportunity in the complex *RB* case mentioned above. Craig (2012) reviews it in detail. Among other points, the Upper Tribunal in *RB* heard no testimony from any independent linguists but invited Språkab's General Manager to testify; they appeared unconcerned about the fact that Språkab's analysts and linguists were routinely anonymous, unlike expert witnesses; and they accepted as adequate the practice of academically untrained analysts working with moderately-qualified linguists who did not know the relevant language. The Tribunal endorsed a process which transfers significant responsibility for determining national origin from UKBA to their linguistic contractor (Craig 2012: 263). The Tribunal concluded:

> where there is clear, detailed and reasoned linguistic analysis leading to an opinion expressed in terms of certainty or near-certainty it seems to us that little more [than a Språkab report] will be required to justify a conclusion on whether an applicant or appellant has the history claimed.
>
> *(RB* para. 171; my insertion in brackets)

In effect the Tribunal waived the usual rules for expert witnesses in favor of Språkab, accepting at face value the view of an interested party – the General Manager – and failing to balance it with informed views from the field. The Court of Appeal for England and Wales endorsed this approach generally in 2012 *(RB (Somalia) v Secretary of State for the Home Department [2012] EWCA Civ 277)*, their only reservation being that the expertise required for a report to a decision-maker (e.g. Språkab's LADO reports) should follow the principles of expert evidence generally – but no instructions or guidance on how to achieve this were issued.

After *RB*, many asylum lawyers saw little point in challenging LADO reports on appeal, and judges who considered them inadequate evidence felt constrained to give them more weight because of the Tribunal's decision. The stifling effect *RB* had on appeals led eventually to a challenge before the Inner House of the Court of Session, Scotland's supreme civil court (which is independent of and equal to the England and Wales Court of Appeal). In 2012, this Court heard two conjoined cases which were very similar on the facts. One judge had ruled that the "Språkab report failed in what it must do" and " . . . is inadmissible"; the other referred to my LADO webpages, quoted the *Guidelines*, and yet "attached considerable weight to the [Språkab] report," following *RB*. An appeal was ordered for the latter, with a senior judge arguing that the lower Tribunal "was not entitled to rely on the linguistic analysis report . . . [which] fails in several important respects to comply with good practice." Such contradictions set the stage for a panel of three judges to reconsider the standards and principles of *RB* (though it was not directly appealed against). I advised and consulted with the two legal teams representing appellants and attended hearings, though as it was an appeal on points of law, I could not file a report as new evidence was excluded.

The Scottish judges took a very different line from their southern cousins: they were unhappy about anonymous experts; they believed the government had to prove the worth of its experts; and they felt *RB* had delegated responsibility for decision-making inappropriately to LADO firms. Moreover, they observed that "being a native speaker of a language does not confer expertise in the identification of dialects within that language, their particular features, or the geographical or social distribution of the dialect," an argument I make in every report.[3] They not only looked with suspicion on Språkab's non-expert native-speaker analysts, but also doubted the linguists, finding that neither report "discloses any intelligible basis of expertise which might justify giving any value to either of their conclusions." One claimant was granted asylum immediately, and the other's case was ordered to be reconsidered.

However, this was not the end. The Scottish and England/Wales decisions were on the same level; to prevent conflicting legal standards, the Home Office appealed to the UK Supreme Court (*SSHD v MN and KY [2014] UKSC30*). Again, I consulted and attended two days of argument; in May 2014, a unanimous judgment sent the asylum tribunals back to the drawing board to reconsider the basis for linguistic evidence in asylum cases – effectively cutting out *RB*, though not directly overturning it. The Supreme Court Justices too felt that *RB* was "unduly prescriptive and potentially misleading" in implying any sort of blanket approval of Språkab's methods, and in allowing routine anonymity of LADO experts. They scolded the agency for going "beyond the proper role of" an expert witness, as these "should never act or appear to act as advocates." In their opinion, Språkab's reasoning should "be better explained and not (as it often currently seems to be) left implicit," while the reports' "comments on knowledge of country and culture were inadequately supported by any demonstrated expertise of the authors." They confirmed the decision for the ASs, who had endured the long-distance legal struggle for over five years. The Upper Tribunal are expected to reconsider the use of linguistic evidence in LADO, hopefully allowing testimony from qualified independent linguists; but what the new standard will look like cannot be predicted. (A year later, this reconsideration has not yet been scheduled.)

I have now been involved in legal challenges to LADO reports for seven years. For much of that time it was difficult to know whether my work had any effect beyond individual cases which represented a small portion of LADO cases in the UK. However, it now seems that persistent casework helped advance the process, by holding up alternative perspectives on good LADO practice. I can only advise anyone contemplating involvement in the legal process as a linguistic expert to be patient and, if possible, enjoy learning about that process itself. As someone who nearly studied law instead of linguistics I have not found this difficult; but it is frustrating to discover that many lawyers are focused almost exclusively on winning their individual cases. As linguist and teacher I want them to understand better what we do and why it is important; and I wish linguistic knowledge and arguments to have more consistent, significant and pervasive impact on decisions – and thus people's lives – or else not to be relied on at all. For long periods of LADO work it has been unclear whether any of this would happen.

Conclusions

While it is fair to say I always intended my LADO work to have impact, the impact did not follow research as cart follows horse. Certainly my training, forensic experience, and previous research led logically to (but did not fully prepare me for) my role. I have drawn connections from specific research to the impact above, and in my 2014 REF impact case study (http://results.ref.ac.uk/DownloadFile/ImpactCaseStudy/pdf?caseStudyId=43408). But in all this, the generation of new research distinctly took a backseat to representing linguistics effectively and fairly to LADO stakeholders who were unaware of what it is, and what questions it can plausibly address.

I cannot overemphasize how much time, persistence, and energy is required to learn even as little as I have about an area as large, diverse, and separate from sociolinguistics as refugee law and asylum policies and practices across three continents. University and department colleagues may be forgiven for initially considering LADO work essentially outwith my job description, much less my research agenda. Indeed, until over halfway through my 12-year acquaintance with LADO, when funding bodies determined 'impact' was to become a criterion for judging research (see Lawson and Sayers, this volume), my work on LADO was an academically unrewarded hobby. More recent recognition within and beyond my university offers none of the tangible rewards that traditionally successful research does. Younger scholars whose ambitions lie in the ever-more-circumscribed sphere of traditional academic success should think twice before taking such a path; those wishing to change the insularity that linguistics sometimes projects, however, may find interesting and satisfying work ahead. Ultimately, useful results emerged from the sustained efforts I and many others have made together, as evidenced by the determined and sometimes unscrupulous opposition they have met with.

In the end, good fortune also played a large role. The conference session in Honolulu might never have occurred. Government policy and judicial views of LADO in the UK might have been set in stone before I ever became involved; I might never have been sought out for casework, especially as I was poorly prepared for it when I began; and the case-by-case battles might have gone on for years yet, before the tribunals and courts attempted to set and refine standards (cf. Coleman, this volume; Levasseur, this volume, on the influence of chance encounters). Meanwhile, in other countries LADO has already been largely discontinued (e.g. Australia, Belgium), recently introduced (Canada, Norway), or has developed along distinct pathways (Austria, the Netherlands), while harmonization efforts across the EU (Tax 2010) and incorporation into broader forensic science regimes (e.g. Netherlands Register of Court Experts, NRGD; cf. Smithuis and van Ruth forthcoming) remain interesting prospects.

Very few scholarly publications directly on LADO exist to date – around 100 items, most of which are descriptive rather than empirical research. Much more research is required before the linguistic problems at its heart can be resolved; while only a few countries (e.g. Sweden) have had public debates about policy or legal aspects. There remains tremendous scope for committed linguistic work to have impact.

Acknowledgments

Although I write in the first person, very little of the work described could have been achieved by one person acting alone. I am especially grateful to Diana Eades and Maaike Verrips for countless hours of discussion, criticism, illumination and peerless support over many years. I am also grateful to Advocate Joe Bryce and his distinguished colleagues, especially Mungo Bovey QC and Michael Howlin QC, for educating me about the arcana of the legal process at an exalted level; and to so many colleagues around the world whose responses have heartened me.

Notes

1 See Inner House decision *M.Ab.N. and K.A.S.Y. v SSHD [2013] CSIH 68*, at www. asylumlawdatabase.eu/sites/www.asylumlawdatabase.eu/files/aldfiles/%5B2013%5DCSIH% 2068.pdf. The Supreme Court decision is *SSHD (Appellant) v MN and KY (Respondents) (Scotland) [2014] UKSC 30*, at www.supremecourt.uk/decided-cases/docs/UKSC_2013_0202_ Judgment.pdf.
2 Enam Al-Wer, Marlyse Baptista, Diana Eades, Helen Fraser, Tim McNamara, April McMahon, John Singler, Gerry Van Herk, Maaike Verrips and others were instrumental.
3 Though few linguists would disagree with Lord Eassie's wording, the role of non-expert native-speaking analysts in LADO – championed by their private and government employers – remains controversial, and research is required. As a first step, in 2011 I convened a meeting involving academic, government and commercial practitioners (including Språkab, Verified and Bureau Land en Taal) to consider ways of making progress (www.essex.ac.uk/larg/events/esrclado2.aspx).

References

Baker, Paul, Costas Gabrielatos, Majid Khosravinik, Michal Krzyzanowski, Tony McEnery, and Ruth Wodak. 2011. « ¿Una sinergia metodológica útil? Combinar análisis crítico del discurso y lingüística de corpus para examinar los discursos de los refugiados y solicitantes de asilo en la prensa británica. » *Discurso y Sociedad* 5 (2): 376–416.

Baltisberger, Eric. 2013. "Letter in support of REF impact case study for Peter Patrick." 9 July 2013, Bern.

Baltisberger, Eric, and Priska Hubbuch. 2010. "LADO with specialized linguists: The development of Lingua's working method." In *Language and Origin: The Role of Language in European Asylum Procedures: A Linguistic and Legal Survey*, ed. by Karin Zwaan, Pieter Muysken, and Maaike Verrips, 9–19. Nijmegen: Wolf Legal Publishers.

Blommaert, Jan. 2009. "Language, asylum and the national order." *Current Anthropology* 50 (4): 415–441.

Bohmer, Carol, and Amy Shuman. 2008. *Rejecting Refugees: Political Asylum in the 21st Century*. Oxon: Routledge.

Broeders, A.P.A. 2010. "Decision-making in LADO: A view from the forensic arena." In *Language and Origin. The Role of Language in European Asylum Procedures: A Linguistic and Legal Survey*, ed. by Karin Zwaan, Maaike Verrips, and Pieter Muysken, 51–60. Nijmegen: Wolf Legal Publishers.

Bryce, Joseph. 2013. "Court of Session rules on linguistic analysis." Accessed 24 July 2013. Available from: https://www.freemovement.org.uk/court-of-session-rules-on-linguistic-analysis/.

Cambier-Langeveld, Tina. 2010. "The role of linguists and native speakers in language analysis for the determination of speaker origin." *International Journal of Speech, Language and the Law* 17 (1): 67–93.

Cambier-Langeveld, Tina. 2012. "Clarification of the issues in language analysis: A rejoinder to Fraser and Verrips." *International Journal of Speech, Language and the Law* 19 (1): 95–108.

Cameron, Deborah, Elizabeth Frazer, Penelope Harvey, Ben Rampton, and Kay Richardson. 1993. "Ethics, advocacy and empowerment: Issues of method in researching language." *Language and Communication* 13 (2): 81–94.

Campbell, John. 2013. "Language analysis in the United Kingdom's refugee status determination system: Seeing through policy claims about 'expert knowledge'." *Ethnic and Racial Studies* 36 (4): 670–690.

Craig, Sarah. 2012. "The use of language in asylum decision-making in the UK – a discussion." *Journal of Immigration, Asylum and Nationality Law* 26 (3): 255–268.

Eades, Diana. 2010. "Guidelines from linguists for LADO." In *Language and Origin: The Role of Language in European Asylum Procedures: A Linguistic and Legal Survey*, ed. by Karin Zwaan, Maaike Verrips, and Pieter Muysken, 35–41. Nijmegen: Wolf Legal Publishers.

Eades, Diana, and Jacques Arends. 2004. "Using language in the determination of national origin of asylum seekers: An introduction." *International Journal of Speech, Language and the Law* 11 (2): 179–266.

Eades, Diana, Helen Fraser, Jeff Siegel, Tim McNamara, and Brett Baker. 2003. "Linguistic identification in the determination of nationality: A preliminary report." *Language Policy* 2 (2): 179–199.

Eriksson, Anders. 2008. "Guidelines? What guidelines?" Unpublished paper to International Association for Forensic Phonetics and Acoustics conference, 20–23 July 2008, Lausanne.

Fraser, Helen. 2011. "The role of linguists and native speakers in language analysis for the determination of speaker origin: A response to Tina Cambier-Langeveld." *International Journal of Speech, Language and the Law* 18 (1): 121–130.

IAFPA (International Association for Forensic Phonetics and Acoustics). 2009. "IAFPA resolution: Language and determination of national identity cases." Accessed 15 April 2015. Available from: http://www.iafpa.net/langidres.htm.

ILPA (Immigration Law Practitioners' Association). 2009. "Response to the UK Border Agency 'NAM+ Asylum Programme' presentation to the National Asylum Stakeholder Forum (NASF) on Thursday 19 March 2009." Accessed 15 April 2015. Available from: http://www.ilpa.org.uk/data/resources/13070/09.04.563.pdf.

Labov, William. 1982. "Objectivity and commitment in linguistic science: The case of the Black English trial in Ann Arbor." *Language in Society* 11 (2): 165–201.

LNOG (Language and National Origin Group). 2004. "Guidelines for the use of language analysis in relation to questions of national origin in refugee cases." *International Journal of Speech, Language and the Law* 11 (2): 261–266.

Lövgren, Petter. 2009. "Språkab's comments regarding Prof. Peter Patrick's report, *The validity and reliability of Språkab analysis generally, and in the case A.H.O.*" Document submitted to the First-Tier Tribunal (Immigration and Asylum Chamber).

Maryns, Katrijn. 2006. *The Asylum Speaker: Language in the Belgian Asylum Procedure.* Manchester: St Jerome.

Norrbom, Torrbjörn. 2014. "Public letter from Språkab Production Manager." 24 November 2014.

Patrick, Peter L. 1999. *Urban Jamaican Creole: Variation in the Mesolect.* Amsterdam: John Benjamins.

Patrick, Peter L. 2002. "The speech community." In *The Handbook of Language Variation and Change*, ed. by J. K. Chambers, Peter Trudgill, and Natalie Schilling-Estes, 573–597. Oxford: Blackwell.

Patrick, Peter L. 2008. "Pidgins, creoles and linguistic variation." In *The Handbook of Pidgins and Creoles*, ed. by Silvia Kouwenberg and John V. Singler, 461–487. Oxford: Blackwell.

Patrick, Peter L. 2010a. "Language analysis of asylum applicants: Foundations, guidelines and best practice." UK Economic and Social Research Council grant (ESRC no. RES-451-26-0911). Accessed 15 April 2015. Available from: http://www.researchcatalogue.esrc.ac.uk/grants/RES-451-26-0911/read.

Patrick, Peter L. 2010b. "Language variation and LADO (Language Analysis for Determination of Origin)." In *Language and Origin: The Role of Language in European Asylum Procedures: A Linguistic and Legal Survey*, ed. by Karin Zwaan, Maaike Verrips, and Pieter Muysken, 73–87. Nijmegen: Wolf Legal Publishers.

Patrick, Peter L. 2012. "Language Analysis for Determination of Origin: Objective evidence for refugee status determination." *The Oxford Handbook of Language and Law*, ed. by Lawrence Solan and Peter Tiersma, 533–546. Oxford: Oxford University Press.

Patrick, Peter L., and Samuel W. Buell. 2000. "Competing Creole transcripts on trial." *Essex Research Reports in Linguistics.* Accessed 15 April 2015. Available from: http://privatewww.essex.ac.uk/~patrickp/papers/CreoleTranscripts.pdf.

Patrick, Peter L., and Nicholas Oakeshott. 2007. "Problems, prospects and perspectives on language analysis in UK refugee status determination." Paper presented to the International Association for Forensic Linguistics (IAFL-7), Cardiff University, Wales, July 2005.

Patrick, Peter L., Monika S. Schmid, and Karin Zwaan (eds.). Forthcoming. *Language Analysis for the Determination of Origin.* Berlin: Springer.

Rickford, John R. 1997. "Unequal partnership: Sociolinguistics and the African-American speech community." *Language in Society* 26 (2): 161–197.

Smithuis, M.M.A., and E. M. van Ruth. Forthcoming. "Forensic science service expertise – not as solid as it seems." In *Language Analysis for the Determination of Origin*, ed. by Peter L. Patrick, Monika S. Schmid, and Karin Zwaan. Berlin: Springer.

Straw, Michelle, and Peter L. Patrick. 2007. "Dialect acquisition of glottal variation in /t/: Barbadians in Ipswich." *Language Sciences* 29 (2–3): 385–407.

Stygall, Gail. 2009. "Guiding principles: Forensic linguistics and codes of ethics in other fields and professions." *International Journal of Speech, Language and the Law* 16 (2): 253–266.

Tax, Blanche. 2010. "The use of expert evidence in asylum procedures by EU member states: The case for harmonized procedural safeguards." In *Language and Origin: The Role of Language in European Asylum Procedures: A Linguistic and Legal Survey*, ed. by Karin Zwaan, Maaike Verrips, and Pieter Muysken, 225–232. Nijmegen: Wolf Legal Publishers.

Tribunals Judiciary. 2010. *Practice Directions: Immigration and Asylum Chambers of the First-tier and the Upper Tribunal, sec 10*. London: Tribunals Judiciary.

UDI (Utlendingsdirektoratet – Norwegian Immigration Administration). 2009. *Specified Requirements for Language Analysis for the Norwegian Immigration Administration*. Oslo: UDI.

UKBA (United Kingdom Border Agency). 2013. "Guidance on language analysis." Accessed 15 April 2015. Available from: https://www.gov.uk/government/uploads/system/uploads/attachment_data/file/370328/Language_Analysis_AI_Public_v18.pdf.

Verrips, Maaike. 2010. "Language analysis and contra-expertise in the Dutch asylum procedure." *International Journal of Speech, Language and the Law* 17 (2): 279–294.

Verrips, Maaike. 2011. "LADO and the pressure to draw strong conclusions: A response to Tina Cambier-Langeveld." *International Journal of Speech, Language and the Law* 18 (1): 131–143.

Verrips, Maaike. 2013. "Letter in support of REF impact case study for Peter Patrick." 30 July 2013, Amsterdam.

Wilson, Kim, and Paul Foulkes. 2014. "Borders, variation and identity: Language Analysis for the Determination of Origin (LADO)." In *Language, Borders and Identity*, ed. by Dominic Watt and Carmen Llamas, 218–229. Edinburgh: Edinburgh University Press.

Zwaan, Karin, Pieter Muysken, and Maaike Verrips (eds.). 2010. *Language and Origin. The Role of Language in European Asylum Procedures: A Linguistic and Legal Survey*. Nijmegen: Wolf Legal Publishers.

Index